Writing South Africa

During the final years of the apartheid era and the subsequent
transition to democracy, South African literary writing caught the
world's attention as never before. Writers responded to the changing
political situation and its daily impact on the country's inhabitants
with works that recorded or satirized state-enforced racism, explored
the possibilities of resistance and rebuilding, and creatively addressed
the vexed question of literature's relation to politics and ethics.
Writing South Africa offers a window on the literary activity of this
extraordinary period that conveys its range (going well beyond a
handful of world-renowned names) and its significance for anyone
interested in the impact of decolonization and democratization on
the cultural sphere. Essays by leading commentators based in South
Africa, Britain, and North America are brought together for the first
time with discussions by some of the most distinguished South
African novelists, poets, and dramatists of our time: André Brink,
Miriam Tlali, Mongane Wally Serote, Elleke Boehmer, Lewis Nkosi,
Zoë Wicomb, Peter Horn, Zakes Mda, and Maishe Maponya.

EDITED BY DEREK ATTRIDGE
AND ROSEMARY JOLLY

Writing South Africa

Literature, apartheid, and democracy, 1970–1995

 CAMBRIDGE
UNIVERSITY PRESS

PUBLISHED BY THE PRESS SYNDICATE OF THE UNIVERSITY OF CAMBRIDGE
The Pitt Building, Trumpington Street, Cambridge CB2 1RP, United Kingdom

CAMBRIDGE UNIVERSITY PRESS
The Edinburgh Building, Cambridge CB2 2RU, United Kingdom
40 West 20th Street, New York, NY 10011–4211, USA
10 Stamford Road, Oakleigh, Melbourne 3166, Australia

First published 1998

Printed in the United Kingdom at the University Press, Cambridge

Typeset in Monotype Fournier 11/13.5 pt
and Bitstream Schadow in QuarkXPress™ [SE]

A catalogue record for this book is available from the British Library

Library of Congress cataloguing in publication data

Writing South Africa: literature, apartheid, and democracy, 1970–1995
/ edited by Derek Attridge and Rosemary Jolly.
     p.   cm.
Includes bibliographical references and index.
ISBN 0 521 59218 6 hardback. – ISBN 0 521 59768 4 paperback.
1. South African literature – 20th century – History and criticism.
2. Politics and literature – South Africa – History – 20th century.
3. Literature and society – South Africa – History – 20th century.
4. Apartheid in literature.   5. Race relations in literature.
6. South Africa – Politics and government.   I. Attridge,
Derek, 1945–   .   II. Jolly, Rosemary, 1963–   .
PL8014.S6W75   1998
809'.8968–dc21   97–17217   CIP

ISBN 0 521 59218 6 hardback
ISBN 0 521 59768 4 paperback

Contents

Contributors

DEREK ATTRIDGE, Professor of English at Rutgers University, is moving to the University of York, England, to take up a Leverhulme Research Professorship. He was born in Dundee, South Africa, and studied at the Universities of Natal and Cambridge. Among his books are *Peculiar Language: Literature as Difference from the Renaissance to James Joyce* (Cornell University Press and Methuen, 1988) and *Acts of Literature* (Routledge, 1992), a collection of Derrida's essays. He is completing a book on J. M. Coetzee and the ethics of reading.

DAVID ATTWELL is Professor of English at the University of Natal in Pietermaritzburg. He is the editor of J. M. Coetzee's *Doubling the Point: Essays and Interviews* (Harvard University Press, 1992), and the author of *J. M. Coetzee: South Africa and the Politics of Writing* (University of California Press, 1993). More recently, he has been working on the cultural history of early black South African literature.

RITA BARNARD is Associate Professor of English and Comparative Literature at the University of Pennsylvania. Born in Pretoria and trained at Stellenbosch and Duke, she has also taught at the University of the Western Cape. Her first book, *The Great Depression and the Culture of Abundance*, was published by Cambridge University Press in 1995, and a second book, *Apartheid, Literature, and the Politics of Place* is under contract with Oxford University Press.

ELLEKE BOEHMER was born in Durban, South Africa. She is the author of *Colonial and Postcolonial Literature* (Oxford University Press, 1995), and of two novels, *Screens against the Sky* (Bloomsbury, 1990) and *An Immaculate Figure* (Bloomsbury, 1993), and co-edited *Altered State? Writing and South Africa* (Dangaroo, 1994). An *Empire Anthology* is forthcoming. She lectures in English at the University of Leeds, England.

ANDRÉ BRINK is Professor of English at the University of Cape Town. He writes in both English and Afrikaans, and has published fifteen novels since the early 1960s, most of which have been translated into several languages. His criticism spans a number of different literary traditions. His latest novel is *Imaginings of Sand* (Secker & Warburg, 1996), and his recent non-fiction includes *Destabilising Shakespeare* (Shakespeare Society of South Africa, 1996) and *Reinventing a Continent* (Secker & Warburg, 1996). A study of narrative language, *The Novel: Language and Narrative from Cervantes to Calvino*, is due in 1997.

JEANNE COLLERAN, born in the United States, is Chair of the English Department at John Carroll University. She has lectured at the Standard Bank National Arts Festival in Grahamstown, South Africa, and served as a dramaturg for numerous North American productions of Athol Fugard's plays. In addition to writing about South African theatre and fiction, she is the editor, with Jenny Spencer, of *Staging Resistance: Political Theatre and Social Change* (University of Michigan Press, 1997).

MICHIEL HEYNS is Professor and Chair in the Department of English at the University of Stellenbosch, South Africa. He was educated at the Universities of Stellenbosch and Cambridge, and has written mainly on the nineteenth-century English novel (notably *Expulsion and the Nineteeth-Century Novel*, Oxford University Press, 1994) and contemporary South African fiction.

PETER HORN is Professor and Head of Department of German at the University of Cape Town. He has published several volumes of poetry, including the prize-winning *Poems 1964–89* (Ravan, 1991), a volume of essays, *Writing My Reading* (Rodopi, 1994), and an anthology of South African poetry in German translation, *Kap der Guten Hoffnung* (Athenäum, 1980). A volume of short stories, *The Kaffir Who Reads Books*, is forthcoming. He has also published widely on German literature.

ROSEMARY JOLLY is Associate Professor of English at Queen's University, Ontario, and Associate Director of the Canadian Research Consortium on Southern Africa. Born in Sasolburg, South Africa, in 1963, she studied at the Universities of Saskatchewan and Toronto. She is the author of articles on South African literature and postcolonial theory, and of *Narration, Violence and Colonization in White South African Writing* (Ohio University Press, 1996). She is currently co-authoring a book with Miriam Tlali on the women of Soweto and working on a study of literature and the culture of resistance in South Africa.

BRIAN MACASKILL was born in Bethlehem, South Africa, and educated at Rhodes University and the University of Washington, Seattle. He is the author of several publications on literary theory and on South African literatures, and is completing a book on J. M. Coetzee. He teaches in the English Department of John Carroll University, Cleveland, Ohio, and has held a visiting position at the University of Cape Town.

MAISHE MAPONYA has taught drama at the University of the Witwatersrand and is currently involved in transforming arts administration in the Gauteng province, working for the Greater Johannesburg Metropolitan Council. He started writing plays and poetry in 1975/6, a key period for the development of critical political consciousness in South Africa. Recent publications include an anthology of five plays entitled *Doing Plays for a Change* (Witwatersrand University Press, 1995).

ZAKES MDA was born in South Africa and has taught in the drama
departments of the University of Vermont and the University of the
Witwatersrand, Johannesburg. He is currently Dramaturg at the Market
Theatre, Johannesburg, and works full-time as a novelist, playwright,
painter, and film producer. His recent publications include *When People
Play People: Development Communication through Theatre* (Witwatersrand
University Press and Zed Books, 1993) and a novel, *Ways of Dying*
(Oxford University Press, 1995).

LEWIS NKOSI is Professor of English at the University of Wyoming at
Larabie. Born in Natal, he began his career as a journalist, writing for
Ilanga lase Natal and then for *Drum* magazine. During the 1960s he was
banned. He studied at the Universities of London and Sussex, and his
many academic positions have included Professor of Literature at the
Universities of Zambia and Warsaw and Regents Professor of African
Literature at the University of California at Irvine. His publications
include *Home and Exile and Other Selections* (Longman, 1965) and the
novel *Mating Birds* (Ravan and Constable, 1986).

BENITA PARRY was born in South Africa, and has written extensively on
colonial discourse analysis and postcolonial theory. She is the author of
Delusions and Discoveries: Studies on India in the British Imagination (Allen
Lane, 1972) and *Conrad and Imperialism* (Macmillan, 1984). An Associate
Research Fellow in the English Department of Warwick University, she
is working on a book on the literature of imperialism.

GRAHAM PECHEY was born and educated in South Africa, to which he
frequently returns. Having held posts at the Universities of Natal and
Zambia, he now lectures in English at the University of Hertfordshire.
He has written a number of articles on the work of Mikhail Bakhtin and in
the fields of Romantic writing, literary and cultural theory, and the
postcolonial.

ALBIE SACHS studied and practised law in Cape Town, until he was forced
into exile in 1966. He lectured at the Universities of Southampton,
Columbia, and Maputo, where he was the victim of a car-bomb explosion
in 1988. As a leading member of the ANC, he played a key role in the
transition to democratic government in South Africa. He is now a Judge
of the Constitutional Court of South Africa. His publications include the
autobiographical works *The Jail Diary of Albie Sachs* (Harvill, 1969)
and *The Soft Vengeance of a Freedom Fighter* (Grafton, 1990).

MONGANE WALLY SEROTE was born in the township of Alexandra. In 1969
he was detained, and went into exile in the early seventies. After his return
to South Africa, he headed the ANC's Department of Arts and Culture
prior to the party's election to government in 1994. He is currently a

Member of Parliament for the North East Rand Area. He is the author of numerous publications, both fiction and poetry. His most recent work, a long poem entitled *Dinouts,* is due in 1997.

MIRIAM TLALI lives both in Hlotse, Lesotho and in Soweto. She is the first black woman to have published a novel in South Africa – *Between Two Worlds,* formerly known as *Muriel at Metropolitan* – and established the first black women's press in South Africa, Skotaville. She is the author of numerous fictional and biographical works, including the formerly banned *Amandla!* and *Footprints in the Quag: Stories and Dialogues from Soweto.* She is currently co-authoring a book on the women of Soweto with Rosemary Jolly.

DENNIS WALDER is Head of Literature at the Open University (UK). He is a Capetonian, and was educated at the Universities of Cape Town and Edinburgh. He has published widely on nineteenth- and twentieth-century literature. Author of the first book-length study of Athol Fugard (Macmillan, 1984), he has also edited Fugard's *Township Plays* (Oxford University Press, 1993), and is currently completing a book on *Post-Colonial Literatures: Theory and Practice,* for Basil Blackwell.

ZOË WICOMB was born in South Africa, and now teaches in the Department of English Studies at the University of Strathclyde, Glasgow. She is the author of *You Can't Get Lost in Cape Town* (Virago, 1988), and stories in such anthologies as *Colours of a New Day* (Ravan, 1990), *The Penguin Book of Contemporary South African Short Stories* (1993), and *The Heinemann Book of South African Short Stories* (1994). She has also published a number of articles on South African culture.

Acknowledgements

Acknowledgement is gratefully made to the Canadian High Commission for South Africa and Ms Lorenci Klopper for permission to reprint two maps of South Africa; to the Hon. Mongane Wally Serote, Malcolm Hacksley and the National English Literary Museum, and Rolf Solberg for permission to reprint the interview with Mongane Wally Serote; to Miriam Tlali for permission to publish Rosemary Jolly's interview with her; and to Justice Albie Sachs for permission to reprint his paper, 'Preparing Ourselves for Freedom'.

The editors wish to thank Laura Moss for research assistance and editorial work and Vanessa Farr for research assistance; and for help with some detailed factual matters, David R. Adler, editor of *Response*, and Alan Jeeves. At Cambridge University Press, Josie Dixon's encouragement and skill have been invaluable. Our greatest indebtedness is to Chris McMullen and Suzanne Hall, who were willing to go the extra mile several times over.

Note on references

Full references to South African literary works in English of the period 1970–1995 are given in the select bibliography at the end of the volume. Full references to other literary works cited, and to critical works cited, are given at the end of each chapter. Wherever possible, references within chapters are given by author's name and an abbreviated title.

South Africa 1970–1996: A chronology

1970   Nelson Mandela and other African National Congress (ANC) leaders have been in prison since 1963. B. J. Vorster has been Prime Minister of South Africa since the assassination of Hendrik Verwoerd in 1966. The Black Consciousness Movement (BCM) is gaining strength. Several neighbouring states have been granted independence.

1971   Formation of the Black People's Convention (BPC).

1973   Widespread strikes by black workers; formation of independent trade unions begins.

1975   Mangosuthu Buthelezi refounds the Zulu cultural organization known as Inkatha, later to become the Inkatha Freedom Party (IFP). Inkatha, some of whose activities are covertly funded by the South African government, is to clash with the ANC throughout the final years of apartheid. Independence of the former Portuguese colonies of Angola and Mozambique.

1976–7   On 16 June, 1976 Soweto children initiate a mass protest, primarily in reaction to the introduction of Afrikaans as the language of instruction in their schools. At least 575 people die as a result of police action in townships.

1976–81   South Africa, following its policy of separate development, 'grants independence' to the scattered territories of the Transkei, Bophutatswana, Venda, and the Ciskei, terming them 'homelands' and stripping their 'citizens' of South African citizenship. The international community refuses to recognize these territories as independent.

1977   In September Steve Biko, BCM leader, dies in detention. He is the forty-sixth person known to have died in detention that year, and his death is later proved to be the consequence of torture. The United Nations Security Council imposes an embargo on arms supply to South Africa. Banning of BCM organizations.

1978–84   P. W. Botha is Prime Minister, after Vorster's resignation due to financial scandal. Proclaims 'total onslaught' against the enemies of the apartheid state, including cross-border raids and invasion of Namibia.

1978   The Azanian People's Organization (AZAPO) is formed.

1979   The Federation of South African Trade Unions is formed. Black trade unions are permitted to register, and gain the right to strike. Wave of strikes, community protests, and student upheavals across the country.

1980 After a decade of warfare Rhodesia becomes independent and is renamed Zimbabwe.

1982 The Black Local Authorities Act establishes puppet municipal governments, contributing to the conditions of township violence during the decade. White right-wing Conservative Party set up under Andries Treurnicht.

1983 Resistance organizations drawn from a wide spectrum combine their efforts in a movement known as the United Democratic Front (UDF).

1984 A new constitution establishes a tricameral parliament of separate houses for whites, Asians, and Coloureds. Asians and Coloureds have limited participation in government; Africans still have no participation. Botha gains the new title of State President. Township insurrections provoke increased state brutality; South African Defence Force troops sent to occupy townships. Anglican Archbishop Desmond Tutu wins the Nobel Peace Prize.

1985 A State of Emergency is declared, instituting emergency powers such as detention without charge and curbs on press reporting. Thousands of detentions are made under emergency laws, which remain in effect until 1990. Foundation of the Congress of South African Trade Unions. COSATU becomes an important organization for resistance among workers involved in heavy industries, such as mining. The government begins to make secret contact with resistance leaders in exile and in prison.

1986 The United States Congress imposes federal economic sanctions against South Africa. Commonwealth Eminent Persons group recommends sanctions. Their visit to South Africa is halted as South African Defence Force launches cross-border raids. The pass and influx control laws and the Prohibition of Mixed Marriages Act are repealed.

1986–95 Violent conflict occurs between ANC supporters and IFP members in KwaZulu-Natal and the Johannesburg area (over 10,000 deaths in this period).

1987 250,000 mine-workers initiate a three week strike. Congress of South African Writers (COSAW) established.

1988 South Africa withdraws from the war against Angola and agrees with the UN to initiate the independence process for Namibia (formerly South West Africa). Intense resistance in KwaNdebele to 'independent homeland' status. Meeting between ANC and a group of Afrikaans writers.

1989 F. W. de Klerk becomes president after Botha suffers a stroke; the ANC presents terms for negotiation to the government (the Harare Declaration).

1990 De Klerk unbans the ANC, the Pan-Africanist Congress (PAC), and the South African Communist Party (SACP), and releases political prisoners, including Mandela. Namibia becomes independent.

1990–91 A series of apartheid laws are repealed, including the 1913 and 1936 Land Acts, the Group Areas Act, the Population Registration Act, and the Separate Amenities Act. The State of Emergency is revoked and the Convention for a Democratic South Africa (CODESA), involving all major political parties, is convened. Widespread violence continues; in October, the Goldstone Commission is established to investigate claims that government organizations are covertly fomenting conflict between the ANC and rival resistance groups.

1992 Whites vote in favour of the negotiation process in a referendum. The Boipatong and Bisho massacres occur. The ANC breaks off negotiations as Inkatha participates in increasing violence.

1993 Negotiations resume; an interim constitution is endorsed. In April, Chris Hani, General Secretary of the South African Communist Party, is assassinated by an agent of the SA Conservative Party; Mandela and de Klerk are jointly awarded the Nobel Peace Prize.

1994 On 27–30 April the ANC wins the first nonracial election in South Africa; Nelson Mandela becomes President on 10 May and forms the Government of National Unity; international sanctions are lifted; collapse of the 'homelands'; South Africa rejoins the Commonwealth. The elimination of remaining apartheid structures and institutions begins.

1995 The Constitutional Court is inaugurated in February and abolishes capital punishment; the Commission for the Restitution of Land Rights and the Truth and Reconciliation Commission are inaugurated; widespread disturbances occur in the universities, related to questions of access and curriculum. Violence in KwaZulu-Natal increases before local government elections.

1996 South Africa continues to deal with the aftermath of apartheid: economic difficulties, widespread poverty and unemployment, and a high crime rate. Evidence before Truth and Reconciliation Commission and in court cases reveals high-level involvement of apartheid governments in criminal activities.

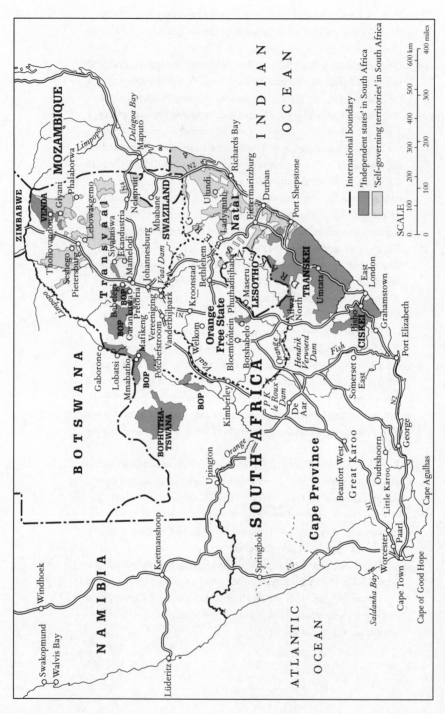

1. South Africa immediately prior to 1994, showing the apartheid 'homelands'

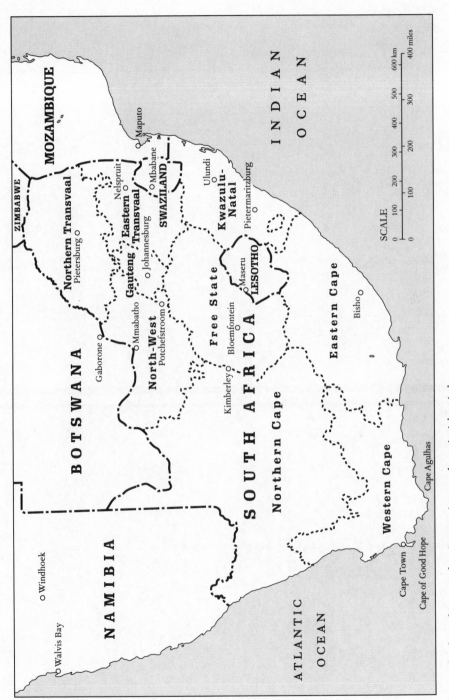

2. South Africa after 1994, showing provinces and provincial capitals

I

Introduction

ROSEMARY JOLLY AND DEREK ATTRIDGE

I

In declining our invitation to contribute an article to this volume, Breyten Breytenbach wished us well but pointed out the impossibility of our task. How can we begin to assess the issues raised by literature written in South Africa from 1970 to 1995, considering our closeness to the event?

Produced during a period of intense political struggle, the literature of the period offers an opportunity to examine a set of complex questions whose importance goes well beyond the boundaries of a single country. Does literature have a distinctive role to play in political life? What is the writer's responsibility in a situation of political crisis? How does the writer's concern with form and language relate to the demands of ethics and politics? How are ethical priorities changing in relation to political developments, and how are these changes suggested or reflected in cultural practices? How do issues of class and gender interact with those of race in an environment that is marked by rapid political shifts?

Such issues inform a further set of questions about the specificity of South African literary traditions. How do these traditions draw on or set themselves against literary developments in the rest of Africa, and in Europe and the Americas? How useful are the terms 'modernism', 'postmodernism', 'postcolonialism', in the description of South African literatures? How does writing by those who were classified as belonging to different racial groups under the apartheid system, by those who speak different languages, by those of different genders and sexualities, differently inflect the peculiar pressures and opportunities with which they were confronted during the past two and a half decades? What specific pressures and opportunities are they are confronted with now?

In the face of the breadth and complexity of these questions, Breytenbach's sense of our project as overly ambitious might appear justified. Yet we pose these questions in the hope not of reaching agreed conclusions but of sharpening the debate and extending it to a wider circle of participants. We regard the cultural history of South Africa in the transition from apartheid to democracy as richly exemplary of the intricate relations among aesthetics, ethics, and politics, and this volume as an opportunity to explore these relations in the light of a new freedom. The freedom to which we refer is not simply the constitutional end of apartheid, but that freedom which cannot be obtained purely in the realm of politics. South Africans during the period which forms the focus of this collection have been and are increasingly at liberty to identify and to reject not only the determinisms of apartheid, but also the determinisms of those systems which, in addition to racism, were implicated in and supported the ideological machinery of apartheid: patriarchy, sexism, homophobia, class and language bias, ethnic nationalism, and so on. The recognition of this (predominantly potential) liberty as a resource in examining the relation between ethical and aesthetic questions forms the context of our exploration.

Yet relinquishing determinism, in the sense of relinquishing ideologies which designate fixed values by assigning negative and positive attributes in accordance with stereotyped notions of essential verities, rather than a sense of the particular possibilities of a given context, is a difficult process. Apartheid, the system of legalized racism, demanded strategic opposition. In this context, such events as the rise of the Black Consciousness Movement in South Africa in the seventies, centred on the figure of Steve Biko, and the creation of the United Democratic Front in the eighties, which drew together a large number of disparate anti-apartheid groups, were accompanied by complementary strategies in the realm of culture. The African National Congress's approach to culture as a weapon in the struggle, and more specifically, the call for literature to represent the victimization of the oppressed in realist form, are instances of such strategies.

Yet an adherence to the ideology of the institutionalized culture of resistance appropriate to the anti-apartheid struggle, but limited by the framework of that time, may prove reactionary rather than liberatory in a post-apartheid context. Thus we find Njabulo Ndebele, as early as 1984, arguing against what he saw as the conservative effects of a realist literature focused on the violence of the apartheid regime as a spectacular object ('Rediscovery of the Ordinary'); and in 1989 Albie Sachs, in a much-discussed paper written for an ANC seminar (reprinted here for the first time in an international publication), denounced the formulation of culture as a weapon of the struggle, arguing for the value of art in terms of its creative ambiguity and contradiction in the struggle against, and not in concert with, the determinism of the gun.

South Africa is in the process of attempting to come to terms with the past in order to build a new future for itself. This is a task that requires balancing the need to view the present as a time of reckoning for those complicit in apartheid's crimes and the need for reconciliation in order to build for the future. This balancing act is being staged most visibly in the form of the South African Truth and Reconciliation Commission, chaired by Bishop Desmond Tutu. The Commission offers a forum for victims to bear witness against the apartheid state and its agents, and offers amnesty to those who confess their implication in state-perpetrated crimes, except in cases of extreme sadism or those that manifest personal vengeance. This is obviously tricky business: as André Brink points out (below, page 24), there may well be no way of avoiding mistakes of judgement in such a context. In addition, the offer of amnesty is, as one would expect, controversial. Nevertheless, the Commission highlights the need to narrativize the past in such a way that the future becomes – unlike the past – bearable. In this light one can view former Prime Minister P. W. Botha's ten-page refusal to admit to any wrongdoing (his response to being subpoenaed by the Commission, having been implicated by other witnesses) as a not-so-extraordinary testimony to the continued existence of those who believe, or claim to believe, that apartheid in and of itself did not constitute a crime, in the face of testimony to the contrary from their cohorts. The secret, despite and partly due to denials such as Botha's, is out.

The Truth and Reconciliation Commission bears the double responsibility of exposure and acceptance. This twin responsibility is at the heart of current debates over the evaluation of literatures produced in South Africa during the demise of apartheid. The need to tell the underside of apartheid history, and to outline its implications for the present and future, is matched by a desire in many instances to find a form of narration capable of acknowledging difference without fearing it and without fetishizing it. The postcolonial world generally faces this task; but the specifics of the South African situation are worth outlining in some detail, as they can form a singular resource for others working on related issues in a postcolonial context.

International responses to South African cultural products, as Jeanne Colleran points out in this volume, have tended to ignore the complexity of work produced by South Africans. This is partly due to the fact that the international consumer of South African culture has been encouraged to view South Africa as an ideological battleground that represents the Manichean conflict *par excellence*. Despite our current critical appreciation of postmodern indeterminacy, we are hesitant or unwilling to recognize in cultural products from both sides of the colonial divide breaches in oppositional logic that could constitute the beginnings of genuine cross-cultural exchange. To insist that South Africa during apartheid should be the emblem of racial struggles internationally, or to use the inauguration of the 'New South Africa' as a symbol of the triumph of multiculturalism over racism and other forms of discrimination, is both simplistic and fallacious. Indeed, brief mention of some of the difficulties attending the initiation of the 'New South Africa', many of which are outlined in more detail in this collection, should be more than enough to give any critic who would see post-apartheid South Africa as an ideal image of postcolonial liberation pause.

The term itself represents the impossibility of trying to narrate the future as though it were severed, in some sort of originary beheading, from the past. As Rob Nixon has emphasized, the phrase 'the New South Africa' was minted by F. W. de Klerk in his speech on 2 February 1990, which proclaimed the end of apartheid, announced Mandela's release from prison, and promised the repeal of apartheid laws; but its conception should not be misrecognized as immaculate: 'The New South Africa would become de Klerk's best-known coinage and an indisputable asset in the astute marketing of his regime as converts to decency and penitence, in a campaign that has seen an instinct for political survival passed off as a species of righteousness' ('"An Everybody Claim Dem Democratic"', 23). Such specious righteousness is evident in National Party condemnations of Inkatha-initiated acts of violence: the 'New South Africa' as event should not disguise the longstanding National Party support of Inkatha's violent expressions of Zulu nationalism (24). Following the announcement in May 1996 of its withdrawal from the Government of National Unity as a prelude to the local elections, the National Party once again demonstrated its 'instinct for political survival' by billing itself as the creator of multiparty democracy in South Africa. 'First we brought you democracy', one of their election advertisements reads, 'Now we bring you multiparty democracy.'

Inevitably, such resurrections produce parodic effects. In statements like the following, the National Party's local election blurb sounds like Desmond Tutu's 'Rainbow Nation': 'The National Party will continue to consolidate its position as a party based on Christian democratic values, uniting South Africans from all communities and all walks of life. Our commitment to reconciliation will form the cornerstone of our new

4

role.' The sense of the ludicrous that this mimicry produces for those aware of the political history of hypocrisy in South Africa was illustrated nicely – if unintentionally – by a Standard Three (Grade Five) student interviewed by a colleague of ours who is working on the new history curriculum for South African schools. When asked in a questionnaire, 'What would you teach American pupils about South African history?', the boy responded: 'I would tell them that we have a Rambo Nation.' This facet of the new South Africa is an encouraging one: the entity that has come into being is far too contradictory to be held up as a symbol of triumph that renders critical vigilance, including self-awareness, redundant. The New South Africa – the Rainbow Nation – is always on the verge of becoming the Rambo Nation.

It is with an awareness of what Elleke Boehmer refers to in her contribution as this 'cusp time', and the importance of teasing out its heady implications, that these chapters, interviews, and position papers have been written. We have included many writers who themselves have made significant contributions to the recent cultural history of South Africa, and who are currently negotiating in their own literary writing the issues discussed here. We have also taken care to ensure a balance between contributors working in South Africa, and contributors in both North America and the United Kingdom. The period we have chosen spans both apartheid's most aggressive phase and its final collapse, a time of intensified oppression and resistance beginning with the rise of the Black Consciousness Movement and ending with the early trials of the young democracy. We focus on writing in English, both for the sake of the coherence of the volume and because it is with this body of literature that South African culture engages most fully with an international audience. However, any attempt to exclude writing in the many other languages spoken in South Africa – the country now boasts eleven official languages – would be highly artificial, and a number of the contributors (who themselves belong to a variety of language groups) extend their discussion beyond works in English. All the major genres are treated, and a number of the contributors respond to the work, creative or critical, of other contributors, reflecting the vigorous debates about South African culture now in progress.

II

Given this context, it is not surprising that many of the debates consider the role of ethics in critical judgement. 'Ethics' is a slippery word, used by different writers for different purposes, but for the present we can take it to refer to the continuing attempt to do justice to others, or, more precisely, 'the other' – the encountered person, group, or culture which does not conform to the set of beliefs, assumptions, and habits that make up the encountering self. Ethics in this sense both precedes and exceeds morality, 'the principles of conduct of both actual moralities (for example, the moral code of Victorian England, or of twentieth-century corporate business) and of ideal morality (the best justified or true moral system)' (Pojman, *Discovering Right and Wrong*, 2). It calls for careful research, for the always imperfect attempt to understand the other without turning the other into a version of the self. Only on this basis is it possible to learn from the other, and thus to engage in a genuine interchange between cultures. Through such institutions as the Constitutional Court, South Africa is self-consciously engaged in an attempt to achieve an agreed moral code that will be adequate to its unique history and complex present; one of the responsibilities of the artist, however, is constantly to test the generalizations of moral systems by confronting them with specific realizations of otherness that demand creative ethical responses.

The temptation to make 'ethical' judgements immediately, that is, before the required research has been carried out, can be overwhelming – all the more so as there is a sense in which *every* judgement is premature, necessarily made before the totality of the evidence can be weighed (a limitation of which literature has often provided powerful instances). Nevertheless, witnessing the proceedings of the Truth and Reconciliation Commission, one notices with interest that the victims testifying are as anxious to know more about the details of their victimization as they are to request reparation from the state; in some cases, when asked what they wanted from the Commission, those testifying requested only information, and not reparation. While retributive justice satisfies a certain sense of symmetry, the witnesses' curiosity about their victimizers' motives and further details of the crimes committed exceeds any closure retributive justice on its own can offer. There is a tension between the desire for reparation – not in terms of the physical comfort it promises but the closure it appears to promise – and the desire for knowledge, which denies any such closure. An analogous contradictory desire characterizes current modes of postcolonial criticism. On the one hand, there is the impulse to name and blame the perpetrators of colonial violence – even if it is the rhetorical violence of the cultural artifact that is at stake, and even if ambivalence is attributed to the colonizing discourse; on the other hand, there is a desire to develop, through an understanding of the other that does not reduce the other to the same, ethical modes of cross-cultural interchange.

South Africa has passed through a period that has for obvious reasons produced a large body of what one might call judgemental texts, both critical and creative; texts that assume an ethical sufficiency to exist in the condemnation of apartheid and its agents. For this reason, the current South African situation forms a productive arena for the exploration of the uses and limitations of, as well as alternatives to, judgemental writing. For one can grant a historical strategic importance to judgemental writing in the struggle against apartheid without denying the fact that it has produced a paucity of options for creative responses to post-apartheid freedoms and their attendant challenges. Indeed, it is remarkable that so many cultural workers from such different backgrounds and producing such differing approaches to South African creative work claim this as the predominant challenge of the current situation, although their delineation of this challenge – as the debate between Benita Parry and David Attwell in this volume illustrates – is as varied as one would expect.

The history behind this challenge relates to the use to which cultural artifacts were put by political organizations during the anti-apartheid struggle. It is ironic that an awareness of the use the apartheid regime made of the management of culture, through its encouragement of certain modes of nationalist discourse and its censorship of others, has given even those South Africans sympathetic to the cause of the ANC and its affiliated organizations a wariness of the use of cultural management to gain specific political outcomes. It was as early as the 1920s that Peter Abrahams, staunch Communist and anti-apartheid writer, refused to accept the Party's demands that he submit his work to be vetted; and as recently as 1993 that André Brink expressed his misgivings over the bureaucratic 'management of culture' by the ANC's Department of Arts and Culture.

As Benita Parry has noted elsewhere, the ANC and other anti-apartheid organizations' tendency to produce doctrinal directives with respect to cultural 'development' can result in a profoundly non-democratic approach to creative activity (the ANC becomes 'donor of knowledge and freedom to the oppressed'), and a separation of the aesthetic and political or ethical ('Culture Clash', 128). This enables, as Parry writes, 'the reification of a stark choice between solipsistic aestheticism and engaged art' (129). The danger of refusing to come out of the shell constructed by such orthodoxies is pinpointed by the ever prescient Ndebele, whose comment is as applicable to much postcolonial criticism as it is to his intended subject, the relation between sociopolitical issues and artistic production: 'The problem has been that questions about art and society have been easily settled after a general consensus about commitment. This has led to the prescription of solutions even before all the problems have been discovered and analyzed' ('Beyond "Protest"', 212): hence the proliferation of premature judgement, of a failure to do justice to the other as other.

Malvern van Wyk Smith's provocative question, 'Why is there so little analysis of the cross-cultural achievements of colonial texts?', can be answered by taking into account Ndebele's identification of 'a general consensus about commitment' as pre-emptive. Clearly postcolonial writing desires to contest the power of the colonizer, and assert the authority of the oppressed subject. It is also clear that some degree of ambivalence has been introduced in critical judgements of colonial narratives; but the potential development of this ambivalence as the basis for cross-cultural exchange has not been realized. The reason for this is the form judgemental writing takes in postcolonial criticism: a general consensus, to use Ndebele's term again, that renders antipathy to the colonizer essentialist. To adhere to such fundamentalism is to ignore those elements of early colonial texts that manifest 'a conscious effort to let the other speak, even – and especially – when the writer's own beliefs were most directly challenged' (van Wyk Smith, 'The Metadiscourses of Postcolonialism', 286). This position also disallows, in a sense, the existence of a post-apartheid South Africa: if we cannot identify the historical gateways to cross-cultural exchange, how can we ever hope to create our own?

Elleke Boehmer points out in her contribution that the narratives of the eighties, written during a period of extreme violence perpetrated by the apartheid regime, relate time as end-stopped, rather than representing indeterminacy as possibility: 'Narrative uncertainty, its suggestiveness and tease, were constrained within the deathly binaries of a long history of oppression and opposition' (below, page 45). Here the unbearable reality of the apartheid world, she suggests, resists the novelistic imagination. There are some periods, it would seem, in which the task of imagining difference – temporally speaking and with regard to the other – is less possible than at other times. In this context, André Brink's description in this volume of fiction as that which is at the margin of what has been and what can be newly conceived, 'as that which inserts

8

itself into the reader's consciousness as an invitation to a moral choice' (below, page 22), underscores the role of the fictive world as a means of exploring the possibilities of ethical cross-cultural intercourse.

This exploration, however, is not one in which there is a single, defined prize to be found. The other is not a trophy to be won in an orientalist game of hide and seek, the dynamics of which depend upon resurrecting the other as a source of authentic knowledge whose authority rests on the ethnic origins of specific 'others', that is to say, real subjects. On this score, the history of South African culture is illuminating for its numerous instances of those who have rejected ethnic identification as a means of negotiating their future because of the bigoted formulation it takes within a racist imagination. (Rita Barnard's contribution to this volume examines some examples of the production of racial difference as myth, as well as some significant counter-mythic endeavours.) Recent South African history is replete with examples of how racial politics render ethnic identification nonsensical. In the fifties, the *Drum* writers and readers rejected the initial editorial direction of the periodical, which was to assume that to be black was to be constantly in search of one's ethnic 'roots', to be on a sort of eternal pilgrimage in the wilderness for one's (lost) self. In the eighties, ludicrous examples of the abuse to which politics puts ethnic identification continued to abound: is King Goodwill Zwelethini, manufactured as King of the Zulus both by whites and Zulus in the interests of ethnic nationalism, the authentic other with which to replace the colonizer?

One could argue that, counter to this politics of authenticity, postcolonialism poses syncretic practice. Yet just as van Wyk Smith argues that the ambivalence of postcolonialism is limited by reliance on a fundamentally Manichean structure, so genuine syncretism is limited by the politics of multiculturalism. While we may read, for example, Wilson Harris's parables of the creativity of cross-cultural fertilization attentively, we rarely produce criticism that recognizes in texts – whatever cognitive limitations they may exhibit – the possibility of interchange between cultures. Part of the problem lies in our fixation on difference, and this is where the suspicion multicultural rhetoric holds for many South Africans – in this volume, Dennis Walder's scepticism of South Africa's 'world cup "nationalism"' say, or Graham Pechey's refusal to believe in secular state politics as an ethical solution, even if they are Mandela's politics – comes in handy as a critique of the essentialism of many postcolonial formulations of hybridity.

Zoë Wicomb's critique of Bhabha's formulation, in her contribution to this volume, is crucial here. She points out that the recent history of coloured politics in South Africa plays havoc with Bhabha's association of a subversive hybridity expressed specifically in terms of biological metaphor. The fact that with the post-apartheid vote coloureds have chosen to align themselves with the tawdry 'multiculturalism' of de Klerk's Nationalists, she argues, speaks to the persistence of shame in the formulation of coloured identity. In this context, the function of the recognition of difference in the subject classified as hybrid is self-abnegation. The South African experience suggests that the fetishization of difference, which takes its form here in terms of the stigmatization of race, produces negative effects. Neither shame, nor its light double, white guilt, are particularly useful resources for a post-apartheid future.

The fetishization of difference – the reading of difference as having an essential and fundamentally incomprehensible content – would appear, then, to be merely another form of Ndebele's moral consensus, in which the recognition of difference becomes a virtue in and of itself; and the institutional ramifications of this practice need to be recognized. Ndebele, in writing of the crisis of culture in South Africa – the great divide that Lewis Nkosi documents and mourns in his contribution to this collection – uses language that tellingly echoes Chinua Achebe's famous comments on racism in Conrad's *Heart of Darkness*:

> Standing between [black and white] is a chasm of engineered ignorance, misunderstanding, division, illusion and hostility. It highlights the national tragedy of people who have lived long together, but could do no better than acknowledge only their differences. They have done so with such passion as would suggest that perhaps they sensed something in common between them, which neither of them was prepared to acknowledge.
> ('Liberation and the Crisis of Culture', 22)

Ndebele's analysis is revealing once it is applied to the field of postcolonial studies as a set of institutional practices. We may not wish to go as far as Anthony Appiah – 'Postcoloniality is the condition of what we might ungenerously call a *comprador* intelligentsia; a relatively small Western-style, Western-trained group of writers and thinkers, who mediate the trade in cultural commodities of world capitalism at the periphery' (348) – but we need to consider that scholars tutored in the paramount importance of difference can fail, at some crucial, ethical level, to respect the subjects of their study.

On the research front, one cannot help but notice the structural similarities between 'multiculturalism' and 'Commonwealth/post-colonial literatures' as categories that produce difference as morality in a form in which only certain kinds of difference, such as national identity, are easily visible and assumed to constitute unproblematic categories. In a 1993 review of Pauline Fletcher's *Black/White Writing: Essays on South African Literature* and Michael Wade's *White on Black in South Africa*, Isabel Hofmeyr notes that 'one striking assumption in both of these texts is that there is indeed a fairly unproblematic thing called South African literature and that it resides in a series of canonical texts' ('Floating in Metropolitan Space', 19). What Hofmeyr takes exception to in these collections is embedded in the institutional organization of post-colonial studies as a whole:

> A few canonical names that signify South African literature are piled up, and then set in the aspic of an introduction. As a result, all of these pieces seem to float in some unspecified metropolitan space. The overall effect is one of muffled distance . . . [producing a sense of] the undifferentiated space that the notion of South African literature – and no doubt other 'Commonwealth'/ 'postcolonial' literatures – occupy internationally. (20)

Here postcolonial studies replicates rather than critiques the conservative dynamics of an image of South Africa that stages the country and its turbulent history as a spectacle for the consumption of an audience whose appetite for the exotic is voracious. Indeed, the success of the market for South Africa-as-spectacle in its domestic capacity has created a tension between those working in theatre-for-development and those in the theatre for commercial profit, a tension evident in Maishe Maponya's outline of challenges facing theatre practitioners in South Africa and one that has recently exploded in the *Sarafina II* scandal detailed by Zakes Mda.

How, then, to go about creating a future in which we can develop alternatives to history 'as the tall story of the ruling classes' (Horn, below, page 35)? In each of these contributions – and markedly so in the interviews with Miriam Tlali and Mongane Wally Serote, in which these authors discuss their own writing directly – there is a sense of a new space, a space filled with the potential to imagine difference differently, but also still jeopardized by the force of an inclusive nationalist rhetoric that ignores questions of power. As Rob Nixon puts it, 'What is needed is an approach to differences that breaks with smiling multiculturalism and its ugly mirror image, apartheid, by recognizing that inequalities in power slice across the sites of identity' ('"An Everybody Claim Dem Democratic"', 32).

If multiculturalism is the latest tall story of the ruling classes, Njabulo Ndebele's now famous call for a rediscovery of the ordinary, made over a decade ago, seems more important than ever. For if one is to combat the sort of social imagination that insists, deterministically, on viewing differences within set hierarchies – just as postcolonialism tends to see nationality or race as the determining factor – a sense of how subjectivity is exercised in everyday instances, in all of its complexity, needs to be conveyed. One of the most powerful resources available for this project is literature. In such a practice, South Africans will no longer be forced to view themselves through and as ghostly colonial spectacles; or to fetishize race, relegating other struggles for justice to the back burner; or to commit all aspects of social life, including cultural production, to the dictates of political exigency.

This is not only a method for envisioning the future, however. It is also a manner of mourning creatively for the losses of the past with which we now live: a poetry of ruins, as Brian Macaskill puts it in this volume. It is a way of revisioning the past in terms of the gateways that past could offer the future. Among what has been overlooked within the overwhelming framework of the anti-apartheid struggle, as André Brink and Michiel Heyns illustrate in their contributions, are the narratives of women and homosexuals. At the close of his chapter, Heyns discusses the work of Koos Prinsloo, noted for its dispassionate register of the events he describes, in terms of its 'refusal to order . . . data in terms of a hierarchy of significance' (below, page 120). In this profoundly non-judgemental form of narrative, the violence of the Emergency finds its context in the violence of the everyday. Prinsloo's refusal to privilege neither the Emergency, nor his own sexuality, nor his impending death from AIDS as points through which to understand the world that produced the narrative paradoxically provides a gateway for identification: 'To read Prinsloo is not so much to understand the Emergency as to experience it, and to see the gay writer not as a marginalized observer but as a participant in a troubled society' (below, page 121). Like Prinsloo's narrative, this collection does not aim to tell the story of South Africa so as to deliver the final word on the decline of apartheid, in a move that would once again distance the reader and produce South Africa as spectacle. Instead, it presents the insights of a variety of writers, drawing from a range of different experiences – as academics, cultural practitioners, creative writers, residents, exiles – as a gateway, necessarily imperfect, to the substance and significance of South African cultural production between 1970 and 1995. The collection does not claim exhaustiveness, which would be as impossible as the ideal ethical judgement we have described; it offers, rather, the perspective of the indeterminate space between the old and the new as valuable in its own right.

Works cited

Achebe, Chinua. 'An Image of Africa: Racism in Conrad's Heart of Darkness'. *Hopes and Impediments: Selected Essays, 1965–87*. London: Heinemann, 1988. 1–13.

Appiah, Kwame Anthony. 'Is the Post- in Postmodernism the Post- in Postcolonial?' *Critical Inquiry* 17 (1991): 336–57.

Brink, André. 'An Uneasy Freedom: Dangers of Political "Management of Culture" in South Africa'. *Times Literary Supplement*, 24 September 1993: 13.

Hofmeyr, Isabel. 'Floating in Metropolitan Space'. Review of Pauline Fletcher, *Black/White Writing: Essays on South African Literature* and Michael Wade, *White on Black in South Africa*. *Southern African Review of Books* (November/December 1993): 19–20.

Ndebele, Njabulo. 'Beyond "Protest": New Directions in South African Literature'. *Criticism and Ideology: Second African Writers' Conference, Stockholm 1986*. Ed. Kirsten Holst Petersen. Uppsala: Scandinavian Institute of African Studies, 1988. 205–18.

'Liberation and the Crisis of Culture'. *Southern African Review of Books* (February/May 1990): 22–3.

'The Rediscovery of the Ordinary: Some New Writings in South Africa'. *South African Literature and Culture: Rediscovery of the Ordinary*. Introduction Graham Pechey. Manchester: Manchester University Press, 1994. 41–59.

Nixon, Rob. '"An Everybody Claim Dem Democratic": Notes on the "New" South Africa'. *Transition* 54 (1991): 20–35.

Parry, Benita. 'Culture Clash'. *Transition* 55 (1992): 125–34.

Pojman, Louis P. *Discovering Right and Wrong*. Belmont, California: Wadsworth, 1990.

van Wyk Smith, Malvern. 'The Metadiscourses of Postcolonialism: "Strong Othering" and European Images of Africa'. *History and Anthropology* 9. 2–3 (March 1996): 267–91.

2

Interrogating silence: new possibilities faced by South African literature

ANDRÉ BRINK

I

One of the most challenging statements I have ever heard came from a wise old Frenchman. 'La parole sert à corriger le silence', he said; adding under his breath, 'Mais le silence est in-cor-ri-gi-ble.' Not that I'm sure language inevitably 'corrects' silence: there would be in such a claim an arrogance I hesitate to endorse; but that the word interminably and indefatigably strives to *interrogate* silence, of that I have no doubt.

The writer's primary engagement, I should like to argue, is with silence. Provided the assumptions underlying the statement are clarified. This kind of interrogation is not a power-play but a dialogue. Silence is not to be thought of as an opponent or an adversary; it is not simply the 'other' of language. If words are indeed, from a certain point of view, wrested from silence, it is equally true that silence may be read to inhere in language itself. This provides a clue to the kind of dialogic writing I have in mind: a coexistence of silence and the word. If all writing demonstrates the tension between the spoken and the unspoken, the sayable and the unsayable, these elements of the dialogue should not be seen as opposites in a binary equation, but at most as end points on a sliding scale – the kind of notion fuzzy mathematics would express in a scale *between* 0 and 1.

This is not intended as fanciful theorizing but as a necessary pre-text to my discussion of new possibilities opening up to South African writers since the dismantling of apartheid (both of its voices and its silences) began.

II

The experience of apartheid has demonstrated that different kinds or levels of silence exist. There is the general silence of which I have spoken above and which exists in a dynamic relation with language/literature; but there are also more specific silences imposed by certain historical conjunctions. If any word involves a grappling with silence, the word uttered in the kind of repressive context exemplified by apartheid evokes an awareness of particular territories forbidden to language. Just as surely as certain sexual relationships were proscribed by apartheid, certain experiences or areas of knowledge were out of bounds to probing in words. These were often immediate and definable: certain actions of the police or the military; certain statements or writings by 'banned' persons; the activities of the ANC or other organizations of liberation.

Behind these loomed larger, greyer areas: whole territories of historical consciousness silenced by the power establishment and invaded by the dominant discourse in order to make them inaccessible to other voices. These included the distortions of the 'right' to the land (even today few white South Africans realize that blacks had settled in the subcontinent many centuries before the first European caravels circumnavigated the Cape of Storms); abuses in the name of Christianity (using the Bible to instil an acceptance by the oppressed of their fate); the extent of miscegenation between staunch Afrikaners and their slaves or servants; the enslavement of indigenous peoples in the interior; strategies to ensure and perpetuate the marginalization of women in both black and white societies; the involvement of 'Coloured' people in the Great Trek; the rape of the environment in the process of 'taming the wilderness'; the tradition of Afrikaner dissidence, etc. These processes of silencing would also include the fabrication of dominant myths about the intervention of God in Afrikaner history (perpetuated even in present-day monstrosities like Michener's *The Covenant*).

Viewed from the opposite end, the very urgencies of a struggle against apartheid encouraged the imposition of other silences (betrayals and excesses within the ranks of the liberation movements; appalling conditions, torture, and murder in the training camps and detention centres of the exiled ANC in Angola, etc.) and produced a sense of priorities which made it very difficult for writers – even for writers who refused to be explicitly harnessed to any 'cause' – to write about certain very ordinary human situations (like a love relationship without direct political connotations) without inviting accusations of fiddling while Rome burns, of suppressing more 'urgent' issues, of avoiding 'reality', or of self-indulgence. It was the kind of situation in which any utterance invited scrutiny in terms of what was *not* said: each word spoken/written implied the imposition of silence on another that might (or even 'should') have taken its place in the paradigm. How often in those years (which already appear immeasurably remote even if they remain distressingly close in time) was one reminded of Brecht's famous dictum about those moments in human history when to speak of flowers means to remain silent about so many other things.

One of the many problems posed by the kind of literature produced in such circumstances is of course the reduction of the co-ordinates in the situation, a tendency towards simple oppositions and binarities. In the best writers these conditions sharpened the imagination, forced it to become more resourceful, refined its subtleties. But contextually the binarities persisted in the tendency to reduce the world to predictable patterns of us and them, black and white, good and bad, male and female. When this climate did not overtly impinge on the processes of writing, at the very least it conditioned the reception of whatever was written. And even the most refined imagination had no choice but to take the bars of the prison as both starting point and point of reference. (Although texts as far apart as *Don Quixote* and the writings of Andrei Sinyavsky have triumphantly demonstrated the scope of the imagination constrained – and challenged – by prison bars.)

The full effect of this burden shouldered by writers under apartheid is only beginning to come to light now that the situation is in the process of changing. An awareness of yesterday's silences – imposed by the binarities; or existing beyond the binarities; or surrounding the binarities; or, in the final analysis, within the binarities – is beginning to dawn. The discovery is both exhilarating and daunting. At last the 'raids on the inarticulate' can assume their full complexity.

III

Throughout the apartheid years the urge to report a cause aright was a prime mover in the work of most writers caught up in the culture of resistance. In the first instance, there was the need for black writers to articulate their oppression primarily to promote the solidarity of internal resistance. Many of these writers were not interested in targeting an international audience: their focus was the local struggle. This state of affairs compounded the irony that during the darkest apartheid years, while the work of a few white writers was avidly read in most Western countries, most of the black writers in South Africa remained unknown abroad. (At least part of this isolation must also, regrettably, be ascribed, I think, to a well-masked racism among readers abroad, who preferred to read works by white writers with whom they felt they could identify more readily, rather than make the effort of coming to terms with a different cultural tradition.) This articulation passed through various clearly demarcated stages – a focus on the urban experience in the work of the *Drum* generation; an exploration of the parameters of oppression after Sharpeville; increasing exploration of literature as 'a tool in the struggle' after the Soweto uprisings of 1976; near-triumphant affirmation during the several States of Emergency since 1986 – but its essential characteristic, whether in poetry, theatre or fiction/faction, remained its rootedness in the 'historical' approach, its faith in the processes of representation. White writers, too, as more and more areas of reportage became proscribed by law and proclamation to the probings of journalism, experienced the need 'to tell things as they are'. If, as Kundera argued in *The Art of the Novel*, the only justification for the novel lies in saying what cannot be said in any other way, then apartheid ironically imposed on the writer precisely the need to report, as this was not permitted to the other media. Whatever else the writer set out to achieve, the need to function as historian – that is, through 'reporting' and 'representing' – informed much of her/his activity and defined much of her/his scope.

But it was a risky enterprise; and the reception accorded a writer like J. M. Coetzee highlighted the dangers lurking within such an approach. The interminable debate between supporters and detractors of his work has carried the claims and counter-claims of 'story-as-story' versus 'story-as-history', of historicity versus (postmodernist) textuality, right through the transition from apartheid into the more open-ended if stimulatingly confusing 'New South Africa'.

Much of the confusion arises from the fact that while both these approaches – the 'historical' and the 'textual' – may be read as responses to silence, they have been regarded for too long, and by too many, as almost mutually exclusive. This is once again the result of strict binary thinking. Surely the point is, once again, that story and history should not be read as choices in an either/or equation, but as markers on a scale. (It is significant that French, like other Romance languages, has but a single word for both genres – *histoire*.)

Within historiography itself, recent years have witnessed an increasing awareness of history not as the representation of fact but as text. Interestingly enough, this is a development presaged by the very origins of Western historiography in Herodotus, who was more concerned with the imaginative structuring of his massive history in terms of the nine muses than with chronology, causality, or even veracity; and in these postmodern times in which the Derridean notion of supplementarity informs so much of our concept of textuality ('Il n'y a pas de hors-texte') it is a sobering rediscovery to find in book IV chapter 30 of Herodotus the caution that 'This history of mine has from the beginning sought out the supplementary to the main argument', an announcement that prefigures Derrida. So it should come as no surprise that in postmodern historiography, in the process of rejoining – and reinventing – its origins, the world-as-text should find itself converging more and more with the text-as-world.

This informs our reading of *both* historiography and fiction and returns us to definitions of postmodernism – particularly in the light of the argument that 'having shed the need for history, South African litera-ture can now at last begin to explore the possibilities of story'; or, in more specific terms, that 'having outgrown its need for realism South African literature can now at last embrace postmodernism'.

The problem, of course, is that postmodernism itself has become sus-pect, especially in the wake of astute theorists like Fredric Jameson who reject the mode because of its alleged congenital inability to enter into alliances with historicity and morality. Postmodernism's focus on 'mere' textuality, these critics argue, removes literature from the materiality that underlies moral choice and historical praxis. They refer to the fact that postmodernism feeds on 'the essentially metropolitan experience of post-1968 disillusionment, its accommodation to the postindustrial age, and its subsequent celebration of relativist experimentation', as David Attwell aptly summarized it in *J. M. Coetzee* (21). This has resulted in the widespread condemnation of postmodernism as a form of neo-conser-vatism because of its alleged inability to act upon the world, its 'self-indulgence', its withdrawal into 'mere' textuality.

It would seem to me that the contrary is true. Wellbery was among the first to point out that, in fact, postmodernism 'is inextricably bound up with a critique of domination' ('Postmodernism in Europe', 235); and Hutcheon argued convincingly for the coincidence of the postmodern 'with a general critical awareness of the existence and power of systems of representation which do not *reflect* society so much as *grant* meaning and value within a particular society' (*The Politics of Postmodernism*, 8). It is becoming more and more likely that the real neo-conservatism of a reactionary mentality is vested, not in the historical or traditional ideo-logical approach, but in the assumption that reality *can* (indeed 'must'!)

be captured and represented, preferably in a prescribed and predictable manner.

Through perceiving the world as a story to be told and endlessly reshaped, I would argue, the reader is actually encouraged to act upon the world. Once the world is perceived as story, with an endless capacity for renewal, metamorphosis, and reinvention, literature becomes more, not less, potent.

The materialist approach runs the risk of sending us back yet again to the dreary binarities of logocentrism (one of whose apotheoses was the apartheid system). It denies the consideration that postmodernism has never been a unitary concept and that particularly in South America (but also in the work of European writers like Hrabal, Kundera, Calvino, and Eco) it has assumed forms of powerful historical engagement without for a moment relinquishing its sense of experiment, relativism, and textuality.

What David Attwell has advanced in defence of J. M. Coetzee – the possibility of discovering historicity *within* postmodernism (and vice versa, of course) – may well outline the basis of an argument in favour of a much more nuanced view of postmodernism in general, and of at least some of the possibilities open to South African writers in particular. This would illuminate the nature of the writer's engagement with the silences of apartheid.

IV

Following the Holocaust, critics like the early George Steiner argued that some experiences belong, through the extent of the outrage and excess they involve, outside language altogether: 'The world of Auschwitz lies outside speech as it lies outside reason' (*Language and Silence*, 108). But it is significant that as the Second World War recedes in the memory, some of these same critics (with the notable exception of a few key figures like Elie Wiesel) have begun to shift their position: in due course Steiner himself wrote a novel about the Holocaust, and pleaded for literature 'to give to reality the greater permanence of the imagined'. Because 'without the arts, form would remain unmet and strangeness without speech in the silence of the stone' (*Real Presences*, 140).

One respects the attitude of critics like Wyschogrod who argue that 'Art takes the sting out of suffering . . . it is therefore forbidden to make fiction of the Holocaust . . . Any attempt to transform the Holocaust into art demeans the Holocaust . . .' ('Some Theological Reflections', 68). Yet, if artists were really to refrain from confronting certain territories of experience, would that not amount to an additional insult to our humanity?[1] If at least a large measure of what makes us human is vested in language (however imperfect, treacherous, or tentative that language may be) then nothing could possibly be excluded a priori from the endeavours of language. Every attempt may indeed be a different kind of failure, but our humanity survives only by virtue of the attempts. Is this presumptuous? If so, we live by presumption.

In any case I doubt that Wyschogrod is right in asserting that 'art takes the sting out of suffering'. Does it not, on the contrary, attempt to *heighten* the perception of that experience and intensify its texture?[2] Or, at the very least, to transform the experience – even if the very 'nature' of the experience appears to lie in the fact that it *eludes* or *defies* understanding – into something that can be grasped by the imagination in order to guard against its repetition? If this is 'blasphemy', as Wiesel contended, or in Adorno's words 'an abomination', then – outrageous as it may sound – it is in these very abominations and blasphemies that the human mind finds its reasons for survival when the only alternative is silence. Our blasphemy, and our one chance of redemption, lies in our

1. And who has the authority to define these silences? The Holocaust undoubtedly represents an extreme of human experience; but does it differ from other horrors in quantity or in quality? If in quantity, where does one draw the line? Would the Holocaust be 'permissible' as a subject for literature if a million Jews were murdered rather than six million? Or a hundred thousand? Or a thousand? . . . If there is a difference in quality, how could this difference be defined in relation to, say, the exploits of the conquistadores in the New World?; the ravages of the Black Death?; the genocides of Biafra, the Congo, Chechnya, Burundi? These questions are by no means to be construed as irreverence towards, and lack of outrage about, the Holocaust, but as mere pointers towards the kind of difficulties one encounters when any attempt is made to impose firm boundaries between language and silence.

2. I am aware of criticism like that of Lilian Kremer: 'To structure a creative response to a destructive force is an anomaly. Nothing about the Holocaust is aesthetic. It is a denial of the creative instinct' (*Witness through the Imagination*, 28). But this would also rule out most of the writing done under apartheid, and deny the contribution of such writing to the gradual creation of a mental climate within which apartheid could ultimately be subverted and eventually destroyed. (I am indebted to Chet Pager for some of the references to commentaries on Holocaust literature.)

indefatigable attempts to speak the unspeakable, to eat of the forbidden fruit.

Critics of Holocaust literature, like many critics who opposed anti-apartheid literature like that of Fugard as a futile 'sugaring of the pill',[3] generally do not object to 'reporting' or 'witnessing' the events – in fact, this is generally encouraged – but only to aesthetic treatment of what is perceived to be too horrendous to be 'reduced' to a play, a poem, a novel. But this is really a curious misconception of literature, once again informed by the dangerous binarism of 'fact' and 'fiction'. Not only is it a sad truth that persistent reportage blunts the mind and diminishes the effect (as any television addict can testify), but we know by now that 'facts' themselves are suspect, and approachable only in a textualized form. 'History' is not a series of events but a *narrated* (and manipulated) series of events; and at any moment in the series a mixture of orientations towards representation and invention is evident. The sliding scale remains with us. Moreover, within certain contexts one end of the scale from 'fact' to 'fiction' may be more effective (in terms of its resonance within a given community); but there are no absolute distinctions.

There was certainly a phase during the apartheid years when eye-witness accounts in the form of a more or less 'realistic' literature stimulated a sense of solidarity among the oppressed while also conscientizing those not immediately involved or implicated in the struggle. But within the changing sociopolitical and cultural context, both inside South Africa and abroad, there are now different expectations of literature. Readers and writers alike have had a surfeit of whatever passed for 'fact'. The reporting has been done, often quite spectacularly; as in the case of post-Holocaust literature, there is now a greater pressure on that end of the scale where the imagination (expressed in the processes of invention, of fiction) acts more freely. 'As we distance ourselves in time from the event, and try to absorb it into consciousness', writes Alvin Rosenfeld of the Holocaust, 'the silence, avoidance or even outright denial will be greater,

3. In a review of *Statements after an Arrest under the Immorality Act,* Elsa Joubert comments, 'The woman must come to terms with her own predicament, and the man's conflict is his own. But what is there for the additional actor, the audience? Must he remain unfulfilled because these statements . . . cannot extend beyond mere statements?' (quoted in Gray, *Athol Fugard,* 87). From a different angle comes Stanley Kaufman's reproach that *Sizwe Bansi is Dead* is 'superficial . . . [and] only about the troubles of South African blacks' (quoted in Walder, *Athol Fugard,* 76).

and the incredibility of the Holocaust will consequently grow to dangerous proportions' (*A Double Dying*, 7). Hence an increasing need for imaginative engagement.

V

History provides one of the most fertile silences to be revisited by South African writers: not because no voices have traversed it before, but because the dominant discourse of white historiography (as well as temptations to replace it by a new dominant discourse of black historiography) has inevitably silenced, for so long, so many other possibilities. And this is an area where postmodernism offers particularly exciting challenges, because the postmodern text is never read 'in its own right' but as a myriad of intertextual relationships, specifically with established discourse(s). In other words, however eccentric or idiosyncratic the new version of a given tract of history (or a figure within it) may appear – like the compacted and compounded War of Liberation in Mike Nicol's *This Day and Age* in which a wide assortment of historical clashes are superimposed on one another – it cannot be discounted as 'mere' eccentricity or idiosyncrasy, but has to be read in its complex interactions with a whole variety of other texts (in this case, various accounts of the Bulhoek Massacre of 1921, for one). In other words, the reader is prompted to compare, and to choose.

It is a ludic enterprise, it is play; but this does not draw its teeth. On the contrary: it becomes a profoundly serious play on the stage of the world-as-story. If stories are retold and reimagined, the re- is of decisive importance: each new invention happens in the margin of the already-written, or against the background of the already-written. This excludes a reading of the new narrative as fortuitous invention, as 'mere fiction', because it engages with the world – the world itself being conceived of as story. It inserts itself into the reader's consciousness as an invitation to a moral choice.

In the suspension of disbelief the reader, after all, does not relinquish his/her faith in right and wrong, but finds him-/herself confronted with the text itself as choice: and each act of choice is inevitably informed by value systems.

In *The Narrative of Jacobus Coetzee*, J. M. Coetzee was able to 'read between the lines' of the historical documents available as *The Journals of Brink and Rhenius* (ed. E. E. Mossop) in order to imagine a story behind history. In writing *On the Contrary*, I was in the happy situation of encountering a historical personage, the eighteenth-century French soldier Estienne Barbier, who in his own letters to the authorities in Cape Town (letters still available in the South African State Archives) already embarked on a series of reinventions of himself; his distortions – some slight, others quite remarkable – provided a starting point for continuing inventions. And the 'point' of these inventions was their interaction with 'factual documentation' from the eighteenth century, most particularly where the latter appeared, in a very literal sense, stranger than fiction.[4]

The new text does not set itself up as a 'correction' of silence or of other versions of history; but through the processes of intertextuality set in motion by its presentation it initiates (or resumes) strategies of interrogation which prompt the reader to assume a new (moral) responsibility for his/her own narrative, as well as for the narrative we habitually call the world.

What interests me particularly at the moment is the link between woman and history: woman as a presence largely excluded from official South African discourses; and history as canon. The Afrikaans poet Antjie Krog has taken a lead in this respect (as in others) by rescuing from oblivion the diaries of a Voortrekker woman, Susanna Smit (the young wife of the elderly preacher Erasmus Smit, whose own diaries have been used for generations in the compilation of official versions of the Great Trek). Her very private experiences and visions shed new light on the historical function and awareness of Afrikaner women. And it seems to me that this kind of enterprise may serve as a starting point of a completely reinvented South African history: history, in fact, reimagined as herstory.

The problem is that historiography has been for so long a male-

4. A case in point: the early German traveller Peter Kolben (or Kolbe, or Kolb) describes an encounter with Governor Simon van der Stel in which the latter narrates how, on a journey towards the mythical kingdom of Monomotapa, he ascended the top of a high mountain 'and discovered from thence very plainly, that the Moon was not so far from the Earth as the Astronomers asserted; for that as that Planet, said he, pass'd at that Time over my Head, the Night being very still and clear, I could plainly perceive the Grass there to wave to and again, and had the Noise of its Motion in my Ears' (*The Present State of the Cape of Good Hope*, 46). Reproducing this passage almost verbatim in chapter 293 of *On the Contrary* created an impression of excessive imagination; yet the source was 'fact' – even if the fact itself was treated by Kolben with the kind of circumspection Sancho Panza tended to bring to the accounts of Don Quixote (who inevitably became another point of reference in the novel).

dominated territory. Even in the novel form, few family sagas have been written by women, with Undset's *Kristin Lavransdatter* as the towering exception, imaging as it does the swirl of several generations surrounding the eponymous heroine as she grows from baby to girl to young wife to matron to ancient widow in the turbulence of the fourteenth century. But in a postmodern age the whole approach to the genre may well have to be rethought: male historiography (though not that of Herodotus!) tends to take genealogy both as its starting point and its justification. A reimagining of South African history in this changed and still changing context may well depart quite radically from this to present its flow as being of another kind altogether – determined not by who-begat-whom but by more subliminal rhythms and contingencies. Such an approach would address two silences simultaneously: that created by the marginalization of women, and that effected by a (white-dominated) master-narrative of history.

In both respects (as in the examples of Coetzee and Nicol referred to above) the crucial new dimension is not the presentation of new historical 'evidence', however important that in itself may be, but the leap of the imagination towards grasping the larger implications of our silences. Ever since 1979, in an essay included in *Mapmakers*, I have been pleading for the need *to imagine the real*. In the new South Africa this would seem to me even more necessary than before.

It has a direct bearing on what is actually happening in the country. Much of the present movement away from the inhibiting mentalities of apartheid and towards a realization of the larger possibilities of democracy is geared to the functioning of the Truth and Reconciliation Commission. This is based on the assumption that societies, like individuals, cannot grow and mature unless they come to terms with the dark places – the silences – in themselves. This process will affect everybody in the country, as comparable experiments have affected post-war Germany, post-unification Germany, or the Argentine in the wake of its military rule. If not handled with great circumspection (and it is almost inevitable that mistakes must be made in traversing such a moral minefield), great explosions may occur; there is so much that can go wrong. And yet the problem has to be addressed. Silence would be intolerable.

I am wary of suggesting that in any given situation writers may have a defined 'function' to perform. (This does not deny that writers do fulfil functions, ranging from the aesthetic to the moral and the political; but this arises from the contexts within which they find themselves, and not from the imposition of any obligation from outside.) But if, as an accompaniment to the processes of such a commission, a new generation of writers would be prepared to confront the *imaginative* challenges of such a situation, some very stimulating texts may come from the experience. I certainly am convinced that without the attempt to grasp, with the creative imagination, the past and its silences, South African society as a whole may get bogged down in mere materialities, sterile rationalizations, and the narrow mechanics of retribution or amnesty.

VI

There is another dimension to the present experience of transition which may inform the new literature in South Africa, and that is the discovery of Africa. Many times in the past Africa has been conquered; its true discovery – certainly in white literature – is still awaiting its moment. This may of course assume innumerable forms; but I am particularly fascinated by what one might cautiously term its magic. Cautiously, because it is such an abused term by now; and if I use it, it has nothing at all to do with the 'heart of darkness', or with 'black magic', with the romantic lure the Haggards and like-minded imperial invaders brought to colonization. It is a magic which can only be set free once the mind has become, in Ngugi's sense of the word, decolonized.

The magic I am referring to has already been demonstrated in the writings of Amos Tutuola; more recently by Ben Okri. But it lurks even amid the more 'realistic' passages in Achebe, Soyinka, even Ngugi himself (and not only in *Matigari*, but in some hallucinatory moments of his novels with a more overt sociopolitical commitment). This magic involves an acknowledgement of a more holistic way of approaching the world, an awareness of more things in heaven and earth than have been dreamt of in our philosophy, a free interaction between the worlds of the living and the dead, a rich oneiric stratum; also of ancestral – historical – commitment of the kind one encounters in the poetry of Mazisi Kunene. It is informed by the thinking Kunene once illuminated for me when he explained why, in taking his leave from someone, he would never use the singular form *Sala gahle* ('Stay well') but always the plural, *Salani gahle*. 'Because no-one is ever alone,' he said. 'You are always accompanied by all your spirits.' I am a multitude, said Whitman; and the concept is expanded by the well-known African proverb, *I am a person through other persons*.

25

The easy intercourse between the living and the dead forms an integral part of African oral traditions in languages like Zulu, Xhosa, and Sotho; and from there it has spilled over into Afrikaans literature, much more than the writing of English-speaking white South Africans – although there are hints of it in some passages of Olive Schreiner's *Story of an African Farm* (for example, the pivotal story of the man who goes in search of the white bird, Truth); and in Herman Charles Bosman. Behind the deft satirical touch in the realism with which Bosman evokes the small racist farming community of the remote Northern Transvaal, there often lurks a sense of the surreal and the inexplicable, an awareness of an altogether different, African, dimension that casts its shadow – or its light – across stories like 'In the Withaak's Shade', in which a magic leopard appears to the narrator in what may, or may not, be a hallucination or a dream; or 'Funeral Earth', in which a band of Boers are confronted with the darker mysteries of Africa in an encounter with a group of women bearing gifts, including transubstantial black earth; or 'Veld Maiden', in which an ordinary love triangle acquires a supernatural allure. In more specifically postmodernist writing this 'magic' has been captured in masterly fashion by the Afrikaans novelist Etienne van Heerden in the novel *Toorberg* (1986; translated in 1989 as *Ancestral Voices*), with its deceptive interweaving of the living and the dead, of past and present.

It is perhaps a pity that the concept of 'magic realism' has become identified almost exclusively, in so many minds, with South America (even though, of course, the term had its firm origins in Europe), for I believe that Africa has a brand of magic realism, peculiarly its own, to offer the world. In black orature in Southern Africa it already has a venerable tradition. In Afrikaans literature, too, it goes back to oral beginnings, *inter alia* in many of the ghost stories first told by trekkers or itinerant traders at the camp fire, before electricity put an end to visitations from other worlds. In written form the way has been paved by short stories (by Eugène Marais, Louis Leipoldt, and others) at the turn of the century; with a startling new impetus in the novels of a writer like C. J. Langenhoven: as early as the twenties he wrote, in deadpan, naturalistic fashion, about a visitor, Loeloeraai, from Venus; and about journeys undertaken in a caravan pulled by an elephant. The outrageous, the wholly unexpected, the truly miraculous, informed much of his fiction. And with the inevitable return to roots which political events and the *fin de siècle* have prompted in South African writing across the cultural spectrum, one may well expect a rediscovery of African magic realism.

Certainly some of the best recent fiction already addresses this long-dormant silence. There is Mike Nicol's *The Powers That Be* (1989), an exorbitant imaginative recapturing of apartheid as a school of Jarryesque violence, intrigue, and corruption, rendered even more explosive through its burst of humour. (It is present also, but in a more contrived and precious manner, in his latest novel *Horseman* (1994), in which an apocalyptic figure from the European Middle Ages gallops across history and geography to reap his grim dark harvest in Africa.) There are the novels of the Zimbabwean John Eppel, most recently *The Giraffe Man* (1994) with its mordant satire of white colonial traditions struggling to survive in black Africa, where a dark magic is revealed to inhere in the everyday. There is also Ivan Vladislavic, who turns recorded history on its head in the short stories in *Missing Persons* (1989), and takes the leap from the ordinary to the fantastic in the construction – and eventual destruction – of a wholly imaginary edifice in *The Folly* (1993).

In the same context, a number of black writers have convincingly reached far beyond all conventions of 'struggle literature' or different strains of realism. Dambudzo Marechera from Zimbabwe (who died at the age of thirty-five in 1987) produced a *tour de force* in *Black Sunlight* (1980), with its exuberant black surrealism and its unsettling allegories released by the confrontation of European and African narrative traditions. In a different vein, but also imbued with the fantastic, Joël Matlou turns 'ordinary' experiences like living on a farm, or working on the mines, or courting a girl, into an extraordinary vision of hell in *Life at Home* (1991).

In these manifestations of what Steiner calls the 'licentious genius of language' (*Real Presences*, 59) I recognize the regenerative powers of South African literature: not simply to escape from the inhibitions of apartheid but to construct and deconstruct new possibilities; to activate the imagination in its exploration of those silences previously inaccessible; to play with the future on that needlepoint where it meets past and present; and to be willing to risk everything in the leaping flame of the word as it turns into world.

Works cited

Attwell, David. *J. M. Coetzee: South Africa and the Politics of Writing.*
Berkeley and Cape Town: University of California Press and David Philip, 1993.

Bosman, Herman Charles. *The Collected Works*. 2 vols. Johannesburg: Jonathan Ball, 1981.

Brink, André. *Mapmakers: Writing in a State of Siege*. London: Faber & Faber, 1983.

Eppel, John. *The Giraffe Man*. Cape Town: Queillerie, 1994.

Gray, Stephen, ed. *Athol Fugard*. Johannesburg: McGraw-Hill, 1982.

Hutcheon, Linda. *The Politics of Postmodernism*. New York: Routledge, 1989.

Kremer, Lilian. *Witness through the Imagination: Jewish–American Holocaust Literature*. Detroit: Wayne State University Press, 1989.

Kolben, Peter. *The Present State of the Cape of Good Hope* (vol. II). London: W. Innys, 1731.

Marechera, Dambudzo. *Black Sunlight*. London: Heinemann, 1980.

Mossop, E. E., ed. *The Journals of Brink and Rhenius*. Cape Town: Van Riebeeck Society, 1947.

Rosenfeld, Alvin. *A Double Dying: Reflections on Holocaust Literature*. Bloomington: Indiana University Press, 1980.

Steiner, George. *Language and Silence: Essays on Language, Literature and the Inhumane*. London: Faber & Faber, 1967.

Real Presences. London: Faber & Faber, 1989.

Undset, Sigrid. *Kristin Lavransdatter*. Trans. C. Archer and J. S. Scott. New York: Knopf, 1930.

van Heerden, Etienne. *Ancestral Voices*. London: Allison & Busby, 1993.

Walder, Dennis. *Athol Fugard*. Houndmills: Macmillan, 1984.

Wellbery, David E. 'Postmodernism in Europe: On Recent German Writing'. *The Postmodern Moment: A Handbook of Contemporary Innovation in the Arts*. Ed. Stanley Trachtenberg. Westport: Greenwood Press, 1985. 229–49.

Wyschogrod, Michael. 'Some Theological Reflections on the Holocaust'. *Response* 25 (Spring 1975): 65–8.

3

I am dead: you cannot read
André Brink's *On the Contrary*

PETER HORN

A voice speaks or writes from the darkness of the slaughterhouse. A voice destined to die violently sets out to tell the story of its existence. Dying, the voice needs a story. Language and story give the functions of an individual meaning, but the individual meaning is always subsumed under the laws of language. Language reaches as far as the supra-individual reality of the subject, because the operations of language are the operations of history (Lacan, 'The Function and Field of Language in Psychoanalysis', 49). The necessity to create a coherent story of oneself, to justify oneself and one's actions by means of language, is the necessity to acquire the agreement, the desire of the other, although Estienne Barbier, the main character of André Brink's *On the Contrary* and its narrator, says: 'I have given up trying to explain either others or myself. This is just a story' (4). But the word 'just' underplays the importance and the necessity of telling the story in the face of imminent, if fictional, death. Stories are always 'just' that, stories, but they are always also more than 'just' stories. Both the story of Don Quixote and the legend of Jeanne d'Arc, integral parts of Brink's novel, demonstrate how 'just stories' determine the content and the style of human lives.

In a wonderful creation myth, attributed to the slave woman Rosette, it was one of those whose voice has been devalued, a woman, who 'spoke a world into being': 'In the beginning there was only . . . a Storyteller and she was a woman'. But then, according to this myth, she was forgotten by the things and beings she had created as a story, and the 'forgotten Storyteller fell asleep into a deep sleep of ages, because they no longer seemed to need her' (184). In the end, in the dungeon, in his last delirious and clear-sighted dreams Estienne Barbier encounters her stories in the landscape he traverses in his imagination for a third time; and he invents another ending for himself than that found in his official historical record: he repents and finds meekness, he implores those whom he had done wrong for their forgiveness, and accepts their punishment as a form of redemption, as a 'necessary purging on behalf of all of us who have invaded this space to subjugate it with our presumption and visit it with our devastation' (359). It is ironic that this oral culture of storytelling – for example, the wonderful story of the girl born from a bird's egg – which is destroyed by the invasion of the colonizer and by his foreign language and literacy, is preserved in the writings of the colonizer (fictionally in Barbier's account, then in Brink's novel) (see JanMohamed, *Manichean Aesthetics*, 283). Yet, of course, this very preservation destroys it finally by fixing it as writing not as a lived cultural environment. The debate around Stephen Watson's adaptations of |Xam (Cape 'Bushman') oral poetry in his volume *Return of the Moon* have called our attention to the dangers of such appropriation by the colonizer culture which extinguished the very conditions in which it could originally exist. And Isabel Hofmeyr has recently pointed out how our concept of incoherence and corruption can impose norms on African oral history which are alien to its own existence in the *bricolage* of the ruined pieces of the past ('Oral History as a Farce?', 49). Even the most sympathetic attempt to fix the oral tradition in writing recreates it as museum of a past destroyed.

The story as it has come down to us in historical documents is interesting enough: the historical Estienne Barbier, a Frenchman, arrived in the Cape some time before 1737 as a soldier in the service of the Dutch East India Company. History describes him as a turbulent character, insolent, eccentric, and quarrelsome, an insurrectionary who became the leader of the white farmers of the Cape interior when they defied the Dutch administration. He evaded arrest for some time, but was captured and tried on charges of treason, leading an armed revolt and inciting the burghers of the colony to evade paying taxes, and causing arson, murder, and pillage. He was sentenced to death, bound to a wooden cross, his head and right hand were cut off and nailed to a stake. The rest of his body was quartered and the portions exhibited – tied to posts in various parts of the settlement. Thus the bare bones of a story. But something is missing in the historical account.

In Brink's novel the story of Estienne Barbier is an imagined story, not only because there is no paper in the slaughterhouse on which to write it down, not only because the story would be confiscated and destroyed by those who are in power, not only because there is no light and no pen in the darkness of the dungeon, but also because the addressee of the story is entirely imaginary: a woman, an escaped slave, whose name might or might not be Rosette, and who might or might not exist. The slave can never be the addressee of history, because history is not written for her but against her. So his last appeal to Rosette is futile if poignant: 'Listen to me, Rosette. Listen well, I am speaking against accepted history, against that version van den Henghel so elaborately formulated in his Act of Accusation, which is the only version the world will know. If they even bother to look it up a hundred, or two or three hundred years from now' (323). And yet this impossible, fictional addressee is the only hope of this fictional refutation of official history.

But the black slave whose proper name has been lost under the super-imposed European name has her own stories, stories which create the land and the paths across the land, stories which create the order in which people can live, but stories, of course, are not histories and her stories are not taken seriously because she is black, a woman, and a slave, thus a loser of history. History is made by the winners. It is they who determine what goes into the documents, it is their voice which assumes the authority to tell it how it is, and who therefore authorize and circumscribe the order which determines the choices we can make in our lives. The documents which come down to us are riddled with lacunae, silences, and with out-right lies. But these documents are the basis and the limit of our constant rewriting of history. Women, slaves, rebels, revolutionaries are not represented in these documents in their own writing, but always only in the writing of their masters.

Where a rebel voice like that of Estienne Barbier tries to set down the truth of an event (as he sees it), his densely inscribed pages are torn out and burnt, one by one, and the more amenable Mentzel substitutes for each of the original pages his own, 'the correct and proper truth' (40), as the authorities want it to be inscribed into the records of their time and the future. All attempts to rewrite history come up against this fact. History cannot normally be corrected because it must exclude accounts of how it could have been from a narrative based on 'authentic docu-ments'. Only fiction can enter that space of the possible which is negated and silenced by the documents that claim to represent the real. Fiction is not about how it really was: fiction is an attempt to keep the story about the past open, an attempt to deny the impression the historians try to cre-ate that what they say is all there is to say about the past. Fiction is about the possibilities (in the sense of Robert Musil's *Möglichkeitsmensch*, who is able to live in a 'real' world without blocking out the fact that reality could be otherwise or even 'contrary'), possibilities which are denied in the official record, therefore it is not dated, it is *sine die*, although it is

ascribed to a known place, the *Cabo de Bonne-Espérance* (3), which, however, as the alienation into Portuguese and French points out, is not the
Cape of Good Hope we believe we know. It is a land 'beyond the calcula-
tions of date and time, everything reduced to mere space' (7). On the
other hand Barbier feels relieved that he no longer has to bear the
responsibility for official truths, where the 'test for the recording of any
observation in my official journal was the sanction of our leader; was
what was judged acceptable to ulterior readers at the Cape and possibly
Batavia and Amsterdam' (26): 'I was free at last to pursue my own, and in
my own way' (41). But this freedom has a curious unreality; in a sense
Barbier is not writing his story and his defence, but he is being written, he
is not observing but being observed (183), 'inscribed as it were by another
pen into [his] journey' (349). It is not only because he is sentenced to
death and his body is about to be torn apart

> *Bound to a cross*, the verdict said, *his right hand and his head severed from his*
> *body, subsequently to be drawn and quartered, the head and hand to be placed on a*
> *stake in the Roodezands Kloof, and the four remaining quarters to be displayed in*
> *four different places alongside the most frequented highways of the Settlement as*
> *prey to the air and the birds from heaven* (3)

that he says: 'I am absent from myself. I am absence' (4). The narrator is
always absent in the narration, because that is the condition of writing: as
he wishes to, and attempts to write his (always fictional) story and to create his (always fictional) meaning, he recreates himself as a monument in
writing which is no longer himself.

The voice which appeals to our sympathies and constantly constructs
and reconstructs its stories is not an unproblematic voice. Not only is it
the voice of a white settler, it is also the voice of a figure who, in his revolt
against government, becomes entangled in the oppression and killing of
the indigenous people, justifying their eradication. Fiction thus deals
with that part of history which has been falsified and silenced, of which
we have no consciousness, and which nevertheless shapes our destiny,
260 years later. No Truth and Reconciliation Commission (such as the
one established in South Africa to investigate the crimes of apartheid) is
ever going to open up that unconscious and make it conscious: the truth
that will emerge will be the one which we will be able to bear, not the one
which is unbearable both to the oppressors and the rebellious oppressed.
Fiction always attempts to cross the border into that region which has
been excluded from language, but its exploits always end, necessarily, in

reconstructions which have no authority, in what official history must call lies. And yet, there is below the rationality of the historical method a silence, an unconscious. The unconscious is that part of its story which is marked by an absence or which has been occupied by a falsehood. The unconscious is that part of our discourse which is not at the individual's disposal, so that it can re-establish the continuity of its interrupted conscious discourse. The truth which reappears in myths and stories is what has been forgotten by history, or to be more precise, what has been repressed – for were it merely forgotten it would not enter our speech, our fantasies, our wishes, our dreams, and our actions with so much force. Were it forgotten, we would be rid of it; instead we still labour under the heavy load of a history which constantly repeats itself, symptom of an unresolved past: 'Sooner or later we are all overtaken by our own stories' (249).

Politics is said to be the game of the possible. This innocent statement is at the root of the falsification of the record of the past and therefore the distortion of the possibilities of the future. The word 'possible' in the first sense excludes all the possibilities which according to the (falsified) record of the past have been judged 'impossible': this includes today such 'impossibilities' as anarchism and socialism. A truly human world without power, anarchic and free, 'a place where life can be once more possible', therefore has become the 'impossible'. Estienne Barbier's inner voice and companion, Jeanne d'Arc, says:

> This is the sin of all of them, all these men who turn to politics as a game to
> be played, a game of the possible. They become powerful because they fetter
> the imagination. That is the very source of their power. They forbid us to
> remember what is truly impossible. And by concentrating only on the
> possible, I tell you, they have made the world an impossible place to live in.
>
> (182)

But, we could argue, this very novel 'shows' that fiction also 'falsifies' the past. The narrator's voice is also the voice of a liar: the voice of somebody constantly rearranging the story of his life to suit his current self/image and the necessities of the situation; it is not a very trustworthy voice, but it is a voice which contradicts the records of official history, a voice which also contradicts itself, a *contrary voice*, the voice of obstinacy, of stubbornness. It is this helpless stubbornness – helpless because it is constantly silenced and confused by the official story – which is the inner resilience of characters like Estienne Barbier, a resilience which makes their lives and their stories such important correctives of the official record. What appears to philosophers like Plato to be lies and contradictions in reality are possible histories, attempts to fill the lacunae of official history. The very fact that the text does not allow us to fix it to only one meaning keeps a multiplicity of possible meanings open against the 'dull grammar of the daily account' (36), the monologue of the official transcript of past events. It is in this sense, opening the canonized text to his searching doubts, that Estienne Barbier asks the question: 'Why does one read the accounts of the convicts as lies, but Don Quixote's inventions as something altogether different?' (122).

That of course is the question directed against all narratives, stories and histories: what more than an ideological play of opinions is any history, what more than a story, a tall story for that, under the guise of a methodologically and theoretically soundly grounded discourse? Writers of fiction, at least in the last 100 years, are well aware of the fictionality of their writing, and it is their awareness which to a degree saves the text: 'This is just a story' (4), it does not pretend to be or do more. The trust between an author and the reader of a fictional account is not that the account can be verified by any of the methods of 'scientific' history, any form of mathematics, statistics, and accounting, but that it has a truth of another order. History as empiricity will always, necessarily, fall short of what fiction can do without that claim to a verifiable truth.

So the question is not: Was Estienne Barbier, as he asserts, a 'very important person', sent by the Lords Seventeen to 'report on the actions and attitudes of the top functionaries' (5), or was that merely the self-aggrandizement of an aimless drifter and adventurer, who shortly after that describes himself as a 'scribe' and a 'corporal' (8)? Or was he, as he later says, one who has lied and cheated his way through the world (196ff)? Bragging is a peculiarly masculine activity (as gossiping is said to be a peculiarly feminine activity): hunters and fishermen, knights, sailors, merchants, and soldiers each have developed their own brand of grandiloquent and self-aggrandizing tall story: while the intention of these stories from the Odyssey down to the present is to heighten the reputation of the hero, the stories become entertainment for an audience which is not all that interested in their accuracy, as long as they are interesting. Interesting is not the little fish who got caught, but the mythical very big one who got away after a super-human struggle. After telling the imaginary story of his discovery of Monomotapa, the narrator says: 'If you will not believe me, how can I persuade you of anything else I witnessed or experienced en route? Is any one phenomenon in this world more amazing than any other?' (225). Such stories in their retelling become more and more elaborate and the various versions become entangled and begin to contradict each other, material for future philologists and mythologists, who do not understand the fascination of the compulsive storyteller and liar with the polyvalence of the story: 'This fascinates me: how each story displaces others, yet without denying or ever entirely effacing them' (134). The reader / listener, however, is like Tante Louise, who 'accepts with great eagerness whatever stories I choose to fabricate ... My whole life I reinvent for her; and alternately she chuckles with glee or sheds tears from her eyes with their whitish-blue film of pearls' (104). It is for the reader to discover 'the truth of my lies' (225).

Such tales of heroic exploits, in the form of praise poems, epic stories, and picaresque novels at first took the place of history – history was, and to certain extent still is, the tall story of the rulers and the ruling classes. Future generations until the age of enlightenment used such fictional material – as long as it was part of the authoritative canon – naively as sources of knowledge, and it is only from the age of reason onwards that a more critical approach attempts to distinguish between fiction and non-fiction. From then on the one who contradicts (himself) can never be the scribe of history: he can only make fictional stories, stories which people know are lies. Yet this liar is 'responsible to the future for the otherwise unremembered past' (7) – because the very process of critical history sifting the sources for their truth value is forced to discard valuable (if fictional) accounts of our past, which say as much if not more than the most severely authenticated account found in state and church archives.

Cervantes' accounts of the exploits of Don Quixote, a book which the hero carries with him all the time and which at times saves his life, form the foil of Brink's own picaresque novel. As Foucault (46) has pointed out, the essence of Don Quixote is language, text, printed pages, already written history. He is born of the contamination of words and he constantly has to consult books in order to know what he needs to do or to say. Just as the novels of knightly adventures are the script of his life, Cervantes' book and the legend of Jeanne d'Arc become the script of Barbier's life. As Don Quixote looks for similarities between his books and the world he encounters, Barbier constantly discovers the world of his book and his legend in the reality of South Africa, imposing European texts on to a reality which has not been described before in European languages. It is not surprising, therefore, that he encounters the unicorn and the hippogryph in the semi-deserts of Namaqualand, and that the inhabitants of his mythical Monomotapa speak Latin and look like smaller versions of Europeans, because as his companion Jeanne d'Arc remarks: 'Monomotapa is a city made of words.' But that, as she says further, 'is no reason to lose faith in it' (253). As long as we recognize that it is made of words. Cervantes lets us understand that the similarities are illusory, and that the adventures of his hero are a delirious vision, while the objects themselves remain in their ironic distance. Brink's ironic stance as a narrator is thus prefigured in the book so beloved by his hero. At the very end Barbier acknowledges that the similarities between the things he knows from Europe and in a European language and the things he encounters in Africa are false:

> The terror lies in knowing that I have no tongue in which to reply. I can say *buttes* or *rocher* or *plaine*, or in the language of this land *heuwels*, *rots*, *veld*: but these remain empty sounds drifting on the wind, as inconsequential as the brittle shiverings of grass. How different is this, *your* language, the world you are speaking into being as I gaze at it: hard sediment, languorous contours, deceptive distances, space, space. (356–7)

But there is another element to Barbier's reading of Don Quixote. The madness of one who sets out on exploits which are doomed to failure from the beginning, because he sees the world as books have described them in the past, fictions, not 'accurate' accounts – although the early 'scientific' accounts of Africa nowadays read like fictions themselves – this madness is another aspect of the contrariness of Barbier, his rejection of the world and of society as it is. When he asks: 'What merit is there in turning mad for a reason?' (76) he really rejects that kind of reason that cannot rise to any form of greatness. This, then, is one of the differences of fictional account and historical report.

The novel creates something more and something less than that account. At first Barbier finds the Afrikaner farmers obnoxious, totally lacking in refinement, ill-mannered and indolent, uncouth and brusque, 'relying on slaves and hottentots for all the work on their farms' (93), yet coming to Cape Town on their wagons to 'lodge interminable complaints about hottentot or Bushmen depredations' (137) while at the same time unwilling to serve as soldiers in the wars against the indigenous people. He sees them as an 'aberrant race' (99), 'who nurse their fabulous dreams of revenge' (7). Not that he himself is much different in this respect: after telling a drunken story of how he cut lieutenant Alleman down to size and emasculated him, he has to admit that 'this is how it should have been' (147), not how it was. Instead of mounting the white horse of his corrupt superior and galloping off in search of his Dulcinea/Rosette, he becomes 'bird-free' (147). Yet after he has been robbed and savagely beaten up by a band of farmers who resent him as a soldier involved in the collection of taxes, he begins to feel empathy towards their attempts to defend themselves against a corrupt regime. Soon he, who has set out to 'bring the light of the law and order to the unruly outlying regions of the colony' (92) and who as a soldier of the company finds 'the unruly nature of the colonists and their blatant attempts to enrich themselves at the expense of the Company' (93) offensive, becomes, as a fugitive from the rule of the Company, a leader of their rebellion against its rule. After he is imprisoned for fighting the corruption of the colonialist Company — 'But the problem is that graft and blackmail and favours and scheming are so commonplace that no one even thinks of it as wrong any more' (101) — and after he is able to flee from prison he gains a new perspective on those he had first seen as 'savages', people 'whose existence showed no difference from that of their sullen cattle, yapping dogs or scratching fowl', being in a 'state of abject lethargy and abysmal ignorance' (229). But as the narrator says: 'this land does not make it easy for a man to hold fixed opinions. There are so few certainties' (245).

Soon it is the native of this land whose humanity comes into doubt: are the 'hottentots' really a species of human beings descended perhaps from the Jews or the Troglodytes? It is here that the uses of analogy for political purposes and as source of doubtful and dangerous knowledge are played out to the full, the idols of the cave are revived in the face of the unknown, which let us believe that things are similar to those we have learned in the past and that the real world is similar to our constructions and theories. Wild and abstruse theories are formed, in the end to justify the subjugation or destruction of others: 'What suggested to me that the hottentots of this land may be considered as much a species of fauna as, say, gazelle or ostrich or camelopard, was — firstly — their language, which (as I had occasion to remark earlier) has nothing of sound or articulation that is peculiar to man in it, but resembling, rather, the noise of irritated turkey-cocks or the chattering magpies' (237). Ironically, they are considered to be on their way towards becoming 'human' when they learn to murder and pillage in the service of their masters (261). Too late Estienne Barbier realizes that the 'hottentots' are not his real enemy:

'The enemy that first threatened me, the enemy I'm still fighting, is in Cabo: it's officialdom, corruption, power. The hottentots are powerless' (326).

What Foucault has said about Don Quixote and similarities should make us wary of drawing all too obvious parallels between the fictional account of an eighteenth-century Boer rebel and current phenomena in the emerging new South Africa. The similarities certainly do not lie on the surface, as a quick reading of the novel might suggest. Ampie Coetzee fleetingly considers Brink's novel as '"politically relevant" within the *ressentiment* politics of contemporary South Africa', but then turns immediately to the theme of the 'disappearing text' (7). What he doesn't seem to see is that it is the *ressentiment* which makes the text disappear. Attempting to inscribe their presence on to that land, they erase any text: 'Likewise, we annihilate kraals and villages and settlements of hostile or indifferent natives, with the single purpose of leaving on that virgin, barren place the scrawl of our progress. *We were there*' (236). There is no communication and thus no text, because: 'Violence our language. A land hostile, empty, strange: it does not talk back, remains inaccessible. Which forces this violence from us, achingly pure' (235–6).

Coetzee does, however, point to an important passage which throws light on the cruelty of the white farmers: 'All of it sprang not from the exaggerated confidence, not even from hate, but from terror: the fear of this vast land, of its spaces, of its unmerciful light, of its dark people' (265). An incidence of this is the impotent rage of Hendrik Ras when his dead daughter is taken from him and he kills one of his servants, 'then hurled away the broken body as one might imagine a rhinoceros tossing in the air the carcass of a victim' (231). That fear breaks out most destructively when the Hottentot servants rebel when they are to be cheated out of the cattle they believed they had won. One of the farmers, Willem van Wyk, is portrayed as defending himself, and in his eyes at that moment is: 'Not rage, not hate, not a lust for blood and violence but, quite simply, fear' (265). Coetzee relates this to the reaction of whites against political change (although of course there is no direct reference in the novel to such change).

It would, of course, be fairly easy to draw copious analogies between the figure of Jan la Grange and other figures from the settlers in the interior and present-day ultra right-wing rebels. The command: 'Get off my farm or I'll shoot!' (140) is one that is still fairly common in certain regions of the country, as is the ingrained suspicion against the govern-

ment of the day which seems to protect and use the indigenous population (despite its colonialist terror against them), and the perspiration of
the underlying fear of the 'Dark Hole' (141) in Cape Town, and the suici-
dal bravery of 'I'd rather kill myself. But first I'll shoot you' (141). At one
point the narrator confesses: 'You may have noticed that I do not particularly like myself' (245). The analogies are clearly intended by the author,
and are meaningful historically alienated descriptions of present-day
paranoias.

There is one passage, however, which comes even nearer to the ultimate silence of the text of Estienne Barbier and his new-found friends and
supporters, the short passage dealing with the herd of *poeskop* elephants –
related by the narrator incidentally with the 'ancient fear of the *vagina
dentata*' (237). The tuskless elephants engender among the hunters a
'kind of precipitate rage' which leads to the senseless total destruction of
the entire herd – senseless because the sole reason for killing elephants are
their tusks: 'Yet in this instance it was the *absence* of tusks that propelled us
into a fury of destruction – as if that abnormality most grievously
insulted us. It went beyond the simplicity of frustration: it was a kind of
vengeance we were compelled to visit upon animals that had attempted to
evade our accepted definition of them' (238). It is precisely that which is
outside the boundaries of their imagination which threatens them even
more than the hated structures of a government with no understanding of
the needs of the settlers. And their fears are reinforced when their helplessness and marginality in the wilds is exposed by an event the following
night: a herd of tusked elephants, like a group of determined guerrillas of
violated nature, within five minutes destroys their camp, kills three of
their servants, and severely maims one of the hunters. This incident is
mirrored by another one when a tribe repossesses the cattle they had
bartered in a similar guerrilla attack, killing two of the hunters, four of
their servants, and wounding another two seriously. The consequence of
this encounter is a considerable hardening of the attitudes of the hunters
against the 'natives': 'Henceforth, on every occasion we came upon a tribal settlement, we took the precaution of first exterminating the hottentots (even those who treacherously pretended to be friendly) before
appropriating whatever sheep and cattle could be rounded up in the envi-
rons. Never again would we be fooled by mere appearances' (243). These
massacres are repeated by the troops of rebellious farmers clubbing
down a group of mainly women and children in a frenzy, 'a lunatic imme-
diacy of slaughtering' and hacking to pieces their dead bodies (315–16).

Coetzee reminds us that 'the protest of the farmers of the interior against the Dutch East India Company and against exploitation was the beginning of Afrikaner nationalism' (8). It is interesting to note how in the novel the community of farmers and hunters grows out of this exclusion of the indigenous population from their definition of human. The hunters who had been but a bunch of individuals 'united only in their common aversion to the authorities in Cabo' but otherwise 'independent to the point of idiosyncrasy' (243) acquire a consciousness of common purpose, even 'a sense of mission into, and in, Africa' (244). But this mission has no real content, it is one of 'pure futurity ... absurdity our only certainty' (247). On their return from their expedition, which ends disastrously with the loss not only of the cattle and sheep they had bartered and stolen from the indigenous population but their own possessions as well, they find that unity again in their fight against what they see as 'oppressors of the people and destroyers of the country' (295). That fight in turn ends ignominiously, despite Barbier's dream that 'the people shall govern' (338). Only in his last dreams in the Dark Hole can he begin to understand that the error of the colonialists is to think in terms of problems ('the native problem') and solutions ('apartheid', 'separate development'): 'The government is here and its soldiers are here, the colonists are here, the natives are here, the earth and dust and scrub and light are here. They are not problems to be solved. They are here, that's all. They can be loved, I suppose' (351). In the end, siding with those who used to be his enemies and victims, he experiences an imaginary passage into another world, the world of the slave woman who is the original storyteller (359), and a strange sense of freedom in his dungeon.

Cultures not only have texts but function largely as texts, as texts describing an imaginary, just as Barbier in the end becomes his own imagining (349). Sentences like: 'A crude land, Africa; only the strongest can hope to survive' (248) form the repertoire of the white settler justifying his existence by tragedy and the ability to survive it. Like any texts they function because of exclusion as much as because of inclusion. The silences and lacunae are the basis of the social contract which makes life bearable for most who live within that prescriptive text, they are a necessary part of the text. With the shifting of political power from one section of the population to another, the truth which was silenced in the previous regime can be rediscovered. The social body is a monument to this lost truth: in its neurotic and psychotic symptoms the forgotten cannot be forgotten. But each such revolution creates a new silence: the political

correctness of a new era makes speechless that which would be unbearable to the bearers of this new social construct. Thus while one domain of
our social history rises into the light of officially recorded history,
another becomes hidden and falls into the domain of fictional speech.

Estienne Barbier in 1993 is as *unzeitgemäß* as the freedom fighter was
in 1983. The question now is, how we deal with that part of our history
that cannot conveniently be integrated into the *grand récit* of our new,
democratic history still to be written, whether we will genuinely be able
to extend the boundaries of the thinkable. This occlusion of elements of
the past is part of every significant reversal or revolution in the history of
nations and continents, when the elements which make up the history are
shuffled to conform to the new consciousness of the nation itself. In
South Africa, for example, an *inside* knowledge of the racist, as opposed
to the knowledge of those who were subjected to racism, might well
become an element of public knowledge which will disappear. A complete knowledge of oneself is always only possible as that which is
deposited in the archive, on the understanding that certain portions of
the archive will be 'forgotten', until their contents become 'relevant'
again. The writer who disregards the rules of the archive will find himself
or herself in the position of an outsider. Will South African writers continue to be 'the anarchist who accepts no authority outside the work itself;
[will they still be] the terrorist who regards nothing as sacred, and attacks
in the name of freedom' (Brink, 'The Social Function', 14), and is that the
answer to the curious question: what will South African writers write
about after apartheid? Or will it forever be that 'for those who speak the
truth there is no shelter in this land' (309)?

Note on André Brink

In 1962 and 1963 André Brink contributed significantly to the development of the modern novel in Afrikaans with *Die Ambassadeur* [*The
Ambassador*] and *Lobola vir die Lewe* [*Lobola for Life*]. With these two
novels he immediately became one of the leading figures of the *Sestiger*
movement (the generation of Afrikaans writers of the sixties). He is the
author of fifteen novels. He soon received international recognition with
the publication and translation of his next novels, including *Looking on
Darkness* (1974), *An Instant in the Wind* (1976), *Rumours of Rain* (1978),
A Dry White Season (1979), *A Chain of Voices* (1982), and *An Act of Terror*
(1991). Not only was he recognized as one of the foremost voices of
South Africa but also as one of the dissident Afrikaner voices during the

apartheid area. His next novels, *The First Life of Adamastor* and *On the Contrary*, continued to probe the colonial past of South Africa with a slight shift in emphasis from the recent years of apartheid to the historical roots of the present.

Works cited

Brink, André. 'The Social Function of the Writer'. *Concept* 2 (July 1970): 9–15.

Coetzee, Ampie. 'Textualising Africa'. *Southern African Review of Books* 5 (1993): 6.

Foucault, Michel. *The Order of Things: An Archaeology of the Human Sciences*. London: Tavistock, 1970.

Hofmeyr, Isabel. 'Oral History as a Farce? – Oral History as a Changing Phenomenon'. *Journal of Literary Studies* 10 (1994): 31–56.

JanMohamed, Abdul R. *Manichean Aesthetics: The Politics of Literature in Colonial Africa*. Amherst: University of Massachusetts Press, 1983.

Lacan, Jacques. 'The Function and Field of Language in Psychoanalysis'. *Écrits: A Selection*. Trans. Alan Sheridan. London: Tavistock, 1977.

4

Endings and new beginning
South African fiction in transition

ELLEKE BOEHMER

In a letter written in 1920 Solomon Plaatje remarks that he had just completed 'a novel – a love story after the manner of romances; but based on historical facts'. It would be: 'Just like the style of Rider Haggard when he writes about the Zulus' (Willan, *Sol Plaatje*, 254). A linguist, historian, nationalist, and founding member of the South African Native National Congress (later the ANC), Plaatje straddled cultural worlds. His novel *Mhudi* (1930), the first work of fiction by a black African to be published in English, itself represents a curious mix – more exploratory in form and as fantastical in conception as the tales of Haggard. Embracing Tswana oral tradition and Shakespearean vocabulary, epic battlefield scenes and romance, speeches of biblical gravity and slapstick tussles with lions, *Mhudi* also looks two ways in time: back to the nineteenth-century wars of the Mfecane, and – as Halley's comet blazes in the sky – to the future and its risks, the danger of deals made between Africans and Afrikaners.

At this time of massive shift and change in South Africa, for which Plaatje did his share of preparation, innovative early writing like *Mhudi* invites another look. In particular the multilayeredness created by Plaatje's variations of voice and register contrasts noticeably with the sense of hesitation, restraint, in some cases of delimitation, expressed both at stylistic and thematic levels in more recent late-apartheid South African fiction. In *Mhudi* a suggestive dissonance carries right through to the ending, which is double. First comes the rout of the Matabele by a combined force of Barolong and Boers, and King Mzilikazi's prescient warning to beware of collaboration with the white man. Then follows a conventional Shakespearean comic ending in which couples are reunited or joined for the first time in betrothal.

The ambiguity of Plaatje's ending – which comes out of a desire not to fix a single frame on the future – recalls another early form-giving South African novel, Olive Schreiner's *The Story of an African Farm* (1883), written when Schreiner was only twenty-one, working as a governess in the Cape Colony. Schreiner's experimentations with narrative style, again carried through to the story's indeterminate ending, began the difficult work of adapting a European realist tradition to non-European surroundings. As the poet and novelist William Plomer once observed: *African Farm* gave 'lasting shape to forms of life hitherto unperceived or unrecorded' (Plomer, *Double Lives*, 155). His own *Turbott Wolfe* (1925), a novel about a quest for new South African identity, is itself a mixed creation, mingling together 'partly satirical, partly lyrical, partly fantastic' elements in 'a spirit of revolt' (Plomer, *Double Lives*, 186; Plomer, *Autobiography*, 170).

The Story of an African Farm has, inevitably, been criticized for its apparent historical weightlessness, or alienation from the Southern African context. Yet, paradoxically, it is Schreiner's struggle to connect with her environment which contributes to her significance in South African letters. The breaks, uncertainties, and digressions in her writing dramatize a central feature of the settler condition, the difficulty of finding the forms to fit a new world. After the first few chapters, the novel's realism is gradually displaced by dream allegory, moral exhortation, flights of fancy. Finally, abandoning caution, Schreiner allows the end of *African Farm* to sink into mysterious silence, a close that is not quite a close, as in Plaatje, suggesting that more might be said, but not quite yet. Waldo, the questing hero, dies quietly, unexpectedly, and apparently for no reason: 'muttering, muttering, muttering, to himself' in his usual way, he falls asleep. However, the finality normally signified by death is avoided. Em, his childhood friend thinks: 'He will wake soon.' 'But', Schreiner adds, 'the chickens were wiser' (281). And falls silent. It is a remarkably evasive, sibylline tease of an ending. Yet it is an evasion that differs in spirit, I want to suggest, from what can be seen as the curtailment, the closing down of prospects, which we find in late apartheid fiction.

When compared to Schreiner and Plaatje, more recent South African novels in English have been distinctly less comfortable with, and less creative, less exploratory about, indeterminacy – by which I mean indeterminacy in form and language as well as in subject matter. Though when it comes to indeterminacy it is difficult to draw clear lines of distinction, it is possible to discern a widely shared mood or trend. Speaking very generally, what a reader picks up in more recent work – especially during the last phase of apartheid – is a suspension of vision, a hemming in as opposed to a convinced and convincing opening up or testing of options. Choices of plot and style are marked by a kind of havering, even (as I will go on to outline) a cultural or artistic pessimism, a loss of will, sometimes also by a concern with stylistic or political orthodoxy. This sense of delimitation is perhaps pointed up most clearly at that place in the narrative which involves both retrospection and anticipation – the ending. And this at a time, significantly, when under the critical banner of 'postmodernism' writers elsewhere were experimenting in any number of intriguing ways with notions of provisionality and undecidability, and with a heterogeneity of narrative techniques.

It is not exactly surprising of course that the fictions of the 1980s – to take that end-time of apartheid as a sample case – might appear to shut down on tomorrow. In other words, again putting it crudely for the sake of the argument, the close of a late-apartheid novel could not in most cases be taken as other than a closing down or narrowing of possibility. A writer was in theory in a position to anticipate, foretell, predict, descry, yet did not ultimately feel capable of doing so. Novels thus give us deaths or near deaths, but without the mystery promised by Schreiner, and escapes, but without clear destinations, departures which are headed for culs-de-sac, caught in a void. What was happening was that the inescapable surrounding reality fenced in the potential questions raised by endings. Narrative uncertainty, its suggestiveness and tease, were constrained within the deathly binaries of a long history of oppression and opposition. Hoped-for but as-yet-inconceivable, the long-delayed moment of liberation, too, forced its own particular hiatus at the end of the South African narrative. What lay beyond that moment was a gap, a space of which it was impossible to imagine the shape. Often, therefore, tales are end-stopped by social breakdown, exile, leave-taking, by the insistent imperatives of commitment to the struggle, or simply by resistances to the novelistic imagination, to envisioning the future, imposed by the apartheid world.

In this chapter it is the meanings and significance of such suspended endings which I want to examine a little more closely, if – at this cusp time – in a necessarily tentative and speculative way. In recent years history has, as it were, leapt across the space which separated the apartheid present from a conceivable future time. With South Africans now in the process of composing a new nation, the years of decline and fall are giving way to a time of fresh starts and apparently reconstructive continuity – what J. M. Coetzee in *Waiting for the Barbarians* (1980) suggestively calls 'recurrent spinning time'. At this moment of transition, therefore, it is worth looking again at some of those fictions of the end-time, of the

1980s, to see what point writing has reached, and also how it might move on from here. Towards the end of the chapter, then, I want to take what I have described as the havering and arrest of the late-apartheid narrative ending, its 'closed openness', if you like, as an occasion to think, rather provisionally once again, about possible changes in fiction in a post-apartheid society. What creative possibilities and prognoses for the future do its particular closings and indeterminacies hold out? If we accept that endings in narrative can be pictured as opening the storyline on to the real-life action that will follow, as offering a set of choices for thinking about the future, can we attempt to discern the ghostly shape of new beginnings in the endings of the end-time, or must we go back to Plaatje and to Schreiner for guidance, for their prescience?

At a time of transformation it is appropriate, too, to look again at form – or a kind of form, the shape of endings, the way writers have organized their closing times. Perhaps for obvious reasons, the heat of opposition to apartheid caused writers to favour certain formal decisions over others, to adopt an upfront, hard-hitting, mimetic aesthetic, and therefore to pay less attention to form as such, to experiment, nuance and the play of ambiguity for its own sake. In progressive circles, literature, viewed as a 'weapon' of liberation, was enjoined to express its message as directly as possible. The call was for a rapid-fire art, for those artists or cultural workers who aligned themselves against apartheid to produce committed work that endorsed or encouraged the formation of a national people's culture. In the case of liberal humanist writers, mistrustful of the indulgence represented by technical experimentation, a narrowly defined classic realism became entrenched as the most reliable and 'relevant' way of capturing the troubling totality of the society. So, as is well known, by the mid-1980s a situation had arisen in which literary critics in the country could claim with equanimity that, unless fiction or poetry could be seen to mirror reality in some immediate way, they attached 'relative unimportance' to textual form.

Now, as writers begin to conceive a post-apartheid art, as they find the opportunity to break away from the mimetic codes of the past, it is significant that a restraint continues to operate. Even while casting about for the symbolic vocabulary with which to imagine and articulate a changing world, writers can still be seen settling for second-hand, borrowed or inherited models: post-structuralist 'play'; magic realist conjuring tricks; the treatment of history as 'discourse' or as fantasy; recuperative autobiography as a way of narrating a self into being (a form which is necessarily end-stopped by the present). Whether it is Mike Nicol's fabulistic and nightmarish retelling of a *longue dureé* of Southern African history in *Horseman* (1994), or André Brink's attempt at composing an originary myth of the Cape in *The First Life of Adamastor* (1993), or whether it is Sindiwe Magona's story of an apartheid childhood and adolescence, *To My Children's Children* (1990), or Achmat Dangor's short story collection, *From Riverlea to Parkview* (1995), mapping his journey from black township to white suburb, whether the form is fantasy or reminiscence, writers appear wary or uncertain about addressing themselves to genuine experiment, to the craft of writing as a movement beyond formula and blueprint, as worth doing for itself.

In general, too, they prefer single, 'pure' models to blendings. And yet, of course, as Bessie Head showed us some time ago in her highly experimental psychological novel, *A Question of Power* (1973), with its combination of personal retrospect, spiritual allegory and, as one final restorative gesture amongst others, a recipe for gooseberry jam – it is the mixing and permutation of forms which in literature gives an occasion and a framework for new imaginings. The structures of art, the organizing plots, as much if not more than the content, create patterns, or a potential syntax of images, within which to think about the unrepresented future. Whether synoptic or dilatory, neatened or fraying, conventionally confirmatory or experimentally interrogative, closed or open, endings offer us different kinds of jumping off places for speculations about what has happened and what is to come.

The suspended and hence often-cited conclusion of Nadine Gordimer's *July's People* (1981) is probably the best-known of late apartheid's blank or so-called 'zero endings' (Visser, 'Beyond the Interregnum', 61–7). A white liberal, Maureen Smales, stranded in an African village following revolution in the city, runs through the bush towards a helicopter that has appeared out of nowhere. Though Maureen has no idea whether the machine 'holds saviours or murderers' (158), her moment of running has been seen as an escape from her old life, and a decisive move towards a new destiny. And yet, given all that has preceded this moment, it could equally be argued that at this stage the significance of her action must remain unclear. Her apparent escape is enclosed by the wider condition of interregnum which is developed throughout the novel, a condition in which, famously, 'the old is dying and the new cannot be born'.

The apparently open yet arrested ending of *July's People* can be seen as emblematic of developments in other 1980s fiction. Maureen Smales is joined in her moment of suspension by, for example, the magistrate in Coetzee's *Waiting for the Barbarians* (1980) or the revolutionary young lovers in Miriam Tlali's *Amandla* (1980), a fictionalized account of the 1976 Soweto uprising. As a young woman watches her lover disappear into the early dawn sky, *Amandla* leaves us with a rather conventional image which gives away little; certainly it forestalls any attempt to envision likely future prospects. Presumably the lover goes to meet his destiny as a freedom fighter, but the episodic quality of the writing, both here and throughout the novel, does not lead us to believe in a messianic outcome. Revolutionary gunmen in the story have tended to be faceless, while the township characters will presumably continue to struggle from day to day, as they have been doing up till now. The young woman's own future in the township, too, remains shrouded in darkness.

Coetzee's *Waiting for the Barbarians*, an allegory of oppressive rule, is perhaps even less sanguine. Self-conscious in its representation of temporality, as Coetzee's work often is, the novel pointedly descends to an entropic ending: an Empire is in decline, its borders are undefended, barbarians are – as indeed they always are – about to invade. Working as a magistrate in an outpost of Empire, the narrator has experienced at first-hand the ways in which imperial authority rules by inventing enemies and crises. He observes that Empire, obsessed with and concerned to safeguard its own survival, compresses the cyclical rhythm of human lives to create 'a jagged time, of rise and fall, of beginning and end, of catastrophe' (133). But, though the magistrate's own time is an end-time, it is an ending that promises no new beginning, no fall and rise again. Instead it is suspended – an endless falling, an always impending disaster.

One could also take this ending, this foreclosure, as a governing sign for other narrative closings under late apartheid. Even though an ending may be plural or indeterminate, even though a sense of things to come may not be completely blocked out, more often than not we encounter a reluctance to speculate or to dream, certainly to give any sort of positive reading about what might happen from now on, other than in the most obvious, formulaic, and limited ways. That is to say, tomorrow is represented as struggle, or cataclysm, or the further disintegration of society. Endings are arrested in a difficult and frozen now: belief in an ongoing, unfolding destiny is largely absent, and this in turn constrains the possibilities for stylistic risk-taking, as well as for a risky making of predictions. Here one of the culminating symbols in Mongane Serote's *To Every Birth its Blood* (1981) comes to mind. At the end of the novel, though 'the Movement' of resistance is growing, a woman is pictured in difficult labour but has not yet given birth. The significance of the image is obvious, yet it is worth noting that even this most predictable of outcomes appears for the time being unimaginable. In the last scene of *Waiting for the Barbarians*, a dream which has haunted the magistrate finally comes to a conclusion, but it is banal and unrevealing. Though the dream offers an ending of sorts, there still seems to be no hope for pain, no promise of release. It is assumed that the barbarians too will be seduced into living the time of Empire.

A slightly later batch of 1980s novels underlines this general sense of descent and loss, without immediate hope of succession. A novel about that archetypal irruption of the repressed under apartheid, forced sex across the 'colour bar', *Mating Birds* (1986) by Lewis Nkosi, closes with the final thoughts before hanging of a young black man who has been convicted for the alleged rape of a white woman. Though critics' interpretations of his crime differ widely, the symbolism of the approaching death as a savage curtailment – execution and then 'cutting down' – is unambiguous. The condemned man is able to hear and feels moved by the freedom songs sung by his fellow prisoners, yet in his 'intolerable' isolation he also concludes 'there are no lessons to be learned from history, only images to be relearned and repeated' (182, 181). That Nkosi's novel represents yet another telling of the sexualized '*swart gevaar*' or 'black peril' plot would appear to be part of, and to reinforce, this sense of entrapping recurrence. In Menán du Plessis's *Longlive!* (1989), a story of (mainly) white activism in 1980s Cape Town, the revolutionary cry of the title is rendered doubly ironic by the two unexpected deaths or near deaths – the heart attack of the aging Afrikaans patriarch, the suicide of the young opera singer – with which the novel ends. And for Coetzee's Michael K in *Life & Times of Michael K* (1983), existence is a perpetual slipping away. As a scavenger and gardener, K has managed to live in the interstices of a civil war zone, 'beyond reach of the laws of nations', and 'of calendar and clock'. He continues at the end to pass unnoticed through the system, 'drifting through time', 'living in suspension', obscure and self-reliant as always (151, 152, 158).

Even in the final scenes of Coetzee's *Age of Iron*, a 1990 novel, the process of falling and lapsing is still not yet completed: the anticipated ending is postponed. Mrs Curren, another representative of suburban liberalism, approaches death in the arms of an adopted guardian and interlocutor, the tramp Vercueil. But because the novel is the testimony of a dying woman, it cannot end at – though it comes close to doing so – her end. Mrs Curren's life, and the humanism for which she stands, 'hover', like dead leaves in the wind, in what she herself calls the *'time being'* which precedes 'the great white glare': the cataclysm which will at last terminate her pain, and presumably her country's insupportable sickness (160; Secker & Warburg/Penguin edition). In Gordimer's *My Son's Story*, also a 1990 novel, the last days of apartheid are upon us, yet here too the ending remains enclosed by silence. A family is dispersed: mother and daughter are in exile; the father, despite a reduced political role, has again been detained. And the son, the non-political family member, who has purportedly written this, their story, claims that he 'can never publish' it (277).

To certain South African critics, most notably the Gordimer scholar Stephen Clingman, the South African novel in the 1980s took the future as its 'presiding' question (Clingman, 'Revolution and Reality', 41–60). Clingman's claim is that South African fiction, which traditionally 'delineated' the phases of history as they unfolded, in the 1980s began to register the collapse of the prevailing 'framework of reality'. However, though considerable fictional evidence might be quoted to support this, the argument needs careful qualification. As the above examples may have begun to show, the ending of the 1980s novel did indeed involve a tailing-off, an unwillingness or an inability to comment on what might follow. There certainly was a widespread perception of an immanent, incipient, or ongoing disintegration in the order of things, but it was accompanied by – and this is the distinguishing element I am trying to outline – a refusal even to go as far as anticipating any ultimate end and therefore any possibility of a new beginning, a diffidence about 'registering' any final 'collapse'. In the eighties such anticipation would have demanded a confidence, even a hubris, that few writers were prepared to risk. In part recognizing this, Clingman finds much richness in the prognostications of narrative allegory. Yet, even in Coetzee, the imaginative challenge of allegory is finally contained within end-stopped structures. Suspension, the zero ending, the dying fall, a closing down of options: in these ways recent South African writers have fallen back into silence.

Because I am working here with such fuzzy ideas as indeterminacy and the imagining of futures, I should try to clarify my point a little further. What I am not saying is that the cumulative effect of endings in recent South African fiction in English involves a denial of provisionality or open-endedness, which might be expected given rule-bound conditions under apartheid. No, what we find is ample, though perhaps also predictable, indeterminacy – the run to the border, the magistrate pressing 'along a road that may lead nowhere' (Coetzee, *Waiting for the Barbarians*, 156). The key difference from a novel like *Mhudi* is that the indeterminacy here happens by default. It rarely promises continuation; it is also rarely creatively disruptive. One gets the sense that the writer's craft is shaped by circumstance, it does not actively *shape*. The indeterminacy, formal or otherwise, justifies itself with reference to a framework of apartheid, which means there can be no surprises, no reversal of expectations. Up to the present, then, the bulk of South African writing seems to have willed an ending to the present state of things, but could do no more – the end was left hanging. Politicians on the right and the left projected apocalyptic visions of the future. As if the initiative had thereby been wrested away, fiction, already hesitant about form-giving, could not or chose not to give the future shape.

'In my end is my beginning.' Perhaps the narrative endings of the apartheid years are monitory not so much in what they say as in what they fail to achieve, in their inevitable closings down. At this moment of transformation in the country, therefore, what we hope for is not so much fictions which imagine the future in detail, but narrative structures that embrace choice or, if you will, stories that juggle and mix generic options. No doubt, as has happened so often before, South African writing will again be whirled into the centrifuge of the country's changed but still-turbulent history. New plots will emerge by and by. Some writers will continue to respond to the demands of realism, seeking to give a full and faithful account, as they have long done. Others may take the parabolic loop away from historical testimony already forged by J. M. Coetzee in order to make sense of a changed polity. But whatever route writers follow, it would be encouraging to see in South African fiction the return of endings that allow for new beginnings, for gestative mystery, the moments and movements following apocalypse, also the dramatization of different kinds of generation and continuity. That is to say, one looks forward to an open-endedness that makes room for new and various ways of thinking about the future – no longer the inevitable interregnum, arrested birth, the moment before death – in short, the foreclosure of the frozen penultimate.

What gives urgency to this hope is again that over the past many decades South Africa has not offered a climate hospitable to artistic explorations. The stylistic achievements of a Coetzee, a Bessie Head, or an Njabulo Ndebele are all the more remarkable for having flourished in this parched place, a society of dead-ends, closures, multiple restrictions on speech and movement, blockages of every kind, spiritual and political. We can predict that the fallout from apartheid's errors will take years to work its way through the culture. For the present, the spread of privilege and access to literacy in the country will remain desperately unequal. Moreover, as more urgent social needs get priority, funding for publishing and writers' projects will be scarce. There are also, of course, mental restrictions which will take even longer to process, what have been called States of Emergency of the mind, both those attributable to the state, and those created within the liberation movement itself. It is interesting that the prescriptive atmosphere of the eighties has permeated into some recent pronouncements on art. In what is said of post-apartheid writing there is still much of 'should' and too little of 'maybe'. Tongue-in-cheek and tentative though it may have been, Albie Sachs's now much-quoted 1989 invitation to South African writers to turn their attention to love was issued, significantly, in the language of injunction: '[We] should be banned from saying that culture is a weapon of struggle' (Sachs, 'Preparing Ourselves for Freedom', 5; see p. 239 below).

The continuing tendency to imitation and cultural obeisance, and the liking for aesthetic orthodoxies, are also in part explained by South Africa's position as a former colony. It remains to be seen whether, in years to come, as the country lifts out of its cultural time warp, literature will make the transition to the creative misreading of sources which characterizes what is called postcolonial writing. The context for these kinds of developments is potentially in place: the mixing of different languages, the cross-fertilization of cultural traditions, even though once stringently outlawed. However, apartheid may have too severely alienated South Africans from an interest in 'native' identities and roots. At present the need to preserve unity, mend divisions, and in general produce a national culture is strong. It may also be that a society which has laboured under a unique situation of internal colonization in a postcolonial world will eventually bypass the teeming dreamscapes that characterize the postcolonial writings of an Amitav Ghosh or a Ben Okri and create something quite its own.

What will South Africans read? What will they write? For the time being these must remain imponderable questions. But perhaps it is worth remembering here that the period between Indian independence, and the efflorescence of the Indian novel in English in the 1970s and 1980s, measures some thirty years. It takes not simply time but important transformations in a society – the widening of an educational system, for example, or the deepening of an indigenous intellectual tradition – for a regenerated national literature to develop.

Yet even if the future is difficult to map out, it does not disallow the making of wishes. The best one can hope for the novel in South Africa is that it will not remain so painfully impaled on that two-pronged fork which is history versus discourse, or reality versus fantasy. The predictability of South African English-language fiction calls out for some sort of disruption – an unsettling of carefully observed familiarity, that documentation of reality which, as Lewis Nkosi has observed, was more often than not addressed to audiences abroad, and which led many readers within the country to dismiss South African literature as 'boring' (Nkosi, 'Constructing the Cross-Border Reader', 37–50). For a long time the novel has been used as a front for other kinds of communication – for political imperatives, for the telling of history, for informing the world about apartheid. Now that freedom has made new kinds of formal and cultural daring more possible, it will be liberating to see the lens of vigilant social observation crack across to give life skewed, fragmented, upended, not by apartheid as before, but as part of the manipulation of aesthetic form, of the testing of visionary, hallucinatory, dislocating, non-camera-ready ways of representing the world. At the same time, with the possible shrinking of its international, politically attuned audience, the terms of reference in the South African novel may become more internal, more domestic. For some writers the loss of the metropolitan connection may prove limiting.

In one of Olive Schreiner's late *fin de siècle* 'Dreams and Allegories', 'Seeds A-Growing' (1901), the Spirit of Freedom, though refusing to say when it will 'gather in [its] harvest', cries out as it flies away 'I cannot die' (143). In 'the sphere of culture', says Albie Sachs in the seminar paper quoted above, we need to accept 'broad parameters rather than narrow ones' ('Preparing Ourselves for Freedom', 7; see below p. 247). His metaphor is worth holding on to, as is Schreiner's motto. The last scenes of *Mhudi* and *The Story of an African Farm* pose the question of the future through their willingness not to foreclose, through what might be called their anticipatory or optative openness. At their end they spread *out*: even if implicitly they allow for a henceforth. Their indeterminacy is an invitation to speculation, to a freeing of words. It is exciting to think that this will happen again in the literature of the new South Africa, that the transformation of the country will loosen up the writing, and invite greater complexity, more exploration, more cross connections, more doubt.

As a way of ending, I want to offer two composite images that, it is gratifying to think, might anticipate the shape of future South African imaginings. One of my images is drawn from a narrative ending, the second comes out of the provocative juxtaposition of issues and themes that, for all its fumbling for a new way of representing itself, may be found on current South African television.

First, at the end of Njabulo Ndebele's story 'Uncle' from the collection *Fools* (1983), there is an impromptu township gathering where jazz is played. The improvised interlinking of 'the gramophone, the trumpet, the concertina, the guitar, the mouth organ, the hooting cars', recalls Uncle's earlier instruction to his young nephew: 'You see, when you are improvising you are free. Completely free. But I'm telling you, you've got to learn to be free. You've got to struggle hard for that freedom' (122; 76–77). Remembering the potential of endings to open out, Uncle has given a timely warning about the difficulty of freedom, and of artistic creation generally. We may have a democracy of new voices in place, but without the structures to combine them, and a constant adaptation, re-adaptation and interleaving of those structures to suit changing circumstances, we will have achieved very little.

'Transformation', Salman Rushdie contends in his essay 'In Good Faith', 'comes of new and unexpected combinations of human beings, cultures, ideas, politics, movies, songs . . . *Mélange*, hotchpotch, a bit of this and a bit of that is *how newness enters the world*' (394). I am aware that citing words of instruction from elsewhere (even where – especially where? – that elsewhere is a highly productive postcolonial narrative space) seems to run the risk, again, of reaching for a second-hand model. I feel it appropriate to mention Rushdie here, however, for two reasons: his inaugural position in Indian postcolonial writing, remembering that *Midnight's Children* (1991), according to Anita Desai, '[loosened]' the tongues of a whole generation of writers (Hamilton, 'The First Life of Salman Rushdie', 104); and because of his resistance to purisms of all kinds. It should also be added that, in different contexts, the conditions and possibilities of transformation offered by intermingling and hotchpotch will be different. But this does not in any way lessen or restrict the potential of 'change-by-fusion', as Rushdie says, or change-by-juxtaposition, as I would want to put it.

My second set of images is taken from a night's viewing on South African television in early 1996. A documentary programme about Mau Mau in Kenya, the retelling of the history of a revolt, was followed by a late-night talkshow slickly hosted by Dali Tambo, son of the late ANC leader Oliver Tambo. His guests on the show were the most recent South African sports stars, the 'Bafana Bafana' football players, fresh from their crucial semi-final victory over Tunisia. On the same day the journalist Khaba Mkhize had ended his regular column in the *Natal Witness*, in which he spoke in patriotic terms of the remarkable 'mixing' in the new South Africa which has been wrought by sport, with a request to Mandela, the 'Praisedent', to 'touch' the team again with his magical touch of victory, and by implication to give the writer yet another cause to enjoy 'barbecued bhabhalaz' (an Africanization of the Afrikaans word for hangover, *babelas*). Mkhize's wish was of course granted (Mkhize, 'The Presidential Touch', 8).

There is something in this partially incongruous juxtaposition of the hype of contemporary stardom with the representation of a struggle of the past, and the living reference to another struggle in the form of Dali Tambo – there is also something in Mkhize's mongrelization of Zulu and English and Afrikaans and his half-parodic legend-making – that it seems to me represents a challenge to writers of fiction, a transformative way of addressing a rapidly transforming world. In the South African novel as in sport, in language, the time for the breaking of inherited rules is here, now. Writers need 'parameters' as broad as it is possible to have, for the metamorphoses that may unfold will, if nothing else, be unpredictable and astonishing.

Works cited

Clingman, Stephen. *The Novels of Nadine Gordimer*. London: Bloomsbury, 1993.

'Revolution and Reality: South African Fiction in the 1980s'. Trump, ed., *Rendering Things Visible*, 41–60.

Hamilton, Ian. 'The First Life of Salman Rushdie'. *New Yorker*, 25 December 1995: 90–113.

Mkhize, Khaba. 'The Presidential Touch'. *Natal Witness*, 2 February 1996.

Nkosi, Lewis. 'Constructing the Cross-Border Reader'. *Altered State? Writing and South Africa*. Ed. Elleke Boehmer, Laura Chrisman, and Kenneth Parker. Hebden Bridge: Dangaroo, 1994. 37–50.

Plaatje, Solomon. *Mhudi* (1930). London: Heinemann, 1982.

Plomer, William. *Autobiography*. London: Cape, 1975.

Double Lives: An Autobiography. London: Cape, 1943.

Turbott Wolfe. London: Hogarth, 1965.

Rushdie, Salman. 'In Good Faith'. *Imaginary Homelands: Essays and Criticism 1981–1991*. London: Granta, 1991. 393–414.

Sachs, Albie. 'Preparing Ourselves for Freedom'. *Spring is Rebellious: Arguments about Cultural Freedom*. Ed. Ingrid de Kok and Karen Press. Cape Town: Buchu Books, 1990. (Reprinted in this volume.)

Schreiner, Olive. *Stories, Dreams and Allegories*. London: T. Fisher Unwin, 1923.

The Story of an African Farm (1883). Johannesburg: Ad Donker, 1975.

Trump, Martin, ed., *Rendering Things Visible: Essays on South African Literary Culture*. Johannesburg: Ravan Press, 1990.

Visser, Nick. 'Beyond the Interregnum: A Note on the Ending of *July's People*'. Trump, ed., *Rendering Things Visible*. 61–7.

Willan, Brian. *Sol Plaatje: South African Nationalist*. London: Heinemann, 1984.

5

The post-apartheid sublime
rediscovering the extraordinary

GRAHAM PECHEY

My concern in this essay is to offer an account of the unfolding post-apartheid condition within which contemporary South African writing takes place; the working premise of my investigation is that that writing (at its best) relates to its environing condition as the latter's most fully reflexive self-knowledge. In thus reading the condition through the optic of the writing (and vice versa), I wish to position myself beyond the space opened up by Njabulo Ndebele when, in the dying apartheid years, he called so eloquently for a post-heroic culture of irony, the local, the ordinary: that is to say, a culture, or a literature, preoccupied not with the polar conflicts of 'the people' versus 'the state' but with textures of life which have eluded that epic battle and have grown insouciantly in the cracks of the structures that South Africa's fraught modernity has historically thrown up.[1] As my guide to occupying this space I have enlisted the work of J. M. Coetzee, and in particular his novel *The Master of Petersburg* (1994). Seemingly poles apart from that of Ndebele, Coetzee's work will nonetheless be seen to stand to Ndebele's in a relation of illuminating complementarity. More to the point: in his most egregious digression thus far from the 'South African' theme, Coetzee licenses me to wander as extravagantly in the territory of history and theory and indeed into the same national culture: that of Russia. Coetzee's use of the late Dostoevsky is, in short, my precedent for drawing on the early Bakhtin. We will not understand the tasks and possibilities of any literature of the colonial margins without first understanding the deep-structural freight of meaning which such a discourse brings with it in its transplantation from the centre and which that transplantation creatively renews.

I

To move 'beyond Ndebele' in the way I have suggested must in no sense be taken to signify a cancellation of what is left behind. It means, rather,

1. See Njabulo Ndebele, 'The Rediscovery of the Ordinary: Some New Writings in South Africa', in *South African Literature and Culture*.

freeing a strand of implication that was in any case already there. One such occluded emphasis is to be found in Ndebele's other writing – in his stories and poems. At least one critic has remarked on the seeming contradiction between his polemical–critical call for a return to 'story-telling', with its strong hint of the traditional, and his distinctly modern practice of short story writing.[2] What is then fascinating is the way that tradition or the precolonial actually surfaces more explicitly in the fiction and poetry. Modern and premodern meet, for example, with a notably unsettling effect in the story entitled 'The Prophetess' (*Fools*, 30–52): a young boy accidentally spills the holy water he has gone to fetch for his mother, refilling the bottle with tapwater that nonetheless helps to cure her after all. As even that bald summary suggests, this story looks Janus-faced towards debunking and towards reaffirmed belief; the special power of the wise woman who gives the boy the water is questioned in a move which (looked at round the other side) works to reinstate the mirac-ulous. The water might almost be a figure for the authenticating inauthenticity of modern writing itself, the boy more specifically a figure for the post-apartheid writer using the bolthole offered by the random-everyday to flee not only the bonds that bind apartheid discourse to its complicit antagonist, but also the very bounds of representation and the probable. In short, it is at the heart of the ordinary that the extraordinary is to be found. Post-apartheid writing turns from the fight against apartheid, with its fixation upon suffering and the seizure of power, into just such stories as these: stories which then open out to transform the victory over apartheid into a gain for postmodern knowledge, a new symbiosis of the sacred and the profane, the quotidian and the numinous.

II

We may begin by specifying in terms appropriate to its literary and other cultural creation what sort of moment it is that South Africa is now pass-ing through. This moment is itself extraordinary: cynics and impossibil-ists may demur, but the predominant tone of response to what has happened, both in print and in common speech, has been one of marvell-ing exclamation. Astonished and thankful hyperbole has seemed to be in order. 'The election was a miracle!' is only the most obvious of the sen-tences cast in this modality to come out of the atmosphere of 1994. And,

2. See Michael Vaughan, 'Storytelling and Politics in Fiction', in Trump, ed., *Rendering Things Visible*.

the rising crime rate notwithstanding, South Africa still bids fair to be the *Gesellschaftswunder* of the late twentieth century. The problems of delivery should not be minimized, and indeed are mounting; there is nevertheless no harm in celebrating the legitimacy we already have; and certainly those who have lived with the incubus of apartheid for most of their lives will, even from afar, have felt the weight of hating and self-vindicating lifted from their shoulders. Those who voted, wherever they were, will have justifiably felt the wonder of doing something quite ordinary.

Let me, then, introduce into the discussion a hint of diabolical advocacy by saying – as neutrally as possible, and perhaps even with the suggestion that this is the best of all feasible outcomes – that South Africa may be entering not exactly a postcolonial phase but the latest of its *neo*colonial phases. Its first such phase (post-1910) may be described as one of British neocolonial hegemony: the empire exploited the charisma of pliant candidates among the leaders of the defeated Boers to secure its interests in the region. The second phase (post-1948) saw the triumphant revenge of those for whom the first was a story of gross anti-patriotic treachery on the part of the co-opted. If to this Afrikaner neocolonial hegemony there has now succeeded an African hegemony of the same essential order, that is because the Afrikaner elite learnt at last to mimic the methods of the old empire, the ordeal conferring charismatic authority upon the new leaders being in this case not a war but the pathos of a long incarceration. If (again) this new phase is indeed neocolonial, then the spread of forces that it has to satisfy makes it perhaps the only phenomenal form that democratic renewal will assume in our epoch. We might say that South African democracy is the effect produced by a neocolonial solution postponed for the time being – perhaps arrested indefinitely – by a powerful counterweight of forces within a civil society still in the making. The prestige of the Bar and the Bench (as witness the appointment of Mr Justice Goldstone to the Yugoslav War Crimes Tribunal) might serve as one index of the suspension of the neocolonial turn. What was true of the country's writers through the whole of the apartheid era – their global acceptance, notwithstanding the cultural boycott – is now true of almost all of its public representatives.

None of this means of course that South Africa's writers must now merge into the diverse traffic of words and bodies to and from a South Africa once again morally in full membership of the world community – that all forms of communication have caught up with the special energizing prescience of literature and theatre. Literature must as much as ever distance itself from the instrumental and ephemeral discourses of the life-world. The writing produced under and after apartheid that we will wish to valorize is that which dramatizes most sharply the high task of all writing within late modernity: to be the witness to that dimension of the interaction of remote contexts which Bakhtin calls 'great time'.[3] It is just this perspective that informs my thesis of South Africa's arrested neo-colonialism, and not at all the cynicism of one who damns all projects of social transformation which are less than classically revolutionary. I am concerned less with the limitations of that country's leaders than with the limits of the political itself. The metanarratives of nationalism and communism alike have proved in too many empirical cases to be instances of that idolatrous *hubris* of modernity which diverts the worship proper only to God or gods on to unworthy worldly objects. Postmodern critiques of modernity have suggested that that heady freedom of the subject's self-grounding which the modern world held out at its beginning turns at length into a bondage. This bondage is then one from which we cannot be freed by a simple return to the premodern: either to the universe of Christian discourse from which secular reason severed itself in early modernity, or to the native spiritual traditions of the colonized world. Opportunities for re-imagining community without setting up the false gods of an overreaching politics open at sundry moments in history; it is as latter-day prophets of these rare moments that we value writers wherever they may be.

III

South Africa today, I would argue, offers one such opportunity. It would seem that categories for understanding this historical opening may be sought in some Russian thinkers of the pre- and immediately post-revolutionary period, and among them most notably one I have already cited: Mikhail Mikhailovich Bakhtin. The parallel is strictly limited: we need not look to the ominous outcome, whereby Bolshevik rule proved in the end to be a neo-absolutism. Instead we might simply note how in both instances the very 'lateness' of the transformation offers, besides evident perils, unprecedented possibilities. The realization elsewhere of possible futures for one's developmentally still-belated home territory gave to the Russian intelligentsia a depth of reflection on the problems of moder-

---

3. For a discussion of this concept of Bakhtin's, see Pechey, 'Eternity and Modernity' (80–2).

nity not available to cultures whose polities and economies had modernized 'on time'. The wish to fashion an appropriate modernity for Russia outside the Bolshevik ambit was not just the knee-jerk reflex of nationalist anti-secularists, but often a real desire to avoid the social and spiritual pathologies that the modern project had spawned in other places. Those seeking to understand the post-apartheid condition in its cultural dimension could do worse than learn from some new readings of Bakhtin.

It is above all in the way Bakhtin rethinks the categories of the aesthetic and of the novel that he speaks most urgently to the post-apartheid imagination. Aesthetic activity is the act by which the other is my author and I in turn his or hers: in his insistence that I can never be the hero of my own life the young Bakhtin encodes his critique of secular modernity's claim to the subject's self-grounding.[4] Turning later to the novel – and in the first instance to the 'polyphonic' novel of Dostoevsky – he makes claims for the hero's autonomy that seem at first to exemplify the fiction of self-authoring he had earlier denounced. It emerges none the less that for Bakhtin the freedom of the hero is nothing apart from the authority of the author; that in pushing the former to the limit we find ourselves back at the latter; and that any other freedom is illusory . Bakhtin enters with gusto into the pluralizing and carnivalizing spirit of modern writing and finds there not faith cancelled in a vertiginous relativism but faith eternally problematized. The obverse of the better-known Bakhtin who novelizes the sacred is the Bakhtin who sacralizes the novel, making of it a talisman we may wear against the temptations of our late-modern world. The objects of modern irony and parody are not the holy or otherworldly as such but their worldly simulacra. Bakhtin wishes us to see that challenges to representation within representation do not threaten what is beyond representation. On the contrary: they reinforce its claim upon our attention; the grotesque no more works against the sublime than incarnation works against transcendence – or the ordinary against the extraordinary. It is in this sense that the novel (like the Gospels) offers at every turn a direct route from the everyday into the most elevated. Every character thanks to the novel's dialogism can be a 'personality', every voice a 'social language'; every element speaks to an infinite context ('Discourse in the Novel', in *The Dialogic Imagination*).

---

4. See 'Author and Hero in Aesthetic Activity', in Bakhtin, *Art and Answerability*; for the turn to Dostoevskian 'polyphony' as the model of modern(ist) writing, see Bakhtin, *Problems of Dostoevsky's Poetics, passim*.

Prototype of all modern writing, the novel is the great generic invention of early modernity by which late modernity might be saved from itself.

Now of course South African intellectuals witnessed nothing so devastating in the way of aggressive and repressive modernization during the apartheid era as did Bakhtin and his contemporaries, and they are in no danger of suffering to that degree now. If South Africa is still far from pacified in the manner of those Western European societies with settled traditions of representation, it has none the less shrugged off the false pacification of the past, when the state and its sworn foes monopolized the cycle of violence. In the new South Africa the threat can now not only come from a variety of points on the political compass but also from quarters for which no known politics can provide reliable bearings. The sublime of terror no longer wears the mask of heroism; death has been freed from its mythologization in both state self-justification and liberation-movement history by the phenomenon of the 'ordinary murder' too complexly overdetermined to serve any partisan agenda. Past deeds of terror are being reinscribed in a new record by the confessions of their perpetrators before the Truth Commission: secular confession as an end in itself is being temporarily institutionalized as the genre in which the Sons on both sides throw off the sins of the Fathers by hearing them out. Meanwhile, though ongoing slaughter and hurting may produce nothing but numbness or panic, this very same condition of moral chaos is one which opens new space for writers to intervene.

We may then ask: what order of answerability is imposed upon literature in a phase when the state no longer murders those it sees as wrongdoers – no longer offers a role model to settlers of scores everywhere by its civil recourse to lethal force? Instead of the sublime of terror surrounding the hanging we have the sublimity of that momentous judicial decision in which the death penalty, having been declared unconstitutional, is given up for good. The word ending the ending of words in killing constitutes the highest reach of the sublime of justice: nothing less than Law and Justice coinciding in a majestic cancellation of the sublime of terror. State-sponsored Truth and Reconciliation, noble as it sounds, partakes more of the beautiful than of that Kantian sublime which has undergone so striking a revival in the anti-foundational philosophies of our time. Writers might in their everyday lives be keen reconcilers, devoted reconstructors-and-developers; their writing has value for us however only insofar as it is no more answerable to those good intentions of the state than it was to the bad ones of the terrorist state of apartheid.[5]

The danger of the post-apartheid condition is that writing will appear to be aligned with the beneficent moves of the state, seeming to have nothing to do after the end of repression. What I have called 'writing' in this chapter is that which can only by an act of hermeneutic violence be read as being *for* any one proposition and *against* another construed as its opposite. We are in the presence of writing in this strong sense when the discourse before us has no designs of assimilation upon other discourses; is unimpressed by the monopolistic claims of any one narrative, even its own; and loves the incommensurability of 'phrasal universes' above all else. The polar contest of apartheid and its antagonists needed for its own purposes to compel an infinity of disparate temporalities and identities into a totality. Writing is under no such necessity, and it is the business of a post-apartheid criticism to respect this discourse, whose agnosticism where centres of power are concerned is absolute.

What does it mean, then, to 'write' in South Africa today? Literature is the unruly child of the birth crisis of European modernity, the disowned brother of Cartesian rationalism – as 'modern' as the latter but still ambivalently freighted with the classical and mediaeval past: freed from the myth of reason by its pursuit of the reason of myth, but fated to be patronized and marginalized by Western knowledge. To write in South Africa today is to take this tradition into a peculiarly complex version of the colonial aftermath and seek to render it indigenous. It is only for nativist or nationalist cultural projects that such an attempt will seem to trespass upon the purity of the precolonial. Such purism is of course founded upon a misreading of the heterogeneity to which colonial cultures are subject from the first moment of colonization. Colonial territories are rich in everyday and up-to-date replays of the crisis of transition which (so Europe tells itself) took place once-off hundreds of years ago: South Africa is especially rich in situations of crossing and of the Protean cultural gaze; it is criss-crossed by margins, a dense texture of boundaries. Russia was (and is) dominated by a single overriding spiritual tradition through which the national community is collectively imagined; South Africa is characterized not only by the thriving in transplantation of all the Abrahamite world religions but also by a plethora of overt spir-

5. See Rorty, 'Habermas and Lyotard on Postmodernity': 'One should see the intellectual *qua* intellectual as having a general, idiosyncratic need – a need for the ineffable, the sublime, a need to go beyond the limits, a need to use words that are not part of anybody's language-game, any social institution' (174).

itual hybrids, scores of 'independent' African churches in which indigenous and imported practices are mingled, Africa's ancestors rubbing shoulders in eternity with the saints of Christian Europe. As Sol Plaatje once observed, his is 'a land filled with prophets'. Its writers therefore have competition, but it is a competition they ought to welcome for its very variety and with which – in their spiritual nomadism, their wandering along and across all margins – they will often find themselves in a dialogical (sometimes a critically ventriloquial) relationship.

Which brings us conveniently back to Njabulo Ndebele and his young boy's resourcefulness. Writers from the majority are the heirs to a powerful meeting and tension of the old wisdom of the forebears and the new street wisdom of the literally and metaphorically 'young' (that is, those only born yesterday into modernity). In one of his most remarkable insights Ndebele suggests that black writing should look to the model of township styles of music and performance, seeking somehow to emulate in words music's negotiation of the passage from the rural world to urban life and wage labour in rhythms that barely need words.[6] Writing would then exercise the adaptive skills acquired over decades by ordinary individuals coming to terms psycho-culturally with the experience of urbanization. For Ndebele such writing would 'rediscover' the ordinary; we might also point to its equal and opposite generation of the extraordinary. The sublime of such writing would be the integral sublime of all music: its challenge to all representation, its assertion of the articulateness of non-cognitive meanings. At the same time it would be as rooted in the humbly ready-to-hand as that popular *bricolage* of worker-performers which submits the gestures of sweated labour to a redemptive choreography, turning the imposed into the chosen, pain into pleasure. The upshot would be a new literacy which renounced the earlier literacy's precipitate leap into a literature and a politics on the metropolitan model, striving instead to embrace the whole range of hybrid articulacies picked up spontaneously by communities as they have historically made a life for themselves under terrible political and social conditions. It would be wrong to trace these observations of Ndebele's back to

6. I have discussed Ndebele's views on the model that the arts of popular performance and of survival present to writing in my Introduction to his collected essays, *South African Literature and Culture*; see especially 8–9, and Ndebele's 'Turkish Tales' in the same volume, 37–8. The present chapter carries forward some of the ideas of that introduction, together with those of the concluding argument in my 'Not the Novel'.

an Africanist or Black Consciousness origin, and label them accordingly. Rather, it is as if Ndebele were calling for the energies of today's South African majority, the product of perhaps three generations, to be directed into the track along which the African diaspora has moved over as many centuries – that is to say, into a cultural expression that has not only evaded the canons of the metropolis but transformed them in a 'reverse colonization' (carried largely by musical forms) which has been nothing less than global in its reach.

IV

So much, then, for the writers of the majority: what of their counterparts from the minorities, and in particular those formerly dominant minorities which hail, historically speaking, from Europe? Clearly they can no more be said to embody some essence of Europe than those of the majority embody an essence of Africa. The privilege flowing from an accident of birth is not a sword with a single edge. It may have cut out a space of dominance, but it has also cut out successive spaces of dissidence, and in the first instance of a liberal colouring. Liberalism in South Africa has historically been the refusal of a 'settler' consciousness in favour of a stance which holds the imperial mission to its nobler promises and sees the bourgeois public sphere as the most precious of imports from the metropolis. From the days of Thomas Pringle it has been culturally speaking – if not inseparable from – then at least strongly bonded with the practice of literature; at the same time its signal political limitation has been its weddedness to a programme of acculturation, its assumption that there is only one modernity and that the benefits of that emancipatory project must not only be extended to all but also internalized by them. Out of white hands, and blended variously with Pan-Africanism and Marxism, liberalism modulates into a nationalism which often fiercely denies its origins.

If Ndebele's version of the post-apartheid imagination might then be more particularly specified as 'post-nationalist' – as occupying a space beyond both the equality politics of the 1950s and the essentialist identity politics which followed in the 1970s – then the corresponding move in white anglophone writing would have to be 'post-liberal'. The best known such voice is that of J. M. Coetzee, whether we think of him speaking as a writer or as that quite other person bearing his name who speaks about his writing. This order of writing which so jealously defends the autonomy of writing has been dismissed by its antagonists as either politically non-accountable or simply a local variety of global postmodernist fashion. Not to see the ethical force of such 'double' (or reflexive) discourse is though not to recognize, first of all, how the valency of literary modes depends almost altogether upon the context of their production and reception. It is also to project one's own dogmatism upon one's enemy, to set up what we might call an inimical dogmatism of sceptical relativism; above all though it is to betray an astonishingly short view of the history of writing within European modernity. The reading I have given above of Bakhtin valuably illuminates the view of writing that we may adduce from Coetzee's practice. Coetzee clearly regards the novel's scepticism-to-the-second-power as a valuable resource, not to be turned to partisan ends but equally not to be mistaken for non-engagement. Defences of Coetzee which read his narratives as allegorized theory are not unhelpful: after all, his other roles as critic and linguist and semiotician make the temptation too great to resist. Where they do not help is in delivering him too easily into global consumption by professional readers in the academy and their acolytes, thereby only confirming the misgivings of his critics at home. Then again, a criticism which too literally historicizes and regionalizes his work courts the other danger of narrowing to nothing the distance between him and Nadine Gordimer, whose equally well-known work takes its cue quite explicitly from the unfolding history of 'the struggle' as viewed through the spectacles of a radical consciousness. To pose his writing as a regional writing of Cape Town against the Johannesburg of Gordimer is to forget that Coetzee's Cape Town is a transcendental as well as an empirical place, capable of cropping up in manifold guises: a focus of cultural meanings in deep chronotopic solution rather than a visitable site.[7] However that may be, any move which takes Coetzee towards the boundary occupied by Gordimer between ethics and politics risks obscuring the strength he derives from straddling that more encompassing boundary between the ethical and the aesthetic, and which gives his work a postcoloniality as peculiar as that of South Africa itself.

Against these misreadings I would argue that Coetzee's way of being postcolonial complements Ndebele's; that the more his work engages the

---

7. Coetzee's status as a regional writer is discussed by David Attwell in his excellent monograph (*J. M. Coetzee*, 25), and has been underlined more recently by Cherry Clayton in the context of a comparison with Gordimer ('White Writing', 155). For an explanation of 'chronotopic' see the next footnote.

Western literary canon of the past, the more it globalizes, without dilution, the particular situation from which it speaks; and that the ethically charged postmodern knowledge which it yields has less to do with some generalized 'postmodernist' textuality than with its highly self-conscious postcoloniality. The sense that literature is the wisdom appropriate to post-traditional communities in all their untotalizable heterogeneity is one that we can get most valuably from both writers; it is also the very note of South Africa today. Each of them shows us that any writing of short-term political commitment is the very reverse of the truly engaged, hitching itself as it does to a perfunctorily localized version of one or other metanarrative of modernity and floating free of the unique existential situation which goes by the territorial name of 'South Africa'. In Bakhtin's terms, they speak to the world by speaking from their own ineluctable chronotope to the chronotopes of their potential readers abroad.[8] If Ndebele's stance is one of positing a knowledge that is so resolutely popular and local that he does not seem to need an addressee in the old metropolis, Coetzee's is one of having so thoroughly and critically internalized the centre's traditions of writing that he can invent in fiction a 'South Africa' which challenges the settled truths of centre and margin alike. Indeed, his work undoes the binary opposition of centre and margin as effectively as it has of late been undone by that most explosive of the newer postcolonialities which has grown up in the metropolis and which has come to be called the culture of 'migrancy'. Coetzee is a textual exile who nonetheless lives at home; his aesthetic migration is exactly the very precondition of his ethical engagement with exactly where he is. As the dimension of metafiction grows in his work, so that work takes on a greater power of intervention in the infinitely many-centred world it shadows forth. Reading him, the world becomes for us politically and culturally – and not just geographically – a sphere, a surface upon which any point is a centre.

Coetzee's nearest approach to a conventionally 'realist' text of the apartheid period is of course *Age of Iron*. That narrative's thematization of its own conditions of transmission is however never swamped in the dramatization of typical characters and historical (let alone, in Ndebele's

8. Bakhtin defines the chronotope as 'the intrinsic connectedness of temporal and spatial relationships that are artistically expressed in literature'. In the chronotope time 'thickens, takes on flesh' while 'space becomes charged and responsive to the movements of time, plot and history'. See 'Forms of Time and of the Chronotope in the Novel', in *The Dialogic Imagination*, 84–5.

sense, 'spectacular') events.[9] Refraction stops short of reflection insofar as Mrs Curren is narrating 'on the threshold', her every word qualified by the death which she awaits. It is in *The Master of Petersburg* that we find the post-apartheid reflexes of which I have been speaking from the beginning coming into full play. The displaced autobiography into which 'all writing' may be resolved here takes the form of a freely revised biographical episode from the life of an actual writer, bringing the story nearer home autobiographically even as it is distanced in a geographical sense.[10] For, perhaps unsurprisingly, the refracting angle in this case passes through not only the Russia without which neither Bakhtin's intellectual formation nor his proffered ethico-aesthetic solutions can be understood, but also the writer who so forcefully reveals to Bakhtin the special *mana* of modern writing: no less a figure than Fyodor Mikhailovich Dostoevsky himself. Coetzee's fictionalized Dostoevsky is the Son who has first found himself in revolt against the Father. We meet him as he suffers in late middle age a painful loss of identity following the death of a stepson whose identity has been forged in a family romance of precisely the same order, at once political and personal. How he has died – was he murdered by the state? or by his terrorist comrades? or did he take his own life? – is less a matter of fact to be established than an index of the shifting state of Dostoevsky's conscience. Coetzee's third-person and historic-present narrative lets us at once see from the outside the creature of needs and infirmities and overhear an inner dialogue which assumes the form of a tortured, mostly unuttered confession.

From the above it will be clear that Coetzee here confronts us with one of those typically Dostoevskian self-undercutting self-accountings which catches its subject in a dizzily relativizing regress only occasionally lightened by a glimpse of that barely imaginable state of all-inclusive forgiveness in which the truth might at last be wholly told. Figured variously either as the serene individual clarity of knowledge in the fall towards death or as the universal exceptionless absolution at the end of all things, this state is in a quite technical sense sublime inasmuch as it almost fails of representation altogether – or is at best only negatively

---

9. Ndebele's discussion of 'spectacular representation' is to be found in 'The Rediscovery of the Ordinary', *South African Literature and Culture*, 41–59.
10. 'All autobiography is storytelling, all writing is biography' – Coetzee, *Doubling the Point*, 391.

representable. Himself no friend of the Russian autocracy, Dostoevsky is rightly repelled by the terrorist's atheistic 'everything is permitted' which enacts syntactically in its passive construction a godless universe where a single imperative reigns over all. In that void individuals are answerable for their deeds only to 'the people', are always-already absolved in the context of an abstract future when what each has willed will be seen to have been effectively willed by all. The followers of such proto-totalitarian 'freedom' may be thought of as holders of moral blank cheques ready for encashing when that future arrives, while the Dostoevsky who thus judges them is very far from such confidence of rightness, seeing himself rather as a gambler willing God to speak in the full knowledge that His grace is a gift and His true speech silence. Now if it is tempting to read Dostoevsky's position between the state and its foes as that of the liberal caught between ideological extremes, that is precisely the precipitately 'political' reading which this text resists. Such an allegorizing reduction can only be forestalled by a reading which understands the transcendental meaning of literary forms, and above all the axiological force of confession and autobiography. Bakhtin will once again prove helpful.

'Confessional self-accounting' in the early Bakhtin is returned first of all to its premodern prototype. Belief is a presupposition of the form: I would not bring up the issue of my life if there were not someone who wished me to be good; trust in absolute otherness is the very foundation of the life I live; faith is implicit in the whole posture of penitence I assume in my earnest self-accounting. When to the tones of penitence are added those of petition, I become explicitly the other-for-God, and confession takes on the special rhythm of prayer that Bakhtin calls 'concord' ('Author and Hero,' *Art and Answerability*, 145). In the confession I acknowledge only one Author; I who utter it am not its author: I am a candidate hero seeking to be written into a role in the cosmic drama of the absolute and ultimate forgiveness of sins. The interest for us of Bakhtin's account of this religious genre is that he sees the characteristic aesthetic and political forms of modernity as transformations of that prototype – as confession diverted or perverted. Irony and cynicism have their roots in confession as theomachy or anthropomachy: verbal fighting against the judgement of God or man, or both (as in many of Dostoevsky's heroes). When Bakhtin cites invective as confession's worst perversion – as the utterance in malicious tones of everything the other might say in tones of penitence about himself, marking him indelibly as the one who has *no other* – we are in the presence of a phenomenon of confession as internalized self-denunciation that both his Russia and Coetzee's apartheid South Africa prolifically exemplified.

Autobiography is confession which has lost the perfect prayerful concord that comes from yielding all author(ial)ity to God, gaining at the same time both narrative values and the subject's freedom to posit a 'possible other' by anticipating others' memories of herself or himself. The result is an aesthetic hybrid: its author is no more the pure artist 'consummating' from without an episode of life-as-it-is-lived than its hero is the purely ethical agent immersed in that life; I as autobiographer forever strive – and forever fail – to put myself in the shoes of posterity. Such a form for Bakhtin is 'highly insecure and precarious' and insistently 'points beyond its own bounds' ('Author and Hero', 165). This ethico-aesthetic hybridity of modern narrative which will later for Bakhtin give it its power to intervene in our late modernity is exactly that which recommends highly reflexive forms of fictional autobiography to Coetzee in the skewed modernity of South Africa. Coetzee espouses these forms not for reasons of fashion or evasion but because he knows with Bakhtin that the constitutively impure aesthetic activity of modern storytelling mimes the characteristically modern gesture of self-grounding whilst averting and neutralizing the pathologies to which the latter has led in historical praxis. Dostoevsky matters so much for Bakhtin because his writing keeps faith with modernity's promise of freedom whilst resisting its will to totality. The polyphonic novel is a space in which cynical and ironic voices are given full weight, where heroes sound like (but are not) authors and the author sounds like (but is not) just one hero among others. Modern writing takes on the aspect of a *felix culpa*, a fortunate fall: grace – the reality of absolute understanding and truth-telling – is expelled beyond the text not in order for cynicism to triumph but to preserve both (human) cynicism and (divine) grace in their benign separateness. Coetzee understands as well as Bakhtin that modern writing works by the principle of the minimum dose: a homeopathic cure for the ills of modernity.[11]

With these reflections behind us, we may now return to *The Master of*

---

11. Readers who know Coetzee's work on confession as a form will recognize some of its terms in this paragraph; see 'Confession and Double Thoughts', in *Doubling the Point*. I am indebted to an unpublished essay by Rachel Lawlan entitled '*The Master of Petersburg*: Confessions and Double Thoughts in Coetzee and Dostoevsky' for drawing my attention to this application of his criticism to his writing.

Petersburg. Coetzee's Dostoevsky becomes in this novel a character rather like one of Dostoevsky's own heroes: in his own eyes not the mediating Christ-figure to which Bakhtin compares the authorial voice in the historical Dostoevsky's novels, but rather the figure of Judas. His end in this episode is however not self-hanging but that other kind of 'fall' or blasphemous temptation of God called writing. The 'master' in writing is the traitor in life. 'Dostoevsky' as a Dostoevskian hero is left writing, on the point of creating the powerful figure of Stavrogin in *The Possessed*; the 'real' Dostoevsky eludes us. Instead of trying on an ethical plane to purge his guilt at forsaking his stepson by merging with him or conjuring his ghost, Coetzee's Dostoevsky embraces the terrorist Nechaev, who incarnates all that he hates and cannot think of his son as embracing. Carrying on the latter's diary, he shifts from an ethical plane to that of 'aesthetic activity' – from futile individual gestures of restitution to the higher, transcendental guilt of writing.

V

The parallels with the writer in the South African situation are obvious: the very name Petersburg conjures up homonymically what might be a South African city; and like Coetzee's Cape Town, in the local context it is by reputation the most 'European' of Russian cities. The low-level insurrection going on around the writer alludes to South Africa at the time of writing; the confession unravelling itself within him suggests the present phase of institutionalized expiation of political sins. The motif of the Father and the Son is also not without a certain resonance in the South African context: it has featured in my argument already; it is prominent in the history of the majority and its phases of struggle; and it is central to the great liberal novel of 1948: *Cry, the Beloved Country*. The trouble though with such a hermeneutic is that it closes Coetzee's text; the parallels should only be the beginning of a (benignly circular) interpretative itinerary, not its end. We need to take the novel's digression from the direct 'South African' theme as seriously as its allusions to that social text: the withdrawal, after all, returns us to the latter with a chastened sense of the possibilities of its recomposition. Lest my focus on this one writer and on one of his works should seem egregious, then, let me say that the power of a work like *The Master* is a power not wholly of its own making. Like Coetzee's earlier fiction, but if anything the more so, it concentrates – only then to displace away from itself – a force of sublime dissonance which it owes to the whole tradition of modern writing. We are not surprised to find Coetzee's Dostoevsky likening himself to a 'cracked bell', given that such a solemn though discordant summons, such affirmation qualified by a flattening irony, is exactly the note that it shares with much of the tradition which it so self-consciously extends (141). To write so much of death in the year of the birth of a new South Africa is not to remind us of the sacrifices that have enabled that birth; this would be to open an ominous and typically modern logic of their heroic sanitization and sublation; it is rather to work an alchemy whereby out of the unthinkable empirical accumulation of deaths death clarifies as the very meaning of community. The Nechaevs of this world will co-opt all such deaths as cases of martyrdom under the rubric of 'the people's vengeance', since it is the way of political discourse of any hue to make a 'work of death' (Nancy, *The Inoperative Community*, 17). Writing like Coetzee's holds itself aloof from, even as it understands ('embraces'), such a will to sublate within a higher sociopolitical totality the sublime extremity of life by which our being-in-common is defined.

Coetzee's writing has suffered perhaps in its reception by being held up as exceptional, when in truth it is only a more thoroughgoing and self-reflexive realization of that vein of the extra(-)ordinary which runs throughout South African literature from its beginning, and which his example has since helped to release in the younger writers following him. To take just one notable instance: the magic-realist experiments of Ivan Vladislavic in *Missing Persons* so elasticize probability, the factual record, and the very dimensions of time and space as to counter that anaesthetizing normalization of South African reality which there is no reason to suppose will have ended absolutely with the formal end of apartheid. In the ruins of Vladisavic's South African allegory the crumbling and neglected surface is a recurring motif; national myth frozen in stone is always a fabric of deterioration; and yet through all of this, against the odds, glimpses of a scarcely representable human life fleetingly show themselves.

Looking not forward but back into the past, we might indeed say that the maturity at which South African writing has arrived was not without hints in its earliest phases. When Olive Schreiner's hero Waldo in *The Story of an African Farm* reflects from his strong 'earthing' in the Karoo upon that landscape as a palimpsest of migrations and exterminations, and latterly as the site of the colonizer's violent obliteration, he remarks that his own micro-community 'will be gone soon' (50). From this we might infer a literature of protest, struggle, 'commitment'; we might also infer from it the fragile finitude of all community. This second perspective, which the dying Bakhtin called that of 'the future without me', is also the perspective for which the present moment of South African history most urgently calls. I 'write' insofar as I turn my 'outsidedness' to the world inside-out, entering imaginatively the world's temporal and spatial outsidedness in respect of me: only in this way can historical processes like that through which the country is passing now resist the birth of a constricted future out of a constricted past. The literature which South Africa's post-apartheid condition both needs and can deliver is the many-voiced discourse of an *ekstasis* which frees us from the future of hopes and fears and admits us to a sphere of 'unexpectedness', of 'absolute innovation, miracle' (Bakhtin, *Speech Genres*, 167). It matters little that the sources of this imagining of the unimaginable – this 'post-apartheid sublime' – are local or global, high-cultural or popular; what language (or silence) it puts to use; or to what genre any one of its texts belongs. It is enough that the writing thus produced should offer from its distance-which-is-not-indifference a model of the ontological priorities appropriate to particular historical phases. Now that South Africa is no longer an object of the world's scrutiny, and that its writers are under no imperative to report from the ground or rally the troops, they are free to polish and infinitely reposition a mirror from which the formerly scrutinizing communities beyond its borders can join all native South Africans in scrutinizing themselves. The field of South African writing is now in every sense without bounds.

Works cited

Attwell, David. *J. M. Coetzee: South Africa and the Politics of Writing*. Berkeley and Cape Town: University of California Press and David Philip, 1993.

Bakhtin, Mikhail. *Art and Answerability: Early Philosophical Essays*. Ed. Michael Holquist and Vadim Liapunov. Austin: University of Texas Press, 1990.

The Dialogic Imagination. Ed. Michael Holquist. Austin: University of Texas Press, 1981.

Problems of Dostoevsky's Poetics. Ed. Caryl Emerson. Manchester: Manchester University Press, 1984.

Speech Genres and Other Late Essays. Ed. Caryl Emerson and Michael Holquist. Austin: University of Texas Press, 1986.

Barker, Francis, Peter Hulme, and Margaret Iverson, eds. *Colonial Discourse/ Postcolonial Theory*. Manchester: Manchester University Press, 1994.

Clayton, Cherry. 'White Writing and Postcolonial Politics'. *Ariel* 25.4
(October 1994): 153–67.

Coetzee, J. M. *Doubling the Point: Essays and Interviews*. Ed. David Attwell.
Cambridge, MA: Harvard University Press, 1992.

'Confession and Double Thoughts: Tolstoy, Rousseau, Dostoevsky'.
Doubling the Point, 251–93.

Gardner, Colin. 'A Poem about Revolution'. Van Wyk Smith and Maclennan,
eds., *Olive Schreiner*, 184–95.

Nancy, Jean-Luc. *The Inoperative Community*. Ed. Peter Connor. Minneapolis:
University of Minnesota Press, 1991.

Ndebele, Njabulo S. *South African Literature and Culture: Rediscovery of the
Ordinary*. Introduction Graham Pechey. Manchester: Manchester
University Press, 1994.

Pechey, Graham. 'Eternity and Modernity: Bakhtin and the Epistemological
Sublime'. *Theoria* (October 1993): 61–85.

'Not the Novel: Bakhtin, Poetry, Truth, God'. *Pretexts* 4. 2 (1993): 68–86.

Rorty, Richard. 'Habermas and Lyotard on Postmodernity'. *Habermas and
Modernity*. Ed. R. J. Bernstein. Oxford: Polity, 1985. 161–75.

Schreiner, Olive. *The Story of an African Farm* (1883). Harmondsworth:
Penguin, 1971.

van Wyk Smith, Malvern, and Don Maclennan, eds. *Olive Schreiner and After:
Essays on Southern African Literature in Honour of Guy Butler*. Cape Town:
David Philip, 1983.

Vaughan, Michael. 'Storytelling and Politics in Fiction'. *Rendering Things
Visible: Essays on South African Literary Culture*. Ed. Martin Trump.
Johannesburg: Ravan, 1990. 186–204.

6

Postmodernism and black writing in South Africa

LEWIS NKOSI

I am concerned in this chapter not with the validity or propriety of post-modernist theory and practice with regard to South African literature taken in its aggregate. That debate has been going on for some time now within the country and in my opinion remains inconclusive. My purpose is to insist that in South Africa there exists an unhealed – I will not say incurable – split between black and white writing, between on the one side an urgent need to document and to bear witness and on the other the capacity to go on furlough, to loiter, and to experiment. This split, apart from the linguistic medium, will find no ready analogy in the difference between, say, Afrikaans and English literatures, a division which is only comparable to the difference between regional literatures in the United States, especially between southern and northern, and between rural and urban writing, a difference which is largely a matter of a constellation of certain themes and preoccupations.

Though often treated as natural, sometimes as a positive sign of our cultural diversity and richness, and as such a reason for celebration rather than regret, this difference between black and white writing can also be read as a sign of social disparity and technological discrepancy. In a post-apartheid South Africa it is clearly a cause for embarrassment. It exists on the one side as a reminder of historical neglect and the impoverishment of black writing and on the other of cultural privilege and opportunity in the case of white writing. While black writing can be said to benefit by being able to draw on its rootedness in the variegated life of the majority, it is also largely impervious for the most part to cultural movements which have exercised great influence in the development of white writing. This discrepancy is particularly noticeable in the domain of theory.

My argument, then, relates first to the colonial status of black writing in South Africa. In the second part of the chapter I deal with what appears to me to be two entirely separate issues. The first of these is the argument that postmodernist theory and practice, as offshoots of poststructuralist thought, have very little to offer oppositional black writers still deeply preoccupied with nationalist agendas and questions of agency. This is an argument which has sometimes been offered by a few black writers sufficiently versed in postmodernist theory to discuss it. On the face of it, this is a straightforward issue of political representation, using a fictional mode. Recent and not so recent criticism of postmodernism, from critics as diverse as Christopher Norris (*What's Wrong*), Aijaz Ahmad (*In Theory*), and Charles Altieri ('What is Living'), can be presumed to lend some support, however limited, to black South African critics who, one imagines, would enthusiastically endorse Norris's attack on post-modernism as tending to sponsor a 'radicalism' which 'has now passed over into a species of disguised apologetics for the socio-political status quo, a persuasion that "reality" is constituted through and through by the meanings, values or discourses that presently compose it, so that nothing could count as effective counter-argument, much less a critique of existing institutions on valid theoretical grounds' (*What's Wrong*, 3–4).

My own ongoing reservations about black South Africans' indifference or impromptu dismissal of postmodernism is that it does not seem to have been accomplished with the necessary theoretical or critical labour, for it is rarely a question of critics who have worked through these theoretical positions and come out on the other side convinced of their hopeless inadequacy or bankruptcy. Quite the contrary; and yet even the most disaffected critics of postmodernism tend to agree that it is not a single monolithic practice. There are at least two distinguishable modes of its operation, one clearly conservative and the other drawing on what Norris describes as a 'continuing critical impulse – the enlightened or emancipatory interest' (5). Finally, is there not a disguised paternalism in the suggestion by some white South African critics that black writers do not 'need' postmodernism, or that it is not 'suitable' for them?

The other question I wish to discuss refers to indigenous African language or vernacular literatures, never even mentioned in most discussions of postmodernism, where I pause to ask whether postmodernism has any contribution to make, and if so, what form both modernism and postmodernism can take in promoting the process of modernization and technical innovation. The reasons for treating this as a somewhat different issue from the first, more technical than merely political, is my conviction that vernacular literatures, through their use of non-European languages, are rooted in or affiliated to other traditions, with different structures and modes of operation. B. W. Vilakazi's doomed experimentations with European prosody in the writing of Zulu poetry early this century provide a cautionary tale, as I shall demonstrate.

I

However, let me turn first to what I have referred to as the colonial status of black writing in South Africa. I wish to argue that its formal insufficiencies, its disappointing breadline asceticism and prim disapproval of irony, and its well-known predilection for what Lukacs called 'petty realism, the trivially detailed painting of local colour': all these naively uncouth disfigurements of which many critics, including myself, have sometimes complained, can be seen to be a result, in part, of a claustrophobia related to this internal colonialism from which, it is hoped, a post-apartheid condition will set it free. Time and again, in its gasps and stutters, in its nightmares and premonitions of a past to be endlessly repeated, black writing shows clearly its relation to this colonial history; the manner, for example, in which it discloses, at the most unexpected moments, its memory of the *sjambok*.

If my analysis is correct, it will surprise no one that black South African writers have shown no particular enthusiasm for postmodernism. Thus, although as another outgrowth of poststructuralist thought and practice, postmodernism appears to have taken some hold in South African literature, it is a movement wholly occupied, managed, and dominated by white writers, with black writers seeming either to ignore it or not even to have heard of it. In the first instance, I wish to argue that the reasons why black South Africans should know so little about these contemporary cultural movements is easy enough to explain. Much black writing, it has always seemed to me, operates in an autonomous region entirely untouched by contemporary cultural theory. In fact, what is so astonishing about Mothobi Mutloatse's introduction to the anthology *Forced Landing* (1980) is a quality of an almost defiant insouciance, an impatient refusal to countenance any discussion of theory as such beyond a succession of normative assertions.[1]

What needs to be emphasized, however, is that for many black writers this seeming indifference to matters of theory is by no means deliberate,

---

1. This impatience is reflected in the modest programme which is however presented in a highly emotive language: 'We are going to pee, spit and shit on literary convention before we are through; we are going to kick and pull and push and drag literature into the form we prefer' (5).

nor is the appearance of innocence a matter of prideful or willed ignorance. Furthermore, what needs to be explained is the wide discrepancy between contemporary theory and black writing as such; but so far much of recent commentary has merely dwelled on what Graham Pechey has correctly diagnosed as a 'bifurcation' between black and white writing without bothering to explain the material conditions which can account for that bifurcation ('Post-apartheid Narratives', 165). Thus, in what at first appears to be an irreproachably nuanced description of 'South African literature', seen in process as developing in relation to the various stages of political resistance, comprising different temporalities while held together by the need to provide simultaneous anchoring to cultural identities and communities living out 'diverse times', Pechey also advances the idea of a South African writing practice which 'has never been anything other than postmodern (as a whole practice, as an institution), though not always (technically, in the sense of its internal textual relations) postmodern*ist*' (165). There is an aporia here in the proposition that parts which have nothing in common with the postmodern somehow begin to share this fate as soon as they are combined into an institutionalized whole. If nothing else, this formulation serves more as a final confirmation of the triumphant rhetoric of postmodernist discourse, rather than offering a convincing argument about an existing state of affairs. Even more suspect is the assertion that South African writing is 'the place where marginalities of *all* kinds can meet and be positively valued' (165). After all, it is black writing which is so obviously marginalized and occupies, in fact, a minority status.

However, putting aside for the moment the obfuscating language, or even the question of how to read Olive Schreiner's 1883 novel as a postmodernist text, what we are offered here is the consolation of a black writing which may be 'postmodern' without being 'postmodernist'. Equally, we are left to wonder at the characterization of black writing as having been 'wakened out of its state-inflicted amnesia' which seems to apportion the blame equally to black writing and state persecution. But what was it that black writing was forced to forget? This is never spelled out. In fact, Pechey's text is riddled with many similar equivocations and evasions which function only to paper over fissures in his line of argument. The general thrust of Pechey's 'Post-apartheid Narratives' is to misrecognize the limitations imposed upon black writing by its colonial situation, in which case it is regarded merely as a reflection of the 'rich diversity' of South African writing.

In that now notorious and much-criticized global treatment of 'third-world' texts, Jameson argued that 'a popular or socially realistic third-world novel tends to come before us, not immediately, but as though already-read' ('Third-World Literature', 65). This 'already-read' quality of much black fiction in South Africa, its tedious quality of inevitability and its inability to surprise the reader, is surely undeniable; but it is important to trace much of the backwardness of black writing to its state of internal isolation and surveillance under the apartheid regime and some of its disabilities to wounds inflicted by cultural deprivation and social neglect. In South Africa the gap between black writing practice and contemporary theory is simply too large to ignore, requiring attention in a concerted fashion, and in terms of remedial action.

Conventional wisdom has it that, until Bantu Education was imposed on an unwilling black population, missionary and provincial schools produced a 'black elite' largely divorced from the social concerns of a black proletariat. Armed with Marx and Gramsci, and writing from the comfortable chairs of 'Whites Only' university departments, these white cultural critics have sometimes managed to produce a profile of a 'black elite' which is hardly recognizable to its supposed members. But even if the charge of 'elitism' could be made to stick, it may be useful to point out here that elsewhere 'elitism' has sometimes been coupled with experimentalism and avant-gardism that have vitalized literatures in Asia and South America; the absence, by and large, of this experimentalism from black writing in South Africa has other roots and remains to be adequately explained. This cannot be done by critics who see Mtutuzeli Matshoba's *Call Me Not a Man* (1979) as an example of ground-breaking innovation.

One result of this kind of critical analysis has been to authorize a view of black writing as wilfully *sui generis* and naturally resistant to any attempts to bring it into fruitful contact with other contemporary movements in world literatures. This kind of analysis assigns a mode of writing to a racial category, then uses this essentialism to simultaneously explain and justify the limits of black realism. Such an approach overlooks the fact that black writers, apart from their isolation from the outside world, and more importantly, their isolation from the development of writing elsewhere on the African continent, until well into the seventies had no ready access to institutions of higher education where matters concerning literary theory, even in its rudimentary bourgeois form, came under discussion.

If we take the so-called *Drum* writers as representative of the fifties generation, it is surprising how few of them had any university education. When I went to work on *Drum* only Can Themba was the product of a university education; Es'kia Mphahlele was then studying for his BA by correspondence. Needless to say, writers inside and outside South Africa have produced excellent work without the benefit of a university education. There is also the added question, much in need of theoretical elaboration, whether one could be a 'postmodernist' without knowing it. In any event, where theory counts for so much – as seems to be the case with current artistic movements – it cannot be an accident that most works that are tuned into contemporary aesthetic movements are by white rather than black writers.

Above all, what the black community must reject is the insultingly patronizing attitude of some left-wing critics who, in their eagerness to privilege text that offers them a slice of black life of which they are ignorant, attempt to foist upon us something like *The Marabi Dance*. Graham Pechey asks: 'Does post-apartheid writing, then, bifurcate into a modernist or postmodernist *white* writing on the one hand and a neorealist *black* writing on the other?' ('Post-apartheid Narratives', 165; emphasis added). The question that Pechey is too embarrassed even to pose is why this bifurcation has taken place at all; instead, he prefers to treat South African writing as 'a rich polyphony of (its) forms and modes' which has 'tended to negotiate the heightening militancy of the struggle: either, on the black side, to thematise "fighting" in cathartic stories of recent struggles and in "battle hymns"; or, on the white side, to let violence have its effects in the formal dislocation of its texts and in its vivid imaging of a chaotic apocalypse' (164–5). Since we are here in the domain of literary production and creative skills and not, except metaphorically, in a zone of combat, given a choice on the one side of 'cathartic stories' and on the other the 'formal dislocation of texts' and 'vivid imaging', we know precisely which texts on the sides of that bifurcation will seem to yield greater aesthetic rewards; for, again to adapt Jameson to the South African situation, certain black South African texts can be read only 'for the freshness of information and a social interest that we cannot share' ('Third-World Literature', 66).

II

I wish to turn now to the two other issues I raised with regard to postmodernism in South Africa, at least insofar as black writing is concerned.

The first concerns the argument often made elsewhere against post-modernism, that it has the effect of 'disempowering' those struggling to dismantle imperialist discourses: the view so powerfully advanced by Nancy Hartsock five years ago, that 'postmodernism represents a dangerous approach for any marginalised group to adopt' ('Rethinking Modernism', 101). From the point of view of many women and minorities, the case against postmodernism is invariably presented as a critique of an epistemological scepticism so extreme that it is seen as politically immobilizing; for it has been argued by many critics, Annamaria Carusi among others, that 'undecidability, multiple and endless possibilities of meaning . . . have no place in the context of real political urgency, where there is a need not for endless self-reflexivity, but for definite decisions to be made' ('Post, Post and Post', 101); and in Kumkum Sangari's assertion about postmodernism, that 'the writing that emerges from this position, however critical it may be of colonial discourses, gloomily disempowers the "nation" as an enabling idea and relocates the impulses for change as everywhere and nowhere'.[2] In my own private discussions with black writers and critics I found them not only hostile to movements like post-modernism; also, they seemed to banish from consideration any form of representation which departs even slightly from their favoured paradigms, including 'magic realism', perhaps because of what Linda Hutcheon calls its 'challenges to the conventions of realism'. For critics who consider literary realism as simply exhausted and who tend to treat *all* realistic representations as necessarily backward, even reactionary, not to have heard of postmodernism signals a species of underdevelopment or worse.

In my study of African literature under the title *Tasks and Masks*, a book completed in the 1970s before the present spate of postcolonial theories, and unashamedly using traditional tools of criticism, I made the observation concerning the fiction of Chinua Achebe that in the light of the history of European denigration of African societies, in the light of the widespread assumption that African societies functioned without family, law, or philosophical thought, the first generation of novelists in post-independence Africa felt it to be their responsibility to re-assemble, re-constitute, and re-present a simulacrum of a precolonial 'Africa'. To the question 'What did Africa look or feel like before the arrival of

2. 'The Politics of the Possible', *Cultural Critique* 7 (1987): 183–4; cited in Adam and Tiffin, eds. *Past the Last Post*, ix.

Europeans?' one could simply pull out *Things Fall Apart* and *Arrow of God* as an adequate reply.

I keep in abeyance, of course, the possible objections to the essentialist turn of such an argument, even the objection to using Achebe's texts in the same way Yoruba cosmogony in Soyinka's plays has sometimes been employed: as essential representations of an African universe. It must also be pointed out that Achebe himself has never authorized that kind of use for his texts. In any case, Achebe's realist procedures would tend to preclude the use of his texts in an allegorical way about African social thought as such: Achebe confines himself rigorously within the Igbo frame. I am also aware that, strictly speaking, the past as such is not wholly recuperable; but where Africa has been essentialized as Europe's other, Achebe's texts have functioned rightly as paradigms of African social thought and organization.

In that chapter, 'In Search of African Modernism', I make the further point that in trying to 'recreate' the past, surprisingly a simple realism 'usually suffices'. Benita Parry misrepresents my argument when she portrays me as 'cool' on African modernism, describing me as 'censoring its linguistic and narrative innovations' ('Culture Clash', 132). What is in question in all these arguments is the role of realism in the representation of the historical process; underpinning Parry's critical writing on South African literature is the notion that realism has run its course and is now politically retardative. She is not alone in holding such a view; in consequence, in spite of its emancipatory gesture, the fiction of writers like Njabulo Ndebele or Alex la Guma is thought to be essentially backward looking. For example, for Parry, La Guma's fiction is nothing more than a 'recycling of stale and purple language, of received narrative practices and exhausted modes of address [which] normalize the fiction's ex-centric material and defuse a confrontational stance' ('Problems', 47–8). One suspects that a certain kind of mechanical, philosophic rhetoric is at work here, a poverty of response which has taken over where a critical sensibility should operate, when a critic can dismiss *A Walk in the Night* as 'a recycling of stale or purple language'. One can even sympathize with Arun P. Mukherjee's impatience with 'the postmodernist tendency to valorize antirealist fiction':

When critics like Catherine Belsey and Linda Hutcheon suggest that
antirealist fiction 'denaturalizes' what we had taken to be real and thus warns
us against being sucked into the illusionist trap set by realist representation by
constantly drawing attention to its process, I feel like telling them that after a

while, the metafictions of postmodernism stop having that effect because of our increasing familiarity with their stylistic manoeuvres.

('Whose Post-Colonialism', 4)

My own quarrel with 'black' realist fiction in South Africa was never premised on the idea that realism as such was outmoded; rather, that it was incompetent, 'technically brittle', to use Emily Apter's descriptive phrase about 'colonial realism'; in fact, quite uncannily, my argument was couched in terms nearly identical with those used by Apter in her criticism of French 'colonial realism' when she suggests that such fiction is in competition with the evidentiary claims of the photographic image; and if one extends this argument to South Africa, this suggests – ironically – that black 'protest fiction' might even be said to serve as the underside of colonial realism:

> Colonial realism's narrative strategies are more technically brittle in their conventional stylizations. Coming apart at the seams, they reveal their fierce competitiveness with the power of the mechanically produced image, given mass appeal by the turn of the century as a result, in part, of the explosion of photographic tourism, ethnography, commercially distributed pornography, national festivals, and world exhibitionism.
>
> (APTER, 'Ethnographic Travesties', 298)

The irony of a politically minded protest fiction in collusion with 'commercially distributed pornography' is too rich not to linger on a little longer; nevertheless, attacks on realism *tout court* cannot ignore the issues raised by Raymond Williams in his essay 'When Was Modernism?', in which he poses the question whether nineteenth-century realism as such is necessarily beyond the modernist pale. Williams makes the interesting point that the intensities in some texts of nineteenth- and early twentieth-century realism – and he would include the canonical texts of high realism by novelists such as Charles Dickens and Gustave Flaubert – show these texts as already constituting instances of, or earlier moments of, modernism. Then the argument to be made with regard to black literature in South Africa or other parts of the non-European world is that black writers there have no obligation to follow every new trend emanating from Europe; they need not dispense with realism altogether until, to their own satisfaction, they feel they have exhausted all the resources which realism was supposed to provide in the first place; and if this argument holds true for the practitioners of realism as a general style, it must also hold for the modernist writer who feels no

83

compulsion to join what Houston Baker would have called 'the post-modernist collective.'[3]

At the risk of being accused of supporting some version of a linear history of development, I think we ought seriously to entertain the idea that black South African writers may not in fact become postmodernists before they have brought to completion their modernist agenda. In what I presume to have been a moment of bad temper, Houston Baker reminded us, if we needed any reminding, that an African–American modernism differed essentially from an Anglo-American version:

> Afro-American scholars, intellectuals, and activists of the late nineteenth and early twentieth centuries were faced with a task substantially different from that of their Anglo-American, British and Irish counterparts. Rather than bashing the bourgeoisie, such spokespersons were attempting to create one. Far from being rebellious dissenters against existent Afro-American expressive forms, they sought to enhance these forms and bring them before a sophisticated public. And far from repudiating the emergent age as 'an old bitch gone in the teeth,' Afro-American spokespersons welcomed a new century as a time when shackles of slavery and impoverishment would fall decisively away. (*Afro-American Poetics*, 7)

Without trying to imply that black writers and intellectuals in South Africa are necessarily striving for identical goals, it is clear that the same historical conditions and divisions which plagued a white-dominated society in America are also at work in South Africa.

III

The final question I wish to ask is what possible reading of indigenous African-language literature can pass unmolested through the grid of the current postmodernisms? Though my intention is not to argue that post-modernism is somehow inappropriate for indigenous-language litera-tures, here I wish to pose the question as to what kind of postmodernism would elicit a response from these literatures: what blending of styles, what quotations and citations, what temporalities would enable these lit-eratures to go beyond their own project of modernization to join the ranks of a postmodern one? Lastly, a more interesting question I wish to

3. In *Afro-American Poetics* Baker refers to the 'myths of non-self', which he says are the products of rhetoricians who are privileged, and goes on to make the point: 'One can, however, always refuse to be part of a deconstructive collective' (4).

ask is whether it is possible to be postmodernist at all without even knowing it? Here I have in mind Tutuola's *The Palm-Wine Drinkard*, which I characterized some years ago as having been a modernist work *avant la lettre*, although on my present reading it may even be said to be more *post-* than modernist.

The work of a 'houseboy' and blacksmith with only a primary school education, Tutuola's text is an amalgam of styles and genres, neither strictly a novel nor a traditional narrative, but a heterogeneous blending of folk-tale, heroic adventure, and dilemma tale, moral fable, quest romance, discourses on law, finance, and commerce, a perplexing pot-pourri of symbolic codes and languages cutting across any strict generic boundaries and cultures, in which the material signs of a modern market economy do not so much replace or displace the traditional barter system, the cowries for the British pound, as merely coexist with it in an unstable heterogeneity. So, too, is a passion for computation a signal of an emergent capitalist formation resembling its manifestation in Defoe's texts three centuries before. In Drinkard's world even 'Fear' and 'Death' are only commodities to be bought and sold:

> Now by that time and before we entered inside the white tree, we had 'sold our death' to somebody at the door for the sum of £70: 18: 6d and 'lent our fear' to somebody at the door as well on an interest of £3: 10: od per month, so we did not care about death and we did not fear again. When we entered inside the white tree, there we found ourselves inside a big house which was in the centre of a big and beautiful town . . . So we met the old woman sat on a chair in a big parlour which was decorated with costly things . . . She took us to the largest dancing hall which was in the centre of that house, and there we saw that over 300 people were dancing all together. The hall was decorated with about one million pounds (£) and there were many images and our own too were in the centre of the hall. (247–8)

What, then, is *The Palm-Wine Drinkard*? A postmodernist text that does not even know its own name? It would be preposterous, of course, to suggest that Tutuola is consciously participating in some postmodernist manoeuvre designed to waylay an unsuspecting contemporary critic; in one of those familiar referential slippages Tutuola explained what he thought he was doing: merely writing a story to 'tell of my ancestors and how they lived in their day'. Michael Thelwell wrote in the introduction to the 1984 edition of this text first published in 1953:

> I shall not speculate – intriguing though that prospect be – on precisely which chords of modern literary sensibility are set resonating under the stimulus of

Drinkard's unique vision. Certainly one can see where certain Jungian and Freudian critics could, with barely compatible assumptions, find much to engage them in its world. So too can surrealists and devotees of magical realism find within it hospitable territory on which to plant their respective standards. (187)

Are we likely ever to encounter in vernacular literature of South Africa a work of such intense hybridity which might be said to resemble *The Palm-Wine Drinkard*? But then, however idiosyncratic his use of it, Tutuola was writing in English, a European language which would make it more than likely that we would read him in ways consonant with our awareness of symbolist and surrealist paradigms. This way of presenting my case allows me to lay further emphasis on the differences between black and white writing in South Africa, this time by way of contrasting European-based and indigenous African languages as media of expression.

Most South African critics eager to participate in the new discursivities made available by the postcolonial condition are equally eager to establish for the two European-based languages, 'South African English', and perhaps with some justification Afrikaans, an *African* identity, though the status of the latter as an 'African' language rather than the creolization of a European one is still in dispute. As in the case of Canadian and Australian cultural critics, this readiness by white South African writers and critics to see themselves as among Europe's 'others' rather than continuers of European traditions in other parts of the globe is surely justifiable on pragmatic political grounds; but it is also probably true, as Fredric Jameson also stated the matter with regard to European radicals like Benjamin, that, like the children of the European bourgeoisie, 'maimed as well as privileged', the children of the colonial settlers in South Africa 'have an interest in lifting the burdens of exploitation [they], too, necessarily suffer'; and that they wish to 'secede' from these colonial settler regimes and 'to enjoy an imaginary identification' with the oppressed majorities or minorities, whatever the case may be (review of *The Correspondence of Walter Benjamin*). What is indisputable is that writers in English and Afrikaans, of whatever ethnic background or race, have a ready access through these languages to European forms of experimentation – I have already mentioned symbolist and surrealist innovations – because these languages, through an accumulation of tradition, through a historical connection with European literatures, are already hooked into European systems of aesthetic forms in a way not readily available to indigenous African-language literatures.

'Available' is perhaps not the right word to use here, since the missionaries tried their best to exercise an influence on the development of local literary traditions which can now legitimately claim John Buchan and Shakespeare as among their 'ancestral fathers'. Nevertheless, most works of African literature written in the native languages are linked to the indigenous traditions in the most obvious ways. They come out of those traditions, confirm their ways of looking at the world and their ways of talking about the world. It would be instructive, for example, to examine how a novel or poem written in Zulu might break with the linguistic habits of Zulu classical poetry which comes to us through the oral tradition. What might a genuinely committed postmodernist Zulu novel look like? We know what a good Zulu poet like B. W. Vilakazi produced in the forties when, in what critics have since considered a misguided experiment, he attempted to modernize the tradition of Zulu poetry in accordance with European norms, first by writing it down where before it had been spoken or chanted, and then by trying to apply the techniques of English prosody to Zulu. According to the Zulu scholar C. L. S. Nyembezi, Vilakazi, in the collection called *Inkondlo kaZulu* (*Zulu Songs*; 1935), was responsible for developing poetry whose form departed from the traditional *Izibongo* (or praise). Instead of adopting the style and pattern of the *Izibongo*, he experimented with European forms. He divided his poems into regular stanzas. He also experimented with rhyme. (See the introduction to Vilikazi, *Zulu Horizons*.) This experiment and its lamentable failure indicated all too clearly that vernacular literatures have prior claims upon them born of different linguistic systems and the oral and narrative traditions from which they partly derive. As one of the scholars and critics pointed out at the time:

> He attempts rhyme, but with limited success, as Zulu syllables, invariably, ending in vowels, do not present the variety of sound and tone that makes successful rhyming possible. Even the forms of English rhythm that he uses do not supply a perfect medium, for Zulu accents and stresses refuse to be bent into conformity with the beat of the music.
>
> (TAYLOR, '*Inkondlo kaZulu*', 164)

A lively question, therefore, is in what form could vernacular works ever insert themselves into the various currents of postmodernist practice which, after all, irrupt from specific disenchantments with various

projects of the Enlightenment, culminating in the now discarded or
largely absorbed modernist experiments? As separate from the problem
of internal textual relations, it is obvious that certain forms of traditional
discourse would have no problem of alignment with the split or decen-
tred Lacanian subject, as the Nongqawuse episode would tend to show;[4]
the art produced under possession is already 'subjectless' and what passes
for the 'subject of discourse' is speaking from many places at once. One
way of reading the Nongqawuse episode, as indeed Bessie Head's
A Question of Power, is by recourse to Shoshana Felman's *Writing and
Madness* and Michel Foucault's *Madness and Civilization*, in which all
normative values and standards regarding the place of madness in society, indeed within the history of Western philosophy and the sovereignty
of Reason within it, are put in question. It is possible, for example, to suggest a link between certain 'mental disorders' in these texts with the
movement of desire in the speaking subject, especially in a struggle
against the curtailment of this movement by patriarchal domination. In
Mtutuzeli Matshoba's fictional version (in *Call Me Not a Man*),
Nongqawuse is presented as a heroine instead of a source of error under
pressure of colonial oppression, as Peires has described the episode in
The Dead Will Arise. Of interest to psychoanalytical thought is
Nongqawuse's 'narcissism', her specular self-identification when she
peers into a pool of water and thinks she can hear voices of the ancestral
spirits speaking to her. Was claiming to have seen visions and to have
heard voices of the ancestral spirits not perhaps Nongqawuse's attempt –
not fully conscious to be sure – to clear space for herself in which as a
woman, traditionally forbidden to participate in political discourse, she
could then speak with some authority and be listened to? What would a
postmodernist feminist discourse do with the *hlonipha* tradition, which
disallows women from uttering certain locutions in the presence of men?

4. There are many accounts, from the tradition and from historical narratives,
the most recent being J. B. Peires's *The Dead Will Arise*, of how in the middle
of the nineteenth century a young Xhosa woman named Nongqawuse,
claiming to have held conversations with ancestral spirits, induced the Xhosa
people to slaughter their cattle and burn corn: 'Nongqawuse said that she had
met with "new people" from over the sea, who were the ancestors of the
living Xhosa. They told her that the dead were preparing to rise again, and
wonderful new cattle too, but first the people must kill their cattle and destroy
their corn which were contaminated and impure' (311). The result was major
catastrophe for the Xhosa, many of whom died of starvation.

If a certain postmodernism is indeed disabling, it is equally true that some form of postmodernism can have potentially subversive and discomposing effects not only on the hegemonic discourses of the imperial centre but on those created by traditions to underpin hierarchical structures of age and patriarchy.

NOTE   This chapter is an expanded version of a paper delivered at the 1995 African Literature Association Conference in Ohio, USA.

Works cited

Adam, Ian, and Helen Tiffin, eds. *Past the Last Post: Theorizing Post-Colonialism and Post-Modernism*. Calgary: University of Calgary Press, 1990.

Ahmad, Aijaz. *In Theory: Classes, Nations, Literatures*. London: Verso, 1992.

Altieri, Charles. 'What is Living and What is Dead in American Postmodernism?' *Critical Inquiry* 22 (1996): 764–89.

Apter, Emily. 'Ethnographic Travesties: Colonial Realism, French Feminism, and the Case of Elissa Rhais'. *After Colonialism*. Ed. Gyan Prakash. Princeton: Princeton University Press, 1995. 299–325.

Baker, Jr, Houston A. *Afro-American Poetics: Revisions of Harlem and the Black Aesthetic*. Madison: University of Wisconsin Press, 1988.

Carusi, Annamaria. 'Post, Post and Post. Or, Where is South African Literature in All This?' Adam and Tiffin, eds., *Past the Last Post*, 95–108.

Felman, Shoshona. *Writing and Madness*. Ithaca: Cornell University Press, 1985.

Foucault, Michel. *Madness and Civilization: A History of Insanity in the Age of Reason*. Trans. Richard Howard. London: Tavistock, 1967.

Hartsock, Nancy. 'Rethinking Modernism: Minority vs Majority Theories'. *The Nature and Context of Minority Discourse*. Ed. Abdul R. JanMohamed and David Lloyd. Oxford: Oxford University Press, 1990. 17–36.

Jameson, Fredric. Review of *The Correspondence of Walter Benjamin, 1910–1940*, ed. Gershom Scholem and Theodor Adorno. *London Review of Books*, 3 August 1995: 8–9.

'Third-World Literature in the Era of Multinational Capitalism'. *Social Text* 15 (Fall 1986): 65–88.

Mukherjee, Arun P. 'Whose Post-Colonialism and Whose Postmodernism?' *World Literature Written in English* 30. 2 (1990):1–9.

Nkosi, Lewis. *Tasks and Masks: Themes and Styles of African Literature*. Harlow: Longman, 1981.

Norris, Christopher. *What's Wrong with Postmodernism: Critical Theory and the Ends of Philosophy* . Baltimore: Johns Hopkins University Press, 1990.

Parry, Benita. 'Culture Clash'. *Transition* 55 (1992): 125–34.

'Problems in Current Theories of Colonial Discourse'. *Oxford Literary Review* 9 (1987): 27–58.

Pechey, Graham. 'Post-apartheid Narratives'. *Colonial Discourse/Postcolonial Theory*. Ed. Francis Barker, Peter Hulme, and Margaret Iversen. Manchester: Manchester University Press, 1994. 151–71.

Peires, J. B. *The Dead Will Arise: Nongqawuse and the Great Xhosa Cattle Killing Movement of 1856–7*. Johannesburg: Ravan, 1989.

Taylor, J. Dexter. '*Inkondlo kaZulu* – An Appreciation'. *Bantu Studies* 9 (1935): 163–5.

Thelwell, Michael. Introduction to Amos Tutuola, *The Palm-Wine Drinkard*. New York: Grove Press, 1984. 177–90.

Tutuola, Amos. *The Palm-Wine Drinkard*. Introduction Michael Thelwell. *'The Palm-Wine Drinkard' and 'My Life in the Bush of Ghosts'*. New York: Grove Press, 1984.

Vilikazi, B. W. *Zulu Horizons*. Cape Town: Howard Timmins, 1962.

Williams, Raymond. 'When Was Modernism?' *The Politics of Modernism*. Ed. Tony Pinkney. London: Verso, 1989. 31–5.

7

Shame and identity
the case of the coloured in South Africa

ZOË WICOMB

> ... Also: brown contains black – (?) – How would a person behave for
> us to say of him that he knows a *pure, primary* brown? We must always
> bear in mind the question: How do people learn the meaning of colour
> names? WITTGENSTEIN, *Remarks on Colour*

In the 1980s South Africans discovered the Khoi/coloured woman
Saartje Baartman, once known as the Hottentot Venus, who was exhibited in London and Paris from 1810 to her death in 1815. In nineteenth-
century Europe, as Sander Gilman points out, the display of her
spectacular steatopygia and its generation of medical discourse on the
Khoi genitalia established the iconographic link between the black
woman and sexual lasciviousness ('Black Bodies, White Bodies', 216).
Since the last decade has seen her well referenced in South African visual
art and writing, popular outrage has moved the government to apply to
France for the return of Baartman, whose remains are still held by the
Musée de l'homme in Paris (though they were removed from public display in the 1980s). Having in the New South Africa become an icon of
postcoloniality, Baartman's case can be seen as one of several initiatives
towards reconstructing a national cultural past.

Although the project of recovery is propelled by the ignominy of
sexualized display before the imperial eye, the discourse around the
return of Baartman is cast in terms of injury rather than shame, and a
question which has not as yet been resolved is what we will do with her
remains. The popular consensus is that the violated body should be cov-
ered with native soil, given a decent Christian burial in her own country,
specifically in the western Cape where she originates, a view that is challenged by the people of Soweto for whom the western Cape can hardly
seem an appropriate site for a national symbol of cultural reconstruction.
Perhaps the more pertinent question is whether her burial would also
bury black woman as icon of concupiscence, which is to say bury the
shame of having had our bodies stared at, but also the shame invested in

those (females) who have mated with the colonizer. Miscegenation, the origins of which lie within a discourse of 'race', concupiscence, and degeneracy, continues to be bound up with shame, a pervasive shame exploited in apartheid's strategy of the naming of a Coloured race, and recurring in the current attempts by coloureds to establish brownness as a pure category, which is to say a denial of shame. We do not speak about miscegenation; it is after all the very nature of shame to stifle its own discourse. What the case of Baartman then shows is how shame, cross-eyed and shy, stalks the postcolonial world broken mirror in hand, reproducing itself in puzzling distortions.

'O shame, shame, poppy shame!' Salman Rushdie, narrativizing shame in his novel about Pakistan and postcoloniality, maps its complexity as he tells the story 'in fragments of broken mirrors' (*Shame*, 16, 69). Its English formulation, 'tainted by wrong concepts and the accumulated detritus of its owners' unrepented past', in other words, by the very shamefulness of colonialism, is replaced by the indigenous term: '*Sharam*, that's the word. For which this paltry "shame" is a wholly inadequate translation... A short word but one containing encyclopaedias of nuance' (39). Rushdie, investing shame with materiality, gives an ironic listing of political chicanery, its shamefulness reflected into that which Sufiya Zinobia Hyder, the character who embodies shame, blushes for. Such acts as

> lies, loose living, disrespect for one's elders, failure to love one's national flag, incorrect voting at elections, over-eating, extramarital sex, autobiographical novels ... throwing one's wicket away at the crucial point of a Test Match ... are done *shamelessly*. Then what happens to all that unfelt shame? (122)

Throughout the novel, shame is connected to concupiscence, to a pathological female sexuality, so that the idiot Sufiya's release of absorbed shame is also finally brought about through the body, in the voracious sexuality and violence of the mass killer.

Following Rushdie's nuanced usage, my project is to find a way of discussing the textual construction, ethnographic self-fashioning, and political behaviour of coloureds in South Africa, which is to say our condition of postcoloniality,[1] through the concept of shame. Stuart Hall's notion of

---

1. I locate the meaning of the term *postcolonial* not in etymology, but rather in discursive fields where it has been shaped through usage and has acquired a variety of meanings, including, for instance, oppositionality, resistance, the practice of radical readings, neocolonialism, as well as the interrogation of the very term.

transcoding ethnicity, of contesting its meaning within a new politics of representation – 'It is only through the way in which we represent and imagine ourselves that we come to know how we are constituted and who we are' ('What is this Black?', 473) – informs my reading of coloured texts. In order to shift the debate out of a local political discourse into culture in the wider sense, I trace the construction of colouredness through postmodernism's reconceptualization of geographical space and of the body. Not only can the body be thought of metaphorically as a text, as explored in recent Euro-feminist theory, but I also wish to consider the actual materiality of black bodies that bear the marked pigmentation of miscegenation, and the way in which that relates to political culture.

Saartje Baartman, whose very name indicates her cultural hybridity, exemplifies the body as site of shame, a body bound up with the politics of location. I adopt her as icon precisely because of the nasty, unspoken question of concupiscence that haunts coloured identity, the issue of nation-building implicit in the matter of her return, her contested ethnicity (Black, Khoi or 'coloured'?) and the vexed question of representation. The Baartman case also neatly exemplifies some of the central concerns of postmodern thought – the inscription of power in scopic relations; the construction of woman as racialized and sexualized other; the colonization and violation of the body; the role of scientific discourse in bolstering both the modernist and the colonial projects – and is thus a convenient point around which to discuss the contested relationship between postcolonialism and postmodernism.

In etymologizing terms the death of apartheid and achievement of liberation from settler colonialism signals a condition of youthful postcoloniality. However, the shameful vote of Cape coloureds for the National Party in the first democratic elections throws such a label into question. Our electoral behaviour, which ensures that the Western Cape is the only region without an ANC parliamentary majority, coincides with the resurgence of the term *Coloured*, once more capitalized, without its old prefix of *so-called* and without the disavowing scare quotes earned during the period of revolutionary struggle when it was replaced by the word *black*, indicating both a rejection of apartheid nomenclature as well as inclusion in the national liberation movement. Such adoption of different names at various historical junctures shows perhaps the difficulty which the term 'coloured' has in taking on a fixed meaning, and as such exemplifies postmodernity in its shifting allegiances, its duplicitous play between the written capitalization and speech that denies or at least does not reveal the act of renaming – once again the silent inscription of shame. Yet, within the new, exclusively coloured political organizations that have sprung up in the Cape since the election, attempts at blurring differences of language, class, and religion in the interest of a homogeneous ethnic group at the same time seem to defy the decentring thrust of postmodernism. What the problem of identity indicates, however, is a position that undermines the new narrative of national unity: the newly democratized South Africa remains dependent on the old economic, social, and also epistemological structures of apartheid, and thus it is axiomatic that different groups created by the old system do not participate equally in the category of postcoloniality. Theoretically, the situation can be cast in terms of the diverging interests of postmodernism and postcoloniality, or it may indicate the need to revise popular definitions of the latter to include the coexistence of oppositional and complicit forms. However, in practice such an absorption into a single category would gloss over the real threat to the task of establishing democracy, at least in the Cape.

The failure, in coloured terms, of the grand narrative of liberation – for how else to describe our vote against non-racial democracy – demands fresh enquiry into the questions of postcolonial 'hybridity' and identity as well as the territorialization or geography of belonging within which identity is produced. This I will attempt through a discussion of cultural practices as, for instance, in our complicit construction of District Six as ethnic homeland. Our postmodern suppression of history demands a strategy of relocating and rehistoricizing our own situation lest we come to believe the myth of our collective birth in Cape Town's District Six in the early 1960s.[2] The making of the subject and the script of shame imbricated in such ethnographic self-fashioning as well as in the discursive construction by others need to be examined in the light of the narrative of liberation and its dissemination in the world media that constructed oppression in particular ways.

District Six, an inner-city community marked by poverty and crime, was destroyed by the Group Areas Act of 1965, which removed people to the dreary, far-flung suburbs of the Cape Flats. Its assumption as ethnic

---

2. An astounding number of 'cultural workers' adopt District Six as place of birth, and CVs for foreign circulation often append to the privileged Harold Cressey High School in the city of Cape Town the barely justifiable address of District Six.

homeland illustrates not only the fictional nature of identity construction but also the postcolonial relationship with a politics of location. Since the earliest fiction by writers like Alex La Guma and Richard Rive, it has become a ready-made southern counterpart to the loaded signifier of Soweto. Site-specific as media signifiers of oppression had become, District Six had the advantage of being urban, demolished and therefore patently about loss, as well as being associated with forced removals to which far fewer coloured than black communities were in fact subjected. The self-fashioning of a totalizing colouredness located in a mythologized District Six of the 1950s and sixties found its expression in the eighties in the popular eponymous musical. Here ethnicity was constructed within a politics of nostalgia that sentimentalized the loss. The contradiction of forging an 'authentic' culture, ironically also the overt theme of 'District Six', through North American cultural conventions and musical forms seemed to escape the mainly coloured audiences enraptured by the process of being constructed in the tepid, amniotic fluid of pastiche. In the heady months before the unbanning of the ANC, the show's self-conscious reliance on pastiche, a mode described by Jameson as 'the imitation of a peculiar mask, speech in a dead language: but a neutral practice of such mimicry, without parody's ulterior motives' ('Postmodernism', 74), signalled its refusal to engage with collocations of colouredness, or with interacting identities in a larger framework of South African citizenship. What is significant is that the musical in fact was produced during the period of mass identification with the liberation movement, that the spatial over-identification with District Six was temporally linked to identification with the black nationalist struggle. In other words, whilst such modalities of belonging clearly existed historically, they did not find their way into a politics of representation. The popular attempt at inventing an authentic colouredness illustrates how representation does not simply express, but rather plays a formative role in social and political life.

The title of Richard Rive's *'Buckingham Palace': District Six* refers to the parodic mode so conspicuously absent in the musical and its sequels. In this work of deliberate generic ambiguity, italicized texts written in the first-person autobiographical genre serve as foreword to each of the three sections of fictionalized vignettes of what we are assured are real-life remembered people: 'And in the evenings we would stand in hushed doorways and tell stories about the legendary figures of District Six, Zoot, Pretty Boy and Mary ...' (4). Thus authenticity is inscribed in a text that apparently already exists in oral and communal representation of these very characters. Whilst neither the place nor the affectionate portrayal of characters is sentimentalized, the autobiographical text is marked by the ethnographic. The past tense modal form, 'we/they would', used throughout these sections, provides nothing less than a generalized customs-and-manners description of coloured life that takes us through the week ending with the Sunday dessert of jelly and custard and the boys' occasional trip to the museum to giggle at 'the models of Bushmen with big bums'. Here Baartman's European viewer is replaced by the puerile gaze of coloured boys, and steatopygia itself is shifted to colonial *representation* of 'primitives' in a museum, a shift that covertly and uneasily refers to shame.

As early as 1962 Bessie Head lamented in her first novel, *The Cardinals* (first published in 1993), the representation of the Coloured and the mythologizing of District Six. Johnny, the voice of truth in the novel, advises his colleague to give up writing:

> I don't even have to read this one to know it's about another prostitute walking down Hanover Street and shaking her behind. Where you see all these prostitutes is beyond me. I've never ever seen a prostitute walking down Hanover Street, shaking her behind. She wouldn't dare . . . Every single story I've read of yours is about the happy little Coloured man and the colourful Malays. Why don't you leave that crap to those insane, patronising White women journalists who are forever at pains to tell the Coloureds how happy they are. (16)

Thus the location of colouredness in the colourful District Six is firmly linked with coloured complicity in their construction, including the stereotype of female sexuality inscribed in the spectacular Baartman-esque behind.

It is instructive to look at how in the sixties, rejecting the label of coloured, Bessie Head in exile in Botswana responds to the question of ethnicity. In an essay called 'Africa' she discusses her identity through addressing the country as a fickle, flesh and blood lover. Her discomfort is stylistically encoded in an archaic, inverted syntax, and using a trope of travelling without direction, she describes her identity in terms of lack:

> Not now, not ever, shall I be complete; and though the road to find you has been desolate with loneliness, still more desolate is the road that leads away from you . . . What do I do now that your face intrudes everywhere, and you

are yet essentially *ashamed* of me as the thing of nothing from nowhere?
Nothing I am, of no tribe or race, and because of it full of a childish
arrogance to defend myself against all of you.
(*The Cardinals*, 121; my italics)

Through the figure of chiasmus shame is identified as the recognition of
being the object of another's shame. Morphological forms of the word
thus indicate changes in meaning that relate to a shifting subjectivity and
to the interrelatedness of different subject positions. (Rushdie's Zinobia
is also wife to Omar Khayyam, who is immune to the feeling of shame.)
For Head this shame is supplanted only by an Africanist politics of liberation which allows her to say of the PAC leader Robert Sobukwe, 'He gave
me a comfortable black skin in which to live and work' (*A Woman Alone*,
97). Here the word 'comfortable' stands in significant contrast to the
word 'proud', a black consciousness term that betrays its continued relationship with shame.

That black nationalist struggles gained an unstable popularity
amongst coloureds is not simply a matter of postmodern scepticism of
grand narratives of emancipation. There is the question of language or
the ways in which political discourse relates to the figuration of colouredness in cultural texts. For instance, apartheid education ensured that
coloureds do not speak the indigenous languages, and the Soweto uprising of 1976, characterized as a revolt against Afrikaans as the language of
the oppressor, produced a movement amongst coloureds in the Cape to
rescue their first language from its association with oppression. Thus
arose in the eighties a flurry of poetry in non-standard Afrikaans that had
only the previous decade along with its lone practitioner, Adam Small,
been pejorated as a shameful 'gamtaal'. Renamed and valorized as
'Kaaps', this local and racialized variety of Afrikaans as a literary language came to assert a discursive space for an oppositional colouredness
that aligned itself with the black liberation struggle. But, as Willemse
points out, English-language writers like Richard Rive saw Kaaps as
'propounding the acceptance of a brand of Colouredism in the face of
strong anti-racism' and falsely claiming 'the right to a special, ethnic
literary existence' ('Die Skrille Sonbesies', 380). This was indeed an
unfounded and linguistically conservative assessment of Kaaps itself,
but raising the spectre of ethnicity at such an unlikely stage was curiously
prophetic of coloured responses to black nationalist discourse in the
nineties when the local variety of Afrikaans is once again appropriated
by reactionary forces.

In literary representations shifts in coloured–black relations are captured in short stories published in 1979 and 1991 by Mtutuzeli Matshoba and Don Mattera respectively. The mood of racial conciliation in Matshoba's 'A Son of the First Generation' is exemplified by an African woman giving birth to a mixed-race child who is forgivingly accepted by her black husband. The story ends with an epilogue in which, stepping outside the fictive, the narrator dedicates the following words to his 'Coloured brothers and sisters': 'To me a so-called "Coloured" human being is a brother, conceived in the same black womb as I. Child of a sister robbed of the pride of motherhood by the man-made immorality laws' (*Call Me Not a Man*, 91). Thus Matshoba's writing of black solidarity embraces the newborn coloured as male, constructed through a narrative of illicit sexuality, female concupiscence, and shame. Don Mattera's 'Die Bushie is Dood . . .' ('The Bushie is Dead . . .', in Robin Malan's collection *Being Here*, 138–42) tells a very different story of ethnic tension confirmed in the death of a coloured youth stabbed at a Soweto rally by black comrades who do not trust coloureds and who question his right to be there, just as the young man's family question his meddling with black politics. The tension in the story is marked by nomenclature: a tussle between the youth and his brother when the latter speaks of 'bantu' and 'darkies'; the use of the derogatory 'Bushie' (from 'Bushman') by a black man to indicate the young man's lack of belonging as opposed to the term 'comrade' used by his friends. Thus the narrative of assimilation witnessed in the political activism of the 1970s and eighties is replaced by Mattera's representation of an ambiguous coloured exclusion and self-exclusion from national liberation politics.

The majority vote in the Cape for the National Party came as no surprise to the ANC. Ozinsky and Rasool, in their discussion of an ANC election strategy for the coloured areas in the Western Cape, offer an account of the history of struggle in this area. The paper, whilst warning against the use of the term *coloured* to cover heterogeneous sets of communities differentiated by class, language, and religion, points out the demographic significance of the group, who comprise 52 per cent of the population in comparison with 25 per cent Africans and 23 per cent Whites in the region. Ozinsky and Rasool comment on the vibrancy of the resistance movement in the eighties when the radical United Democratic Front captured the determination of diverse coloured constituencies not to be co-opted into the ruling block. The paper asks the following rhetorical questions: whether a legacy of organization and structures had been left in coloured communities; and whether the 1980s had indeed created non-racialism, acceptance of African leadership, and a sense of common nationhood. The failure of the movement since its unbanning is attributed to the fact that after its legal relaunch, the ANC was not seen to have a clear programme for work in communities. When politics became centralized, there was no focus on mass work, and the racial tension that developed when the oppositional coloured Civic organizations that had contributed significantly to the demise of apartheid and now became subject to the ANC is quaintly characterized as an 'ambiguity'. This, Ozinsky and Rasool argue, 'led to the dissipation of much of the inherent strength of mass politics in coloured areas' (2). What the document does not address is the question of regionalism and ethnicity, the way in which coloured activists considered themselves to be marginalized since the dismantling of the UDM. Its rehearsal of the party line, 'the main content of our national liberation struggles is the liberation of the African majority. The African majority is the most reliable force for the completion of the tasks of national liberation', thus fails to take into account the reality of regionalism, that the majority in the Cape are in fact coloured. The working paper ends limply with recommendations for more ANC branches focusing on community issues in the Cape. What the ANC had not predicted was that the National Party, with its superior resources, would mobilize working-class coloured communities around issues like housing, and, with propaganda about alien concepts like affirmative action, would lead them to believe that Africanization necessarily meant depriving them of their homes, schools, and jobs, and ultimately their culture.

The *volte face* of the National Party's false appeal to a shared culture centred in the Afrikaans language, the Dutch Reformed Church, and mutton bredie was overlooked as Cape coloureds cast their shameful vote. And the shame of it lies not only in what we have voted against – citizenship within a democratic constitution that ensures the protection of individual rights, the enshrinement of gay and lesbian rights, the abolition of censorship and blasphemy laws – but in the amnesia with regard to the National Party's atrocities in maintaining apartheid. Our postmodern effacement of history stretches back to the very memory of our origins. Robert Ross in his study of the history of slavery at the Cape remarks on the difficulty of research when virtually nothing by way of folk-tales, stories, or songs has been retained and when the only sources are records of the Court of Justice covering the period of the Dutch East

India Company rule. His account of the rebel slave Leander Bugis and his band of runaways at Hanglip, their insurrection including an attempt to burn Cape Town to the ground in 1736, is indeed of a figure ripe for legend and mythology, but such stories have not found their way into folk history. Ross explains the amnesia in terms of social history, but also in terms of denial: 'The continued oppression of large numbers of ex-slaves by their ex-masters and . . . the concern of those who had escaped from this position to set themselves apart from the rural scene' (*Cape of Torments*, 76).

This failure or inability to represent our history in popular forms and consequently the total erasure of slavery from the folk memory presumably has its roots in shame: shame for our origins of slavery, shame for the miscegenation, and shame, as colonial racism became institutionalized, for being black, so that with the help of our European names we have lost all knowledge of our Xhosa, Indonesian, East African, or Khoi origins. Significantly the reference to slavery in our self-naming as *Gam* originates not in memory but rather in apartheid's legitimizing reference to the Old Testament narrative of Noah's son Ham, who looked upon his father's nakedness and so earned the curse of slavery. It is no coincidence that the very word *shame* has acquired a peculiar semantic attenuation into an utterance of tenderness, sympathy, or empathy so that we would exclaim 'Shame!' on seeing a baby or a beggar, whilst the meaning of disgrace has been excised in common usage.

The shame-bearing coloured finds her literary origins in Sarah Gertrude Millin's eugenicist novel *God's Step-Children*, where miscegenation, as J. M. Coetzee points out, is expressed in terms of 'blood, flaw, taint and degeneration' (*White Writing*, 136–62). Similarly, in the first African Nationalist novel, Sol Plaatje's rehabilitated Mzilikazi in his grand nation-making speech warns against the Bechuana's alliance with the Boers, who will 'take Bechuana women to wife and, with them, breed a race of half man, half goblin', although he wrongly predicts that 'they . . . will waste away in helpless fury till the gnome offspring of such miscegenation rise up against their cruel sires . . .' (*Mhudi*, 175). Shame is still inscribed in the tragic mode routinely used to represent coloureds where assumed cultural loss is elevated to the realm of ontology, as in Liz Gunner's enigmatic story 'You, the Lioness'. Here a black singer speaks of 'women [who] heal with water and prayers – things I half understand because it's only half mine, and we of mixed blood, Coloured, that word! . . . I don't know where we belong' (15). (The answer, I fear, is in the

Cape!) Such perception of culture as something divorced from the performative and curiously defined as that in which you do *not* participate is
typical of this mode; more worrying is the metaphysics of race which
allows difference to exclude an individual from what others in her own
community intuitively know.

As Gunner suggests, the shame is located in the very word *Coloured*, a
category established by the Nationalist government's Population
Registration Act of 1950, when it was defined negatively as 'not a White
person or a Black'. But it is worth remembering that as several groups
found the term unsuitable, amendments to the act for additional categories such as 'Other Coloured' or 'Griqua' were made. Subsequent
shifts in nomenclature have further supported the idea of a fragmented
coloured subject as a postmodern 'ontological "fact" that can only "find"
itself in language' (Hebdige, *Hiding in the Light*, 193). Postcolonial theorizing of the coloured also takes its cue from the notion of fragmentation, as witnessed in Homi Bhabha's analysis of the following passage
from Nadine Gordimer's *My Son's Story*.

> Halfway between: the schoolteacher lived and taught and carried out his
> uplifting projects in the community with the municipal council seated under
> its coat-of-arms on the one side of the veld, and the real blacks – more, many
> more of them than the whites, 'coloureds' and Indians counted together – on
> the other. His community had a certain kind of communication with the real
> blacks, as it did with the town through the Saturday dispensation; but rather
> different. Not defined – and it was this lack of definition in itself that was
> never to be questioned, but observed like a taboo, something which no-one,
> while following, ever could admit to.   (21)

Gordimer's representation of racial identity in terms of the popular
nationalist discourse of the authentic selves of 'real blacks' and coloured
indeterminacy is taken up in orthodox postcolonial terms by Homi
Bhabha. Bhabha makes an ontological leap from the mytho-geographi-
cal, so that the 'borderline existence' for the coloured marks a 'deeper
historical displacement' and represents a 'hybridity, a difference
"within" a subject that inhabits the rim of an inbetween reality' (*Location
of Culture*, 13). Here, surely, are echoes of the tragic mode where lived
experience is displaced by an aesthetics of theory. How, one is tempted to
ask, do people who live in communities inhabit, spookily and precari-
ously, a rim of inbetween reality? Symbolically, of course, and therefore,
according to Gordimer, in silence, the shame of it all encoded in the word
taboo. Surely relegation to such a space relies on an essentialist view

which posits a 'pure' reality that is experienced in the space inhabited by the racially pure.

Continuing the metaphor of the home suggested by Gordimer's narrative, Bhabha speaks of the halfway house of 'racial and cultural origins that bridges the "inbetween" diasporic origins of the Coloured South African and turns it into the symbol of the disjunctive, displaced everyday life of the liberation struggle' (13). This link, assumed between colouredness and revolutionary struggle, seems to presuppose a theory of hybridity that relies, after all, on the biological, a notion denied in earlier accounts where Bhabha claims that colonial power with its inherent ambivalence itself produces hybridization:

> Produced through the strategy of disavowal, the *reference* of discrimination is always to a process of splitting as the condition of subjection: a discrimination between the mother culture and its bastards, the self and its doubles, where the trace of what is disavowed is not repressed but repeated as something different – a mutation, a hybrid. (111)

In this language of eugenics, Bhabha explains how ambivalence revealed within the discourse of authority enables a form of subversion; however, in the case of the coloured, racial hybridity, as in the previous quotation, is somehow itself responsible for a necessary subversiveness – much like Plaatje's prediction of a hybrid race rising against its sire![3] But in the very narrative that he examines, coloured complicity rather than subversion is affirmed: Gordimer's schoolteacher, who becomes an ANC activist, remains after all an anomaly in his extended family who continue uncommittedly to 'picnic in the no-man's-land of veld'; there is no coloured community of activists. And the narrative charts Sonny, the activist's, decline in the movement because of his sexual relations with a white woman.

Bhabha's theory of hybridity cannot account for the current coloured politics, where it is precisely the celebration of inbetweenness that serves

3. Robert Young's *Colonial Desire* (published since this paper was first delivered at the African Literature Association Conference, March 1995) dismisses the postcolonial concept of hybridization as one that 'assumes . . . the prior existence of pure, fixed and separate antecedents', and that is 'still repeating its own cultural origins'. Thus he claims that 'the threat of degeneration and decay incipient upon a "raceless chaos" has not yet been fully redeployed and reinflected' (25). This claim is summarily dismissed by Stuart Hall as a simple coincidence of using the same terminology that bears different meanings ('When Was "The Post-Colonial"?').

conservatism, as in the use of the word *brown*, introduced into the unwieldy title 'Coloured Liberation Movement for the Advancement of Brown People', launched at the beginning of March 1995. Slipped in tentatively as a prepositional phrase, the word bears the trace of shame in its capitulation to the National Party's expedient use of 'Brown Afrikaners', which successfully drew in the coloured vote, as well as in its evocation of country-folk, an attempt at fabricating a traditional past to foster the notion of a coloured nation. The association of brown with mid-century Afrikaans-speaking farmworkers whose customs and manners had been ridiculed and whose difference has been racially codified by Afrikaner writers like Mikro shows both the amnesia and the contradictory nature of this construction: the apposite terms of *liberation* and *advancement*, *Coloured* and *Brown*, thus have the task of amelioration that will efface history and reconcile contradiction. Amnesia is most crassly demonstrated in another new coloured political party, the Kleurling Weerstand Beweging [Coloured Resistance Movement], with its unseemly echo of the Afrikaner right wing.

That coloured politics presents a problem for representation seems to be a central concern in Nadine Gordimer's *My Son's Story* (1990). Gordimer, who is admirably free of the postmodern anxiety about representation and has never missed a chance to comment on the good, strong legs or large buttocks of black female characters, problematizes the representation of the coloured in her very title. The narrative is of Sonny, the coloured teacher turned political activist, who has an illicit affair with a white woman. It is his son, Will, consumed with disgust and anger on his mother's behalf, who writes the story of his father's infidelity and his mother's subsequent adoption of the struggle as a gunrunner. The final words of the novel, 'I am a writer and this is my first book – that I can never publish', present a deictic complexity that points to the displacement of the 'my' in the title, where the pronoun in the phrase 'my son's story' refers to Will's father, the man who cannot represent his own shameful story. (Rushdie's ironic reference to extramarital sex as a source of shame is pertinent here: it is, of course, a shame refracted through the comrades' ejection of Sonny.) In the very act of representing the coloured activist, the possibility of representing him is disavowed in Will's final words. What cannot be represented, one suspects, bearing in mind Gordimer's careful charting of the history of the struggle, is not the coloured, but the coloured activist within the ANC whose relations with the organization turn out to be problematic, not least because of his concupiscence. In contrast, J. M. Coetzee's virginal coloured vagrant, Michael K, whose life remains isolated from a community or a resistance movement of which he has no knowledge, even as the revolution rages about him, is indeed representable.[4]

The narrative voice in Gordimer's text alternates between Will's first-person account and a third-person centre of consciousness, itself focalized through either Will or his father. But we are told at the end of the novel that the events focalized through Sonny had all been Will's inventions; in other words, Sonny as source of the information about himself is denied; he cannot tell his own story. Will is able to write their story as a private act, precisely because he has been excluded from liberation politics, a decision that much to his resentment is taken by his mother, Aila. But he cannot publish it. The coloured story is destined to be suppressed; the narrative of Aila's surprising contribution to the struggle is marked by silence: in the space between writing and making public lies an unacknowledged shame steeped in its originary interracial sex.

Gordimer's account of the 'spectator status' that coloureds adopt as they speak of black insurrection from a distance is communicated in an imperfect transcript of direct speech in the Afrikaans syntax that characterizes ordinary coloured language:

> There was fervent stoep and yard talk, *they going to moer the lanies   you'll see ou   they quite right make the Boers shit their pants there in Pretoria   what you think you talking about they going to get a rope round their necks   that what they putting up their hands for, bracelets man bullets up the backside you can't win against whitey.* (23)

This curious discourse, situated somewhere between the political and idle gossip, significantly takes place on the stoep or in the yard, the ambiguous space between inside and outside, between public and private, which makes it possible to present the dialogue between indistinguishable participants as if overheard. Thus it is marked by ellipsis, the most marked being the indicator of direct address, the *ou*, a modifier which is never used in face-to-face communication without being followed by an addressee's name. Instead of identifying the speaker there is typographic

---

4. David Bunn's essay, '"Some Alien Land"', refers to Arthur Nortje's problematic relationship with the ANC. This is suggestive in relation to the explicit, self-loathing references to miscegenation and colouredness in Nortje's poems.

space, a replication of the symbolic no-man's-land where the unpoliticized Sonny and his young family used to picnic. The dialogue, drawing attention to itself through italics, presents the available positions of resigned acceptance of the power of apartheid as well as a vague empathy with Black resistance, but not of active participation in the Movement. Thus Gordimer's unidentified speakers, represented through ellipsis, express through their own enunciation their political identity as lack.

Significantly, this family do not live in the Cape, home of the coloured, where we find instead of an articulation of lack of identity, a shameful excess, an exorbitance of identity currently expressed in the construction of coloured nationhood that has surfaced since the elections. This situation questions several of the metropolitan articulations of postcoloniality. For instance, Homi Bhabha's location of the condition in the 'history of postcolonial migration, the narratives of cultural and political diaspora' (*Location of Culture*, 5) would seem to prove inadequate for a group who in the suppression of their diasporic slave origins have adopted an excessively proprietorial attitude towards the Cape. Similarly, the indigenists' dismissal of the postmodern critique of nationalism as imagined community needs to be reconsidered in the light of the new fissures. The coloured valorization of rootedness at the Cape also brings to mind Aijaz Ahmad's sneer at the postcolonial myth of ontological unbelonging that is linked to diaspora (*In Theory*, 128–34). In his critique of *Shame*, Ahmad complains about postmodern dislocation and the fact that 'the idea of belonging is itself seen now as bad faith, a mere myth of origins, a truth effect produced by the Enlightenment's "metaphysic of presence"' (129). However, such bad faith may well serve as antidote for the equally mythical excess of belonging or exorbitance of coloured identity. Instead of denying history and fabricating a totalizing colouredness, 'multiple belongings' could be seen as an alternative way of viewing a culture where participation in a number of coloured micro-communities whose interests conflict and overlap could become a rehearsal of cultural life in the larger South African community where we learn to perform the same kind of negotiations in terms of identity within a lived culture characterized by difference.

As I write, there is news of Winnie Mandela declaring the ANC Women's League an Africanist organization, the meaning of which we euphemistically choose to construe as a riposte to the League being called a feminist organization. News also comes of the walkout at the ANC Youth League's annual general meeting in the Western Cape by coloured comrades who claim that discrimination against them has become intolerable. The comrades' choice lies in either being shamefully aligned with the Browns or remaining silent on the margin of the movement, hugging to themselves their refracted shame. Otherwise there is the retreat into culturalism with a rallying mumble of diversity that hardly constitutes the excision of shame that we would like to think it is.

It is in the spirit of the new postcolonial internationalism that I choose to end with the African–American artist Carrie Mae Weems's image-text work, *THEN WHAT? Photographs and Folklore,* recorded in an artist's book of fold-outs. One of these constitutes a series of black and white informal photographs of six young black people with a continuous text running below:

DEEP BLACK, ASHY BLACK, PALE BLACK, JET BLACK, PITCH BLACK, DEAD BLACK, BLUE BLACK, PURPLE BLACK, CHOCOLATE-BROWN, COFFEE, SEALSKIN-BROWN, DEEP BROWN, HONEY BROWN, RED BROWN, DEEP YELLA BROWN, CHOCOLATE, HIGH-BROWN, LOW-BROWN, VELVET BROWN, BRONZE, GINGERBREAD, LIGHT BROWN, TAN, OLIVE, COPPER, PINK, BANANA, CREAM, ORANGE, HIGH YALLA, LEMON, OH, AND YEAH CARAMEL.

In this self-consciously discursive text, where a speaker rattles off gradations of colour, ending affirmatively with the remembered 'Caramel', difference is linguistically inscribed in the range of metaphoric colours. But in the disjuncture of accompanying images of black people who are of the same colour, difference is also at the same time disavowed: at the intersection of image and text there is a space where people can resist received racial descriptions, where they make their own meanings, oh and yeah, new discursive spaces in which modalities of blackness can wipe out shame.

Works cited

Ahmad, Aijaz. *In Theory: Classes, Nations, Literatures.* London: Verso, 1992.

Bhabha, Homi. *The Location of Culture.* London: Routledge, 1994.

Bunn, David. '"Some Alien Land": Arthur Nortje, Literary History, and the Body in Exile'. *World Literature Today* 70. 1 (Winter 1996; "South African Literature in Transition"): 33–44.

Coetzee, J. M. *White Writing: On the Culture of Letters in South Africa.* New Haven: Yale University Press, 1988.

Gilman, Sander L. 'Black Bodies, White Bodies: Toward an Iconography of Female Sexuality in Late Nineteenth Century Art, Medicine and Literature'. *Critical Inquiry* 12 (1985): 204–42.

Gunner, Liz. 'You, the Lioness'. *Southern African Review of Books* 6. 2 (1994). 14–15.

Hall, Stuart. 'When Was "The Post-Colonial"? Thinking at the Limit'. *The Post-Colonial Question*. Ed. E. Chambers and I. Curtis. London: Routledge, 1966. 242–59.

'What is this Black in Popular Culture?' *Popular Culture*. Ed. Gina Dent. Seattle: Bay Press, 1992. 465–75.

Head, Bessie. *The Cardinals – With Meditations and Short Stories* (1960–2). Cape Town: David Philip, 1993.

Hebdige, Dick. *Hiding in the Light: On Images and Things*. London: Comedia, 1988.

Jameson, Fredric. 'Postmodernism, or The Cultural Logic of Late Capitalism'. *Postmodernism: A Reader*. Ed. Thomas Docherty. Hemel Hempstead: Harvester Wheatsheaf, 1993. 62–92.

Millin, Sarah Gertrude. *God's Step-Children*. London: Constable, 1924.

Ozinsky, Max, and Ibrahim Rasool. 'Developing a Strategic Perspective for the Coloured Areas of the Western Cape'. *African Communist* 133 (second quarter 1993): 39–47.

Plaatje, Sol. *Mhudi* (1930). Oxford: Heinemann, 1978.

Ross, Robert. *Cape of Torments: Slavery and Resistance in South Africa*. London: Routledge & Kegan Paul, 1983.

Rushdie, Salman. *Shame*. London: Picador, 1984.

Weems, Carrie Mae. THEN WHAT? *Photographs and Folklore*. Buffalo: CEPA Gallery, 1990.

Willemse, Hein. 'Die Skrille Sonbesies: Emergent Black Afrikaans Poets in Search of Authority'. *Rendering Things Visible: Essays on South African Literary Culture*. Ed. Martin Trump. Johannesburg: Ravan, 1990. 367–401.

Young, Robert J. C. *Colonial Desire: Hybridity in Theory, Culture and Race*. London: Routledge, 1995.

8

A man's world: white South African gay writing and the State of Emergency

MICHIEL HEYNS

Traditionally, gay writing has found its subject and its political agenda in the perceived plight of the gay person in a world indifferent or hostile to homosexual desire. E. M. Forster's Maurice, resolutely confronting the responsibility, the penalty, and the reward for loving his own kind, was declaring a secession from 'normal' relations that has remained implicit in much gay writing:

> He knew what the call was, and what his answer must be. They must live outside class, without relations or money; they must work and stick to each other till death. But England belonged to them. That, besides companionship, was their reward. Her air and sky were theirs, not the timorous millions' who own stuffy little boxes, but never their own souls. (*Maurice*, 208–9)

Though, obviously, much has changed since poor Maurice attempted to have himself 'cured' by hypnosis, his sense of being outnumbered and outlawed would be recognizable to many of the protagonists of more recent gay novels and stories. That 'happier year' to which Forster dedicated his novel in 1914 has been, in this respect, elusive. In spite of, and perhaps partly because of, much more liberal official attitudes, prejudice and intolerance persist.

In South Africa, of course, prejudice and intolerance have long been much more visible as institutionalized racism than as homophobia; but even here, gay literature frequently records the experience of discrimination and oppression. In Zirk van den Berg's 'Voor die trein' ['Before/In front of the train'], for instance, a homosexual man commits suicide after overhearing the homophobic anecdote which forms the main body of the story ('As daar een ding is wat ek nie kan vat nie, is dit 'n moffie' – 'If there's one thing I can't stand it's a faggot'): the thuggish narrator recalls, to the delight of his fellow-commuters, how he and his cronies raped a homosexual on a railway line (75–6). And in Hennie Aucamp's 'Vir vier stemme' ['For four voices'] a sensitive young

Englishman who falls in love with an Afrikaans farmer is driven to shoot himself when he is contemptuously raped by the man he loves. Both these examples would seem to suggest, through their use of rape as expression of aggression, that homophobia is frequently a perverted redirection of a suppressed homoerotic impulse.

Maurice's plight thus persists (although often, as in these cases, manifested more luridly than in Forster's novel), as does the countervailing valorization of individual desire over the conventional feelings of the 'timorous millions'. Thus Hennie Aucamp, in his editorial discussion of a volume of Afrikaans gay writing, refers to the need for the 'recognition of a state of emergency – in this case, the incompleteness of self' ('Nawoord', 214): Aucamp is evidently claiming for individual feeling the relevance normally reserved for overtly political themes. But many of those acquainted with what they might want to call the *real* State of Emergency would have little sympathy with this appropriation of the term to a cause with which they have no reason to identify. From the perspective of the State of Emergency in South Africa in the 1980s, with its brutal repression of the most basic human rights, the 'incompleteness of self' may come to seem effetely irrelevant, and male homosexuality in particular may become branded as yet another white privilege trying to pass itself off as a right in a democratic society. Ruth Mompati, a member of the National Executive Committee of the ANC, is on record as saying in 1987: 'I cannot even begin to understand why people want gay rights. The gays have no problems. They have nice houses and plenty to eat. I don't see them suffering. No-one is persecuting them' (Gevisser, 'A Different Fight for Freedom', 70).[1] Gays, from Mompati's perspective, are screaming for cake where others are denied bread. One thinks also of Winnie Mandela's defence when charged with abducting four youths from the Methodist Manse in Orlando West: she argued that she was rescuing them from the sexual abuse – for which read homosexual practices – allegedly occurring at the Manse. 'Homosex is not in black culture' read a placard held by one of her supporters outside the

---

1. The whole of Gevisser's survey is highly informative on the relation between the fight for gay rights and the larger struggle for basic political freedom in South Africa. For a fascinating account of the attitude within one left-wing organization – in this case the End Conscription Campaign – to the homosexuality of one of its high-profile members, see Ivan Toms, 'Ivan Toms is a Fairy?'.

court. By the same token, homosex was not an issue in the larger liberation struggle.[2]

And yet, of course, the lesser injustice remains unjust, and its relative
unimportance in the hierarchy of human suffering may not reconcile its
victims to their lot. This is expressed with brutal candour in Johan
Bruwer's politically very incorrect sketch "'n Moffie chaff 'n Kaffer' ('A
Faggot Chats Up a Nigger' would more or less render the register of the
Afrikaans), a bar-room monologue in which a white homosexual
vociferously declares the black man to be privileged in at least having a
revolutionary agenda:

> jy het alles. jy't jou siel aan jou kant. jy't jou siel aan jou kant en jou fokken
> gewete en jou trots. jy het die *reg* om veronreg te wees. jy't 'n fokken blaze of
> glory. dis wat jy het, jou doos . . . ek's jaloers, want daar's geen marx vir
> moffies nie, my china. there's going to be no bloody revolution for us queers,
> my dear. you won't see us sitting and knitting before the scaffold. never.
>
> (116–17)

> [you've got everything. you've got your soul on your side. you've got your
> soul on your side and your fucking conscience and your pride. you've got the
> *right* to be aggrieved. you've got a fucking blaze of glory. that's what you've
> got, you cunt . . . i'm jealous, because there's no marx for faggots, my china]

The speaker defiantly adopts the racist and homophobic vocabulary of
the society which oppresses both blacks and homosexuals, claims equality or even superiority in suffering, and then comes to the point of the dia-
tribe: 'wat ek wou vra is: kom jy saam na my flat?' (117) ['what I wanted to
ask was: are you coming to my flat?']. Rather oddly, this brutally
offensive monologue ends up, as far as its political priorities are concerned, not too far away from Forster's *Maurice*, with sexual attraction
overriding class or in this case race differences, whether as a gesture of

2. 'Mandela's defence case, conducted by George Bizos, codified homosexuality
   as sexual abuse, and characterised homosexual practice as a white, colonising
   depredation of heterosexual black culture . . . The trial demonstrated the
   obstructive degree to which heterosexuality and 'the family' dictate social and
   political organisation – even within constituent parts of a radicalised
   liberation movement, in this case the African National Congress' (Holmes,
   '"White Rapists Made Coloureds (and Homosexuals)"', 284–5). Subsequent
   developments, such as the inclusion of a sexual orientation clause in the new
   Constitution, suggest a much more tolerant attitude on the part of the ANC to
   homosexuality, recognizing freedom of sexual choice as also a basic human
   right.

solidarity in the face of mutual oppression, a deliberate violation of a tribal taboo, or just a straightforward expression of desire.

In Alexis Retief's 'Ek en my Ghoffel' ['My Nigger and I'], another plain-spoken monologue, the speaker, a white working-class outlaw who retains many of the racist attitudes he grew up with, nevertheless cherishes his sexual relationship with his black fellow-outlaw, and even aspires to a romantic release: 'Ek druk hom teen my hart, ons sal eendag vry wees soos sysies, ou. Ons sal gaan waar ons wil. Ons sal mos vlieg, ek en hy' (106). ['I press him to my heart, one day we'll be free as birds, my man. We'll go where we like. We'll fly, won't we, him and me.']

In these stories, the political is subsumed in the personal, in that the fact of sexual desire between the races is automatically imbued with the whole charge of racist politics. Stephen Gray has said apropos his own sex-across-the-colour-line novel *Time of Our Darkness*, that 'the entire apartheid policies go to bed with you' (Ludman, 'Much to Learn', 23). This has of course long been the implication of what Gray calls 'that old South African sub-species of fiction', the '"immorality" novel'; but he dismisses the earlier specimens of the genre as 'little more than a pitifully bourgeois shocker that needed drastic renovation if it was to reflect the post-Immorality Act intrusion of the law into private loves' ('An Author's Agenda', 26). Certainly *Time of Our Darkness* brings the genre up to date by concentrating on the relationship between a white schoolteacher, Peter Walker, and his thirteen-year-old black male pupil Disley Mashinini – a configuration that would of course attract the attention of the law even in countries not plagued by apartheid. The uncharitable suspicion that the political angle serves mainly to lend respectability to a form of specialized erotica could claim some support from the very detailed descriptions of the various (and varied) sexual encounters in the novel: whatever their political implications, they are clearly offered for the pleasure of like-minded readers (though Gray includes a heterosexual encounter for readers with more conventional taste).[3] Pleasing the readers is of course a perfectly legitimate aim for an author; but it does complicate Gray's claim to be depicting 'the history of black liberation, especially in its relation to women's liberation and then gay liberation'

3. See also Gray's short story 'The Building-Site', in which a white home-owner takes in a black worker from the site next door. The narrator, motivated wholly by sexual desire, and proceeding entirely by showering gifts and favours on the object of his admiration, considers the political situation only insofar as it may render the desired liaison slightly awkward.

('An Author's Agenda', 26). In the novel itself, too, Gray's protagonists are presented as the harbingers of a new order. Attending his first political rally, Walker discovers his affinity with the forces of change: 'For the first time I felt eased into the situation. I think we were the germs of the new South Africa; old South Africa was out there, declining' (106). And close to the end of the novel, he imagines his bond with Disley and with Jenny, the British anti-apartheid activist, as constituting the unit of the future:

> In our age, even in backward South Africa, relationships could no longer flow in the old nuclear-family system. Certainly no one I knew lived in a stable parent–children unit any longer. The new family, for a while, comprised Jenny, me and Disley – a trio improvised for the occasion, dissolved by law.
>
> (304)

So here the homosexual is seen as sharing the oppression of the black and of the woman: there is really no sense of possible complicity on the part of the narrator with the system that ultimately kills Disley (even though it is Walker who has arranged the meeting with the police during which Disley is shot). Indeed, whether intentionally or not, Gray has created a remarkably complacent narrator, who seems not to be aware of his own self-deception and condescension, and of his part in Disley's co-option by the snobbish tokenism of Saint Paul's private school, where he is the single black pupil.

The tendency, nevertheless, in Gray's novel as in the short stories mentioned above (and also in Gray's other novel, *Born of Man*, in which a team of adoring black servants assist in the pregnancy, confinement, and motherhood of Kev, the first man on earth to give birth), is to see the homosexual and the black as common victims of an oppressive system.[4] Similarly, Matthew Krouse, in introducing the predominantly white short stories in his collection of gay writing, says: 'The content of the military theme [of the short stories in the collection] adds a new voice to the existing outcry against conscription and ultimately places these writers in solidarity with those whom they are conscripted to oppress' (Krouse and Berman, eds., *The Invisible Ghetto*, xv). This view, valid as far as it goes, ignores the position of the white man at least partly inside the dominant structure. What distinguishes Damon Galgut and Koos Prinsloo, the two writers to whom I want to devote the rest of this chap-

---

4. For the contention that Gray's novels, in spite of their undefensive presentation of homosexuality, 'enact their own range of deferrals and inner contradictions', see de Waal, 'A Thousand Forms of Love', 239.

ter, is that in their very different ways, they do consider the white gay man as *white man* in a racially divided society, and thus suggest ways of positioning a gay agenda in a context with, as it were, other things on its mind.

The title of this chapter is derived from Damon Galgut's novel *The Beautiful Screaming of Pigs*, which won the prestigious CNA Literary Award in 1992: Malcolm, the impeccably masculine brother of the narrator, taunts him with 'It's a man's world, Patrick' (19; citations from 1992 edition). The bond between Malcolm and their father becomes to Patrick representative of that whole world of male camaraderie from which he is excluded, and which is ultimately responsible for the Border war in which he finds himself implicated without loyalty and without faith. Galgut is on record as saying 'the values that made apartheid possible are extremely male values . . . I see apartheid in its entirety as a male mythology' (Rosenthal, 'An Extended Cry', 34). There is much in his novel that may be taken to demonstrate this view: Patrick's father is recognizable as that kind of South African male that is readily available as explanation of a whole pattern of oppression, and that is perhaps even more common in literature than in life: 'He was a hunter, my father; and the walls of his study bore witness to this fact' (10). From these masculine exploits both Patrick and his mother are excluded:

> She never went with him on these trips of his. He would go in the company of men: loud, hairy, intense as he. I had seen them often, my father's friends, as they congregated on the lawn outside. Beers in their hands, their worn boots creaked as they moved. They were – and behaved like – people in no doubt of themselves: they laughed out loud and slapped each other on the back. They had names that asserted their natures, these men: they were Harry or Bruce or Ivan or Mike. There was Fanus, whom I had seen pissing in the roses once. And Terrence. Like my father, they were all successful men, who could afford to hide their status in their outdoor clothes. They bared their teeth when they smiled. They hunted animals with guns.
>
> I never went on trips with them. But Malcolm did . . . (14–15)

These hairy creatures baring their teeth and violating the roses do not really present a very complex moral problem: they have a sort of elementary awfulness that requires only rejection, as much on aesthetic as on moral or political grounds. But Galgut insists on the connection between this form of male camaraderie and a political system that finds its logical conclusion in killing: Malcolm, the natural inheritor of this world, becomes a Defence Force instructor, training recruits for that war on the Border that has become such a powerful trope in South African literature: 'Dwelling, as I imagined him, in his kingdom of dust, my brother embodied the land I'd grown up on: brutal and tall, he helped people learn how to kill' (20).

Against this background, the novel's single sexual encounter figures as an act of rebellion against the man's world. Patrick is drafted into the army, to come under the command of Commandant Schutte, another of those men completely at home in this world: 'He resembled, disturbingly, my brother. He was utterly terrible, splendid and mean. He had a moustache and a laugh full of scorn' (68). Schutte forces the recruits to play rugby as a sort of general training in masculinity, and Patrick discovers a friend in Lappies, to whom he is driven as much as attracted by their common helplessness in the presence of a rugby ball:

> We suffered our isolation without much complaint. We had always contained it within us. There was, you see, a brotherhood of men, to which we could never belong. My father, my brother, the boys at my school: they knew things that I didn't know. There was that in their hands that helped them catch balls; that helped them see objects in flight. Lacking this vision, I felt myself blind. I had watched, through the years, the grace of these men, that left shimmering trails on air. (70)[5]

The inarticulate friendship between Patrick and Lappies never really develops beyond a mute recognition of common exile; but one evening on guard duty, they make fumbling sexual contact, more in agony than in passion:

> Tugging and gasping, we moved our wrists in rhythm. It was an act of revenge, undertaken in pain: against men, who had made the world flat. 'Leave me,' I gasped, but it wasn't to him: I was speaking to Malcolm, my father, to Schutte. 'Leave me,' I called down the well of my past, to those who'd colluded against me. (76)

Lappies is killed in action and Patrick is left alone to deal with Schutte and with his father, twin figures of repressive authority. Situating the

5. Rugby, like hunting, figures frequently as an icon and measure of white South African masculinity. Thus the aggrieved white homosexual in ''n Moffie Chaff 'n Kaffer' claims more extensive knowledge of oppression than his black counterpart, because the latter has not had to live up to that particular criterion: 'jy sal nie weet nie. hoe sal jy weet as jy nognie rugby gespeel het nie. of *nie* rugby gespeel het nie. skande. skande op die huis' (117) ['you won't know. how can you know if you've never played rugby. or never *not* played rugby. shame. shame on the house'].

political situation within the family, Damon Galgut traces a relatively neat correspondence between the father and the authoritarian structure that puts in place both apartheid and the war: 'I don't know why,' Patrick says to Lappies, 'but I can't help feeling as if . . . as if men were responsible for this. I mean . . . women couldn't have made things like this' (73). The father in Galgut is thus almost purely a figure of rejection, and this model of the patriarchy would seem to establish a self-evident link between gay identity and political dissent: to dissociate oneself from the heterosexual patriarchy is to disown also the political situation which it has wrought.

But for all the honest pain with which it is posited, this is perhaps too easy an attitude. In the first place, there is a good deal of ambivalence in Patrick's attitude to the 'brotherhood of men': as described, it is, with all its grossness and insensitivity, a matter also of 'knowledge', 'grace', and 'vision', for the want of which Patrick is sensibly the poorer. Even apart from this, amongst the many male possibilities in the novel there are at least two, possibly three, that are potentially liberating: Andrew Lovell, the political activist who is assassinated on the eve of South West Africa–Namibia's first free election; and Godfrey, the black SWAPO activist and lover of Patrick's mother. The third, more ambiguous, possibility is that presented through rather than by Lappies, the potential acceptance of love between men as offering not only revenge upon what is, but an affirmation of an alternative and liberating way for men to be in the world. There seems to be the dawning of some such realization – that he had been in love with Lappies – in Patrick's interchange with his mother:

> 'Have you ever been in love?'
> 'Yes,' I said. 'Once.'
> 'You never told me.'
> 'I don't think I knew at the time.'   (109)

Men, in other words, even in Galgut's novel, are not *only* the bringers of war, and the man's world not the creation of *all* men. Nor is it the creation *only* of men: in this novel, as in Galgut's other works, the attitude to women is far from untroubled. If the father is the hunter, the rugby player, ultimately the soldier and the killer, what is the mother who chose to marry him and to bear his children? At first, she is predictably the sensitive victim of male brutality, adapting to the role imposed upon her:

> She was Afrikaans; [my father] hated that. She had grown up on a farm: he hated that too. Resolutely, with wordless determination, she had constructed

herself along different lines. Practising English, practising style, she had
gradually acquired values that weren't truly her own. She was a housewife, a
mother, a maker of homes. (8)

Thus, alienated from her background at her husband's insistence, and
then from him by his insensitivity, she and the young Patrick develop a
classic *Sons and Lovers* closeness: 'We walked through Sea Point, arm in
arm, holding ice-creams in our hands. My mother was white and cold and
long, like any ice-cream cone' (16–17). But if she is all that the boy
requires, she needs more excitement than he can offer, and she drifts from
lover to lover and from self-image to self-image. Her involvement with
Godfrey is thus a self-conscious attempt to identify with Africa rather
than an appreciation of any quality of the man himself. In the novel's
central section, the voyage to the about-to-be-independent Namibia, she
changes allegiance from the SWAPO ex-terrorist to a meat-eating white
Afrikaans farmer who maintains: 'Man is a hunter by instinct. A killer.
The world is a jungle' (168). Patrick ends up seeing her as merely 'a dis-
torted white woman, lost on her way. She was part of nothing at all' (158).

For Patrick himself, the primary liberation, the one that is not mentioned at all or only by implication, would presumably be an acceptance
of his sexual identity. But the single sexual encounter is, as we have seen,
not an affirmation as much as a denial: the two men are only momentarily
united in their rebellion, to be thereafter even more deeply alienated from
themselves and others: 'My solitude, perhaps, had begun in that moment,
as we hastily did up our flies' (112). Sexual liberation is glimpsed only as a
kind of understudy of the struggle; the concern with self is seen, at least
through Godfrey, as an effete neurosis of white people:

> 'White people,' he said. 'You make me laugh.'
> 'Why is that?'
> 'You're so . . . concerned with yourselves. Your own little lives. You have no
> nation. Just people. You're so . . . so . . .' He fumbled in the air with his hands.
> 'Narcissistic?'
> '*Ja*. Introspective. Neurotic – you're neurotic.' (134)

The two males with whom Patrick finds most rapport are both politically
and sexually active; and whereas their politics are, in pre-independence
South-West Africa, dissident, their sexual orientation is perfectly
conventional. If Patrick is rejected by the man's world as exemplified by
his father, he is also refused entrance to that other world symbolized for
him by Andrew Lovell. Before Lovell's funeral he tries to make contact

with the dead man's girlfriend, but she is clearly too much involved in her own grief to share or understand his, and rebuffs him in words echoing his own rejection of the man's world: "'I don't know what you want," she said. "I don't think I'm able to help you. It's been a bad time for me. I'd appreciate it, I really would, if you would just leave me alone'" (140).

Perhaps what Galgut's novel most effectively dramatizes is the perplexity of the white male homosexual in South Africa, who cannot allow himself even the luxury of a struggle for his own liberation. When, near the end of the novel, Godfrey tells Patrick 'You'll live here [in Namibia] till your country is free', Patrick replies: 'There are other kinds of exile' (165). Distancing himself from what he regards as the man's world, Patrick thus has to disown also gay desire, which is after all centred on the male. His exile is as much from his own nature as from the man's world.

If Koos Prinsloo's stories, by contrast, are brutally unapologetic about the homosexual nature and acts of the protagonist, they are also more ambivalent in their implied attitude to the world of male activity and sexuality.[6] Prinsloo's provocatively autobiographical characters exercise their sexuality as both rebellion against and complicity in that man's world that is desirable and repulsive at the same time. In 'Promise You'll Tell No-one', which assumes the form of autobiographical recollections, he establishes a direct link between his sexual experiences and his position as a member of the dominant race: he recalls an incident in which two black boys 'pinned a third down on the ground. He laughed and struggled, but they held him down and undid his fly buttons. Later they also egged me on to push my hand into the front of his khaki shorts and to feel. I was six years old, but I was the son of the *baas*' (320). This early memory points forward to the story's last paragraph, in which the protagonist, by now an adolescent, expresses in the language of his race and class the desire that is his privilege; going for a walk on a Sunday afternoon ('My dad had forbidden us to swim on Sundays' he adds parenthetically), he comes across a black man 'in a khaki shirt and pants' masturbating:

> His muscled diaphragm was moving up and down rapidly. Then I said: 'I want your thing.' I pointed at his pants. 'No, he hasn't got money, baas,' he replied, flustered. (324)

6. I have as far as possible concentrated on such stories as have been translated into English, and in such cases I have cited the commercially available translation. Uncredited translations are my own.

Presumably this is not what the boy's father had in mind as an alternative to Sunday swimming, but that point is not spelt out. Prinsloo doesn't interpret his little incident for us – Prinsloo is not an interpreter – but he leaves us free to establish the troubled relation between the young boy demanding 'I want your thing' and the narrator recalling the apparently disparate experiences of a childhood in the bosom of a close but fraught family.

'Promise' is in fact a chronicle of the narrator's developing sexuality, from 'the first time I touched somebody else's cock' (319) through the grotesque sexual instruction and induction of childhood ('babies grow from "pus"', 321) and the early experiments, to the first open expression of desire : 'I want your thing' (324). The apparently unrelated events in the story form a coherent if not reasoned account of burgeoning sexuality as part of the processes of family, race, and country: his sister who has to leave home to have an illegitimate child under cover of a spinal operation; his father, presumably under the pressure of this event, giving the narrator the only hiding he ever gets (322); the Mau Mau uprising (the early part of the story is set in that other State of Emergency, in Kenya in 1963); the death of Verwoerd. Sexuality is contextualized without being in any way 'explained'. The man's world, it is clear, is a white man's world, and the protagonist experiences it as 'the son of the *baas*'.

In '"Border Story"' Prinsloo, like Galgut, connects his own sexuality with the war on the border, but much more obliquely. Even the title, with its fastidious quotation marks, announces Prinsloo's self-conscious distance from what has become in South African literature, more specifically in Afrikaans writing, the strong subgenre of 'Border stories': narratives of that war on the South African–Namibian border which came to represent to many young South Africans the insane limit (and price) of Nationalist rule. The opening paragraph sustains the balance between distance and engagement: 'I was on the Border (90 days' ongoing military training) when she died between 18h00 and 19h00 on the evening of 1 August 1983. She was twenty-four years old. I used to tell people she's "my closest girl-friend"' (134). This opening seems to point in two directions: the Border war and the loss of a girlfriend; but by the end of the story we are not much closer to defining the relation between the two or their common relation to the gay subtext. We have been given a dispassionate record of experience – sexual, military, even emotional (and a dispassionate account of emotion is not, given Prinsloo's style, the contradiction in terms it would seem to be). The young soldier-protagonist whose 'fiancée' is killed records her death, the speech of the chaplain, the crater blown by a land-mine which reduced two 'locals' to a body-bag of remains, a poodle's attempt to copulate with an Alsatian, all with the same detachment. The narrative voice participates equally laconically in '90 days' ongoing military training' and in the funeral of the dead woman: 'The memorial service was held at 11h00 on Friday 5 August 1983, after which she was cremated' (138).[7] In the same functional vein he records: 'That afternoon after the funeral I went to a Turkish steam-bath and health clinic in the city centre where I picked up a man. He had prominent eye-teeth, acne and a short chin' (139). We do not know if there is any affective connection between the funeral and the visit to the steam bath; but this is followed by the only offer of emotion in the story: 'When he penetrated me, with my knees bent over his shoulders, I cried for the first time. The afternoon sun shone through the Sunfilter curtains on the damp white sheets' (139). We don't know what it is that he cried for, and certainly there is no suggestion of catharsis or of even a moment of tenderness with the man he has picked up: 'The man said he liked my "bush cut" and wrapped a towel round his waist' (139). The haircut, as mark of involvement in the war, has no significance other than titillation.

In keeping with this moral neutrality, the figures of authority are more ambivalently represented than in Galgut's novel: they are half-comical, half-threatening functionaries of an absurdist regime. The guardians of the country are cynically taking part in a farce which has lost its meaning ('You are not allowed to talk religion or politics, or to say kaffir,' the commandant counsels the new troops [137]). The causes of the war are obscure even to the racist imagination:

'This camp is P. W. Botha's fault, the black-bitch-fucker,' said a man with frizzy blond hair and pimples.

7. Biographical assumptions are dangerous with Prinsloo, in that he uses incidents from his own life in an apparently documentary fashion, but adjusted to the particular effect the story requires. Still, it seems likely that this account was based on the death of Prinsloo's friend Helena Stark, which, according to her mother, was 'a great blow' to Prinsloo, contributing to the 'considerably more cynical' tonality of *Die Hemel Help Ons*, in which '"Border Story"' first appeared (Schoombie, 'Die woedende woord', 74) – in other words, that the disillusioned tone of '"Border Story"' may be partly owing to the traumatic effect of an incident which he now describes in an apparently detached manner.

'How come?' asked the thin man with the ears.

'Well, he wants us to marry the kaffirs now.' (136)

The idea of the president of white South Africa as exponent of trans-gressive sexuality exemplifies the inversion of 'normality' in the name of normality itself.[8] Sexual dissent is placed within a context of 'normality' that is itself so bizarre that the term loses its meaning.

Prinsloo's stories do not comment explicitly on the political situation in which they are steeped; rather, they are themselves embodiments of that situation, apparently amoral and fragmented recordings of data, with no single experience privileged over any other. '"Border Story"' ends with an ever-faster intercutting of references to the Border, the encounter in the bath house, and a moment three weeks after the woman's death, when the narrator opens a letter from her forwarded from the Border. He puts a recording of the Mendelssohn octet on his NAD turntable, notes that the scherzo was inspired by four lines from part 1 of Goethe's *Faust*, quotes the lines (ending on 'Und alles ist zerstoben' – 'And everything is dispersed'), and then records, as the closing sentence of the story, that 'The Viennese Octet plays the scherzo in this recording (Decca Jubilee JB 128) in 4 minutes and 41 seconds' (139–40). The lines from Goethe and the playing time on this particular recording are accorded equal status with each other and with all the other constituents of the situation; it is left to us to construct a hierarchy, to reflect that the music is the *raison d'être* of the paragraph, the poetry the inspiration for the music, the Viennese Octet the interpreters, and the playing time only a mechanical detail. The last line from Goethe may be an elegy for the loss recorded in the story, or it may be only a piece of information taken from the record sleeve.

This refusal to order his data in terms of a hierarchy of significance means that in Prinsloo's work sexual encounters, disturbingly, seem no more and no less meaningful than the atrocities and trivialities he records so dispassionately. Whereas, say, André Brink (in *States of Emergency*) can from a heterosexual perspective use sex as the alternative, the momentary escape from the Emergency, and to Galgut sex between men represents an act of defiance, to Prinsloo sex is itself part of the

---

8. The reference to Botha as 'black-bitch-fucker' (or *meide-naaier* in Afrikaans) cost Prinsloo two publisher's rejections and the lucrative and prestigious Rapport Literary Prize, which was awarded to him and then withdrawn. (He sued and got the money.) See de Waal, 'A Thousand Forms of Love', 243.

Emergency, an assertion of the predatory nature he, as 'son of the *baas*', has in common with the male society to which he is nevertheless in important respects an outsider. If in his stories sex itself often seems like an atrocity committed upon a consenting partner, that may be a measure also of the meaning of desire in a violent society. Prinsloo's world is horrifying because it seems valueless; but it is conscious of its own valuelessness, and records that loss truthfully.

That Prinsloo's dispassionateness is not simply indifference to the plight of others is suggested by the fact that in his last published stories before his death from AIDS (in March 1994) he refers to his own illness with equal neutrality – in 'Die Storie van My Neef' ['The Story of My Cousin'], for instance, literally subordinated, in the last line of the story, to the account of his cousin's death from AIDS :

> Terwyl ek op my regtersy draai sodat die dokter met sy witgepoeierde
> rubberhandskoene na die koorsblaartjies tussen my boude kan kyk (hy het
> gesê die twee groot ulkusse het mooi genees en nog Asiklovir voorgeskryf),
> dink ek skielik weer aan die hele palaver rondom my neef en aan een van die
> goed wat Philip my in die wagkamer meegedeel het: Bennie het vir sy ma-
> hulle gesê hy het dit van 'n bloedoortapping gekry. (64)

> [While I turn on my right side so that the doctor with his white-powdered
> gloves can examine the little fever blisters between my buttocks (he said that
> the two large ulcers had healed well and prescribed more Asiklovir), I
> suddenly recall the whole palaver around my cousin and one of the things
> that Philip told me in the waiting room: Bennie had told his mother and the
> rest that he had got it from a blood transfusion.]

This detachment, when applied to the political context of much of Prinsloo's fiction – his matter-of-fact, apparently indifferent, recording of the atrocious, the obscene, and the trivial – forces the reader to engage directly and actively with the blurring of values, the problematization of normality, that characterized the Emergency. To read Prinsloo is not so much to understand the Emergency as to experience it, and to see the gay writer not as a marginalized observer but as a participant in a troubled society.

Note   This is a revised version of a paper given at the Modern Language
Association Convention, San Diego, in December 1994. The financial
assistance of both the University of Stellenbosch and the Council for Science
Development of the Human Sciences Research Council of South Africa is
gratefully acknowledged.

Works cited

Aucamp, Hennie. 'For Four Voices'. 1981. Trans. Ian Ferguson. *Armed Vision: Afrikaans Writers in English*. Ed. Martin Trump. Craighall: Ad Donker, 1987. 130–50.

'Nawoord'. *Wisselstroom: Homoërotiek in die Afrikaanse verhaalkuns*. Ed. Hennie Aucamp. Cape Town: Human & Rousseau, 1990. 188–214.

Bruwer, Johan. ''n Moffie chaff 'n Kaffer'. Aucamp, ed., *Wisselstroom*, 114–17.

de Waal, Shaun. 'A Thousand Forms of Love: Representations of Homosexuality in South African Literature'. Gevisser and Cameron, eds., *Defiant Desire*, 232–45.

Forster, E. M. *Maurice* (1914). Harmondsworth: Penguin, 1972.

Gevisser, Mark. 'A Different Fight for Freedom: A History of South African Lesbian and Gay Organisations from the 1950s to 1990s'. Gevisser and Cameron, eds., *Defiant Desire*, 14–86.

Gevisser, Mark, and Edwin Cameron, eds. *Defiant Desire: Gay and Lesbian Lives in South Africa*. Johannesburg: Ravan, 1994.

Gray, Stephen. 'An Author's Agenda (3)'. *Southern African Review of Books* (February–May 1990): 26–7.

Holmes, Rachel. '"White Rapists Made Coloureds (and Homosexuals)": The Winnie Mandela Trial and the Politics of Race and Sexuality'. Gevisser and Cameron, eds., *Defiant Desire*, 284–94.

Ludman, Barbara. 'Much to Learn. But Do We Want To?' Review of Stephen Gray, *Time of Our Darkness*. *Weekly Mail*, 27 May–2 June 1988: 26.

Prinsloo, Koos. '"Border Story"'. Trans. Laurens Seliye. *The Invisible Ghetto: Lesbian and Gay Writing from South Africa*. Ed. Matthew Krouse and Kim Berman. Johannesburg: COSAW, 1993. 134–40. Translation of '"Grensverhaal"'. *Die Hemel Help Ons*. Emmarentia: Taurus, 1987. 34–43.

'Die Storie van my Neef'. *Weifeling*. Groenkloof: Hond, 1993. 58–64.

'Promise You'll Tell No-one: A Memoir'. Trans. Johannes Bruwer. Gevisser and Cameron, eds., *Defiant Desire*, 319–24. Translation of 'Belowe Jy Sal Niemand Sê Nie'. *Slagplaas*. Cape Town: Human & Rousseau, 1992. 100–9.

Retief, Alexis. 'Ek en my Ghoffel'. Aucamp, ed., *Wisselstroom*, 104–6.

Rosenthal, Jane. 'An Extended Cry Against Male Mythology'. *Weekly Mail*, 14–20 August 1992: 34.

Schoombie, Schalk. 'Die woedende woord: huldeblyk'. *De Kat* (May 1994): 70–7.

Toms, Ivan. 'Ivan Toms is a Fairy? The South African Defence Force, the End Conscription Campaign, and Me'. Gevisser and Cameron, eds., *Defiant Desire*, 258–63.

van den Berg, Zirk. 'Voor die trein'. *Ekstra Dun vir meer Gevoel*. Cape Town: Tafelberg, 1989. 75–6.

9

The final safari: on nature, myth, and the literature of the Emergency

RITA BARNARD

In April 1988, while the second official State of Emergency was still in effect in South Africa and the international clamour for sanctions against the apartheid regime was growing louder, a startling full-page advertisement appeared in the *Washington Post*. It featured a picture of a zebra caught in a rifle gunsight, accompanied by the slogan 'Shoot it in the white and the black also dies' (20 April 1988). This maxim (which had for years been a favourite weapon in Foreign Minister Pik Botha's rhetorical arsenal) is on a certain level undeniably true. The text's deviousness lies elsewhere, in the analogy between the signifier (the zebra) and the signified (the South African state). It is an analogy which turns something that has been constructed – constructed by people and through history – into something that is natural and given. With ostentatious candour the advertisement seems to address the matter of racial difference, but it renders the meaning of that difference innocent, even decorative. It turns the deep contradiction of a society in which some are rich at the expense of others into a matter of surface contrast: the elegance of the zebra's stripes. In its address to a foreign audience, moreover, the image positions its reader as a tourist on safari. It invites him or her to think of South Africa not as a site of political strife, but as an exotic beast, best looked at through the photographer's telephoto lens: as something to be celebrated and conserved – emphatically not something to take pot shots at.

The advertisement, though clearly the work of political lobbyists, operates in much the same way as the modern 'myths' analyzed by Roland Barthes. It is, in a sense, 'depoliticized speech' in that it addresses the contentious matter of sanctions through an image that sublimates all human and historical complexities (*Mythologies*, 143). The purported sponsors of the ad are careful to deny any political agenda: 'We are not politicians,' the small print reads, 'only color-blind businessmen with a deep concern about the future of our country.' It is precisely this kind of (ostensibly) apolitical reasonableness – the assumption that it is only natural that 'we' should think this way – that is the problem: by 'emptying things of history' and 'filling them with nature', Barthes argues, myth alienates men and women from their power to act upon the world. It 'stifle[s]' human beings 'in the manner of a huge internal parasite' and 'assign[s] to [their] activity the narrow limits within which [they are] allowed to suffer without upsetting the world'. The pseudo-nature of myth becomes essentially 'a prohibition for man against inventing himself' (155). The image of the black-and-white zebra thus functions as a kind of stop sign: a prohibition not just against sanctions, but against the invention of a new non-racial South Africa.

As I thought about this advertisement and reread Barthes's *Mythologies*, I was struck by how powerfully its concluding essay (now almost forty years old) seemed to speak to the South African literary scene of the 1980s. On the most fundamental level – the level of ethics and political commitment – the essay's allegiances and passions are in line with the creation of a culture of resistance, a revolutionary culture of the sort that emerged in South Africa during the past decade or so. Barthes's critique of myth rests on a vigorous endorsement of language that is actively directed towards a world yet to be made. The details of his analysis are also strikingly relevant. Indeed, I would argue that the triad of oppositional discourses outlined in the 'Myth Today' essay (the revolutionary language of the oppressed, 'myth on the left', and the 'artificial' or 'second-order myth' of certain kinds of ironic fiction) offers us a useful way of describing the literature of the South African Emergency: the period of intensified political struggle demarcated (roughly) by the rise of the UDF in 1983 and the official unbanning of the resistance movements and the release of Nelson Mandela in 1990.

In this chapter, I examine a few examples of each of Barthes's discursive modes in order to suggest something of the formal range of South African writing during these years of crisis. Implicit in my analysis is a sense that the context of political violence produced a characteristic 'structure of feeling', palpable in certain recurrent motifs and narrative situations. In the texts I discuss, this pervasive violence is explored through a set of related motifs (animals, eating, hunting, and, more abstractly, the food chain) all of which are readily connected to my opening image of the zebra in the gunsight. I offer, in conclusion, some reflections on the task of criticism – on what Barthes would call the enterprise of 'mythology'. I am aware that my recourse to a French theorist will raise the eyebrows of purists who insist on the exclusive use of indigenous theoretical models; it is, however, my firm belief that theories are no less capable than other cultural objects of becoming hybridized and transformed in different political contexts. I would argue, further, that the applicability of *Mythologies* to the literature of the South African Emergency is by no means a matter of coincidence. *Mythologies*, we must recall, is a meditation on French bourgeois culture at the very moment of decolonization: it appears only two years after the humiliation on the battlefield at Dien Bien Phu. Barthes's consciousness of this moment is clearly marked in the text: his key example of mythic discourse is a photograph of a Sudanese soldier saluting the French flag, and one of his most powerful definitions of myth is the 'robbery by colonization' (132) of pre-existing signs. While nobody would wish to equate De Gaulle's France (the world of *Elle*, the new Citroën, the jet-man, and the striptease) with P. W. Botha's South Africa (the world, shall we say, of *braaivleis*, *Forces' Favourites*, Sun City, *The Cosby Show*, and such institutions as the Tricameral Parliament and the Department of Cooperation and Development), one might nevertheless note an important connection. In both instances we are dealing with moments when a colonial power is forced to recognize the subjectivity and power of the other, even as it avoids naming and recognizing itself (whether as 'bourgeois culture' or as 'apartheid' politics). Both historical moments present a situation that is likely to augment the fundamental though often unconscious hypocrisy or *masking* that, as Barthes suggests, is the primary motor for the production of myth.

I

If myth is to be grasped as an erasure of history, its most direct antithesis would obviously be a discourse that is concerned not so much to represent as to intervene in history. From this perspective the most important cultural development of the South African Emergency must surely be the forging of a 'people's culture', of a variety of popular forms of expression explicitly engaged with the liberation struggle. This kind of discourse is described with great power and clarity in *Mythologies*. The language of the oppressed, Barthes asserts, is by definition 'poor', not only in the sense that it speaks for the destitute, but in a very specific rhetorical sense. While myth can produce a wealth of images to forestall the transformation of the status quo, the oppressed 'has only one language: the language of his emancipation' (149), a language concerned not so much with the making of images but with the single purpose of remaking the world.

A representative example of this discursive mode is offered by the poem 'The Tears of a Creator' (written for the launch of the Trade Union Movement COSATU in 1985 by Alfred Temba Qabula and Mi S'dumo Hlatswayo). Addressed specifically to workers, like those assembled in King's Park Stadium for its first performance, the poem intones:

> Your labor
> Has turned you
> Into prize-game
> For the hunters of surplus
> . . .
>
> You are the raw meat
> The prey
> For vultures
> Are you not the backbone
> Of trade?
>
> Now
> You are a nameless breed of animals
> A stock of many numbers
> And your suppressor's lust
> To suck you dry
> Recognizes neither day
> Nor night
> . . .
>
> Maker of all things
> . . .
> They scatter you about
> With their Hippos
> With their vans
> And kwela-kwelas
> With their tear gas
> You are butchered
> By the products of your labor
> These are the cries of the creator of all this
>
> COSATU
> Woza 'msebenzi, woza COSATU, woza freedom.
>
> (BUNN AND TAYLOR, eds., *From South Africa*, 286–8)

If these lines seem flat as they are reproduced here, we should remember that in performance the words – which may sometimes be Xhosa or Zulu words (Qabula and Hlatswayo switch languages depending on the occasion) – would be interrupted with chanting, ululation, improvisation, and audience responses. Yet even on the page the poem's purpose is clear. Though it also evokes images of African wildlife and the hunt, the poem is the complete antithesis of the *Washington Post* advertisement. For one thing, the poem's audience is identified with the animal and not with the hunter/spectator; they stand framed by the gunsight, rather than fingering the trigger. South Africa is figured here not as an organic unity with surface differences, but as a parasitical system whose creatures feed off each other. (It is not incidental, especially given the authors' identification with a radical trade union organization, that the conflict is represented not as one of colour but of social class.) There is an important sense, however, in which the poem's natural imagery is finally irrelevant: the poem is, as Barthes might have put it, concerned to represent 'nature' only insofar as the speaker wishes to transform it. In its assertion of revolutionary commitment, the poem is an instance of 'the language of man as a producer' (146). It interpellates the audience not as spectators, but as participants, actors, makers of the world. It is an act, rather than a gesture; and in this lies both its 'poverty' and its power.

II

A more complicated relation to myth is revealed in the writing of more privileged South Africans, who, while opposed to apartheid, cannot properly claim to speak with the 'poverty' of the oppressed. Their message is perforce 'richer', more metalinguistic, and therefore more capable of lying – something which language as act, strictly speaking, cannot do. Both the possibilities and problems of such writing can be illustrated with regard to Nadine Gordimer's 1990 collection *Jump and Other Stories*: a volume which is centrally concerned with diagnosing the 'morbid symptoms' (174) of the Emergency situation. There is no question that Gordimer's work generally challenges the myths of apartheid, and *Jump* is no exception. Indeed, one story, 'The Ultimate Safari', is explicitly intended to counter a text that is rather similar to the anti-sanctions ad: a travel advertisement published on 27 November 1988 in the London *Observer*. The slogan is reprinted as the story's epigraph: 'The African Adventure Lives On', it reads, 'You can do it! The ultimate safari or expedition with leaders who *know* Africa' (31). The narrative that follows, however, is not the hunting story in the mode of Hemingway that these lines might lead one to expect. It describes instead the experience of a group of starving refugees, fleeing from war-torn Mozambique to a dismal refugee camp, a place which the narrator, a young girl, can only think of as 'away'. This journey takes the group on foot through the famous Kruger National Game Reserve; and they do, in a way, experience the 'ultimate safari' – especially compared to the comfortable visitors in the rest camps, whose cooking the hungry refugees can smell on the evening air. The Mozambiquans, following their guide's instructions, 'move and eat like the animals', and they observe the beasts (with 'big shiny eyes like [their] own' (38)) from an uncomfortably intimate vantage – as competitors for food in a country ruined by political strife.

Gordimer's story, then, deliberately reverses the characteristic operations of myth: it returns the human dimension to the spectacle of nature, and chastises the (probably foreign and probably already chastened) readership for its complicity in such reifying exoticism. It does so, in this particular instance, with a shrewd recognition of the author's own (potential) position of spectatorship in Africa. At the end of the story, a white woman comes to the camp and ineptly questions the narrator's heroic but embittered grandmother about her experiences. The significance of this character is underscored if we recognize her relationship to the author: Nadine Gordimer herself visited these refugee camps in connection with the script she wrote for the 1989 BBC series *Frontiers*. Through this autobiographical figure, she inscribes in her text a curiously self-deconstructing element, a warning against the very real possibility that the hunger of Africa's people, no less than the feeding habits of its wildlife, may provide fodder for the naturalizing and spectacularizing operations of myth – literary or otherwise.

Another story from *Jump*, entitled 'Spoils', takes on a similar set of images, but does so in a rather more problematic fashion. The story reveals something of the character and the limitations of what Barthes calls 'myth on the left'. This discursive strategy involves – as does bourgeois myth – a certain masking of the political agenda. It arises, Barthes argues, when the left chooses to hide its name and marks the moment when it becomes a kind of institution, when it is no longer revolutionary in the rather austere sense suggested by the idea of 'poor' language. The most obvious examples of this mode may of course be found in the meagre official discourse of the former Soviet Union: for example, in such notions as the 'Genius of Stalin', a phrase from which the sense of historicity has been drained and a concept reiterated with such frequency that it becomes almost a kind of litany. Strictly speaking, 'myth on the left' cannot be produced in a time of revolutionary struggle like that of the South African Emergency. Even though there might be formal resemblances between a poster depicting the face of Stalin superimposed on a hammer and sickle and a poster depicting the face of Walter Sisulu framed in the ANC's gold and green, the political and semiotic differences are key. The latter, though also stylized and celebratory, represents a kind of transitive, operational utterance; it is designed to change the world, rather than to preserve it as an image.

This said, it seems to me that there is a certain context in which, even in this period, one could appropriately speak of myth on the left. I am thinking of realist fiction by political radicals, especially those who still claim an artistic autonomy for the text and therefore engage in a certain masking of their political agenda. This masking is perhaps inevitable: after all, the constraints of realism require that the message should seem to emerge 'naturally' from the characters and the action. What often happens, then, is that such texts, despite the radical intentions informing them, end up borrowing masks from the richer pre-existing store of bourgeois myth. Their subversions, in other words, risk becoming mere deviations: variations on the dominant themes of bourgeois representational strategies.

This risk is evident in much of Gordimer's work (as has recently been suggested in Kathrin Wagner's analysis of the persistence of stereotype in Gordimer's novels) and 'Spoils', it seems to me, allows us to characterize this problem with some precision. The story explores a vision of society reminiscent of certain passages in Norbert Elias's *The History of Manners*. It experiments with the idea, suggested by Elias, that the basic grammar of society (especially its hierarchies of power) can be read in the practices surrounding the consumption of meat: in who eats, who carves, and who divides the spoils of the hunt. For the protagonist of this story, such a vision is a nightmare. He is nauseated by the endless narrative of human brutality he hears on the radio: the story of a boy who had both his arms broken by the police, or that of a girl doused with petrol and burned alive as a traitor. This violence amounts, in his mind, to a kind of feeding frenzy of rapacious individuals scavenging off the carcass of a rotting society, an activity in which he himself unavoidably participates. In fact, the story begins with the protagonist's (and our) disgust at his own fart, which smells of the lamb chops he devoured the previous night: 'another corpse digested', he thinks, a corpse decorated with 'an undertaker's paper frill on the severed rib-bones' (161). The man's impulse is to have 'no part' in this 'daily necrophilia' – and this key phrase, 'no part', is repeated throughout the story. But since in his imagination *all* social relations are translated into a grammar of meat-eating, it is impossible for anyone to opt out of this vicious food chain. His wife's superficially practical advice – 'Become a vegetarian, then!' (162) – offers no solution to the moral and political dimension of his disgust.

The theme of meat-eating is also a dominant concern in the main part of the story, in which the scene shifts to a Transvaal game farm. It recurs on the literal level of event and conversation (the visitors grill meat, argue about a woman's leopard-skin coat, and see a pride of lions feeding on a zebra). It is also developed on the metaphorical level: one guest, a young revolutionary who has spent time in detention, is described as one who is 'brave enough to swallow' the 'carrion of brotherhood' without gagging (168). The conclusion of the story again plays on this motif. When the company returns to the site of the lions' kill, Siza, a black man who works on the farm, takes his panga and carves himself a piece of meat from the carcass: 'not a chunk or hunk', Gordimer is careful to insist, but 'a portion'. When asked why he does not take a larger piece, Siza explains: 'The lions, they know I must take a piece for me because I find where their meat is. They know it. It is all right. But if I take too much, they know it also. Then they will take one of my children' (179).

The abrupt ending of the story with this statement suggests that it must be read symbolically. Siza's action and his words clearly suggest a kind of middle ground, a normative position – a lesson in how one might participate in the spoils of society. Instead of taking 'no part' (like the troubled protagonist) or swallowing the violent present whole (like the young revolutionary), Siza takes only a 'portion' and thus signifies a new order, a balance between the violence of the killer and the greed of the scavenger. The ending is, in this sense, politically utopian; and it is significant, moreover, that the person who does the dividing, who holds the symbolically important knife in his hand at the end, should be a black man. But there is something troubling here as well. The resolution offered by Siza's act and words is in fact strikingly *depoliticized*. The white characters in the story explicitly articulate connections between the natural and biological and the political (they joke, for instance, about the idea that the hegemony of class society can be explained by the fact that you can't smell blood on a full stomach). But the black character, performing a simple task, becomes essentially a vehicle – a metaphor – of a political vision. At the moment of closure, when the realist text is, as it were, ratcheted up a notch to carry the political message, the black man becomes mythic. The story relies, finally, on our acceptance of his closeness to nature and his knowledge of nature's ways. We may recognize in this symbolic figure certain disquietingly familiar traits: the features of that old colonial stereotype of 'the guide who really knows Africa' – the very stereotype Gordimer criticizes in 'The Ultimate Safari'. This unconscious retreat into the old repertoire of South African myth demonstrates the difficulty of attaching new kinds of revolutionary affirmation to literary forms which have their own naturalizing force. 'Unfortunately', as Barthes laconically observes, 'there is no antipathy between realism and myth' (136–7).

III

The problems besetting Afrikaans writers opposed to apartheid have been even more fundamental than those confronting the realist writer in English. For it is fair to say that apartheid, linked as it has been with the Afrikaner's struggle for political power, has rendered the entire Afrikaans language mythic. Under the forty or so years of Nationalist rule, it was no mere system of linguistic signs (as evident in the very existence of the Afrikaans Language Monument in Paarl – surely the only monument ever to memorialize a living language). The language itself became a second-order signifier, attached to a larger concept of the Afrikaner's 'national identity'. Myth, consequently, is hard to avoid in Afrikaans, and perhaps especially so in literary Afrikaans, which in the past has so readily been turned into a safe cultural treasure to be 'appreciated' by the Afrikaner establishment.[1] The dissident Afrikaans writer is, therefore, confronted at the outset with the task of writing against the system in the self-same language that has been used to justify the system and to express the colonizers' claim to African soil.

1. The reception of Elsa Joubert's *Die Swerfjare van Poppie Nongena* [*The Long Journey of Poppie Nongena*], for instance, is a fairly recent case in point. This novel offers a detailed narrative of a Xhosa woman's sufferings under the Group Areas Act in the Cape: it is the story of a life shaped by very specific historical conditions. Yet many readers, and even to an extent Joubert herself, tended to read it mythically, i.e., as a representation of human suffering and endurance, or as another jewel in the crown of Afrikaans – as a text which for the first time puts a certain vernacular form of the language (the Afrikaans of Xhosa speakers) to literary use. We see here a strategy that Barthes identifies as typical of bourgeois myth, namely *inoculation*: a resistant voice is incorporated in a tolerable dose and nicely watered down in such a way as to render its troubling political implications almost invisible.

While Afrikaans has often been turned to ironic use (as, for instance, in Etienne Leroux's *Magersfontein, O Magersfontein!*), it seems to me that the crisis of the 1980s marked the emergence of a number of texts which are almost entirely absorbed by the task of reiterating and exploding the increasingly threadbare myths of Afrikanerdom.[2] The discursive strategy we see in such texts is accurately defined in the 'Myth Today' essay as a retaliation *in kind* against myth: if myth, as Barthes argues, is a kind of 'language robbery' or 'parasitism', the best weapon against it would seem to be a kind of second-order parasitism, the creation of a counter-myth out of already existent mythic discourses. This is an anarchic or (in Barthes's neologism) a 'semioclastic' practice, one that is closely allied with his own critical project as mythologist (7).

Such a strategy is strikingly exemplified in a 1988 musical revue by Gerrit Schoonhoven entitled *Piekniek by Dingaan* [*Picnic at Dingaan's*], a text obsessed with the abuse of the Afrikaans language, especially during the second State of Emergency. The very first number describes, by way of a pseudo-biblical myth of origins, the way in which language has been invaded by and saturated with the paranoia of apartheid:

> In the beginning was the Word
>> And the word was God
>> And the word became flesh
>> And the flesh fear
> And it came and got scared here among us – and
>> white . . .
>
> [In die begin was die Woord
>> En die Woord was God
> En die Woord het vlees geword
> En die vlees vrees
> En het onder ons kom bang word – en wit . . .][3]

2. Though I shall be analyzing texts by white writers here, it should be noted that the problems I have described also affect black writers in Afrikaans in perhaps even more profound and contradictory ways than their white counterparts. Poets like André Boezak, Jan Wiltshire, and Vernie February have put the ironic strategies of 'second-order myth' to excellent use in their parodies of a variety of Afrikaans classics. For a discussion of these writers see Willemse, 'Die Skrille Sonbesies' (especially 381–4).

3. Citations from *Piekniek* are transcribed from a tape recording of the final performance; translations are my own. Thanks to Ian Glenn for drawing my attention to this text.

The performance that follows constitutes an effort to discover or invent a way in which the 'word' might cease to be purely 'white': how one might, as one of the revue's more raucous rock-and-roll songs puts it, 'kaffergaan' (i.e., 'get down', 'go wild', or more literally 'go *kaffir*') 'in Afrikaans'. The risky use of the racist slang word here suggests the answer: it may be necessary to inhabit the ugly myths, the ugly words, of apartheid in order to subvert their racist, separatist significations. The revue, accordingly, takes the form of an extraordinarily bitter parade of empty cultural forms: hymns, popular songs, inspirational legends, political speeches, celebrities, and news sensations of yesteryear. It is a veritable encyclopedia of all the old codes, transmogrified to express the anguish of the current moment. In the final number, for example, the national anthem, 'Die Stem van Suid Afrika' ['The Voice of South Africa'] is transformed from a nationalist rallying cry to a statement of disloyalty and an expression of suffering: the call of the nation no longer resounds (as it does in the original) across empty plains and crags, but across a landscape of devastated neighbourhoods and burnt-out school buildings; and the 'groan' ['kreun'] of the anthem's emblematic ox wagon is replaced by that of hungry children. This savagely ironic ending links back to the musical's first rollicking anthem: an invitation to all Afrikaners to sing the 'lullaby of anarchy' ['die wiegelied van anargie'].

Piekniek's counter-mythic strategy, as well as its bitter, almost nauseous structure of feeling, is also evident in more literary Afrikaans texts. The emerging fiction writer Jeanne Goosen's curious 1987 novella *Louoond* is a case in point.[4] *Louoond* (the word refers to an oven at a low temperature or to a plate-warming drawer) is not a realist text, nor is it in any obvious way politically committed. Yet it is clearly 'about' the violence of the Emergency, a topic it approaches from an almost comically alienated vantage. The narrator is a white woman confined to her kitchen – imprisoned, as it were, in the narrow space defined by a table, two chairs, a stove, a fridge, and a garbage can. This confinement is underscored by the obsessive way in which the woman's rather erudite meditations revert to the mundane matter of food: to lists of ingredients, or to grisly descriptions of the preparation of meats. The kitchen becomes a

---

4. Goosen was introduced to an international readership with her short story 'Wat Sag is Vergaan', translated as 'The Soft Has No Durability' and collected in Bunn and Taylor, eds., *From South Africa*. *Louoond* has not yet been published in English; the translations given here are my own.

symbolic expression of the beleaguered and paranoid separatism of the Afrikaner. Though figured as an orderly, white enclosure – a world in which 'Surf' reliably 'removes the most stubborn stains' ['Surf verwyder die hardnekkigste vlekke' (30–1)] – the kitchen is not so insulated from the rest of the world as the narrator likes to think. The surrounding air smells of burnt rubber and the newspaper brings home frightening images which relentlessly 'open the door to the outside' ['maak die deur na buite oop' (19, 33)]. Seated at her kitchen table, the narrator is drawn into the grey landscape of a news photograph depicting a pile of corpses at the Crossroads squatter camp, and the effect of the image on the narrator is described in terms that suggest a kind of boiling – an acceleration, not only of the ink particles in the photograph, but of body parts: 'The heap of people begins to spread out, it clumps together again, explodes: portions of limbs, intestines, chunks of faces and heads fly through the air, colliding with each other' ['Die hoop mense begin vanmekaar sprei, beweeg, dan klomp hulle weer saam, ontplof: stukke ledemate, binne-goed, stukke gesig en kop vlieg deur die lug, bots teen mekaar' (34)]. This horrifying experience elicits a nausea even more intense than that which afflicts the male protagonist in Gordimer's 'Spoils': the distinction between inside and outside is rent apart as the narrator vomits up decayed 'pieces of meat and juice and soup' ['stukke vleis en sap en sop' (34)].

This important and disturbing passage allows us to grasp the meaning of the 'warming oven' referred to in the title. Cooking, which the novella recurrently represents in scientific terms as intensified molecular activity, or as a process of chemical reconstitution, becomes a metaphor for the political situation in South Africa: an agitated state of transformation. 'Things are bubbling inside my casserole on the stove', the narrator observes. 'On the atomic level the traditional world no longer exists' ['Binne-in die kastrol op die stoof borrel dit. Die elementêre hoë-energie partikels bots' (54)].

The narrator's confinement to the kitchen and its prescribed round of activities serves an additional expressive function. It allows Goosen to subvert one of the Afrikaner's most fondly held stereotypes: the traditional image of the woman, the *volksmoeder*, as nurturer. This image is parodied in the figure of the narrator's grandmother, Ouma Sannie. 'She is my history' ['Sy is my geskiedenis' (52)] the narrator resignedly observes, an embodiment of all the old clichés: a veritable 'motto' ['leuse' (51)] in human form. Ouma Sannie defines her world with stern housekeeping maxims – 'Show me your dish towels and I will tell you

exactly what kind of woman you are' – and grim nationalistic pieties –
'We bought this land with our blood' ['Wys my jou vadoeke . . . en ek sê
jou presies watter soort vrou jy is'; 'Ons het hierdie land met ons bloed
vrygekoop' (50, 44)]. This coexistence of domestic virtue and racist
bloody-mindedness is central to Goosen's critique: the novella consis-
tently describes Ouma Sannie's kitchen activities in such a way as to suggest her complicity with the violence of the emergency – with the
mutilation and burning of human bodies in the world beyond the kitchen
door. Her techniques of food preparation are presented as nothing short
of murderous: she decapitates carrots, tortures cabbages, and executes
chickens with callous efficiency. Her manners, moreover, express a
vicious gluttony, the political dimension of which is underscored by the
novella's frequent references to the hunger of the oppressed. We see
Ouma Sannie stuffing a slice of cake into her mouth in the same breath as
she spews the tired tautology: 'A kaffir is *always* a kaffir' [''n Kaffer bly
áltyd 'n kaffer' (18–19)]. She dies, appropriately, with 'her body still half-
full of groceries' ['haar lyf nog halfvol kruideniersware' (52)]. With all
her traditional domesticity, Ouma Sannie is a horrifying grotesque,
emphasizing the fact that the mythic white world, the 'security zone'
['veilige domein' (51)] of the kitchen, is no refuge from violence nor from
guilt.

The myth that *Louoond* is most centrally concerned with, however, is
a biological one: a conception of human society as homologous with (or
as a mere part of) the age-old evolutionary competition between species.
This vision of 'nature red in tooth and claw' – with its grim message, 'if
you want to live you must fight otherwise *you* get bullied!' ['as jy wil leef,
moet jy baklei anders word *jy* geboelie!' (27)] – is one the narrator finds
strangely compelling. Her meditations on this theme are often presented
with the apparent objectivity and assertiveness of a textbook on natural
history:

> In the past the pendulum of evolution has swung many times and it will swing
> again in the future to instal yet another species at the apex of the foodchain. The
> fossil animals of the wetlands and marshes, among other things, provide us with
> evidence of the emergence of two vast classes of animals, which each in turn would
> dominate the earth.
>
> [Die evolusieslinger het in die verlede al baie keer geswaai en dit sal in die toekoms
> nog so swaai om elke keer 'n nuwe dieregroep aan die spits te plaas. Die fossieldiere
> van die vleie en moerasse gee naas ander dinge ook insig in die verskyning van twee
> groot diereklasse wat elk op sy beurt heerskappy oor die aarde sou voer. (17)]

It is clear, however, that, irrespective of its scientific validity, this 'survival of the fittest' idea serves a suspect political function. It suggests that the violence of the Emergency – so powerfully rendered in the description of the newspaper photograph – should be seen as just another instance of the innate violence of life on earth: much like the aggressivity of the narrator's Dobermans, who instinctively go after chickens on rainy days (11). The woman even comes to compare the political commitment of such human collectives as the AWB, the ANC, the PLO, and the Ku Klux Klan to the instinctive devotion of ants or flies to the survival of their species. This fatalistic and ahistorical analogy eventually leads her to propose an utterly fantastic solution to South Africa's problems: specialized drugs which would suppress the violent urges inherent in the human brain.

The effect of the novella's elaborate meditations on evolutionary myth, however, is curiously distancing: *Louoond* ultimately undermines and ironizes the narrator's obsessions. The limitations of her biologistic vision are first revealed in a wonderfully absurd scene in which she imagines that in that proverbial time after-the-revolution, she will have to beg her ex-maid (who now lives in her erstwhile madam's house and wears her best 'slacksuit') for her Maria Callas tapes – the one cultural treasure she cannot do without. Her argument is strictly in accordance with the vast perspective of natural history that she finds so fascinating:

Listen Anna, let me explain carefully: in the Triassic, millions and millions of years ago, long before the continental drift, we were both flying reptiles. We ruled the earth. We lived peacefully scale to scale in the Moordenaarskaroo, grey, grotesque, and pacifistic . . . I appeal to you today on the basis of our ancestral connections, and I ask you nicely, Anna, please save my Maria Callas.

[Luister Anna, laat ek mooi verduidelik: in die Trias, miljoene en miljoene jare gelede, lank voor die kontinentale drif, was ons albei vlieënde reptiele. Ons het heerskappy oor die aarde gevoer. Ons het vreedsaam skub teen skub in die Moordenaarskaroo gewoon, grys, grotesk en pasifisties . . . Ek beroep my vandag op ons voorvaderlike verbintenis en ek wil jou mooi vra, Anna, spaar asseblief my Maria Callas. (21–2)]

This strange pseudo-scientific plea (appealing to 'nature' in order to preserve a specific kind of 'culture') is comically ineffective. It entirely fails to overcome the former maid's dislike of 'that Callas woman' ['daardie Callas-vrou' (22)] who, after all, gave her splitting headaches in those days when she still had to polish the kitchen floors. Besides, as an

ANC supporter, Anna's notion of equality and of 'Darwinistic struggle' ['Darwinistiese worsteling' (22)] is political and practical, not a
matter of dinosaurs and ferns. She is far more interested in the white
woman's next desperate offer: to teach her how to can meat and bottle
Coca-Cola.

The most potent criticism of the narrator's evolutionary myth, however, is the simple fact that she herself finally finds little consolation in it:
'It is the politics of an insane system' ['Dit is die politiek van 'n waansin-
nige stelsel' (27)], she admits, and it leaves her crying at the thought that
evolution will eliminate all human sensitivity (55). Even when she tries to
live by her own survival-of-the-fittest code, resolving at least to extermi-
nate the insects who invade her kitchen, she is left feeling impotent and
ridiculous: 'I stand in my kitchen, I stand knee deep in a world of flies'
['Ek staan in my kombuis, ek staan kniediep in 'n wêreld vol vlieë' (27)].
The tinge of a dark, absurdist humour is unmistakable here; and it
emerges again at the end of the novella, when the narrator and a friend
are out in a sailboat, arguing bitterly about nature, politics, and violence,
and suddenly find themselves drifting through a veritable sea of shit –
sewage from a nearby military base. Such symbolic situations are clearly
intended to deflate the profundities of the narrator's meditations.

Louoond is by no means an ironic romp like Barthes's classic example
of 'artificial' or second-order myth: Flaubert's *Bouvard and Pécuchet*. Yet
it is fair to say that it operates in a similar way; with its strange, unreal narrative, and its various 'supplementary ornaments which demystify it'
(Barthes, *Mythologies*, 136), *Louoond* ultimately denaturalizes the narrator's biologistic ideology. It forces us to gaze on the myths it evokes as
political evasions, as symptoms of the 'controlled hysteria' ['beheerde
histerie'] of a racist culture in the violent moment of its decline.
Implicitly *Louoond* calls for a radical remaking of all culture, literature
included. It is no accident that the narrator keeps her own writings – a
notebook entitled 'KITCHEN BLUES' ['KOMBUIS-BLUES' (32)] in the warming oven: the implication is that writing too must be reconstituted, must
expand and vibrate, transform itself, if it is to address a world in crisis.

IV

The texts I have juxtaposed here as examples of three different anti-
mythic strategies have also revealed certain important commonalities.
They share, as we have seen, a preoccupation with a set of related motifs
(hunting, cooking, eating – especially meat-eating – and the food chain):

motifs that allow the writer to explore the most fundamental relations of power and the most basic differences between nature and culture. This nexus of themes (which can be traced back to J. M. Coetzee's prescient *Life & Times of Michael K* (1983), a novel obsessed with food, power, and parasitism) may yet emerge as one of the more significant and characteristic in the literature of the Emergency. Each of these texts, furthermore, has suggested a model or paradigmatic activity through which political change may be imagined and effected – whether it be production (Qabula), redistribution (Gordimer), or a radical 'molecular' reconstitution of the world (Goosen). This marked emphasis on social change surely challenges us to ask some questions about the task of critical writing, especially in the context of a new South Africa. Now that apartheid is officially a thing of the past, has it not become problematic to classify texts in terms of their relation to the hegemony of myth? Does an emphasis on demystification and a suspiciousness towards discursive orthodoxies not simply perpetuate an oppositional stance at a time when the old verities are in fact disappearing? Has the task of the critic not changed – to the point where he or she need no longer be a mythologist, need no longer (as Barthes does in 'Myth Today') conceive of the task of the critic as essentially negative and closed off from the utopian dimensions of other forms of discourse?

These are not questions that can simply be brushed aside. There is clearly a need for affirmative cultural work in the new South Africa: a task of discovering a new ordinariness, a new set of ideas that will eventually be taken for granted – a new culture, in short, with a richness that has been unavailable to the 'poor' discourse of revolution. It is likely that this task will carry, for some time yet, a sense of newness, an awareness of the human agency and creativity that shape both language and the world. However, it seems to me that even in a time of reconstruction, there is bound to be a need for a literary or cultural criticism conceived of in demystificatory terms. The idea of 'myth on the left' suggests, after all, that even such radical changes as a successful revolution will not necessarily mean the end of myth. For myth, in the sense I have tried to use it here, is not merely a set of received ideas, but the erasure or masking of the historicity of our language and our images. And historical thinking is not always easy to do. There is clearly a danger that the 'Greatness of Mandela', like the 'Genius of Stalin', may become a myth. Indeed, to judge by a travel advertisement in the June 1996 issue of the British Airways magazine *High Life*, such a process is already well under way.

Urging readers to visit Pretoria ("'n Lekker place to be '), the ad features a collection of images of Mandela's smiling face. More precisely, it reproduces twelve times the pleasant mug shot that appeared on the 1994 ballot, but in each case modifies the image in order to associate the great man with the city's various tourist attractions: he is shown in a Voortrekker hat and bandolier ('Historical Monuments'), in a safari hat and binoculars ('Game Parks'), in Zulu headgear with leopard skins and beads ('African Art'), in a hard hat and mine lamp ('Mine Tours'), and so on. Though the caption – 'SEE PRETORIA THROUGH DIFFERENT EYES. HE DID.' – explicitly reminds the reader of history and historical change, the eye-catching illustration does the opposite. By implicitly equating such diverse institutions as the gold mine and the Voortrekker Monument (both become pure spectacle), it erases their specific histories and social significance in classically mythical fashion. We are back, it would seem, on Pik Botha's mythic safari, in a world where images are more important than human experience and collective creativity.

The Pretoria advertisement is, of course, an easy target, and before we smile too easily at its effects, we should consider the fact that myth can also colonize the work of the critic. The discourse of criticism, like any other discourse, is not immune to a hypostatization of its terms. As Rosemary Jolly has shown in her recent essay, 'Rehearsals of Liberation', there is a danger that critics too – even critics on the left who are consciously committed to a decolonizing political stance – may cease to be 'mythologists' and may come to ignore the historicity of their own discourse. A fixation, for instance, on apartheid as 'Racism's Last Word' (a formulation which in the present context presents a special danger of complacency) may generate a critical practice which turns the now-abolished apartheid into an evermore remote spectacle of racist horror. The vigilant negativity which Barthes associates in 'Myth Today' with the attitude of the mythologist will therefore remain essential, even as the task of cultural reconstruction continues. It is an attitude which, as Barthes frankly admits, presents difficulties: difficulties 'in feeling, if not in method' (*Mythologies*, 146). Since criticism is not the same order of discourse as the language of revolution (it is, after all, metalinguistic, concerned in the first place with representations rather than things themselves), it can bring about a sense of distance or vicariousness. But Barthes's meditations offer some reassurance as well: if criticism does not exactly *make* the world, it can ethically, as an act of unveiling, '*harmonize* with the world, not as it is, but as it wants to create itself' (146). This affiliation with a changing world must continue to underpin our reading and writing now that apartheid is over.

Works cited

Barthes, Roland. *Mythologies*. Trans. Annette Lavers. New York: Noonday Press, 1991.

Elias, Norbert. *The History of Manners: The Civilizing Process*. Trans. Edmund Jephcott. Vol. I. New York: Pantheon, 1982.

Goosen, Jeanne. *Louoond*. Pretoria: HAUM Literêr, 1987.

Jolly, Rosemary. 'Rehearsals of Liberation: Contemporary Postcolonial Discourse and the New South Africa'. *PMLA* 110 (1995): 17–30.

Joubert, Elsa. *Die Swerfjare van Poppie Nongema*. Cape Town: Tafelberg, 1978. Translated as *Poppie*. London: Hodder & Stoughton, 1980.

Qabula, Alfred Temba and Mi S'dumo Hlatshwayo. 'The Tears of a Creator'. David Bunn and Jane Taylor, eds., *From South Africa: New Writing, Photographs and Art*. Chicago: University of Chicago Press, 1987. 285–9.

Wagner, Kathrin. *Rereading Nadine Gordimer*. Bloomington: Indiana University Press, 1994.

Willemse, Hein. 'Die Skrille Sonbesies: Emergent Black Afrikaans Poets in Search of Authority'. *Rendering Things Visible: Essays on South African Literary Culture*. Ed. Martin Trump. Athens: Ohio University Press, 1990. 367–401.

10

Interview

MIRIAM TLALI,
INTERVIEWED BY ROSEMARY JOLLY

I interviewed Miriam Tlali in December 1994 at the Harbour Castle Hilton
in Toronto. She was attending the African Studies Association of America
meetings as a guest speaker, and trying to combat the Canadian winter at
the same time. We attended a reception in her honour hosted by the South
African Consulate. The master of ceremonies was polite, but failed to
pronounce Miriam Tlali's name, or the titles of her books, correctly. It was
clear that the end of apartheid did not signify the end of an entrenched
ignorance of 'non-white' writing.

RJ How did you get interested in literature? It is not common, I think,
for people who came from your situation to be interested in writing.
MT It's not. I didn't sort of sit down and say, hum, I'd like to be a writer
one day; this was never the case. I admired good writing and read a lot,
whatever I could get hold of. I was introduced to the idea of books, of
learning and so on, because when I grew up trying to understand things
around me, I heard my grandmother and my mother speaking about my
father. They would speak about this teacher, and to me that was one of
the first things that I put in my mind – that he must have been some kind of
special person. Especially in the forties teachers were so special.

And then when I went to the high school [in Western Native
Township], where the principal of the school had been one of the first
two African students ever to enter a white university. So our school had
this man as headmaster, and as you can expect, he influenced us. He was a
man who could devote the first forty-five minutes to speaking about the
excellence of learning. In his effort to make an impression on us, he
would unwittingly take up the first period. He spoke about how you
ought to give something to your society. And one of the things that this
man would do was he would touch on the political set up. Very lightly,
because they were not allowed to preach politics to us, but he would touch
on it. He would speak about discrimination, about how people are being
ill-treated in the towns and how intolerable it was and so on . . . So that's
the kind of man who loosely inspired me.

I lived with my grandmother for a long time, and fortunately for me she was involved in her own business; she was what you call a witch-doctor now. And she would be busy with her herbs and so on, which also I came to know. She would leave me to sit, you know, and these books and the little pamphlets and the magazines that I got hold of were my school-mates. She would let me read by candlelight and do my homework. And then I learned how to admire literature, and to know about excellence in writing, to admire it, to appreciate it, even at that stage ...

And then of course there were in Sophiatown at the time, the activities of the ANC. And, then, the Communist Party and so on. But as girls of course you were never allowed to move out of the house and to attend these things. But I would hear about them and you know, I would know about the ANC, the fact that there are political movements which are prepared to face the government. And in addition, living in Sophiatown, we had what we called the *Bantu World*, the African newspaper. So we knew about the *Bantu World*; that my uncles were reading these papers, about politics and so on.

And then again, you felt the fact that you are black, that there are certain things you are not allowed to do because you are black. I remember it used to surprise me, you know, such things. For instance during Christmas we would have to go into town, to be taken into town by my grandmother, by my aunt, and so on, to go and buy Christmas clothes. And then we would notice that there's a problem here. That we are supposed to be given socks, kind of socks to wear, before we can pick [try on] shoes. And we couldn't try on shoes here in public. We had to, to be, you know ...

RJ Around the back?

MT Around the back somewhere, a dingy little dark place where you [as a black person] are allowed to try on shoes and so on. And we wouldn't be allowed to go through this entrance and [only] be allowed to go to that one. And then later on, of course, with the Nationalist Party coming into power, the signs were now very visible. There were signs 'Europeans only', 'non-Europeans only', you know. The idea that you are a kind of person who is not supposed to do things – you wonder what's wrong with you. You cannot sit on this bench, you cannot walk here, you cannot enter there.

And then there were the strikes, or there would be fighting somewhere inside town between blacks and whites, and this would affect the trams which passed on the way to Newlands. These trams of course were segregated for non-Europeans and Europeans. And whenever there was something going on in town, the trams would be affected in that they [the black passengers] were constantly throwing stones at the whites, and what not. And we would also join in that, and throw stones, and we learned now to fight. We were divided by Toby Street from Westdene – a white suburb – on the one side and Sophiatown on the other. And we used to play with these white children on the other side of the street. But whenever there was this fighting then we would throw stones at them, and we wouldn't even know why we were doing it.

And then of course I went to university. For the first time in my life I was working towards this quality of life and getting books and reading! The books! Oh my god! Oh!

RJ Well, even where you live now, you're not close to a library.

MT The so-called libraries which were there were destroyed by the kids. They are very intelligent, these children. Those are some of the first things we went for, to burn them down, because they were really structures which were full of stupid books, really degrading stuff. [Recently, some of the 'old' libraries have been rebuilt, and stocked with new materials.]

RJ They were part of the whole Bantu Education system?

MT Right. Which was to educate you to accept the fact that you are a lower being, you know. As for the history, that was the limit.

RJ Garbage.

MT It's real garbage. Which my grandmother used to shake her head at years ago . . . She couldn't express it, but I knew she knew it was rubbish, you know.

RJ So how did you come to write your first book?

MT Well, I worked at this departmental store called Mayfair Radio and Appliances. In my book, I called it Metropolitan Radio. The original title of the book was *Between Two Worlds*, which the publishers changed to *Muriel at Metropolitan*. I left university (then known as Pius XII University College in Lesotho) to go and have a baby and try to get some work. I worked at this store, all the time striving for a better position, fighting hard and so on. It was so painful – to see what was happening, and to experience also what was happening to black customers and other black workers in the store.

RJ And to be part of it?

MT And be part of it. By that time I knew what all the intricacies were legally, because I had studied African Administration and I had had a lot of reading about this. And it was hard, because it [the store] was like a kind of stage where the whole of the South African scenario was being played out.

RJ A microcosm.

MT Right. Like a whole microcosm.

RJ The funny thing about teaching *Between Two Worlds* is that students in North America are not used to reading for certain things. They read your book. And then I ask them, did you see that she was calling for a general strike? And they don't read for that; they can read for the story but, because they're not used to a society in which to strike is illegal, they don't recognize what kind of book they have read.

MT They don't understand. And my writing has been said to be didactic, which is exactly what it is. And I did it intentionally.

RJ That's the point?

MT That's the point. All political organizations – the PAC and the ANC and others – were all banned. Political meetings were not allowed. We had no platform at all. There was very little protest and I was restless and worried. At university I had met all these very wonderful people, all the politicians who would come and give us a lecture, and teach us about the system. And that broadens you up. For the first time in my life I was exposed to that kind of thing. And, then, I had also studied English, and I knew that to write a book where you are busy preaching is not right. You know it's not good literature. I knew all of that and I did not care. I did it deliberately, I preached with the very first chapter. And they [the publishers] left that out with that first issue of the book. They cut out all these parts where I was preaching. And I was creating my own platform, it was deliberate. You know I didn't care to adhere to the so-called aesthetic.

RJ Aesthetic standards?

MT I didn't want to do this because it would waste my time. What I was interested in was to get anybody, any African who read the book, to be conscious of the system. That was my intent.

RJ Do you think that you write with the same things in mind now?

MT I wouldn't now. It's not necessary, is it?

RJ No.

MT Well, perhaps it would be necessary in the case of the dis-advantaged. The situations in which, say for instance, women have found themselves . . . I have now started to write like a novelist, you know, try-ing to write what is regarded as a good novel.

RJ So you think that now there is a changed situation?

MT Yes, it's a relief to me to be able to go back to writing like a free person, you know, to write about life generally.

RJ And do you think of *Between Two Worlds* as being a novel that is participating in an activist kind of approach to writing?

MT Yes, it is. When I wrote this one [*Between Two Worlds*], I decided to do it in a very diplomatic manner, and to hit at the same time, to cover up as I went along with it. Hitting while appearing not to do so. I tried to use a lot of that. But with this one, you know [points to a copy of *Amandla!*], the system had become much more oppressive. It had become, you know, openly so, almost trying to destroy us, and I decided to hit at it without any reservation at all. That is what this book is about.

RJ It's different [from *Between Two Worlds*] in that way.

MT It's even more activist.

RJ It's very direct.

MT Right, yes. And it was banned immediately.

RJ And did they [the security forces] bother you personally?

MT Yes, oh that. Oh, Rosemary! They did. In fact right now, I have been talking to my husband about it. It's high time we dig up in the yard and decide where I have been hiding all the books. Yes.

RJ You buried books in the ground [to hide them from the security forces]?!

MT Yes, in the ground, to dig up later. I must get a . . .

RJ A forklift truck.

MT A forklift truck. [Much laughter.] Yeah, we must get all the books. And be careful not to destroy them. Yes, they are somewhere in the yard there, wrapped in the aluminium foil. I don't remember where I used to bury them!

At this lecture [given earlier by Miriam Tlali] there they were asking me, tell me, now what are you going to write about now seeing that things have changed and so on. Oh, I'll write like you people write here in free societies. I'll write about love, about girl loving boy and dreaming, dreams, love, write about the moon and sky, I'll write about everything that is beautiful and so on. I didn't have time to notice the skies. We were busy fighting.

RJ But the funny thing is, now that it is over, you have other things that you are also still fighting about, or working on, with the issue of women.

MT Yes, my last book, this one [points to *Footprints in the Quag*]. Yes, yes, yes. Dealing with the problems women face — women in the trams for instance.

RJ And the question of sexual harassment?

MT Yes, yes. The fact of our culture being destroyed. Like with Paballo, the one who moves around the townships when she doesn't know where to go [after being maltreated by her husband and her in-laws].

RJ You've been talking about how violent the situation is right now. Do you think it's worse for women than it is for men right now, or is it just bad for everybody?

MT No, it is bad for everybody, but the worst for women. That is the second war that is going on.

Because the men are so frustrated, they're so disgruntled. And some of them seem intimidated by the choices that are made by women. For instance, I want to do a lot of research about women who had decided to go out of the marriage, you know, in order to buy their own houses to be on their own, and to have their own businesses, because they were held like this [makes a fist] by the men in the system. They couldn't do anything, you know. Even if you earned a lot of money trying to sell vegetables and fruit and so on, you had no business to buy a table like that. Those are some of the things I left out in this book [*Between Two Worlds*], [things that] emphasize the plight of the women. There were cases, for instance, [at the store at which Miriam Tlali worked] where a woman would want to buy a radio and the husband would resist, you know, and she'd be frustrated, and she would have the money and she wouldn't be able to do anything with it.

RJ Because of her husband?

MT Exactly.

RJ Why did you leave these scenes out of the book?

MT Partly because, you know, I did not want to overemphasize the problem between the men, African men and African women, because the success of the struggle depended on how united we were against it. If I were to emphasize that – for me to bring some kind of trouble between men and women, as far as the struggle is concerned – it would be confusing, it would confuse the struggle.

RJ Right. And now you think there's room to do that?

MT Exactly. Oh yes, oh yes, definitely.

RJ And it's necessary.

MT Yes. In fact I've been thinking that I should rewrite [*Between Two Worlds*] and include these stories, these things that used to take place at this place [the store], that affected men and women, you know, especially blacks.

RJ Relationships between men and women?

MT Yes, yes. I left out the ideas of love relationships, deliberately. There was a lot going on besides just selling furniture and so on. I thought it was irrelevant. I mean, because this was a book that had . . .

RJ Had a very strong focus?

MT Right.

RJ But now you're doing it with these new stories [*Footprints in the Quag*]?

MT Yes. I'm exposing a lot of [male–female relationships], yes. A lot of them [women who have a case of abuse to report] are inhibited even by the society itself. They don't report it, because most of them feel so insecure. What if my husband discovers I have reported him? What if my mother-in-law knows that I have reported her son? What if this happens and so on?

There are a lot of stories here by women who come to me. [They tell me about] beating up the wife and so on.

RJ So one of the things that you're doing there in your house in Soweto is actually recording stories for people who cannot record them for various reasons themselves?

MT Right.

RJ You've been talking about how Soweto is very violent right now, and that the whole fabric of society is so broken and destructive. And I was wondering, what do you think young writers can contribute to this situation? What do you think the pressures are on young writers right now? You've spoken to me now about not having space, no computer or anything like that, no time. What do you think that concerns of the younger generation of writers will be?

MT It should be how society can be run in such a manner that these things, everything is put in its place. For instance, that the infrastructure is such that women are able to get access to electricity and water, to work, and perhaps facilities for women who have children and so on, to be able to write. You have to push for such things, organize . . .

RJ And if the writers write about these issues, then there's the possibility of trying to undertake education in a place like Soweto, where there has been no education to speak of for years.

MT But you know they have to learn how to write. You have to learn how to read.

RJ But there is no written culture in that way, in at least two generations of children.

MT That's the thing. That's what I'm talking about. I'm saying, okay, they [cultural workers] might be engaged in trying to encourage writers to write. For instance, they asked me to go and provide a workshop, at the Windybrow Theatre. I was too busy, but I said okay I'll go and do this. Notices had been sent out asking aspirant writers to come for help with their short stories and so on. I sat there for two hours, but there was nobody. Nobody turned up. Because there are other factors which are pertinent which have to be dealt with, and which have not received attention. It's not enough to say just sit down there and write a story. How can you say that to a person who is concerned about how to survive, where to get the next meal. It's still fighting against the odds. You have to remove all these problems that prevent people from sitting down, reading the books, appreciating them and developing their own writing.

Speech and silence in the fictions of J. M. Coetzee

BENITA PARRY

I

David Attwell maintains that Coetzee's novels are 'directed at under-standing the conditions – linguistic, formal, historical and political – governing the writing of fiction in contemporary South Africa'. In turn, he offers the volume of interviews and essays he has edited as reflecting 'on an encounter in which the legacies of European modernism and modern linguistics enter the turbulent waters of colonialism and apartheid' (Coetzee, *Doubling the Point*, 3). This is an apt and elegant designation of the fictions' moment and space, and I use it as a starting point for considering the ways this fraught confluence is negotiated in self-reflexive novels which stage the impossibility of representation, estrange the norms of reality, and work, in Coetzee's words, to 'demythologize history'.

Metropolitan reviewers, as well as those critics whose attention, when reading South African novels, was focused on detecting condemnations of an egregious political system, have been predisposed to proffer Coetzee's fictions as realist representations of, and humanist protests against, colonial rapacity at large, and in particular against the intricately institutionalized system of racial oppression that until recently prevailed in South Africa.[1] Other critics whose concern is with the radicalism of Coetzee's textual practice, and who foreground parody and reflexivity as oppositional linguistic acts, argue that the authority of colonialism's narratives is undermined by subversive rewritings of the genres traditional to South African fiction – the heroic frontier myth, the farm romance, the liberal novel of stricken conscience[2] – hence opening conventions to scrutiny and confronting the traditional and unquestioned notion of the canon (see Attridge, 'Oppressive Silence').

1. See, for example, Gallagher, *A Story of South Africa*, and Penner, *Countries of the Mind*.
2. See Dovey, *The Novels of J. M. Coetzee*, and Attwell, 'The Problem of History'.

Such readings have come from Coetzee's most attentive critics, amongst some of whom there has been a tendency to construe the fictions as calculated transcriptions of the author's known critical stances on the instability of language and the unreliability of narration. The consequence is that paradox and impasse, gaps and silences are accounted for, not as textually generated through the interplay of the referential and the rhetorical, or by the interruptions of incommensurable discourses, but as the planned strategy of a highly self-conscious practice which displays the materials and techniques of its own process of production.

What I will be considering is how novels that weave a network of textual invocations traversing European literary and philosophical traditions, as well as contemporary theory from linguistics and structuralism to deconstruction, circumvent, or rather confirm, that quandary of white writing's insecurity or dislocation in South Africa which Coetzee as critic has detected. For the principles around which novelistic meaning is organized in Coetzee's fictions owe nothing to knowledges which are *not* of European provenance, but which *are* amply and variously represented in South Africa; while the disposals of Western interpretative paradigms are disseminated in a poised, even hieratic prose uninflected by South Africa's many vernacular Englishes.

That Coetzee's novels interrogate colonialism's discursive power is indisputable, through estrangement and irony making known the overdeterminations, fractures, and occlusions of colonialist utterance; while their excavations of the uneasy but timid white South African liberal consciousness are amongst the most far-reaching in South African writing. All the same, I want to consider whether the reverberations of Coetzee's intertextual transpositions, as well as the logic and trajectory of his narrative strategies, do not inadvertently repeat the exclusionary colonialist gestures which the novels also criticize. Let me, then, put forward the polemical proposition that despite the fictions' disruptions of colonialist modes, the social authority on which the rhetoric relies and which it exerts is grounded in the cognitive systems of the West. Furthermore, I will suggest that the consequence of writing the silence attributed to the subjugated as a liberation from the constraints of subjectivity – a representation to which I will return – can be read as reenacting the received disposal of narrative authority.

The paradox as proposed by this hypothesis is that in the double movement performed by Coetzee's novels, the subversions of previous texts enunciating discourses of colonial authority are permutated into renarrativizations where only the European possesses the word and the ability to enunciate, the lateral routes of the virtually plotless novels taking in nothing outside the narrators' world-views and thereby sustaining the West as the culture of reference. A failure to project alternative perspectives might signify Coetzee's refusal to exercise the authority of the dominant culture to represent other and subjugated cultures, and might be construed as registering his understanding that agency is not something that is his to give or withhold through representation. Yet I will argue that the fictions do just this, because of which European textual power, reinscribed in the formal syntax required of Literature, survives the attempted subversion of its dominion.

For whereas the novels do enact the discursive processes whereby 'Bushman' and 'Hottentot' in 'The Narrative of Jacobus Coetzee' (*Dusklands*), the Barbarians in *Waiting for the Barbarians*, the servants in *In the Heart of the Country*, the gardener in *Life & Times of Michael K*, and the enslaved black Friday in *Foe* are muted by those who have the power to name and depict them, or as in *Age of Iron*, are subjected to acts of ventriloquizing, the dominated are situated as objects of representations and meditations which offer them no place from which to resist the modes that have constituted them as at the same time naked to the eye and occult. The question however has been differently phrased to privilege the transformative force of an unspoken presence: do these figures, as Derek Attridge maintains, perform 'the capacity of Coetzee's work to engage with – to stage, confront, apprehend, explore – *otherness*', in this engagement broaching 'the most fundamental and widely significant issues involved in any consideration of ethics and politics' ('Literary Form and the Demands of Politics', 244)?

In 'The Narrative of Jacobus Coetzee' (*Dusklands* (1974)), for instance, the conflicting enunciations in the making of a colonial discourse are ironically rehearsed. But what is there, in a narrative that dramatizes a metaphysics of conquest, to contradict Jacobus Coetzee's doomed discovery that 'in that true wilderness without polity ... everything, I was to find, was possible' (66), since the Khoi-Khoin are relegated as being unable to impinge on and participate in annulling the discourse of mastery disclosed by an autocritique? Is the silence of these 'strange' and defeated people deployed here as a textual strategy which counters the colonizing impulse and impudence in simulating another's voice? Alternatively can it be construed as a mute interrogation and disablement of discursive power? – a possibility offered by Attridge, who reads Coetzee's fictions as a continued and strenuous effort in figuring alterity as a force out there disrupting European discourse, a force which is both resistant to the dominant culture and makes demands on it, not by initiating dialogue, but by 'interrupting or disturbing the discursive patterns in which we are at home' ('Literary Form and the Demands of Politics', 250). On the other hand, can this narrative muteness be read as intimating a narrative disinclination to orchestrate a polyphonic score? And if so, then the consequence is that the silenced remain incommensurable, unknowable, and unable to make themselves heard in the sealed linguistic code exercised by the narrating self, and hence incapable of disturbing the dominant discourse?

Tzvetan Todorov, whose discussion of the other constituted by colonialism enlists the work of Levinas, has written that 'one does not let the other live merely by leaving him intact, any more than by obliterating his voice entirely. . . . Heterology, which makes the difference of voices heard, is necessary' (Todorov, *The Conquest of America*, 250, 251). This suggests a notion of commerce with alterity as a contact taking place in an intersubjective space where the non-identity of the interlocutors is respected and retained, and which leaves both 'I' and 'you' separate and intact but enhanced. A text written from within this interval or 'in-between' would register the opening of one's own discourse to strange accents and unfamiliar testimonies, but without suppressing or erasing difference, without pretending to simulate another's authentic voice or speaking on another's behalf, and without imprinting an absolute dissimilarity which simultaneously offers an explanation of, and excuse for, oppression. Such a procedure would engender a multiple, 'neologistic' idiom, which because it inscribes alterity not as a disarticulated presence but as an interlocutor, would counter what Levinas names (in *Totality and Infinity*) 'the eclipse, the occultation, the silencing of the other'.

II

Within the discussion of colonial and postcolonial discourse, silence has been read as a many-accented signifier of disempowerment and resistance, of the denial of a subject position and its appropriation.[3] In keeping with this recognition of the multiple resonances to silence, critics

3. On silence as a privileged signifier of postcolonial writing, see Ashcroft, Griffiths and Tiffin, *The Empire Writes Back*. See also Paulo Freire's writings, where silence signifies a culture of defeat and resignation.

have construed Coetzee's deployment of the topos as if this is notated by the text to be intelligible as an emblem of oppression, or to be audible as that unuttered but inviolable voice on which discourses of mastery cannot impinge and, thus, as an enunciation of defiance.[4] However, I will suggest that the various registers in which silence is scored in the novels speak of things other than the structural relationship of oppressor/oppressed, or the power of an unuttered alterity to undermine a dominant discourse, and that these other things are signs of the fiction's urge to cast off worldly attachments, even as the world is signified and estranged. I have already noted how in 'The Narrative of Jacobus Coetzee' the process of muting is staged as an act of conquest. My hypothesis about Coetzee's figures of silence in the subsequent novels is that although they are the disentitled, and are therefore available to be read as manifesting subordination to, and retreat from, a subjugated condition, the potential critique of political oppression is diverted by the conjuring and endorsing of a non-verbal signifying system.

Shared by Coetzee's protagonists of silence is an absence or economy of speech which is, in all cases, associated with sexual passivity or impotence: the hare-lipped Michael K, a gardener and progenitor of fruits and vegetables, lacks a father, a patronymic and sexual desire, and remains bonded to the mother; it is intimated that the dumb Friday is without tongue and perhaps without phallus; while the taciturn Vercueil in *Age of Iron* is perceived by the narrator as unable to beget children, his semen imagined as 'dry and brown, like pollen or the dust of this country' (180; refs. to Secker & Warburg/Penguin edition). These deficits have been read as signalling their location on the fringes of the phallocentric social order, whose dominance through their speechlessness and asexuality they evade.[5] Yet although the silence of each of these figures has a distinctive tenor, what all signify is not a negative condition of lack and affliction, or of sullen withdrawal, but a plenitude of perception and gifts: Michael K's aphasia facilitates a mystic consciousness; the verbal abstinence of the drunken and incontinent Vercueil, who means more than he says, is appropriate to his metaphysical status as the unlikely incarnation of an annunciation – 'verskuil' in Afrikaans means to obscure, conceal or mask; while the outflow of sounds from the mouth of Friday gives

---

4. See Spivak, 'Theory in the Margin'; Huggan, 'Philomela's Retold Story'; Splendore, 'J. M. Coetzee's *Foe*'; Attridge, 'Oppressive Silence'; Castillo, 'Coetzee's *Dusklands*'.

5. See Kristeva, *Desire in Language*.

tongue to meanings? desires? which precede or surpass those that can be communicated and interpreted in formal language. It could be argued, then, that speechlessness in Coetzee's fiction exceeds or departs from the psychoanalytic paradigm it also deploys, to become a metaphor for that portentous silence which signifies what *cannot* be spoken.

Coetzee's figures of silence are not without a quotidian dimension, and an inequality in social power is marked by the disparity between the obsessional will to utterance in Coetzee's female and European narrators, who literally perform the constitution of the subject in language and are authors of a discourse of the body, and the inaudibility of those who are narrated: Michael K, who is cryptically identified as coloured (96), is a unpropertied labourer; Friday is a black slave; and Vercueil is a tramp of unspecified race. However this incipient critique of how deprivation inflicts silence on those who are homeless in a hierarchical social world is deflected by the ascription of value to the disarticulated body, since the reader is simultaneously offered intimations of a non-linguistic intuitive consciousness, and is invited to witness the fruits of speechlessness when there is a failure of the dialectic between the 'Imaginary' and the 'Symbolic', or, in Kristeva's vocabulary, between the 'semiotic' and the 'thetic'.

Both surmises can be referred to Michael K, who is written as a being without an identity, outside the writ where the Law of the Father runs, and as the exemplar of a mind turned inward. Spoken for in the narrative – his representation depends on 'he thought', 'he found', 'he said' – Michael K is interpreted as being too busy with fantasy 'to listen to the wheels of history' (217); he is 'a soul blessedly untouched by doctrine, untouched by history' (207) who lives in 'a pocket outside time' (82), has access to a numinous condition when he 'emptied his mind, wanting nothing, looking forward to nothing' (74), and attains an ineffable state of bliss on eating a pumpkin he had reared in a parodic act of parental nurturing.

Although the narrative gloss has him likening himself, a gardener, to 'a mole, also a gardener, that does not tell stories because it lives in silence' (248), Michael K is attributed with an ambition to interpret his own solitary, eidetic consciousness: 'Always when he tried to explain himself to himself, there remained a gap, a hole, a darkness before which his understanding baulked, into which it was useless to pour words. The words were eaten up, the gap remained. His was always a story with a hole in it' (150–1). Here failure to attain and articulate self-consciousness is not rendered as disappointment, since silence is privileged as enabling the euphoria of desire unmediated by words; and if Michael K is perceived as dramatizing the inability to achieve a voice in the 'Symbolic' order, then we can note that his 'loss of thetic function' is not represented as a lapse into psychosis but as a path to the visionary.

Because Friday's inner consciousness is not narrated, his silence is more secret, and less available to the attention of conjectural readings, a sign of which is that he is offered alternative futures by the fiction, one within and the other outside the formal structures of language. In her discussion with Foe on how to bring Friday into the realm of representation, Susan Barton protests at Foe's proposal that he be shown writing, believing that since 'Letters are the mirror of words', Friday, who has no speech, can have no grasp of language. For Foe, on the other hand, writing is not a secondary representation of the spoken word but rather its prerequisite: 'Writing is not doomed to be the shadow of speech ... God's writing stands as an instance of a writing without speech' (142, 143). It is Foe's view that would seem to prevail in the first narrative turn, where the prospect of Friday as a scribe is prefigured. Formerly the pupil of an Adamic language taught by Cruso and a pictographic script offered by Barton, Friday, who had previously uttered himself only in the 'semiotic' modes of music and dance, now takes his seat at Foe's desk, and with Foe's quill, ink, and paper, and wearing Foe's wig, appropriates the authorial role.

His mouth likened by Barton to an empty buttonhole, Friday begins by forming *O*s, of which Coetzee has written: 'The O, the circle, the hole are symbols of that which male authoritarian language cannot appropriate' (cited by Dovey, *The Novels of J. M. Coetzee*, 411). All the same it is intimated that Friday will go on to learn *a*, a portent of his acquiring linguistic competence. There is, however, yet another narrative turn, when the dream-like quest of a contemporary narrator for Friday's story takes him into the hold of a wrecked ship. This time, Friday does not cross the threshold into logical and referential discourse, remaining instead in that paradisal condition where sign and object are unified, and where the body, spared the traumatic insertion into language, can give utterance to things lost or never yet heard, whose meanings, we are given to understand, will water the globe:

> But this is not a place of words . . . This is a place where bodies are their own signs. It is the home of Friday . . . His mouth opens. From inside him comes a slow stream, without breath, without interruption . . . it passes through the cabin, through the wreck; washing the cliffs and shores of the island, it runs northward and southward to the ends of the earth. (157)

It would seem, then, that although the various figures of silence in Coetzee's fictions are the dominated and, hence, intimate disarticulation as an act of discursive power, they are not only 'victims' but also 'victors' accredited with extraordinary and transgressive psychic energies. Furthermore, since it is explicitly posited in the fiction that writing does not copy speech and is not its symbol or image, might we not consider whether for Friday, and the other disempowered figures who cannot or will not make themselves heard in the recognized linguistic system, their bodies are to be read as encoding a proto-writing? Friday's mythic home is designated as 'a place where bodies are their own signs', and to the Magistrate in *Waiting for the Barbarians* (1980) who cannot understand the gestures of the barbarian girl, and can communicate with her only in makeshift language without nuance, her body is a script to be decoded in the same way as the characters on the wooden slips he has excavated.

It is therefore notable that when Coetzee's novels stage another discourse of the body, it is not in the scripted silence of the lowly and the outcast, whose oppression is also the condition for their access to transcendence and/or intuitive cognition, but as the progeny of women who speak, albeit uneasily, from a position of entrenched cultural authority, while also articulating their homelessness in and opposition to the patriarchal order. Three of Coetzee's narrators so far have been women, and while it could seem that he is enlisting the notion of the body as progenitor of woman's language – a notion posited by several feminist theorists – it is less certain that the writing he invents for them does transgress standard usage to register the irruptions of repressed libidinal elements into the performative text.

What is evident, however, is that Coetzee's female narrators explicitly represent the body as the agent of language: Mrs Curren, in *Age of Iron*, declares in her letters to an absent daughter that her words 'come from my heart, from my womb' (133), assigning to writing the properties of the genetically communicated code, of the phylogenetic inheritance made flesh in print: 'These words, as you read them . . . enter you and draw breath again . . . Once upon a time you lived in me as once upon a time I lived in my mother; as she still lives in me, as I grow towards her, may I live in you' (120). In another register, Susan Barton, in *Foe*, who asks 'Without desire, how is it possible to make a story?' (88), asserts that 'The Muse is a woman, a goddess, who visits poets in the night and begets stories upon them' (126); while Magda, in *In the Heart of the Country*, rejects her 'father-tongue' as a language of hierarchy which is not 'the language my heart wants to speak' and longs for 'the resonance of the full human voice ... the fullness of human speech' (97, 47).

All Coetzee's female narrators resolutely position themselves as authors of their own narratives:

> I have uttered my life in my own voice. . . I have chosen at every moment my own destiny. (Magda, 139)

> I am a free woman who asserts her freedom by telling her story according to her own desire . . . the story I desire to be known by is the story of the island.
>
> (Susan Barton, 131, 121)

> How I live, how I lived: my story . . . my truth, how I lived in these times, in this place. (Mrs Curren, 140, 119)

However, in terms of dis/identification with masculine narrative traditions, each produces a differently accented script: the recitations of Magda and Mrs Curren ostentatiously enunciate maternal desire, whereas Susan Barton, who insists on her freedom as a woman to choose her speech and her silence, affirms her wish to be 'father to my story' (123). By resisting Foe's determination to write 'the history of a woman in search of a lost daughter' (121), Barton thus refuses to be party to a discourse of motherhood.

Furthermore, alone amongst Coetzee's narrators, Barton articulates a reluctance to exert the narrative power which she as an Englishwoman, however disreputable, holds over those who are muted, when she resists Foe's urgings to invent Friday's story, 'which is properly not a story but a puzzle or hole in the narrative' (121). It is above all in *Foe*, which amplifies its status as a book about writing a book, that the disparate stratagems of novelistic authority are conspicuously and self-reflexively dramatized. The dialogue of Foe and Barton condenses a contest between protagonists holding different positions on language and representation. With her commitment to the priority of speech, Susan Barton formulates the task as descending into Friday's mouth, seeking a means to use Friday as an informant in order to fill the hole in her narrative: 'It is for us to open the mouth and hear what it holds' (142). But to the exponent of writing's primacy and the father of linear realist narrative – 'It is thus that we make up a book . . . beginning, then middle, then end' (117) – it is the author's brief to fabricate another's consciousness and circumstances: 'We must make Friday's silence speak, as well as the silence surrounding Friday . . . as long as he is dumb we can tell ourselves his desires are dark to us, and continue to use him as we wish' (142, 148).

Is Coetzee's fiction free from the exercise of that discursive aggression it so ironically displays, since it repeatedly and in different registers feigns woman's writing? The artifice of the rhetoric perhaps serves to foreground the fact that these texts are artefacts contrived by a masculine writer pursuing the possibilities of a non-phallocentric language. But why does a male novelist take the risk of simulating woman's speech, indeed her self-constitution in language (Magda declares 'I create myself in the words that create me', and Mrs Curren writes 'I render myself into words') while this same white novelist refrains from dissembling the voices of those excluded from the dominant discourse (where such voices are audible, their status as written by a white narrator is made apparent), instead elevating their silence as the sign of a transcendent state? If, as I have suggested, both the topos of silence and the imitations of a woman's writing act to transcribe and valorize the body as an agent of cognition, then both the claim that the fiction contrives to manifest an identification with feminism, and the charge that it consigns the dispossessed to a space outside discourse, could be dismissed as irrelevant to the novels' interests. Such an argument overlooks the fact that the effects of bestowing authority on the woman's text, while withholding discursive skills from the dispossessed, is to reinscribe, indeed re-enact, the received disposal of narrative power, where voice is correlated with cultural supremacy and voicelessness with subjugation; just as the homages to the mystical properties and prestige of muteness undermine the critique of that condition where oppression inflicts and provokes silence.

III

I have attempted to argue that Coetzee's narrative strategies both enact a critique of dominant discourses and pre-empt dialogue with non-canonical knowledges through representing these as ineffable. I now want to consider whether the noticeable absence of inflections from South Africa's non-Western cultures in the narrative structure, language, and ethos of Coetzee's fictions registers and repeats the exclusions of white writing, omissions on which Coetzee has commented in identifying 'the baffling and silencing of any counter-voice to the farmer/father' in the South African farm romance (*White Writing*, 135). The eclipse, the occultation, the silencing of the other is what South Africa's settler colonialism, as the self-appointed representative of Western civilization in Africa, was intent on effecting. Hence, the cognitive traditions and customs of South Africa's indigenous peoples were derogated and ignored, as were those of the practitioners of two world religions whose communities in South Africa were initially brought as slaves from the Dutch East Indies in the seventeenth century and as indentured labourers from the Indian subcontinent in the nineteenth century.

The paradox is that whereas the institutional structure of the previous South African regime internally duplicated the divide between the hemispheres, and its state apparatus exercised an imperialist ascendancy over neighbouring and *de jure* autonomous territories, within the orbit of imperialism's global system it was an outpost complicit with but on the boundaries of the West's power centres, its white comprador class deferential to the cultures of the metropolitan worlds. Such subservience was perpetuated, as Coetzee has shown in his essays, in the adoption/adaptation of established European fictional genres by both English and Afrikaans literatures, which, until the 1950s, were overwhelmingly aligned with, and served to naturalize, the ideology of white supremacy and segregation coterminous with Afrikaner, British, and subsequent diverse European settlement. Such writing is now virtually extinct, while a literature predominantly in English, but also increasingly in Afrikaans, positioned itself as opposed to the former status quo. But whether it was to classical and modernist realism or to postmodernism that they turned for inspiration and sustenance, writers until now have been dependent on metropolitan modes – although critics are now claiming that the later Nadine Gordimer, and those younger white writers who have transgressed cultural insulation and have assimilated knowledges and accents from which previous generations were through circumstance and choice isolated, are on the brink of inventing other forms in their plurally located and multiply voiced 'post-apartheid' novels.[6]

Meanwhile, the predominant mode of the South African novel, white and black, has remained social realism, a mode from which Coetzee, in his critical writings and novelistic practice, has intimated his distance.[7] If

6. On Gordimer, see Cooper, 'New Criteria'. The notion of the white 'post-apartheid novel' has been mooted by Graham Pechey in numerous reviews that have appeared in the *Southern African Review of Books*; see also his contribution to this volume.

7. The question of which mode exercises the most subversive power under contemporary South African conditions has been raised by Neil Lazarus, who argues for the subversive power of modernism; see 'Modernism and Modernity' (131–55).

Coetzee's own writing defamiliarizes the practices of white South African fiction, then its subversions of the representational paradigm also set it apart from black writing, which, for complex historical reasons, was similarly indebted to established Western modes, despite the ambition to register the heterogeneous black experience in its own oppositional terms and its own resistant voice.[8] The preference for a responsible realism aimed at reclaiming black history and registering black agency was reinforced on different grounds by 'cultural agendas' devised during the 1980s by the most visible organizations of the liberation movement. These decreed that writers commit themselves to developing a purposeful, expressive, and accessible literature depicting oppression, illuminating the struggle, and serving to raise consciousness. Such demands in turn generated a 'solidarity criticism', which by arguing that evaluation should be based on cultural function, inhibited the debate on what might constitute a revolutionary literature and art.[9] A climate in which established Anglo-American critical paradigms vied with political programmes for the arts is now changing. This is evident in the self-interrogations of critics and writers who as members of one or other community were aligned with the struggle against an oppressive regime, and who, as scholars, are aware that the discussion on autonomy and commitment in the arts in South Africa is in urgent need of redefinition.[10]

IV

It is from within this specific literary landscape that I now want to look at Coetzee's implementation of what he has referred to as 'a politics of writing for postcolonial literatures'. Detached from the hitherto predominant modes of South African writing, obliquely situated to the prevailing intellectual formations of his native land, whether white nationalism, liberalism, socialist-liberationism or black consciousness, and little touched by the autochthonous, transplanted, and recombinant cultures of South Africa's African, Asian, and coloured populations, Coetzee negotiates 'South Africa' as a referent in his fictions through defamiliarizing strategies that efface its spatial and temporal specificity,

8. See the essays by Nkosi, Ndebele, Parker, and Morphet. In a longer version of this essay, I attempt to address the different articulations of black writing by using the work of other critics (*New Formations* 21 (Winter 1994): 1–20).

9. See de Kok and Press, eds., *Spring is Rebellious*.

10. See Trump, ed., *Rendering Things Visible*, and de Kok and Press, eds. *Spring is Rebellious*.

denying it the identity of a social space and rejecting it as a site of cultural meanings. In one of the Attwell interviews, Coetzee, while speaking with admiration about the 'passionate intimacy with the South African landscape' of fellow-writer Breyten Breytenbach and the ostensible pleasure which playwright Athol Fugard takes in the beauty of South Africa (*Doubling the Point*, 377, 369), explains his own refusal to contrive 'nature description' of the Cape on the grounds that this represents no challenge to his 'power of envisioning', threatening 'only the tedium of reproduction' (142).

Such abstinence, I would argue, has further implications. In his critical writing, Coetzee has detected an impulse in the South African pastoral mode 'to find evidence of a "natural" bond between *volk* and *land*, that is to say, to naturalize the *volk's* possession of the land', observing too that 'the politics of expansion has uses for a rhetoric of the sublime' (*White Writing*, 61). It is these connections between landscape and the legitimizing narrative of the white nation which the novels sever by ostentatiously failing to register any signs of splendour in the very scenery that has inspired rhapsody.

Hence the terrain mapped by 'The Narrative of Jacobus Coetzee' constitutes an ideological cartography, the naming by an eighteenth-century explorer and proto-colonialist of rivers and mountains, and the designation of flora and fauna as yet uncatalogued in European taxonomies, establishing the authority of the invader's nomenclature and marking the act of territorial acquisition. Magda, in *In the Heart of the Country*, atones for her confession 'I am corrupted to the bone with the beauty of this forsaken world' (138) by spurning the favoured images of the South African pastoral tradition and rendering the scene as existentially sterile, her lapses into humanizing the spectacle being swiftly followed by recantation. The pastiche of naturalist conventions in the litany of place names that tracks Michael K's journey through the Cape Province registers the past occupation of the territory by Afrikaner and British settlement, but screens the meticulously inventoried locations from the infiltration of affect. In *Age of Iron*, the romance and promise with which European voyagers infused their accounts of the fairest Cape in all the world, the Cape of Good Hope, are demystified when the majestically serene and smiling peninsula of legend is configured in a rain-soaked suburb built with bricks made by convict labour, and the drably named 'False Bay' is redesignated a 'bay of false hope'.

In thus estranging and voiding of emotional investment a landscape named as the Cape, Coetzee's narrators effect a distancing from the historic claim to the land celebrated by white settler writing. But does not rendering a locale as null and void repeat that 'literature of empty landscape' which Coetzee has designated a literature of failure because it articulates a homelessness in Africa? Further, does not restricting the site of the colonial drama to the Cape act to produce a truncated version of the narrative of conquest which the fiction invents in 'The Narrative of Jacobus Coetzee'? Because the beginning colonial confrontation is played out here between Afrikaner and Khoi-San, the so-called Hottentots and Bushmen, whose resistance was effectively crushed, whose populations were decimated and whose cultures were dispersed, the boundedness of the staging excludes the violent and prolonged struggles that took place between the white settlers as they moved across the southern subcontinent and the Nguni- and Sotho-speaking peoples, struggles in which military defeat and dispossession did not entail genocide. And indeed, since Coetzee's fiction only leaves the Cape and its immediate hinterland for the unnamed and unspecified imperial frontier of *Waiting for the Barbarians*, and the textually received locations of *Foe*, it might perhaps even be seen as turning its face from Africa.

When Africans do enter the recent past of South Africa in *Age of Iron*, the passing of so pitiless an era is contemplated by the narrator as a return to kinder times, to the age of clay, the age of earth. A novel which speaks an intimacy with death was welcomed in reviews as an allegory where the narrator's affliction with cancer is a figure of a diseased body politic – and certainly this is a connection which her rhetoric insistently makes. But since the narrative of Mrs Curren's dying occupies a different discursive space from the story of South Africa's bloody interregnum, her terminal illness is detached from the demise of a malignant social order; while her salvation, effected by Vercueil, the tramp-as-figure-of-deliverance who ensures that in the disgraceful state of the old South Africa she will die in a state of grace, also draws attention to the absence of any prospect of another, transfigured social order. This withholding of a gesture to the politics of fulfilment in a novel which does intimate a personal redemption is made all the more conspicuous because the aspiration of the oppressed for emancipation detaches the narrator from an attachment to a liberal–humanist ethic; and the text's refusal to countenance the hope for a tomorrow – 'the future comes disguised, if it came naked we would be petrified by what we saw' (149) – is perhaps the strongest signification yet of the fiction's urge to mark its disengagement from the contingencies of a quotidian world in transition from colonialism.

All the same, another ending narrated by *Age of Iron* has very different resonances, for in taking to its limits the only political discourse to which she has access, the narrator recites a requiem for South African liberalism. For when she discerns the exclusions in an old photograph taken long ago in her grandfather's burgeoning garden, self-exculpation of her own ideology is suspended, and nostalgia for the golden days of her childhood, 'when the world was young and all things were possible' (51), is annulled:

> Who, outside the picture, leaning on their rakes, leaning on their spades, waiting to get back to work, lean also against the edge of the rectangle, bending it, bursting it in? . . . No longer does the picture show who were in the garden frame that day, but who were not there. Lying all these years in places of safekeeping across the country, in albums, in desk drawers, this picture and thousands like it have subtly matured, metamorphosed. The fixing did not hold or the developing went further than one would ever have dreamed . . . but they have become negatives again, a new kind of negative in which we begin to see what used to lie outside the frame, occulted. (102–3)

That this act of erasure in white self-representation cannot be restored by Mrs Curren's story is the burden of a narrative whose efforts to bring the blacks into representation issues in bathos, when pastiches of a benign naturalism and moral outrage all too familiar in the South African protest novel are offered, and the exhaustion of the liberal tradition of white fiction which this signals is confirmed by the death of its author. But does not this extended metaphor of the eclipse, the silencing, the occultation of the other in the chronicle of white South Africa have yet further reverberations which hark back to the exclusions, the holes in the narratives, 'the baffling of counter-voices' in Coetzee's own novels?

In protesting against the predicament of writing's compliant instrumentality, Coetzee as his own critic appears determined to detach his novels from their worldly connections. While it does not follow that his novels are so dissociated, I have considered here whether a body of fiction which is at such pains to avoid playing 'the flat historic scale' does not position barriers against readings that would privilege its secular particularity. The apparent referents of Coetzee's fictions have encouraged their literal interpretation as protests against colonial conquest, political torture, and social exploitation, while critics have argued that by subverting colonialism's oppressive discourses, his work performs 'a politics of writing'. What I have attempted to suggest is how a fiction which in its multivalence, formal inventiveness, and virtuoso self-inter-rogation of narrative production and authority remains unmatched in South African writing, is marked by the further singularity of a textual practice which dissipates the engagement with political conditions it also inscribes.

NOTE Although I am aware that they will continue to dissent from the revi-sions, I am indebted to the stringent criticisms made of an earlier version by Derek Attridge and David Attwell, which prompted me to reformulate some of the arguments.

Works cited

References to J. M. Coetzee's novels are to the Penguin editions, excepting
  Age of Iron, London: Secker & Warburg, 1990.
Ashcroft, Bill, Gareth Griffiths, and Helen Tiffin. *The Empire Writes Back:
  Theory and Practice in Post-colonial Literatures*. London: Routledge, 1989.
Attridge, Derek. 'Literary Form and the Demands of Politics: Otherness in
  J. M. Coetzee's *Age of Iron*'. *Aesthetics and Ideology*. Ed. George Levine.
  New Brunswick: Rutgers University Press, 1994.
  'Oppressive Silence: Coetzee's *Foe* and the Politics of the Canon'.
  *Decolonizing Tradition: New Views of Twentieth-Century 'British' Literary
  Canons*. Ed. Karen R. Lawrence. Urbana: University of Illinois Press,
  1992.
Attwell, David. 'The Problem of History in the Fictions of J. M. Coetzee'.
  Trump, ed., *Rendering Things Visible*, 94–133.
Castillo, Debra. 'Coetzee's *Dusklands*: The Mythic Punctum'. *PMLA* 105
  (1990): 1108–22.
Clingman, Stephen. *The Novels of Nadine Gordimer*. London: Allen & Unwin,
  1986.
Coetzee, J. M. *Doubling the Point: Essays and Interviews*. Ed. David Attwell.
  Cambridge, MA: Harvard University Press, 1992.
  White Writing: On the Culture of Letters in South Africa. New Haven: Yale
  University Press, 1988.
Cooper, Brenda. 'New Criteria for an "Abnormal Mutation": An Evaluation
  of Gordimer's *A Sport of Nature*'. Trump, ed., *Rendering Things Visible*,
  68–93.
de Kok, Ingrid, and Karen Press, eds. *Spring is Rebellious: Arguments about
  Cultural Freedom*. Cape Town: Buchu Books, 1990.
Dovey, Teresa. *The Novels of J. M. Coetzee: Lacanian Allegories*.
  Johannesburg: Ad Donker, 1988.

Gallagher, Susan VanZanten. *A Story of South Africa: J. M. Coetzee's Fiction in Context*. Cambridge, MA: Harvard University Press, 1991.

Huggan, Graham. 'Philomela's Retold Story: Silence, Music and the Postcolonial Text'. *Journal of Commonwealth Literature* 25. 1 (1990): 12–23.

Kristeva, Julia. *Desire in Language: A Semiotic Approach to Literature and Art*. Ed. Leon S. Roudiez. Oxford: Blackwell, 1981.

Lazarus, Neil. 'Modernism and Modernity: Adorno and Contemporary White South African Literature'. *Cultural Critique* 5 (1986/7): 131–55.

Levinas, Emmanuel. *Totality and Infinity*. Trans A. Lingis. Pittsburgh: Duquesne University Press, 1969.

Morphet, Tony. 'Cultural Imagination and Cultural Settlement'. *Pretexts* 2. 1 (Winter 1990): 94–103.

Ndebele, Njabulo. 'Redefining Relevance'. *South African Literature and Culture: Rediscovery of the Ordinary*. Introduction Graham Pechey. Manchester: Manchester University Press, 1994. 60–74.

Nkosi, Lewis. 'The New South African Novel: A Search for Modernism'. *Tasks and Masks: Themes and Styles of African Literature*. Harlow: Longman, 1981. 53–75.

Parker, Kenneth. '"Traditionalism" versus "Modernism": Culture, Ideology, Writing'. *The African Past and Contemporary Culture*. Ed. Erhard Reckwitz, et al. Essen: Die Blaue Eule, 1993. 21–42.

Penner, Dick. *Countries of the Mind: The Fictions of J. M. Coetzee*. New York: Greenwood Press, 1989.

Spivak, Gayatri. 'Theory in the Margin: Coetzee's *Foe* Reading Defoe's Crusoe/Roxana'. *Consequences of Theory*. Ed. Jonathan Arac and Barbara Johnson. Baltimore: Johns Hopkins University Press, 1991. 154–80.

Splendore, Paola. 'J. M. Coetzee's *Foe*: Intertextual and Metafictional Resonances'. *Commonwealth* 11. 1 (1988): 55–60.

Todorov, Tzvetan. *The Conquest of America: The Question of the Other*. Trans. Richard Howard. New York: Harper & Row, 1982.

Trump, Martin, ed. *Rendering Things Visible: Essays on South African Literary Culture*. Johannesburg: Ravan, 1990.

12

'Dialogue' and 'fulfilment'
in J. M. Coetzee's *Age of Iron*

DAVID ATTWELL

Conceding that J. M. Coetzee's fiction 'remains unmatched' in South African writing for its 'multivalence, formal inventiveness, and virtuoso self-interrogation of narrative production and authority', Benita Parry argues that Coetzee's writing 'dissipates the engagement with political conditions it also inscribes' (above, p. 164). In its general terms, a similar argument had a fair hearing as the most widely held view of Coetzee amongst the left in South Africa until about the mid-eighties, a view which was prominently endorsed by Nadine Gordimer in her review of *Life & Times of Michael K* in the *New York Review of Books*. There would be little point in turning over all this soil again; however, Parry's challenging critique raises certain issues that might profitably be taken up as a way of enabling us to understand more fully the dynamics of Coetzee's writing of the Emergency period. I refer here to the late eighties when the shreds of what passed for civil society under apartheid seemed finally to give way under the immense strains of the political struggle. The novel produced under – and in response to – these conditions was, of course, *Age of Iron*.

The two, I believe central, terms in Parry's argument that I shall take up are 'dialogue' and 'fulfilment'. With respect to dialogue, the 'principles around which novelistic meaning is organized in Coetzee's fictions owe nothing to knowledges which are *not* of European provenance' – the West therefore remains 'the culture of reference' (pp. 150–1). In addition, the argument is that Coetzee seems disinclined 'to orchestrate a polyphonic score'; that is to say, there ought to be a 'commerce with alterity' in which the other is represented 'not as a disarticulated presence but as an interlocutor' (p. 152). In relation to fulfilment, Parry laments 'the absence of any prospect of another, transfigured social order' and the 'withholding of a gesture to the politics of fulfilment' (p. 162). In this respect, Coetzee repeats the literature of empty landscape about which he himself is so trenchant in *White Writing*, where homelessness in colonial and settler writing is read as symptomatic of the failure to imagine Africa as a place of community.

In response, firstly, to the strictures concerning dialogue, one must begin by remarking that if Coetzee were to engage with 'non-Western' knowledge systems – assuming he had ready access to them – and if he were to 'orchestrate a polyphonic score', he would not make the West any less the principal 'culture of reference' in his fiction. Parry's concern, as I read it, is largely with the problem of authority, and in this regard if Coetzee were to make the gestures being called for, this would not solve the problem – if anything, it would surely compound it, for Coetzee, like any 'postcolonizing' writer, could only make such gestures from within the limits of his historical and epistemological position. Even if a writer of Coetzee's skill could pull it off, avoiding serious blunders of cultural misrecognition, he would in effect only be consolidating the authority which Parry accuses him of wielding without sufficient deference. But there is another layer of awkwardness here which has to do with the nature of fictional language. The demands Parry makes on Coetzee would have more obvious relevance to a writer who sought an unqualified assent from the reader to the fictional world, an assent in which the gap between fiction and reality is reduced by convention to the point of being inconsequential; that is to say, the argument's purchase depends on the notion of a fairly simple correspondence between the play of events in the narrative and the kind of social order that well-meaning people would like to see brought into being. However, self-evidently, while Coetzee's work does invest in the construction of a fictional world to which we give partial assent – we cannot discount this dimension of narrative, since it is the source of much of our experience of pleasure or pain as readers – it also forces us to recognize the distance between itself and the real (and between itself and the political notion of an imminently benevolent society), thus inviting us to attend more closely to the performative features of the language. Since this is Coetzee's narrative mode, if it is to encode a social vision it will do so *in terms of* its commitment to aesthetic self-reflection. We need to recognise that a novel like *Age of Iron* will not stage certain interclass and intercultural encounters purely as object-lessons in social conduct; it will be about alterity itself, in both the thematic and performative senses – in other words, the work thematizes, performs, and thus reflects on, various modes of alterity. As we shall see, the polyphony Parry desires is present in full measure in *Age of Iron*, but it is also shown to be entirely contingent on an aesthetic mode of discourse whose social power – and, judged in a certain light, lack of social power – is made the subject of reflection. But let me proceed more slowly.

In part, in its handling of alterity *Age of Iron* breaks ground which had been somewhat intractable in Coetzee's previous novel, *Foe*. In that work, the tongueless Friday represents the unassimilable other whose silent presence overshadows the authority of the two author-figures, Susan Barton and Foe himself. Although he is there to reveal the contingency and precariousness of the voices of those who can speak, Friday is not indeed, in Parry's terms, an interlocutor, for while he produces meaning by other symbolic gestures (music, dance, the scattering of petals) he remains silent. In *Age of Iron* it is quite different; here, ethnographic and class differences are revealed in their specific detail. Far from being thematized as a rather inscrutable if compelling force, alterity is given a social density in the later novel. In one especially memorable moment, Mrs Curren is forced to acknowledge that the unnamed township dweller who rebukes her efforts to articulate a position on the violence around her – 'To speak of this', says Mrs Curren, 'you would need the tongue of a god' – is quite correct: '"This woman talks shit," . . . "Yes," I said, . . . "you are right, what you say is true"' (91; references to Secker & Warburg edition). Undoubtedly, it is an interlocutor in Parry's sense to whom Mrs Curren is speaking – and there are other such interlocutors: Florence, Thabane, the boy who partly to rebuke Mrs Curren calls himself 'John'. The novel recognizes that there is polyphony, but not enough *reciprocity*: as Mrs Curren says, 'To have opinions in a vacuum, opinions that touch no one, is, it seems to me, nothing. Opinions must be heard by others, heard and weighed' (148).

The self-consciousness about alterity that we find in *Foe* is therefore present in *Age of Iron*, though on new terms. Mrs Curren, in fact, makes several cogent efforts to engage with what she understands to be the life-world and subjectivity of those who are most socially distant from her. Such moments deserve some attention in the light of Parry's accusation that Coetzee's narrators seldom project themselves out of their own sphere. One such moment involves Mrs Curren's giving Florence a lift to her husband's place of work, where she discovers that his job is to kill chickens. The repetitive and desultory violence of the task leaves Mrs Curren bewildered at first but later she reflects on what she has seen in terms that comprise a startling description of the effects of racial capitalism in South Africa – perhaps the country's unique contribution to the project of modernity:

But my mind would not leave the farm, the factory, the *enterprise* where the husband of the woman who lived side by side with me worked, where day after day he bestrode his pen, left and right, back and forth, around and around, in a smell of blood and feathers, in an uproar of outraged squawking, reaching down, scooping up, gripping, binding, hanging. I thought of all the men across the breadth of South Africa who, while I sat gazing out of the window, were killing chickens, moving earth, barrowful upon barrowful; of all the women sorting oranges, sewing buttonholes. Who would ever count them, the spadefuls, the oranges, the buttonholes, the chickens? A universe of labour, a universe of counting: like sitting in front of a clock all day, killing the seconds as they emerged, counting one's life away. (41)

Could the materialist reader wish for a more satisfying picture of alienated labour? Coetzee's interests, of course, go directly to what it means to the worker and his family – and more immediately to the observer of the work, in this case Mrs Curren – that he should be habituated to a daily grind involving such perfunctory carnage. Surprisingly, as part of the answer to this question, Coetzee suggests that William (as he is known by Mrs Curren) and his family are not, in fact, in any way afflicted by psychic terror as a result of the work he performs:

Five o'clock came, the end of the day, and I said goodbye. While I was driving back to this empty house, William took Florence and the children to the living-quarters. He washed; she cooked a supper of chicken and rice on the paraffin stove, then fed the baby. It was Saturday. Some of the other farm-workers were out visiting, recreating themselves. So Florence and William were able to put the children to bed in an empty bunk and go for a walk, just the two of them, in the warm dusk. (39)

The point of the passage is that it continues Mrs Curren's efforts to come to terms with a particular kind of alterity. It goes on to describe events of the following day: a leisurely Sunday in William and Florence's household, with a visit to Florence's sister where the family gathers for lunch, sleepy children, a careless dog, the exchange of money for a child's upkeep, and in the evening, the long journey by several buses back to Mrs Curren's house in the suburbs. In other words, despite the stark otherness registered by Mrs Curren when she confronts the material base of urban black life, she refuses to allow it to condition her apprehension of Florence's world entirely. The refusal is explicit: 'All of this happened. All of this must have happened. It was an ordinary afternoon in Africa: lazy weather, a lazy day. Almost it is possible to say: this is how life should be' (40). Is Mrs Curren trying to disavow the knowledge the visit has afforded her, and is her voice being presented ironically, as lacking all credibility? Surely not: the detailed description of the casual Sunday activity in Florence's household is convincing – so much so that it would be easy to forget that it is all Mrs Curren's construction – and its purpose, rather, is to oppose the possibility of an alterity so radical that there are no grounds for intersubjective recognition. The key phrase here is 'an ordinary afternoon in Africa', with the word *ordinary* invoking, no doubt – at this moment in South African literary debate – Njabulo Ndebele's much-discussed critique of the 'spectacular' in black South African fiction. 'Ordinariness', as the valued alternative to the 'spectacular', represents Ndebele's attempt precisely to define a mode of oppositional writing which declined the radical antitheses of apartheid, and which also affirmed the capacity for survival in the day-to-day ingenuity of township dwellers, children particularly, but also mothers, commuters, teachers. Like Ndebele then, Coetzee associates the creative transgressions of which narrative fiction is capable with a refusal to participate in the kind of dogmatic insistence on absolute difference which has been the bane of everyone's existence in South Africa, and his particular contribution to this debate is to note the uncanny coexistence of ordinariness with the routinized violence of certain forms of labour in black life. There is more than a 'commerce with alterity' here; there is also a minor polemic about how alterity is to be weighed and understood in context.

Mrs Curren is capable not only of refusing to see the other as non-human, but also of reading herself *through* those whom she is disinclined to love. This is apparent, for instance, in her efforts at imagining the last moments of 'John' before he is shot dead by police in the servant's quarters of her backyard, ostensibly as a member of a guerrilla cell. Whilst her distance from John is not sentimentalized – she imagines him sitting facing the door through which the gunfire will burst in and destroy him, fondling a pistol between his knees in a gesture of masturbation which emulates the masculine heroism she abhors – nevertheless, she concentrates her efforts on reconstructing his encounter with death precisely because his anticipation of it mirrors her own:

> His eyes are unblinking, fixed on the door through which he is going to leave the world. His mouth is dry but he is not afraid. His heart beats steadily like a fist in his chest clenching and unclenching.
>
> His eyes are open and mine, though I write, are shut. My eyes are shut in order to see.

Within this interval there is no time, though his heart beats time. I am here in my room in the night but I am also with him, all the time . . .

A hovering time, but not eternity. A *time being*, a suspension, before the return of the time in which the door bursts open and we face, first he, then I, the great white glare. (159–60)

The paradox of Mrs Curren's eyes being shut 'in order to see' – and to write – raises Coetzee's emphasis on allowing writing to circumvent prevailing socio-ethical conditions and to assert an alternative frame of reference. In *Doubling the Point* Coetzee reflects on the imaginative confinement which seems endemic to the South African situation, and compares South Africa with Eastern Europe before 1989. Whereas Zbigniew Herbert, in a poem such as 'Five Men', could assert the social vitality of a pastoral convention in response to political barbarism, Coetzee feels that in South Africa such traditions do not have the same purchase: 'In Africa the only address one can imagine is a brutally direct one, a sort of pure, unmediated representation.' And he qualifies the remark thus: '"The only address one can imagine" – an admission of defeat. *Therefore*, the task becomes one of imagining this unimaginable, imagining a form of address that permits the play of writing to start taking place' (67–8). This is characteristic of much of Coetzee's later writing, which derives in part from a struggle with what, in his Jerusalem Prize acceptance speech of 1987, he calls 'truth by the bucketful'. On this occasion, Coetzee compared his situation to that of another Eastern European, Milan Kundera, the previous recipient of the Jerusalem Prize, who in his acceptance speech had paid tribute to Cervantes. What is it, Coetzee asks, that prevents the South African writer from shaking the dust of La Mancha off his feet like Don Quixote and entering 'the realm of faery'?

What prevents him is what prevents Don Quixote himself: the *power* of the world his body lives in to impose itself on him and ultimately on his imagination, which, whether he likes it or not, has its residence in his body. The *crudity* of life in South Africa, the naked force of its appeals, not only at the physical level but at the moral level too, its callousness and its brutalities, its hungers and its rages, its greed and its lies, make it as irresistible as it is unlovable. (*Doubling the Point*, 98–9)

Interestingly, the Polish critic Stanislaw Baranczak uses a similar metaphor to Coetzee's notion of imagining the unimaginable when describing the situation of the Eastern European before 1989. Extrapolating from a satirical story by Stanislaw Lem, Baranczak describes life under an 'Immovable History' as 'breathing under water', suggesting the unreality of the politically admissible language. Under such conditions, the task of a 'Recalcitrant Literature' becomes one of doing what comes naturally – in other words, coming up for air (*Breathing Under Water*, 6). That Baranczak can link literary language with the natural air we breathe is a good illustration of Coetzee's point: 'imagining the unimaginable' very precisely involves finding a language that *does not* come naturally. This is a measure of how far Coetzee feels himself to be *detached* from Europe – to return briefly to Parry's point in this regard – since its conventions seem to have no ready connection with the context. Coetzee's relation to European traditions is perhaps not altogether unlike Mrs Curren's attempts to listen to classical music on the short-wave radio: 'If one persists into the unlikely hours of the night there are stations that relent and play music. Fading in, fading out, I heard last night – from where? Helsinki? the Cook Islands? – anthems of all the nations, celestial music, music that left us years ago and now comes back from the stars transfigured' (20). At the very least, Coetzee knows only too well that the traditions of Europe need to be reconfigured if they are to be made to speak to Africa. The question arises: is Coetzee's 'unrepresentable Africa' the same kind of disorientation of European perceptions on the African landscape that we are familiar with since at least *Heart of Darkness*? Or is it rather the result of contemporary political conditions which are more than usually stressful? I would of course argue the latter, partly because with all her political credentials, Nadine Gordimer shares Coetzee's concerns when she says that in South Africa the 'morality of life and the morality of art have broken out of their categories in social flux. If you cannot reconcile them, they cannot be kept from one another's throats, within you.' Speaking confessionally, she adds, the 'coexistence of these absolutes often seems irreconcilable within one life, for me' (quoted in *Doubling the Point*, 385). Both Coetzee and Gordimer attest to an agonistic condition in which the writer in the Emergency years is forced to reconstruct the literary enterprise in the teeth of a historical situation which seems confining and/or predatory for writers. The responses of the two authors to their predicament are, of course, markedly different, and Coetzee's sense of Gordimer's achievement is that 'she does not thrive on strife': 'She is not even, in a fundamental sense, a political writer. Rather, she is an ethical writer, a writer of conscience, who finds herself in an age when any transcendental basis for ethics (as for aesthetics) is being denied in the name of politics' (*Doubling the Point*, 387–8). In this reading, Gordimer's *œuvre* is a record of her efforts to heal the wounds of self-division. By contrast, Coetzee has chosen to represent the conflict over the status of fictionality *within* his fiction: where there is loss of authority, where imaginative possibilities seem curtailed by historical forces, Coetzee has reached more deeply into the traditions of his formation in order to subsume and, indeed, transcend the agonistic position. His project thus renders the aesthetic more resilient, enabling it to speak to the political on more or less equal terms.

I turn now to Parry's point concerning 'fulfilment', the idea being that Coetzee's fiction is marked by the absence of a 'transfigured social order'. Some of the discussion in *Doubling the Point* anticipates Parry's argument in this respect, for when I put it to Coetzee that while contemporary white literature has been more successful at 'subverting colonial traditions than at replacing them with the imaginative possibility of a moral community', this was his reply:

> I agree with every word you say; I hesitate only in the face of the shadow of an implication . . . that imagining such a possibility is a duty that falls upon writers (white or black or neither white nor black), one they have failed to perform. And my hesitation is not in relation to the notion of the duty itself (that is another story for another occasion; I will accept it as given in the present argument), nor in relation to the failure to perform that duty, but in relation to the question of where that duty comes from. To me, duty can be of two kinds: it can be an obligation imposed on the writer by society, by the soul of society, by society in its hopes and dreams; or it can be something constitutional to the writer, what one might loosely call conscience but what I would tentatively prefer to call an imperative, a transcendental imperative. All I want to say here, in this tiny demurral, is that I would not want to favor the first definition unhesitatingly over the second. (339–40)

Parry's demand, it seems to me, is expressed very much in terms of the first duty defined here, whereas Coetzee wishes to protect the space of the second, that which is 'constitutional to the writer'. Elaborating on the notion of a 'transcendental imperative', which he sees as intrinsic to this second concept of duty, Coetzee explains that he does not see himself as a herald of community – '[t]o be a herald you would have to have slipped your chains for a while and wandered about in the real world' – but as someone 'who has intimations of freedom . . . and constructs images of people slipping their chains and turning their faces to the light'. His role, he adds, evoking Kant, is not to represent freedom 'an sich', since freedom itself cannot be imagined (341). The metaphor of confinement in this instance is, of course, Platonic – the metaphor of the cave – and the analogy is between confinement in a hostile historical situation and the cave of ordinary experience from which, Plato argues, we cannot directly apprehend the essences of things. We shall have to account for Coetzee's dabbling in the language of the sublime through his allusions to Kant and Plato; they are, it is true, striking in a writer whose work is demonstrably sensitive to its own historicity – the paradox will have to be carefully understood. But first I shall return to *Age of Iron* in order to establish whether, and in what form it contains the notion of a 'transcendental imperative', for the answer to Parry's charge must obviously be sought here.

Commentators who – with the 'literariness' of *Foe* in mind – have remarked on the strongly 'realist' qualities of *Age of Iron* (referring to what I have called the novel's social density, the graphic depictions of township violence, and so on) have played down the transformative role played by the novel's mode of address and by Vercueil. Coetzee has done this to us before, of course: in *Life and Times of Michael K* we have a lavishly specific account of a civil war into which is inserted a leading protagonist who is able not to feel the weight of that history bearing down upon him. The interest lies precisely in the tension between the closely realized social texture and the literary re-working of that ground in the name of another, transformative level of consciousness. *Age of Iron* combines similar elements: Vercueil is not a historical being, or if he is that – as a recognizable tramp surviving in the crannies of the suburbs – he is so only in part. Attempts to fix Vercueil's social position ethnographically, as several critics have done abroad (where it seems South Africa's history of racial othering is at times mesmerizing) are particularly misconceived. Vercueil's role – as with Michael K's – is to serve as an Archimedean point of reference outside of the dimensions of what is recognizably real, and outside of Mrs Curren's world, and thus to enable her to speak from within her consciousness of impending death. 'Why do I write about him?' she asks. 'Because in the look he gives me I see myself in a way that can be written' (8). Similarly, the mode of address in *Age of Iron* is refracted back, as it were, from the moment of death: in order to participate in the novel's meaning, we accept the impossibility of Mrs Curren's narration of her own death, and of her making the manuscript – with its description of the 'final embrace' which takes her life away – into a parcel which she entrusts to Vercueil to mail to the daughter in the United States. As readers, we 'intercept' this process and become privy to a text which is intended only for the eyes of the daughter. The significance of this refracted narration can be read in various ways: as reflecting the ungroundedness of meaning in postmodern culture, perhaps, where value has no existence apart from the acts of language in which it is realized; or as reflecting something of Coetzee's own situation as a white writer in South Africa, that is, his having to speak, rather like Mrs Curren herself, from a tenuous historical position. Neither of these explanations, however, accounts for the urgency of the narrative voice and the anguish we are made to share as the recipients of a strikingly intimate presence, one whose dis-embodiment is palpable. Quite apart from his being linked in Mrs Curren's mind with the news of her condition (he arrives on the day she hears it, thus acquiring the status of her 'Angel of Death'), Vercueil's presence and the mode of address are clearly connected: 'If Vercueil does not send these writings on, you will never read them. You will never know they existed. A certain body of truth will never take on flesh: my truth: how I lived in these times, in this place' (119).

The question, then, is not what the novel can or cannot achieve by its grappling with historical time as an approximation of South African conditions, but what it achieves by its *suspension* of historical time through the narrative conventions it deploys, and whether that suspension can be said to have a reciprocal effect on our perceptions of what is socially possible. In this respect, it seems to me that what the novel achieves is to stage, or to have performed, a certain consciousness which the society would ordinarily choose to ignore or to deride. Through the apparent unreality of its aesthetic code, the novel gives consideration to those things for which in a revolutionary situation there is literally no time: 'I am trying to keep a soul alive in times not hospitable to the soul' (119), says Mrs Curren. Vercueil is by no means a conscious agent of sublime transformation: handed a charitable mug of coffee, he spits at Mrs Curren's feet, at which she realizes his corporeality only too well: 'His word, his kind of word, from his own mouth, warm at the instant when it left him. A word, undeniable, from a language before language' (7); nevertheless, Mrs Curren projects on to him associations drawn from her education and reading which grant him multivalent powers. As a former seaman he is her Ulysses, charting elements as unfamiliar as those she will shortly travel; as Virgil to her Dante, he will enable her to discover her own powers of articulation over the realm of the dead; as her Angel of

Death, he seems, among other things, to be living confirmation of the grim message she has received from Dr Syfret, a message whose alterity is perhaps the most difficult of all. Whilst his full significance must always remain partly obscure (in Afrikaans, 'verskuil' means hidden, 'verkul' deceived), he is also a paradoxically enabling presence who reminds Mrs Curren of boundaries to be transcended.

And so we return to Coetzee's 'transcendental imperative'. Since they make it possible for Mrs Curren to speak that which otherwise would not be spoken, the presence of Vercueil and the refraction of the narration back from the moment of death would seem to be the narratological forms taken by the transcendental imperative in this novel. The significance of the formal innovation – which amounts to a strategy of tactical circumvention – is felt ultimately in the novel's treatment of the subject of ethics. We are not speaking here of this or that particular ethical code, but whether the society in question has a culturally embedded code of ethics to which most of its members have shared access. And of course, in the absence of such a shared basis for judgement, the novel performs an ethical consciousness in the place where it has been vitiated, simply because there is no alternative to doing so – ethics, in this sense, is what we turn to because we lack secure foundations for conduct. Mrs Curren makes the point directly: 'Because I cannot trust Vercueil I must trust him' (119), and later, 'the inexplicable: the ground of all ethics. Things we do not do' (180). In larger cultural terms, this imaginative re-creation of the grounds of ethical consciousness is the positive side of the absence of a highly conventionalized language such as Coetzee regrets not having when he refers to Eastern Europe, for the lack forces him into reconstructing the language of value in a manner which immeasurably enriches his writing.

Coetzee does allusively give positive content to certain ethical propositions in *Age of Iron*, although these propositions are always offered, as it were, in the subjunctive mood. The novel's ethics work partly by counterposing the degenerate age of iron in Hesiod's *Works and Days* – whence the novel's title – with the redemptive figure of the Angel of Death. Whilst there might be a tenuous association here with the biblical angel who appears at the first Passover – Vercueil would preserve the bond between mother and daughter by passing on the letter – there are more obviously relevant allusions to Angels of Death in Tolstoy's story 'What Men Live By', and in Kant's early work, *Observations on the Feeling of the Beautiful and the Sublime*, which

Hannah Arendt reads as a precursor to the *Critique of Judgement*. The age of iron as it appears in Hesiod has since become conventionalized as a time of moral inversions and distortions: 'Father shall not be like to his children, neither the children like unto the father: neither shall guest to host, nor friend to friend, nor brother to brother be dear as aforetime: and they shall give no honour to their swiftly ageing parents, and shall chide them with words of bitter speech, sinful men, knowing not the fear of the gods' (Hesiod, *Poems and Fragments*, 7). As Susan Gallagher has shown, the novel exploits these inversions, paying particular attention to the effects of revolution on childhood and the relationships between parents and children. In this context, Tolstoy's angel comes to teach the shoemaker, Simon, and his wife that 'though it seems to men that they should live by care for themselves, in truth it is love alone by which they live' ('What Men Live By', 81); appropriately, Mrs Curren learns to love those whom she is least inclined to love, notably Bheki and his friend 'John'.

In Kant's *Observations*, the Angel of Death appears in a 'thought-experiment' in which the miser, Carazan, is admonished by being made to experience the horror of eternal silence and solitude. Arendt reads this as an important moment in the development of the Kantian notion of 'sociability', that is, the idea that people 'are interdependent not merely in their needs and cares but in their highest faculty, the human mind, which will not function outside human society' (*Lectures on Kant's Political Philosophy*, 10–12). I have turned to Arendt's reading of Kant because it enables us to put Coetzee's dabbling in the language of the sublime into proper perspective: the allusions to Kant (as well as those to Tolstoy and Plato) contribute to a strain of muted ethical utopianism that one finds without searching too far in most of Coetzee's fiction, a utopianism that amounts to an attempt to work around the denial of reciprocity that seems entrenched in colonial relationships. Just as Arendt, in the wake of European fascism, turns to Kant's notions of 'communication, intersubjective agreement, and shared judgement' in an attempt to construct, or more accurately to *reconstruct* 'an account of moral life that recognizes the nonself-evidency of moral propositions' (in Arendt, *Lectures*, 112), so Coetzee turns to similar resources in an attempt to achieve what he somewhat misleadingly calls transcendence, that is to say, to project, through self-consciously textual performance, the possibility of an ethical community in a society which historically has shown little propensity to achieve such a state. As with Coetzee's handling of alterity, there is most certainly a gesture towards what Parry calls fulfilment, but it is a question of understanding it first on its own terms, and then in relation to its situational context.

I shall close on a different note. Despite the substantive ethical 'load' which can be deduced from the allusions in Coetzee's treatment of ethics in *Age of Iron*, we also need to bear in mind the novel's insistence that its ethical propositions are grounded – so to speak – only in its textual performance. Mrs Curren does not bequeath meaning to the daughter in any final sense: what the daughter receives – and what we who intercept the memoir actualize for ourselves – is the staging of that meaning. As Mrs Curren is metamorphosed from the half-life or 'doll-life' that she is reduced to by her social position and history, she thinks of herself as a moth that 'will brush your cheek ever so lightly as you put down the last page of this letter . . . It is not my soul that will remain with you but the spirit of my soul, the breath, the stirring of the air about these words, the faintest of turbulence traced in the air by the ghostly passage of my pen over the paper your fingers now hold' (119). Derek Attridge speaks of the need to think of Mrs Curren's ethical sensitivity in a verbal sense, that is, to see it 'as an activity that does not correspond to a noun. The gift that the letter represents can only be produced and received as an act' (3). And Michael Marais usefully points out that this self-conscious textualization effectively transfers authorial responsibility to the reader ('"Who Clipped the Hollyhocks?"', 23). As Coetzee himself put it in *Doubling the Point*, before *Age of Iron* had appeared in print:

> There is no ethical imperative that I claim access to. Mrs Curren is the one who believes in *should*, who believes in *believes in*. As for me, the book is written, it will be published, nothing can stop it. The deed is done, what power was available to me is exercised. (250)

Works cited

Arendt, Hannah. *Lectures on Kant's Political Philosophy*. Ed. Ronald Beiner. Brighton: Harvester, 1982.

Attridge, Derek. 'Trusting the Other: Ethics and Politics in J. M. Coetzee's *Age of Iron*'. *South Atlantic Quarterly* 93 (1994): 59–82.

Attwell, David. *J. M. Coetzee: South Africa and the Politics of Writing*. Berkeley and Cape Town: University of California Press and David Philip, 1993.

Baranczak, Stanislaw. *Breathing Under Water and other East European Essays*. Cambridge, MA: Harvard University Press, 1990.

Coetzee, J. M. *Doubling the Point: Essays and Interviews*. Ed. David Attwell. Cambridge, MA: Harvard University Press, 1992.

Gallagher, Susan VanZanten. *A Story of South Africa: J. M. Coetzee's Fiction in Context*. Cambridge, MA: Harvard University Press, 1991.

Gordimer, Nadine. 'The Idea of Gardening'. *New York Review of Books*, 2 February 1984: 3, 6.

Hesiod. *Poems and Fragments*. Trans. A. W. Mair. Oxford: Clarendon Press, 1908.

Marais, Michael. '"Who Clipped the Hollyhocks?": J. M. Coetzee's *Age of Iron* and the Politics of Representation'. *English in Africa* 20. 2 (October 1993): 1–24.

Tolstoy, Leo. 'What Men Live By'. *Twenty-Three Tales* (1906). Trans. Louise and Aylmer Maude. London: Oxford University Press, 1960.

13

Interview

MONGANE WALLY SEROTE,
INTERVIEWED BY ROLF SOLBERG

This exchange is abstracted from an interview recorded in Cape Town on 9
May 1995. It was edited by Malcolm Hacksley and published by the National
English Literary Museum in Grahamstown, South Africa, in a collection of
interviews with black South African writers entitled *Reflections: Perspectives
on Writing in Post-Apartheid South Africa (1996)*.

RS Would you fill me in briefly about your personal background, some
of the factors that formed the writer and politician Wally Serote as he
appears today?

MWS I was born in Alexandra, a highly politicized community. For one
reason or another, I thought I wanted to write and I started writing at quite
an early age. The two, politics and writing, have played a key role in my
formation as a person: the two feed on each other. My political involvement, being an active member of the ANC, MK, and the underground
structures of the African National Congress, has helped me to understand the dynamics of people. That in itself has fed into what I write.

RS You served time in detention. Was that in the early seventies?

MWS I was detained in 1969.

RS Were you subjected to harsh treatment?

MWS First of all I was detained under what they called the Terrorism
Act, Section 6, which means that you were kept in solitary confinement,
incommunicado. You were entirely in the hands of the security police. I
was harshly tortured, physically. There are two things we should talk
about here. The first is the spiritual, psychological torture. I was in solitary confinement for nine months. That in itself is extreme torture for a
human being, but we were also physically brutalized. However, in circumstances of that nature one discovers, if one has convictions, a human
treasure: resilience. That contributes towards continuously rebelling
against what is unjust. Rather than having been subdued, many of us
came out feeling very strongly that something had to be done to overcome the evil of the apartheid system.

RS If I may turn in the direction of literature now: Albie Sachs suggested putting a ban on the Struggle as a theme for writers. In one of your essays in *On the Horizon* you compare the effects of protest and resistance poetry with soap: it cleanses. You go on to say: 'Like soap, that poetry is finished. It's gone. It's done its job. Screaming poetry has rendered the poet hoarse. And those who wrote swearing poetry must only be a bit embarrassed by it now.' Would you like to comment on that?

MWS One must recognize that I was speaking about a spirit and a consciousness of defiance. I don't want to call anything protest poetry. It is a very unfortunate category and name. I do recognize that there are phases that a writer moves through. Writers are the most unfortunate artists because they grow through speaking loudly in public and everybody remembers what they say. Lots of other people also do that, but then people forget what they have said. That's why I don't like to call it protest poetry. There is a growing process where one is outraged, where one wants to say that in one's clearest voice and one uses all sorts of mechanisms to do that. Some of this in our time was the swearing poetry, the sloganeering poetry. It served its purpose at that time. We should not discard it. It is part of ourselves.

I am calling writers to realize that even when we were doing that we were addressing a key issue which is going to remain with the human race forever, and that is human nature and human relations. The crisis before us is about this, but so is the ecstasy of being alive. This is what we writers must fine-tune and sharpen our skills to deal with and understand and write about.

RS You come from a socialist background. Would you define yourself today as a socialist, a communist?

MWS I have learnt a lot by having been a communist. One basic thing I learnt was the value one places on life, human nature, human relations, and people. I think this is the basic principle of communism. It always tries to address those issues. I think I have developed and become a broad-minded person through having been a communist. I still want to be a communist. I realize that certain things happened in the Eastern Block which challenged some of the fundamental principles and issues raised by communism.

But I want to say this: there is nothing which communism did – talking about the history of the Eastern Bloc – which capitalism did not do. Nothing! Human suffering, totalitarianism, harsh reality for people, all of those things are happening today as well. The fact that capitalism at present still maintains power and control in the world is a different issue. I do not accept capitalism as an alternative for anything.

We now have to address the question of what we can actually do to change relationships in the world, so that more and more people have access to quality of life. South Africa was one of the capitalist countries that articulated how human values and human rights can be absolutely violated. I have still to see one country in the world which has not done that.

RS In a paper at a UNESCO seminar in Dakar in 1989 on 'Cultural Resistance, Mobilization and People's Freedom' you talk about three films on South Africa. You say that the film *A World Apart* 'expresses strength by basing every detail of its story on the organized masses', while André Brink's *A Dry White Season*, on the other hand, 'lacks this important element, is weakened by using individuals as the basis of history'. Would you like to enlarge on these statements?

MWS I come from a culture of struggle. My childhood, my youth, my adulthood were spent in struggle. I have come to understand very clearly that the condition of the world is not changed by fate. Nor is it changed accidentally or by individuals. Changes take place when people are informed, when people are conscious, when people identify common goals and common objectives, and in certain circumstances are prepared to make sacrifices for that. When masses of people do that the world can be changed. It is a very important phenomenon of change and it is my point of reference for charting what happens in the world. That is what we mean by democracy, rule by the majority, and the majority must consist of increasingly greater numbers of people.

RS But wouldn't you say that, for the viewer to become emotionally involved in a film, the individual is important? Wouldn't the masses be much too general for the film audience to achieve a sense of personal involvement and identification with them? It is that element of identification which, in my view, the Brink film does have.

MWS It is very important that the masses are involved in everything. Within the context of the masses of course there will be individuals who excel, who do outstanding things, but when that happens it happens precisely because one also has the backing of the masses. I don't subscribe to the manner in which films are made in Hollywood where individuals can change the whole world, nor do I subscribe to the simplistic approach of some European novels where one person is a hero or a heroine. There is nothing like that, it's fiction. I come from a culture and a struggle which has created millions of heroes and heroines in the context of the masses. People excel in different ways.

RS What kind of themes do you see on the horizon for the young guard of black South African writers?

MWS At a certain point we were really charged with compassion and idealism. Now we are living a real reality. For a long time the two opposites, the ideal world and the real world, are going to form the basis of a very strong articulation on the part of the writers. I am in the fortunate position that I understand how the state machinery, the so-called bureaucratic machinery, works. I can see the gulf between that machinery and the perceptions of need and the reality of ordinary people outside all that. There is a very big gulf. Our challenge is to narrow this gap.

Government has to start with the process of legislation. I look at the process itself – it's a very long-drawn-out thing – and I am hit by reality. It is important that the process should take the route that it takes, that it is debated in the manner that it is, but the worst part is that there is no mechanism that explains these processes to the ordinary people.

I hope that writers will enter this area and objectively assess it. On one hand I am saying that there should be high expectations, it's correct for people to have high expectations. On the other, I also expect there to be debate about legislation. There is a contradiction in what I am saying. We have to look at this contradiction and say: What do we do? What is the humanly possible thing to do in these circumstances? There is a challenge here, looking us straight in the face.

RS Turning to language, you say in your poem *Come and Hope With Me* (1994), 'we must delight in the orchestra of our many languages', and you have stated very clearly that you support the idea of having eleven official South African languages of equal status.

MWS When it comes to the cultural aspect, I would say it is wrong for any country to suppress people's cultures. I associate the question of multilingualism with the multicultural nature of our country. It is very important for South Africa to stimulate and to promote multiculturalism to its full blossoming, as we should also do with its languages. By doing so, we are empowering the nation itself and the individuals and collectives within the nation. This is very important. I don't think it is correct, as happened in the past, that 'literate' means you can speak English. There are many people in this country who are literate but don't speak English, and there are many who are literate but can't speak Afrikaans. These people must come to the front and be recognized for what they are.

The other important thing is that having been dominated by European culture in this country, we have almost completely sacrificed the wisdoms, gems, and treasures of African culture. It is high time that those are articulated through the African languages in this country.

RS May I bring up another issue, a major issue also in South Africa – that of women's liberation? Your poetry breathes love and respect for woman – both mother and lover. I am thinking especially of a poem like 'No Baby Must Weep', but one finds this attitude all through your work. Clearly a lot of South African men do not share this attitude. Is this an issue that ought to be addressed with a view to changing male chauvinist attitudes throughout the 'Rainbow' spectrum?

MWS Yes, I think so. Let me state two points. Firstly, it is correct that there was inequality between the sexes in our traditional cultures. We must make sure that we protect equality between men and women in South Africa. I draw a distinction and say that I don't think it is correct to say that men and women are the same. It can never mean that, it must not mean that! If we say that, we are going to violate human nature itself. It is important that women are women and that men are men, but we are all equal. We must find out what our role is as men and as women in that equation. Equal but not the same.

The second point is this: the liberation of women should not be championed by women only. I want to participate in the liberation of women because by so doing I will be educated about women, but they will also be educated about me, as a man. It is important, now in the nineties, that all of us, men and women, stand together in addressing this issue.

RS Did I detect a rather harsh criticism of the youth generation in *Come and Hope with Me*? I am thinking of the way they have taken a course of extreme violence, necklacing and so on.

MWS There are certain issues related to the Struggle which hit me, for one, very hard as a human being. One of these things was necklacing. I remember when I first saw that on the television screen. I asked myself, in all honesty: what has gone wrong with our people? How is it possible that these young people, conscious and able as they are, could do what they are doing? It is not in our culture. It is inhuman. Intellectually I understood perfectly well where it came from. I understand the results that it achieved, but still I do not accept it. I will not accept it in the future either, but we are capable of that as human beings. When I saw that on TV it was for me one of the saddest moments of the Struggle. I was deeply saddened by it, but I cannot entirely place the responsibility for that on the youths. It is the responsibility of the South African people as a nation. We created conditions that could result in that state of affairs and we must now take full responsibility as a nation.

RS I enjoyed very much reading *Come and Hope with Me*. There is a series of recurrent motifs: the return, the tentative motif of hope in humanity that runs like a red thread through the poem. Do you have a particular strategy when you set out to write a long poem like this one? Do you consciously use technical devices or do you go where your creative impulses take you?

MWS It is very funny that you should ask me that question because just this morning when I woke up and switched on the television, I saw what the world was doing about the celebration of the fiftieth anniversary of peace. I thought there was something very beautiful, warm, and compassionate in this, when people got together and said 'This far, no farther' to the Nazis, made the intervention that they did, and created the solutions that they came up with. Not perfect solutions, because we still have some of those problems, but on that 8th of May 1945 you saw a moment of high and dramatic creativity by human beings to claim life.

Now, I take that – and I also take the fact that we ourselves as a nation during these last four years have been engaged in negotiations – as a high drama of compassion, of seeking a solution to make life worth living.

The two things this morning have sparked my life. I have been walking around knowing that I must find a format that I must catch them in. This is what is important to me as a writer, more important than the mechanics. I know that one day I will sit down and say: 'This is how I will articulate that compassion – the two compassions, that which happened fifty years ago, and this that happened four years ago in our country.' These were very important moments in history, but not in history as a technical thing.

I am very attracted when I see human compassion taking control, choosing the direction of things. I always ask myself: 'What must we do to nurture this so that it becomes the main issue of our lives? What is it that we must do?' I don't know if I'll write a poem about it, or a novel, or an essay, but it is something that has captured my mind, and at present I am conserving it. It wants to come out and soon it will.

RS One of the key words of *Come and Hope with Me* is 'return'. In addition to the obvious return of South Africans from exile, were you also thinking of a return to the African values that you cherish?

MWS In one sense all South Africans were in a kind of exile. If you look at South Africa as a country, you will find that the whites pretended to be Europeans, and just by having committed such grievous crimes against humanity, they were in exile from humanity. Of course, there was also the literal exile that some of us were in. Because of strife, war – which breeds mistrust, anxieties, insecurity, defensiveness, alienation from other people, discrimination – we sacrificed what was essential to human nature, to human relations.

To come out of that, one has to search for the basics in human life. We must return to that to try and resolve the problems facing us. This country is still torn between whites who are defending their interests, and blacks who are saying 'We are tired. We don't want this any more.' This country was saved largely by black people. In a sense, white South Africans must learn humility and modesty. Despite the whites' lack of these things, there is enormous good will among blacks. While I am talking of good will, I do not want to see a stage where that good will changes into anger among the people who are oppressed, underprivileged, and marginalized. We must not risk that.

14

Inside out: Jeremy Cronin's lyrical politics

BRIAN MACASKILL

Jeremy Cronin's poems collected in the single and singular volume *Inside*, the interviews he has granted in conjunction with the publication of this volume, and his critical essays on literary culture, mostly concerned with ideological configurations in black South African poetry of the 1970s, all in one way or another address the relation between public and private, rearticulating a tension common to recent South African literatures: the disparity, perhaps only an ostensible disparity, of demands for revolutionary struggle on the one hand and aspirations for a more private aesthetic on the other.[1] Amid the poems in *Inside*, I shall argue, Cronin commonly achieves a surprisingly secure viewpoint for ideological critique. And no small part of the surprise in which this viewpoint is secured is that it should be secured here, inside a volume of poetry, rather than 'outside'; rather, that is to say, than in the critical essays where Cronin directly addresses the issue of ideology, or rather than in what for him must be the political domain of that public performance for which some of the poems are expressly composed. Cronin's ideological critique, I shall further argue, derives its security from a less predictable event than the ruin of hegemonic order that the order and ordering of his poems frequently seek; the force of his critique will instead be linked in the end to the collapse of order in which these poems themselves come to participate.

I

Charged in 1976 under the Terrorism and the Internal Security Acts for his participation in the then-banned African National Congress, Jeremy Cronin was sentenced to seven years' imprisonment, part of which term he served with death-row inmates at a maximum security prison in Pretoria. Detained at Pollsmoor and other prisons in Cape Town during

---

1. Occasional sentences in this chapter are based on my brief account of Cronin in the sixth edition of *Contemporary Poets*. A longer version of the essay refers for further substantiation to several more of Cronin's poems.

the two months before his trial, he began to compose works which, together with poems illegally recorded in Pretoria and smuggled out of prison or memorized for later reworking, would come to be published as *Inside*, the twenty-first volume in the Ravan *Staffrider Series* from Ravan Press. Having already published *Ideologies of Politics*, a 1975 collection of academic essays by various and authoritative hands for which Cronin and de Crespigny as co-editors wrote an 'outer' introduction, after his 1976 arrest Cronin thus embarked on an 'inner' and more private record of how 'the diverse senses of "ideology" tell us much about the wanderings of our own recent history' (de Crespigny and Cronin, *Ideologies*, 5). Furthermore, the 1983 publication of this inside and private account publicly joined Cronin and the poetic wanderings of his own recent history to a considerable corpus of South African prison writing, some of whose most familiar voices have included those of Herman Charles Bosman, Ruth First, Albie Sachs, Alex La Guma, Dennis Brutus, D. M. Zwelonke, Hugh Lewin, John Ya-Otto, Indres Naidoo, Molefe Pheto, and Breyten Breytenbach.[2]

Although Cronin acknowledges a particular debt to Dennis Brutus (from whom 'I learnt that one could write an extended book of lyrical poetry out of a prison existence') and a general debt to what he calls a 'tradition' of local writing that presents prison 'as a paradigm for South Africa' (Gardner, interview with Cronin, 23), the contributions from *Inside* nevertheless stand out against the voices adduced above: exceptionally so, at times, and for a variety of reasons, beginning with their reception. The first publication in the *Ravan Staffrider Series* by a white writer – that is, an exceptional event in South African publication history – *Inside* curiously garnered more attentive praise from the Afrikaans press than from the English, though individual English-language academics and poets would soon come to valorize the collection as a 'major text' (Driver, 'South African Literature in English', 567) and as 'the leading example of materialist poetry in South Africa or Africa' (Gottschalk, review of *Inside*, 58). To the materialist tradition out of which it stems, moreover, the volume itself seems exceptional in its apparent reliance on a core of lyrical feeling that nourishes the collection through an umbilicus

---

2. Breytenbach's *The True Confessions of an Albino Terrorist* is roughly contemporaneous to *Inside* in publication date; more recent accounts have since joined the list, including Breytenbach's *Judas Eye*, and works by Tshenuwani Farisani, Caesarina Kona Makhoere, and Emma Mashinini.

of love and landscape poems, not (yet) to dwell on the fact that many of the most interesting poems rely substantially for their effects on an expressly Christian mythopoetics. Even the more overtly political poems in the collection, marshalled especially in the first section subtitled 'Inside' and asserting their presence again in the sixth and last section, 'Isiququmadevu', are nurtured by the autobiography more properly the property of the love poems and other poems of placement situated in sections between one and six; thus a reader is drawn throughout the volume to imagine the source of the collection's life-blood as auto- and biographed in, as it were, the placenta of the personal, its author.

In an interview with Stephen Gray, Cronin confesses an early interest in lyric poetry, despite 'feeling very paralyzed about writing it, principally because it seemed so self indulgent' (Gray, interview with Cronin, 34). In almost identical terms he speaks to Susan Gardner of a paralysis imposed on his production by a 'disjunction between the realities in South Africa on the one hand, and [his] aesthetic predilections for the lyrical mode on the other' (interview, 18). In both interviews, Cronin explains that incarceration freed him from fears that a lyricism 'concentrated largely on subjective feelings and emotions' is self-indulgent in the context of oppression: 'One of the advantages of being in prison, at least for me, was that I suddenly felt that it wasn't such an indulgence to be able to write about my own personal feelings; what I was experiencing in prison was to a large extent the effect of the apartheid system, of which I too was a minor victim' (Gray, interview, 34). An insistence on the 'ordinariness' of his life experiences and (literary) work experiences punctuates these interviews, which seek to sign themselves on behalf of collective struggle. Hence for instance:

> I'd been in prison, I was a white, had been a member of the African National Congress, and in the course of my imprisonment my wife had died. So a number of apparently exceptional personal things happened to me, and what I've endeavoured to do, both in [*Inside*] itself, and in the way I present the poetry at readings, is to insist that my situation is *not* exceptional, it's only apparently so. My gaol sentence, for instance, is something that is far from exceptional in the South African situation. The same can be said about separation from one's family, since migrant labour, pass laws, influx control and the Bantustan System separate hundreds of thousands of families.
>
> (GARDNER, interview, 14)

Thought of in such terms, lyrically expressed emotion can mediate 'the consequences of apartheid'. The emotions thus put to work are 'not exceptional, but exemplary of the oppression that other [South African] people feel,' and through their emotive agency 'the subjective and the public [can be] held together in a dialectical relationship rather than being simply different one from the other' (Gardner, interview, 18).

II

Inside indeed bears testimony to an often surprising dialectic. The sense of surprise the volume evokes begins with some of the thematic turns to which the title entitles the collection. 'Inside' of course refers in one sense to the documentation of solidarity with and among political prisoners inside a contaminated penal system, a sense placed first in the collection by the defining character of those poems gathered together under the initial subtitle 'Inside'. Such solidarity can be expressed epigrammatically, as in the two lines prefatorily offset from the remainder of a short lyric like 'For Comrades in Solitary Confinement': 'Every time they cage a bird / the sky shrinks. A little' (25; citations from the Ravan Press edition, 1983). Or, solidarity might be subjected to more sustained treatment, as it is in 'Death Row' or 'Walking on Air'. But 'inside' refers also – by placement in a secondary though no less striking sense – to the autobiographical sequence of childhood reminiscence recorded under the lemma of 'The Naval Base' in the second section, and to the autobiographical interiority of poems written for the wife who died while Cronin was imprisoned, an interiority that fuels the lyricism of such poems as 'A Prayer in Search of Beads' from the fifth section of the volume, 'Love Poems'. 'Inside' further refers to the mouth cavity, whose innards, organs of articulation, are especially celebrated in the third and median grouping of poems, 'Venture to the Interior', where the mouth serves as a metonym for historical and geological formations of paleographic interiority.

While the conjunction of these three or more senses of 'inside' is perhaps not in itself exceptional, the linkages Cronin effects among levels of interiority are enriched by the modulations of this polysemantic term that begins by signifying political incarceration but that manages despite incarceration to venture outward to various topological exteriors and to venture also inward to various autobiographical interiors. And what remains exceptional in the coupling of personal and institutionalized senses of 'inside' here operative is that the titular metonym of this collection usually turns out (or in) to refer neither to private lyricism nor yet to public politics in any disjunctive sense.

The amalgam of lyrical expression and extended narrative that constitutes 'Walking on Air', for instance, enacts in every respect a politics of resistance. In the prison workshop, 'also known as the seminar / room', where 'work is done by enforced dosage, between / political discussion, theoretical discussion, tactical / discussion, bemoaning of life without women, / sawdust up the nose', prisoner John Matthews 'speaks by snatches' the political autobiography that has led to his continued incarceration (5–6). He tells of a life and makes contraband goods, working thus for himself and for others like himself, but '"not for the boere"' (5). That the life story thus embedded inside the poem is of consequence outside itself is testified to in the first instance by the biographical unfolding of the poem's narrative: beginning with a '*Prologue*' that strategically insists on the poem's setting as a locus of resistance – prison workshop, but also seminar room – the poem leads to a narrative climax in its account of how the prisoner and his wife, the latter 'not political at all' (13), agree that continued and lengthy incarceration is preferable to turning state witness.

But the poem itself resists being reduced only to this political triumph of continued resistance, since its unfolding – from setting to climax – along the way joins as much as it celebrates Matthews's love and craftsmanship. In the prison workshop Matthews illegally fabricates contraband goods of 'oh, delicate dovetailings' (6). Accepting as its legacy from Matthews's story the 'lifelong / love for the making / and fixing of things' that Matthews acknowledges as an inheritance from his father (7), the poem likewise and also illegally (given the circumstances of its production) reinvests with care that heritage of love for the making and fixing of things over the gradual revelation of its ten-page-long life. Not coincidentally – and this coupling provides a second testament to the pertinence of John Matthews, of his story, and of the poem Cronin crafts out of his story – 'Walking on Air' is one of three poems Cronin includes with invariant regularity in 'outside' or public performances of his work, presumably not only for the didactic potential of political configurations within the poem, but also for its 'delicate dovetailings' of the personal and the public, the interior account and its exterior shaping, for the way it embodies Cronin's experience of writing poetry, an experience he elsewhere describes – learning, as it were, from John Matthews and borrowing his words – as 'a productive activity, one requiring an apprenticeship, constant practice and keeping one's hand in, also a lifelong love for the making and fixing of things' (Gardner, interview, 19).

'Walking on Air' thus blends together from the inside out the personal and the political: in its affect as much as in its technical mixing of lyric and narrative, in its celebration of craft as much as in its promise of didactic utility. While the poem remains 'political', one sees in it also a love poem not limited to the story it tells of husband and wife.

III

In the most successful political poems, such as 'Walking on Air', Cronin resurrects what has been or what might otherwise be forgotten, and thus creates what could be otherwise. What remains is to emphasize the perhaps even more surprising triumph achieved by some of the love poems and some of the poems of childhood reminiscence, an emphasis which in due course will lead to a consideration of that other sense of 'inside' so far only intimated: the metapoetic celebration of mouth and tongue. 'A Prayer in Search of Beads' from the 'Love Poems' section leads the way, beginning as it does with a childhood recollection poised above what becomes a triumphant transformation of self-portraiture and its algorithms, blindness, and loss:

> As a child I learned
> to follow blind the circular path
> where the hand was guide to the tongue
> each bead unlocked
> its own particular prayer.

Here the rosary's mnemonic function blindly practised in youth – to recall words of spiritual praise – is substantiated and yet powerfully transformed by a more mature practice enacted in and by the poem's second stanza. In the blindness of having been removed from the presence of an intimate and her body, Cronin closes his eyes in the second stanza and, accepting blindness, reinvents by inversion the childhood act of the first stanza, making his words now invoke a carnal palpability whose spirituality is verbally incarnated as the capacity to imagine beads of sight despite blindness and loss:

> But now I have to hope
> for some reverse palpability to emerge.
> I close my eyes – fervently,
> *Un ʒip . . . Un ʒip* I intone
> fumbling with its sounds
> as if I hoped to touch

> in that word, bump, bump,
> the tingling, the warm
> rosary down your spine.   (70)

Although the touch evoked in this second stanza remains literally impalpable, a tangibility predicated of hope with no guarantee of sensory gratification, a 'reverse palpability' does here materially emerge in the agentive inversion between the two stanzas: the tongue that once blindly followed the hand now comes literally to lead through darkness the fettered hand, enabling that hand to record in concrete figures the tongue's praise and so enabling a new prayer for changed circumstances, perhaps even a prayer for change.

Thus drawing strength more than consolation from an absent spine, say, or from imaginative revision of absent eyelids ('Who can forget how they'd unveil / – between blinks, / through all tears – / an unbreakable strength' ('Eyelids', 79)) Cronin stiffens his resolve to look also at himself in the mirror of those remarkable reminiscences perhaps more accurately called recreations of identity 'against an impassable glass frontier' ('Mirror', 82). In the autobiographical sequences entitled 'The Naval Base' and 'Some Uncertain Wires', sequences that together most closely approach the act of confession that pumps at the heart of all autobiography, Cronin tries from inside to re-see his own body – personal, familial, and politic – as it extends outward through a 'nostalgia / [that] is thicker than water', in generational spaces 'half filled with childhood rhymes, joined / by some uncertain wires' ('My grandma had been getting old . . .', 64).

Most tellingly, in the first of 'The Naval Base' series we see – through the initially closed eyes of an autobiographical 'I' – the onset of a hide-and-seek game in which the Cronin contemporaneous to the composition of the poem will search for himself, looking first for the grammatical third-person of a 'five-year-old / kid',

> nose pinched
> to stop his sneeze – the point
> being not to be found
> too soon[;]

and then for the grammatical second-person:

> your nose pinched
> hidden in the deepest ignorance
> of the bulldozers moving on the zinc camp,

of the trek fishermen group area'd
out for the submarine pens[.]

Finally, when the seeker's feet come closer and thus according to the vernacular of this game get 'w-a-r-m-e-r', we see Cronin seek himself out as the grammatical first-person:

Me hiding in there, ears pricked up.
Me out here circling about. There is
between the two of us, in this
necessary space, nothing,
nothing that could be learned,
or forgotten now
by backing off.   (35–6)

The subsequent poems in this series indeed refuse to 'back off' from what might be forgotten or from what already has been forgotten, from what must now be sought out of hiding. Nor, as the third poem in the sequence makes clear, can the first-person seeker 'disclaim that string-thin, five-year old boy / with big ears and bucked teeth' once he has been found, even though the finding reveals him to be the one 'Who polished with envy and Silvo his pa's ceremonial sword':

That boy, that endless earache, who knew at five,
because learnt by heart, the naval salute, the sign of the cross,
the servant's proper place, and our father who art.

While the hegemonic values so economically distilled in the two lines immediately above – education, militarism, theism, colonialism, and rationalization – can obviously not be espoused from within the poem or from its locus of (resistant) production, their presence in the five-year-old child is not only acknowledged, but claimed, again by means of a deictic shift. *That* boy of the poem's beginning becomes *this* boy of its ending in the subsequent two lines, lines still subsumed by the poem's opening utterance:

I cannot disclaim that string-thin, five-year-old boy
. . .
– This five-year-old boy, this shadow,
this thing stuck to my feet.   (39)

A homology between two different but still related states of being is here discovered and uncovered in the course of a game of hide-and-seek – minted, so to speak – then confirmed through an illocutionary act of claim.

By accepting the blindness of the child he once was – a blindness that includes the child's ignorance of bulldozers moving on shanty towns near the naval base, an ignorance as impervious to the bulldozers' synecdochic representation of the power on which the naval base is founded as it is impervious to the fishermen 'legally' moved to make way for submarine pens – by joining again for a while that blindness to count his way into a childhood game ('I close my eyes', the first poem begins), Cronin comes to see the homology he cannot disclaim and begins again to seek responses inside a familial closet to 'Mothballed shoes, cuffs, legs, / Arms, amongst my solemn / Ancestral ranks with their wire / Question marks for heads' ('Clothes', 102).

IV

The processes of reclamation thus inaugurated primarily by the love poems and by the self-portraiture poems profitably bring blindness and insight to bear upon ruins of the past and of the present. These poems recognize a past ruined by the wilful ignorance of a racial policy blindly followed, say, and recognize too a childhood passed in ignorance of such ruin, a childhood innocence since become aware of consequences attending the ruin of lives that has led to this present incarceration, this sometime opening and reopening of eyes held captive still, this ruin of innocence, this struggle with and against blindness. As such, these poems enable further poetic excavation of the past and the present for the potential benefit of a time still to come. Incarcerated inside one sense of 'inside', the collection begins there but soon finds other insides to pursue. Contiguously folding personal autobiography into excavations of forgotten history, the collection follows its various insides through darkness, bringing to light among other remnants the ruins of a language once spoken by a vanquished and now vanished people whose autochthonous tongue it seeks to commemorate.

The 'Venture to the Interior' sequence of poems, replete with allusions to the mouthings of a vanished Khoi culture, excavate among ancient African ruins a language left behind by the gestation of a modern colonial nation. Seeking in an expanded and now more accommodating English to celebrate a lost Khoisan tongue, these poems pay sometimes erotic tribute to the Khoi remnants they resurrect out of the ruins of a cultural past long ago flooded by colonial languages. In 'Our land holds ...', for instance, the mouth consulted and attended to in a quest for 'hard / Wooden truths' held by the land is first the wind becoming visible as it blows over and past the cooling towers of the nuclear power plant at Athlone to 'zig-zag, / Through the khaki bush', humming. According to the 'fancy' of a witness, the voice of the wind here 'mourns, thin / Thin with worries'. But the semblance of mourning has in more concrete terms already been celebrated by the poem as a musical performance played on autochthonous and non-European instruments. The wind 'hums' through the desiccated foliage of indigenous khaki bush, and 'tongues' its 'gom-gom' (above all an onomatopoeic resonance, but by allusion also those hollow iron bowls struck for musical effect with a rod or stick and called the *gom-gom* or *gum-gum*, names presumed to derive from a Malay dialect). The accompaniment passes to that ancient and uniquely Khoisan stringed wind instrument the wind then 'frets' – the *gorah* is a hollow stick strung like a bow with sheep entrails and equipped with a quill mouthpiece at one end – before it finally gives song to 'The names of decimated / Khoikhoin tribes', thus linking in commemoration its passage with their passing.[3]

Thus, rather than passing away or following into death those ancient Khoikoin warriors 'Charging zig-zag into musket fire', the voice of the wind zig-zagging through the khaki bush persists in passing on an answering activity, an 'unfinished task', in which the poem's phonological commemoration has already participated:

> Those warriors who've left behind
> Their fallen spears that our land
> Like a peach its pip
>> Holds now:
> This unfinished task. (50)

The 'unfinished task' is a military one, a relay for the picking up of fallen spears. (We need only recall that *Umkhonto we Sizwe*, the military wing of the African National Congress, often shortened to just *Umkhonto*, means 'Spear of the Nation', or simply 'Spear'.) But the 'unfinished task' is also an archaeographic one that Cronin further digs into at other autochthonous mouth-sites: in a poem called 'Cave-site', for instance, which meta-

---

3. Most of the names here adduced refer to Peninsular clans of the Khoikhoi in the vicinity of Table Bay (the Goringhaicona, Goringhaiqua, and Gorachouqua all acknowledged the authority of a single overlord), as well as to chiefdoms immediately to the east of Table Bay (the Hessequa) and to the north (the Cochoqua). For a brief history of these peoples, see Elphick and Malherbe, 'The Khoisan to 1828'.

poetically conjures attempts 'to prise carefully / sound / from sound / to honour by speaking / (and sometimes to discard) / . . . shells of meaning / left in our mouths / by thousands of years of / human occupation' (46). Or in the remarkable compression of a poem that links a mountain spring to speech, specifically to indigenous sounds of African speech ('dropping dental, lateral / Clicking in its palate like the flaking of stone tools'), and then to the flow of history, agriculture, and industrial labour, all to identify 'The River That Flows Through Our Land' and to celebrate the 'many tongues' this river 'carries . . . in its mouth' (57).

The poems that undertake a 'Venture to the Interior' stage their digging as activities congruent to autobiographical ventures already discussed. A poem like 'Litany' thus pays homage to the coming of language by telescoping together the tongue's evolutionary birth out of 'primal swamps' with the moment of the poem's composition, a second coming in which the tongue is now figured as a Christian dove 'bearing the leaves of speech' (47). Such a poem surely and justifiably celebrates the tongue as an instrument of linkage: an instrument capable of effecting linkage despite its archaic descent, capable of uttering links alternate to those captured by the 'Great White Hunter' Cronin acknowledges as his ancestor (55), capable of articulating materialist interests through religious imagery, capable even, why not, of granting and accepting forgiveness. Such a tongue should be well-prepared 'To learn', as the last poem in the sequence puts it, 'how to speak / With the voices of this land'.

V

But 'To learn how to speak . . . ', probably the most widely anthologized and thus – for his minority audience of literates – probably Cronin's best-known poem, internally bears the striations of its difficult birth into a position of authority. If a reader follows the poem's determination 'To understand the least inflections', she will notice that the poem appears to hesitate between the expression of a desire 'To learn how to speak / With the voices of the land / To parse the speech in its rivers' and a desire 'To learn how to speak / With the [human] voices of *this* land' (my italics):

> To write a poem with words like:
> I'm telling you,
> Stompie, stickfast, golovan,
> Songololo, just boombang, just
> To understand the least inflections,
> To voice without swallowing

Syllables born in tin shacks, or catch
the 5.15 ikwata bust fife
Chwanisberg train, to reach
The low chant of the mine gang's
Mineral glow of our people's unbreakable resolve. (58)

In one sense the hesitation is negligible, since by the last lines of the poem, lines that articulate in summary the second desire – 'To learn how to speak / With the voices of this land' – the two projects have become one. In another sense, however, the hesitation is crucial. Like several of its predecessors in the sequence, this poem indubitably achieves the first objective: in its phrasing, the poem demonstrates a considerable ability 'To catch in the inarticulate grunt, / Stammer, call, cry, babble, tongue's knot / A sense of the stoneness of these stones / From which all words are cut'. Such lines successfully imitate in their performance the delicate difficulties of chiselling through to the strata of a stone age. But the distance between digging sites and long-buried layers of sedimentary words is perhaps here too great to warrant the poem's desire for connection.

The chiselling of words out of stones from the past to prefigure the poem's concluding lines takes determinate form as the poem lexically mimics its wish 'To trace with the tongue wagon-trails' by cutting off endings from Afrikaans place names, 'Saying the suffix of their aches in -kuil, -pan, -fontein, / In watery names that confirm the dryness of their ways'. Indeed, the already-quoted profusion of South African idiom that materializes the poem's desire 'to speak / With the voices of this land' emerges directly out of its first-person speaker's ache 'To bury my mouth in the pit of [the land's] arm; / In that planetarium, / Pectoral beginning to the nub of time'. And the words that emerge – *stompie, stickfast, golovan, songololo, just boombang*, and so on – are in their variety clearly meant to slake a thirst occasioned by the monological dryness of that untranslatably Afrikaans word, *apartheid*.

Oddly enough, however, only one of these words – *songololo*, the millipede that curls itself into a coil when disturbed – is etymologically related to any language possibly descended from some primordial African utterance at the 'nub of time', coming as it does by way of Nguni (Xhosa *i-songololo*, Zulu *i-shongololo*, from *ukushonga*, to roll up).[4] The

4. I gratefully acknowledge the assistance given me by Penny Silva, Director
   of the Dictionary Unit for South African English at Rhodes University,
   Grahamstown, South Africa, whose new *Dictionary of South African English*

remaining words and expressions here celebrated as the speech of this land, cut from its rocks, are again derived from that recent language of European descent, Afrikaans (*stompie*, for example, a cigarette butt or the stump of a vine or candle, and hence also figuratively a short person or worthless remnant); or, in the case of *golovan*, a mine trolley, the word is reached by way of its close association with Fanakalo, the creolized labour-esperanto fabricated to serve the interests of capital in South African gold mines; or, as in 'the 5.15 ikwata bust fife / Chwannisberg train', an expression is achieved by informal phonetic transcription of how some black South Africans might pronounce in English the 'quarter-past-five Johannesburg [commuter] train'. Even the sole more-or-less authentically African word here, *songololo*, is, I suspect, more commonly used in South African English and in Afrikaans than either 'millipede' or its Afrikaans equivalent, 'duisendpoot'. [5] While these linguistic circumstances hardly allow one to claim, as David Schalkwyk does, that Cronin employs in the poem 'no true examples of the black vernacular', and while it is even more difficult to agree with Schalkwyk that the poem (consequently?) 'offers no syllables "born in tin shacks"' ('Confession and Solidarity', 42), it clearly remains possible to see the poem's verbal display in terms of a polemic that militates against its desire for and achievement of a coherent paleographic connection. [6]

A more likely reading of the poem's intentional interests is of course to see here an attempt vocally to participate in the speech of labour, an attempt motivated by identifications that violate the distance between stone and industrial ages, and between languages of conquest and submission. Even under such circumstances, however, and even if the

on Historical Principles was published in 1996 by Oxford University Press, Oxford and Cape Town.

5. The paucity of black vernacular here is made all the more remarkable by Cronin's strategic use of Khoisan, Nguni, and Sotho languages elsewhere in the collection. I have already illustrated Khoisan evocations in the text above; for Cronin's use of Sotho in a prominently titular position, see 'Motho ke Motho ka Batho Babang' (18); Nguni utterances are incorporated into 'Death Row' (26–31), and – again titularly – in 'Isiququmadevu' (85–6).

6. Although I dispute the details of Schalkwyk's reading, I agree with his overarching sense that 'Both the tenets of Cronin's historical materialism and his own cultural and political history speak obliquely against the grain of this poem', and find intriguing his claim that this cross-grain friction turns the poem 'into a kind of unconscious confession' ('Confession and Solidarity', 42).

paucity of black vernacular were thus allowed to vindicate the persistence of a spirit resistant to linguistic domination, the poem brushes
against ruin and collapses under the weight of its tendentiousness. No
longer as securely footed in that play of identification the deictics and
pronouns of poems like 'The Naval Base' sequence undertake, nor yet as
multiply rooted in the many-tongued river that 'flows through this land',
'our land', the 'this' and the 'our' of 'To learn how to speak ...' are signed
on more tenuous authority and come to constitute less convincing signs
than their tendentiousness promises. If 'our people's unbreakable
resolve' were changed to read, say, 'the people's unbreakable resolve',
the poem might present fewer difficulties; and it would hereby only pay
the price of explicitly committing itself to a desire for a state yet to come
rather than prematurely presuming itself as the achieved enactment of
that state.

But enough has been said, I trust, to serve my principal observation:
that this celebrated poem is itself implicated in the collapse of a coherent
language of resistance to that incoherent and fundamentally linguistic
dream we know as apartheid.[7] Under the difficulty it experiences uttering
a celebration of 'the voices of this land' without also testifying thereby to
the ostensible triumph of apartheid's language, 'To learn how to speak
...' collapses into ruin. Nevertheless, the poem's critical force remains
linked precisely to the resistance it displays against the contagion of
apartheid's dream despite being itself infected by the language of that
dream. Again, it would seem, the 'exceptional' – here (perhaps) Cronin's
best-known poem – becomes exemplary of the struggle the volume
undertakes against limitation, even to the point (perhaps) of making one
want to question the purity of this poem's 'exceptional' status.

My more embracing point, of course, is that the ideological critique
so effectively pursued by *Inside* is most effective where we might least
expect it to be: in the interiority of an autobiographical practice that is
first lyrical, then more commonly political, in the reseeing of childhood
as a reclaimable fragmentation, in the palaeographic recreation of lin-

---

7. Writing of apartheid, Derrida reminds us that 'there's no racism without a
   language' ('Racism's Last Word', 292). Paying close attention to the language
   of one of apartheid's seminal theoreticians, J. M. Coetzee reads apartheid
   'from inside' this language as 'a dream of purity, but an impure dream'
   ('Apartheid Thinking', 165). For a more detailed account of Derrida and
   Coetzee on apartheid thinking, see also Macaskill and Colleran 'Interfering
   with "The Mind of Apartheid"'.

guistic remnants, in the eye of an autobiographical 'I' seeking to see again lost intimacies, including itself, even when it purports to report on behalf of a trans-individual collectivity; to be brief, in the ruin already there from the beginning. This ruin already there from the beginning is not only – as we might expect it to be – the devastation wrought by an apartheid that preceded the birth of Jeremy Cronin's generation, but also the collapse of the seemingly exceptional into exemplarity, a collapse that has shaped the conception of *Inside* from the outset and that furthermore encourages re-evaluations of, for instance, the exceptionality and even the exemplarity of a poem as well known as 'To learn how to speak . . . ' The force of ruin in this latter sense is critically more potent in *Inside* than the critique inscribed in Cronin's expository discussions of, say, limitations inherent in ideological notions 'of "privileged access" into the "black soul"' ('"The law that says . . ."', 44), or in his inquiries concerning an insurgent South African poetry 'that can only be understood and analyzed in its relationship to a range of traditional and contemporary oral and verbal practices' ('"Even under the Rine of Terror"', 12); more passionately present in *Inside*, that is to say, than in the essays upon which Cronin's reputation rests for being a pioneer in the deployment of materialism 'as a semiological conception' (Klopper, 'Ideology', 259).

Perhaps this is so for reasons similar to those J. M. Coetzee posits concerning what can and cannot be accomplished in discursive and more literary writing. Speaking of passion, for instance, 'where a strange logic prevails', Coetzee suggests that while a novel or poem 'allows the writer to *stage* his passion', 'when a real passion of feeling is let loose in discursive prose, you feel that you are reading the utterances of a madman' (*Doubling the Point*, 60–1). Cronin's poems stage a passion unavailable to the discursive logic of his critical essays and inaccessible even to the logic of order upon which the arrangement of poems in *Inside* appears to rest. Far from building incrementally alongside the inversions of public and private that the subdivided structure of the collection undertakes, the passion *Inside* enfolds to embrace and to reveal is that of a child-like intensity strictly speaking out of place in discursive domains, an intensity that militates against stricture to the point of embracing collapse. In ways my discussion has sought to demonstrate, *Inside* fruitfully reduces into rich collapse the distance between outside and inside, between politics and autobiography, between exemplarity and the exceptional. Articulating themselves against an outside political order, an exceptional law of ruin known as apartheid, and announcing their insides as not exceptional but exemplary of the conditions wrought by that law, these poems engage the state of forced partition in the most powerful manner possible: they take exception to it. And the exception they take is already exemplarily there in the opening poem of the collection, 'Poem-shrike', where items from a prison inventory list and other assorted objects are transformed into a (predatory) bird-poem. In an act as impossibly childish as that of a defiant child whose behaviour is sure to prompt some adult authority into exclaiming 'impossible', the poem is launched 'over the high walls' and out of the prison: 'sshrike!' (3).

Works cited

Bosman, Herman Charles. *Cold Stone Jug: Being the Record of a Somewhat Lengthy Sojourn in Prison* (1949). Cape Town: Human & Rousseau, 1969.

Brutus, Dennis. *Letters to Martha and Other Poems from a South African Prison.* London: Heinemann, 1968.

Coetzee, J. M. *Doubling the Point: Essays and Interviews.* Ed. David Attwell. Cambridge, MA: Harvard University Press, 1992.

'Apartheid Thinking'. *Giving Offense: Essays on Censorship.* Chicago: University of Chicago Press, 1996. 163–84.

Cronin, Jeremy. '"Even Under the Rine of Terror . . .": Insurgent South African Poetry'. *Research in African Literatures* 19. 1 (1988): 12–23.

'"The Law That Says / Constricts the Breath-line (. . .)" South African English Language Poetry Written by Africans in the 1970s'. *English Academy Review* 3 (1985): 25–49.

de Crespigny, Anthony, and Jeremy Cronin, eds. *Ideologies of Politics.* Cape Town: Oxford University Press, 1975.

Derrida, Jacques. 'Racism's Last Word'. Trans. Peggy Kamuf. *Critical Inquiry* 12 (1985): 290–9.

Driver, Dorothy. 'South African Literature in English'. *Encyclopedia of World Literature in the 20th Century.* 5 vols. General ed. Steven R. Serafin. New York: Ungar, 1981–93. Vol. v, 565–8.

Elphick, Richard, and V. C. Malherbe. 'The Khoisan to 1828'. *The Shaping of South African Society, 1652–1840.* Ed. Richard Elphick and Hermann Giliomee. Middletown: Wesleyan University Press, 1989. 3–65.

First, Ruth. *117 Days.* Harmondsworth: Penguin, 1965.

Gardner, Susan. Interview with Jeremy Cronin, 27 April 1984. *Four South African Poets: NELM Interviews Series Number Two.* Grahamstown: National English Literary Museum, 1986. 13–27.

Gottschalk, Keith. Review of Jeremy Cronin, *Inside. Critical Arts* 3.2 (1984): 52–9.

Gray, Stephen. Interview with Jeremy Cronin. *Index on Censorship* (March 1984): 34–7.

Klopper, Dirk. 'Ideology and the Study of White South African English Poetry'. *Rendering Things Visible: Essays on South African Literary Culture.* Ed. Martin Trump. Johannesburg: Ravan, 1990. 256–94.

La Guma, Alex. *The Stone Country.* London: Heinemann, 1967.

Macaskill, Brian. 'Jeremy Cronin'. *Contemporary Poets.* 6th edn. Ed. Thomas Riggs. Detroit: St James Press, 1996. 205–6.

Macaskill, Brian, and Jeanne Colleran. 'Interfering with "The Mind of Apartheid"'. *Pretexts* 4 (1992): 67–84.

Sachs, Albie. *The Jail Diary of Albie Sachs.* London: Harvill Press, 1966.

Schalkwyk, David. 'Confession and Solidarity in the Prison Writing of Breyten Breytenbach and Jeremy Cronin'. *Research in African Literatures* 25. 1 (1994): 23–45.

15

Spinning out the present: narrative, gender, and the politics of South African theatre

DENNIS WALDER

I

In 1988, a time of the most massive repression the country has ever known, the 500th anniversary of the 'discovery' of South Africa by the Portuguese explorer Bartolomeu Dias was commemorated in the small seaside resort of Mossel Bay. Three white actors in a rowing boat landed on a 'whites-only' beach, there to be welcomed by seven more whites wearing curly wigs and painted black. This simple ceremony was applauded by some 2,000 people, including the then President, P. W. Botha, in full regalia, with his cabinet. The spectacle would have been complete were it not for the absence of the local black population – an action precipitated by a 'Coloured' high-school teacher, who had warned the authorities that unless beach apartheid were ended, he and his pupils at least would not welcome Mr Dias back.

This event demonstrates a number of things. First of all, it suggests the complex absurdity of race politics in the country. Secondly, it registers the importance of theatrical representation or performance, broadly defined, in constructing a people's view of themselves – in this case, that of the white ruling class. And thirdly, it reveals the peculiar and persistent nature of the colonial imagination in a society which, although nominally independent, has long continued to exhibit the typical features of a colonial culture. Not only do the whites enact a version of the country's history which begins with the arrival of the Europeans; but the social, political, and legal superstructures they have set up exclude black people, so defined, even from this representation. Moreover, what is known of the paradigmatic, initiating colonial encounter itself gets almost completely reinvented, and the possibility of indigenous resistance elided, since according to the da Gama Diary, Dias and his men were pelted with stones when they landed, to which Dias retaliated by killing one of the inhabitants with a bolt from a crossbow (da Gama, 'Diary', 6). As Fanon long ago pointed out, apartheid is but an extreme example of the colonial condition, in which it is the 'settler' who thinks he (and it is 'he') makes history, while the 'native' does not (39–40). Worse: it is as if the colonized are outside the imaginable, the settlers appropriating for themselves the identity of 'native' too; whence the laughable sight of whites embracing whites as a representation of European arrival upon the alien shore.

Now that we have entered the 'post-apartheid' era, in which the laws if not the underlying structures of apartheid have been dismantled, political prisoners released, exiles returned, and a democratically elected, nominally multiracial state set in motion, how does the state see itself? And where does theatre as a defined cultural practice come in? These are large questions, which it would take a lot more space than I have here to begin to answer – even supposing they could be, at this early stage of the 'New South Africa'.

But consider another, more recent public event, which may usefully be set beside the Mossel Bay show: the winning of the Rugby World Cup in South Africa by South Africa. Unlike the Dias commemoration, the World Cup was performed before millions of people worldwide, as well as a large local audience, having been set up as part of South Africa's international acceptance after decades of sanctions and boycott. Such an event was hardly conceivable in 1988, and hardly possible until the release from prison of the regime's most abhorred opponent, and his election by a majority as the country's first black president in 1994. The climax of the tournament took place on 24 June 1995, when President Mandela, wearing an exact replica of the Springbok jersey worn by the captain of the South African team, appeared before some 60,000 people in the country's premier sporting venue, Ellis Park, Johannesburg, there to congratulate his own victorious captain. Before doing so, the president executed a little victory shuffle, both hands raised in the air, a gesture amplified by delirious crowds congratulating themselves around the country, as if to reinforce the captain's assertion after the game that triumph had been ensured by the support of the entire nation.

The whole occasion was evidently intended to signal a nation-building, 'post-apartheid' moment to the country and the world at large. Earlier attempts to alter the team's symbolic springbok had failed, and the absence of black players in the South African side (with one exception), was apparently overlooked. By donning the Springbok shirt Mandela proposed the incorporation of one of the most potent, if reviled symbols of Afrikaner nationalist supremacy within the new government's Rainbow Nation project; the victory confirmed it. What about the hopeless millions in squatter camps and townships still without proper housing, jobs, or education? Even if they looked to the World Cup win as an authenticating sign, there remained some troubling images to cloud this representation of nationhood. For example, the glimpse before an earlier match, after a torrential downpour delayed the start, of a group of middle-aged black women sweeping puddles off the pitch. Cameras swung away without comment from this scene, as if embarrassed by the survival of all-too familiar power structures into the new epoch.

Forging a new nation gives the necessary illusion of inclusiveness, but it is an illusion not a reality. This is not to deny the massive, enforced exclusiveness of the old system, represented so well at Mossel Bay in 1988; rather, it is to suggest that the euphoria generated by the radical changes which have overtaken South Africa should not blind anybody to the problems inherent in the decolonizing process. This is as important for distinct cultural forms such as the theatre, as it is for related forms of cultural self-representation such as those I have been describing. The boundary between theatrical performance and other kinds of cultural activity is not always easy to define. But at least there is growing agreement about the need to understand the former in terms of the latter – to understand, in other words, the linkage between varying cultural forms and social power, as recent theorists of South African theatre agree (for example, Hauptfleisch, Steadman, Kruger, Orkin). The difficulty, however, is that those of us brought up within the dominant colonial tradition may misperceive the cultural potential of the wider society – a misperception far less culpable in the search for authenticity in terms of alternative or oppositional voices, as in presuming their non-existence; but a misperception nonetheless. After all, how can we claim more autonomy or detachment from our own backgrounds and environment than we allow the cultural producers we observe?

One way of working towards a more self-critically aware position, it seems to me, is to review and revalue one crucially influential, if not dominant, strand of cultural life, the English colonial tradition in South Africa. A starting point for such revision could be taken from Barbara Masekela's leading speech in Grahamstown, the historic heart of English-speaking culture, during the 1990 National Arts Festival. 'National' in this context meant to begin with in 1966 a celebration of the cultural contribution of the 1820s settlers; by 1984, and after huge new sponsorship by the Standard Bank, its remit had broadened, but was still overwhelmingly white and Anglocentric. Boycotted until the late eighties by community groups for this bias, the festival had further broadened its reach by the time of Masekela's invitation to speak. Yet her address was the first delivered there by a black woman, moreover an ANC activist returned from exile; and its importance for liberal dissent was underscored by the fact that until the last minute the ANC's own Cultural Desk opposed her visit; after which her speech was published in full in *Die Suid-Afrikaan*, a bilingual product of late eighties' Afrikaner liberalism originating at Stellenbosch University. Masekela struck hard by claiming that 'the people's voice' had long been poorly represented at the festival, and that to begin to make up for the lack, culture needed redefining as a carrier of the community's values, rather than in terms of the dominant, oppressive, and patriarchal view implicit in the position of the ruling white groups. 'English and Afrikaans-based cultures', she said, 'are a valid part of the whole rich tapestry of South African culture – but a part – not the sun around which the whole cultural universe revolves.' Instead of looking to 'ersatz European high culture' for guidance, what was required was 'an aesthetic which is uniquely South African' (Masekela, 'We Are Not Returning Empty-handed', 38–40).

This is the familiar theme of the contestation of values between the metropolitan and the local; familiar, too, is the demand for a more broadly based and therefore authentic national culture. But according to Masekela, it is the culture of the English-speaking community which has been 'the most exclusive and resistant' to the other voices needing to be heard – notably those of people in the rural areas, women, and children. Language, education, and the erosion of 'our own folk tradition' by the migrant labour system were all factors in allowing the continuance of this exclusivity. So, too, was the prominence of the voice of the well-financed cultural elite, who enjoy 'disproportionate access to national and international media. Their voice is often assumed to be our voice, simply because it is the only one anyone has heard.' There is some irony involved in attacking the Eurocentrism of the English-speakers' cultural attitudes from a position based upon a European, neo-Marxist form of cultural analysis. But the perception remains that there is an historically dominant, elitist English tradition, which has been validated by external, metropolitan cultural mediation.

On the other hand, that tradition has been neither monolithic nor impermeable; not only should we recall (as Masekela does) the complicating growth of Calvinist Afrikaner hegemony since the early years of this century, but also the fact that from the start South African writing in

English has been predominantly non-generic, consisting of diaries, travel, journalism, tales, sketches, and hybrid oral forms such as Andrew Geddes Bain and Frederick Rex's *Kaatje Kekkelbek* (1838) – a theatrical 'review' in which the Khoi girl of the title (played by a white man) satirized Grahamstown life in a rich mix of indigenous Cape dialects (see Gray, *Southern African Literature*, 52–7). Naturally the establishment version of this writing emphasizes the growth of generic establishment forms, and the importance of imported work, from Goldsmith to Shakespeare – still used to reinforce conventional universalist interpretations of literary production, which in turn help maintain the long-term, colonialist divisions of South African life and culture. But the perspective to adopt now, if we are to attend to the hitherto unheard or new voices which Masekela and others insist on, is to look to those areas of literary or cultural production and reception which have avoided the constraints and distortions of colonial or neocolonial structures, areas associated with the relative freedom of the domain of the spoken or performed. I say relative freedom, because of course these areas have also been subject to the political and commercial pressures of the media. But if we should not underestimate the importance of the 'conscientizing' function of performance in the last two decades of crisis and instability, its limitations have become apparent – the 'simplifications, romanticism and contradictory formulations' identified for instance by Bhekizizwe Peterson ('Apartheid and the Political Imagination', 245). During the period of repression which culminated with the Botha regime, this work did, after all, testify to the potential of performance, scripted or otherwise, as an area of dissent.

Further, the appearance over the last two decades of a wide variety of hybrid, yet specialized forms, from trade union and workers' theatre to the rural community theatre which saves lives by teaching people about AIDS and child nutrition, suggests the importance of freeing up the preconceptions about theatre held by most of us who comment on it – although this also makes theatre more difficult to judge, since the criteria are going to be more various, and less stable, too. But at least we should now habitually recognize the characteristically mixed origins of the work we are dealing with – Masekela's uniquely South African aesthetic – and the changing contexts of its production, reception and status.

II

This chapter, therefore, is simply intended as a contribution to the rewriting of South African theatre history currently in process. Rewriting that history is dependent upon the gradual accumulation of evidence about its barely known past, and proceeds despite the distortions, gaps, and fissures inevitably attendant upon its present. To be more specific, then, I will consider one aspect of this theatre as it may be rediscovered within some of the work associated with the country's leading and still most active practitioner, Athol Fugard; a 'rediscovery' which cannot now be made without considering the new voices of women playwright-performers such as Gcina Mhlophe and Fatima Dike, for reasons which I hope to make plain. In any case, Fugard's work should never be considered in isolation, nor as if it were in any simple sense the product of his individual genius. The importance of viewing the plays – whether jointly or singly authored in name – as texts open to performative reinterpretation has never been more apparent than today, when so much theatrical performance – from the Junction Avenue Theatre Company, to the Soyikwa Group, from the Maratholi Travelling Theatre to the *Asinamali!* company – has operated as a way of bringing together diverse cultural forms, including mime, music, and movement as well as dialogue, role-playing, and storytelling, so as to find a voice for the voiceless. Perhaps most *sui generis* has been the emphasis upon storytelling, or narrative, in South African theatre today, including Fugard's. It is striking how far Fugard, the complete 'man of theatre', sees himself as 'a storyteller . . . the only truly safe place I have ever known is when I am in the middle of a story as its teller' ('Some Problems of a Playwright', 384–5).

This seems to imply a claim on authorial control which in practice his work often belies. Partly this is the result of the automatic, patriarchal Western assumption that narrative implies a linear, one-way hierarchy – author, narrator, audience. Partly it is because the significance of the collaborations involved in Fugard's 'township plays' has not yet been fully acknowledged, nor do we have all the detail we need about the creative input of key performers in all the work associated with Fugard – performers such as Zakes Mokae, John Kani, Winston Ntshona, and, especially, Yvonne Bryceland. Their input was registered not only in the obviously 'collaborative' works such as *Sizwe Bansi is Dead*, but even in such apparently 'private' and conventionally structured and produced plays as *Dimetos*, which contains key speeches scripted by Fugard from Bryceland's own words during pre-rehearsal workshops. As if to reinforce the point, Fugard's production *My Life*, premiered at the Arts Festival in Grahamstown in July 1994 and not yet published, placed five young women from different backgrounds on stage to perform extracts from their personal diaries – a performance filled with adolescent pathos and naivety, yet directly associated with the historic changes of the present. Most interesting from the point of view of narrative, however, is the fact that this offered a kind of group presentation implicitly challenging the 'normal' structure of storytelling – a 'recital', Fugard's co-director Rebecca Waddell said they called it, 'not a play' (quoted in Bowker and West, Interview with the cast of *My Life*, 57).

Although a slight work, *My Life* hinted at new possibilities for the Fugardian form of theatre, even a turning-point; while other productions at this, the first national arts festival after the April 1994 watershed in South African political life, seemed merely to reflect nostalgia and uncertainty. Among the most successful plays, Reza de Wet's powerful exercise in Afrikaner grotesque, *Drif*, was set in the early thirties, and Barney Simon's engaging version of a Can Themba story, *The Suit*, was set in fifties Sophiatown. Even Fugard's early *Nongogo*, revived under Jerry Mofokeng's astute direction as 'a play about overcoming the past', served only to recall the fact that its final message, on the contrary, was to suggest the survival of old structures, and the impossibility of liberating oneself from the past. In this context *My Life* – its title derived from a pop song the girls use for the aerobics class which frames their performance – was unexpectedly fresh and contemporary, while relying on the manipulation of familiar, everyday techniques of storytelling. Perhaps the most consciously self-effacing of any of his contributions to the theatre, *My Life* was set up by Fugard as a different, a new kind of theatrical expression to suit the new times: it 'taps into the same source of energy' as the workshopped pieces with John Kani and Winston Ntshona, Fugard told an interviewer, but whereas he had been 'quite ruthless' with 'John and Winston's raw material', he had, he said, 'tried to be totally respectful of this material' (Sichel, 'Confessions of a Passionate Patriot', 9); a view apparently confirmed two months later by the cast, who summed up the development of their production thus: 'Nothing was changed out of what we said except that he just put it in the order that he wanted it . . . if he liked some of the stories, then he would include them' (Bowker and West, interview, 54–5).

The strength of the cast's performance lay in the engaging embodiment through these stories of the everyday surfaces of their lives, while circling familiar themes of guilt, fear, and anxiety. By offering a mouthpiece for their stories, Fugard directed attention away from the desire to tell his own (channelled meanwhile into his memoir *Cousins*), and towards the potential of the female cultural producer. And yet, defusing the patriarchal presumption of female selfhood as a construct within the dominant culture may not have been entirely successful, since theatregoing audiences would have been aware of Fugard's name and presence behind the production. As if in recognition of this, he placed himself on-stage as the self-styled Author in his next play, *Valley Song* (1995), where he is revealed resisting the struggle towards expression of the young Cape coloured girl Veronica. *My Life* represents the furthest Fugard has managed to go in trying to absent himself from the process of offering to speak for the voiceless. As I have suggested elsewhere, for all the evidence of earlier productions such as *The Island* of the liberal playwright offering an empowering voice to those broken, imprisoned, or otherwise silenced by the apartheid regime, there has also always been potential or actual compromise involved in simultaneously defining the terms in which the colonized 'other' could be expressed ('Resituating Fugard', 353ff). The multiple monologues of *My Life* have been structured so as to contrast while interweaving the experiences of the young women as different but related in a way which suggests the playwright's hand: the predictable focus upon black resistance and aggression (Shoki tells of refusing to confess after being caught up in the burning of her school by young comrades) is contrasted with white ignorance and guilt (although Heather denies feeling guilty when she realizes how sheltered her life has been compared to the others), in an echo of the speeches of Thami and Isabel in *My Children! My Africa!* And the concluding 'message', that 'our main problem in South Africa is a lack of communication', sounds a familiar, rather facile didacticism.

At the same time, however, the unexpected insistence of the young Tamil woman Gamy that her 'traditionalist' beliefs about marriage be respected, the struggle of the 'Hotnot, Kapie' woman Riana to draw on her Sotho grandmother's strength against male violence, the sheer drive of the performers to demand recognition of their identities, constitute a surprising move across familiar race and gender if not class boundaries — a move more evident in performance than in the script. Have the performers successfully resisted Fugard's appropriation? 'These are our lives. What about yours?' asks for a more considered, active understanding from the audience than usual in Fugard. Overall, the performance of *My Life* touches on the complex origins of oral traditions, of storytelling as an everyday as well as historically grounded, communal activity in older societies; yet transformed to serve the purposes of a hybridized present struggling to move away from the monolithic, high-cultural European forms so angrily anathematized by Masekela.

It is striking that after lengthy auditioning Fugard seems to have been unable to find any young men to offer themselves in this way. Were there really none available? The drive towards finding a place for the woman's voice in his work has been constant since at least the mid-sixties, and it may be that this has less to do with his individual make-up than with a deep sense that what he has been looking for on some level is a gendered tendency towards the more interactive, group storytelling so noticeable in *My Life*. Researchers have drawn attention to the non-hierarchical, non-linear structure of the kernel stories that frequently dominate the storytelling practices of women in many cultures, enabling a group identity to emerge which implicitly challenges male-dominated discourses, as well as the latter's tendency to regulate and silence women's voices (Langellier and Peterson, 'Spinstorying', 157–79). These women's stories, it is claimed, spiral from conversation to story to conversation in a curvilinear structure in which the personal narratives of the group 'spin connections and interweave women's lives' (173). The normative male narrative in cultures in which a boundary between 'story' and 'conversation' is marked becomes a boundaryless continuum, in which co-operative interruption rather than competitive domination is the norm. The process implies group interaction rather than the familiar Western, one-way speaker–listener dyadic model, and participatory identification rather than a struggle to assert or maintain individual identity (174).

The tendency towards multiple monologue and circularity in Fugard's work is generally ascribed to the influence of modernist European theatre, from Beckett to Grotowski; and there can be little doubt of the effect that modernist practice has had upon plays from *Boesman and Lena* to *Orestes* and *Sizwe Bansi is Dead*, as the playwright himself has often testified. But it is also striking how far, at certain moments in his career, Fugard has been specifically concerned to tell the woman's story, with varying results – including, however, such truly remarkable theatrical performances as Yvonne Bryceland's embodiment, in *Boesman and Lena*, of the despised Lena's spiralling search for 'someone to listen' to her. Fugard cast Bryceland as Lena, one of a pair of Cape coloured derelicts evicted as 'white man's rubbish' at the start of the play, in which almost the entire action is their attempt to construct a shelter for the night upon the desolate mudflats outside Port Elizabeth – except for the arrival of an elderly African, who comes out of the dark to share their fire, cannot speak or understand their language, and who dies after Lena tries to tell him her story. His story, it is obvious even to audiences unfamiliar with his language (Xhosa in the original production), is a sorry tale of lonely wanderings around the countryside, a kind of ground bass to Lena's.

In an important sense, the shape of *Boesman and Lena* is derived less from the European tradition of absurdist drama, than from the impact upon an experienced, practising South African playwright of close, almost unbearable contact with the demand to be heard of the disenfranchised peoples around him – including especially the doubly disenfranchised black women. 'Black' here is not to be understood as in any simple terms the 'other' of postcolonial theorizing, as Lena's mixed status as a 'Hotnot meid' insists: 'Hotnot' (the word she uses of herself as given) is the abusive term derived from the earliest naming by Dutch settlers of the original, precolonial inhabitants of the Cape, the Khoisan whose stones greeted the Portuguese explorers in Mossel Bay, and a people whose intercourse with the dominant newcomers was only matched by the latter's persistent attempts to deny or downgrade their existence.

Persistent indeed: in 1984 officials of the Cape Department of Education ordered all copies of *Boesman and Lena* in their schools to be burned, after complaints that the language of the set text was 'foul' – that is, precisely the bastardized or illegitimate discourse of the 'Hotnot'. Certainly the text is replete with offensive vulgarisms such as 'poep' (shit), 'moer' (cunt), and so on, which school authorities are likely to object to, no matter how prevalent they are in fact among the people the play is about (and others), or how carefully they are stitched into the dialogue, to create a kind of poetry of despair. 'Hotnot' is an offensive version of the earlier 'Hottentot', given by early travellers to describe the indigenous people of the Cape, supposedly in imitation of a word in their songs, and more recently applied to any mixed-race or coloured person by whites, hence even among the people themselves a term of abuse. Earlier liberal humanist, universalist readings of *Boesman and Lena* at home and abroad had led to a presumption on the part of the school authorities that the play was as safe as – Shakespeare, perhaps. Suddenly they were obliged to listen to it, and participate in its mediation, in their own peculiarly pernicious way.

That way was the way of book-burning, thus of a piece with the violent exclusions of Calvinist ideology long at work in South African society, with its draconian censorship provisions, its deafness to dissent in any shape or form, its rejection of the people that served the elect. From Fugard's earliest published writings, the impulse to acknowledge the way of speaking, the lives, the very existence of those excluded is evident. In *Boesman and Lena* this is confirmed by the fact that the play was one result of repeated attempts to render with fidelity the story of a rejected, wandering, nameless Cape coloured woman encountered in the desolate Karroo region in 1965. The woman's story, about being cleared off a farm after her husband's death, was told to one of Fugard's collaborative black performers, Serpent Player Mabel Magada, in the playwright's car when they gave the woman a lift. She told Magada a simple tale of being sent off the farm, which was her livelihood, because her husband who worked there had died. She was many miles from anywhere, and did not know the whereabouts of her nine children. She would probably sleep in roadside drains.

Having heard this tale, Fugard confided to his notebooks that he would 'never escape' it (*Notebooks*, 129). When he recalled watching her walk off under the blazing sun, all her possessions on her head, he saw 'no defeat – there was pain, and great suffering, but no defeat', and it struck him that two of his female characters already seemed to have made that walk – Hester (*Hello and Goodbye*) and Milly (*People Are Living There*) (124). Yet they were 'poor whites', and it was her later reincarnation as the miserable derelict mixed-race Lena which effectively witnessed to the lives and suffering of women like the one who told Mabel Magada her story, scrabbling for a living in drains or on the mudflats of the eastern Cape.

As *Boesman and Lena* made its own way through production and performance beyond Fugard's original, local conception of it, he tried once more to articulate the story of the woman on the road. This was in *The Road to Mecca* (1985), ostensibly a celebration of the life and work of Miss Helen Martins, a Karroo recluse whose neighbours turned against her when she began producing curiously pagan sculptures in her garden, and who finally committed suicide. Yvonne Bryceland played the main role, without being able to rescue the play from its uncertainties – uncertainties generated, it seems to me, by an implicit acknowledgement of Fugard's struggle to meet the challenge of the woman on the road, and this play's incomplete or fractured mediation of her story, which reappears as something told, rather than embodied. The failed mediation registers the larger failure of the English liberal tradition, a failure fully to acknowledge the voiceless, even as it gestures towards their presence: a gesture variously represented in the nameless black corpse floating through Nadine Gordimer's *The Conservationist* (1974), the ventriloquized black workers of Jeremy Cronin's much-anthologized poem 'To learn how to speak . . .' (*Inside*, 1983), or the apparently tongueless black servant of Coetzee's *Foe* (1986). In Fugard's play it is the troubled young white schoolteacher, Elsa Barlow, who wishes to admit the voice and sufferings of the oppressed, above all the sufferings of the woman she met on the Karroo road while on her way to visit her friend, Helen Martins – to whom she tells of the encounter. The meeting between anguished liberal protester and stoic victim is referred to three times in the play, but remains marginalized by Fugard's focus upon the central character, the lonely Miss Helen, and her battle to save her artistic vision.

Elsa's encounter as described in the play recalls both Fugard's earlier encounter with the woman on the road, and one more recent, when he asked the name of a black woman walking the same dreary way and she replied, 'My English name is Patience'. This was in fact the first title of *Mecca*, dropped when he realized she was not to become as important as he had first intended, thereby losing an opportunity to challenge the dominant white construction of black people by confronting not only Elsa, and the eccentric Miss Helen, but also the patriarchal Afrikaner Calvinist minister Byleveld, who wishes to have Miss Helen consigned to an old folks' home. The acceptance of Patience's English name – as we are smugly reminded in the play, 'Patience is a virtue, virtue is a grace' – blocks the possibility, at least partially evident in the characters of women like Lena, of defiance, if not affirmation, by constructing her as suffering object.

III

The defining contrast to one-directional, ultimately excluding works such as Fugard's *Mecca* is provided by *Have You Seen Zandile?*, whose appearance coincided with it. One of a very small but growing number of plays conceived and created by women since the 1970s, *Zandile* began when the young journalist, poet, and actress Gcina Mhlophe sought her own voice through a series of diary entries written after the death of her mother. Commissioned by director Marilyn Vanrenen for a festival of women's plays at the Market Theatre in Johannesburg, and workshopped by Vanrenen, singer Thembi Mtshali, and Mhlophe (who performed the leading role herself), *Zandile* depicts the development of self-awareness in a schoolgirl who realizes she is a black woman in a society which denigrates her race and gender; and who goes on to turn herself from the object of others' perceptions into an active subject, by telling her story and affirming her identity. Mhlophe thereby mediates her own experience in a way Fugard is debarred from offering by race, gender, and position, although as the black women performers of Lena have demonstrated, the potential remains in at least that role for resistance, for reappropriating the stories he has drawn upon for its writing.

Like her creator Mhlophe, Zandile is illegitimate, and lives at first with her storytelling grandmother near Durban. The grandmother's ambitions for the girl's education, with her qualified reverence for traditional values, reflect a clear-eyed grasp of the complexities of urban culture, and prepare Zandile well to resist the oppressive, patriarchal side of rural life after her mother's family abduct her to the Transkei. Exploring the girl's inner world through continuous, interwoven, and multilingual monologue, mime, role-play, and song, Mhlope enacts the profound 'refashioning' of cultural categories which, according to Barbara Masekela, 'will allow new voices to be heard' ('We Are Not Returning Empty-handed', 40).

Apartheid may be gone, but as I write, despite the proposed liberalization of the new constitution, African women remain marginalized 'minors' (see Cock, *Colonels and Cadres*, 43; Women's Charter, *Learn and Teach*, 7); and so it is understandable that feminists should quickly claim Mhlophe's voice, although she herself to a degree resists that claim, as a white metropolitan imposition. For her, refashioning the culture of silence in South Africa means more than allowing new voices to be heard, entering if not appropriating the realm of the 'other', it means creating a new medium and audience for her own voice – a process she furthers by reactivating oral, participatory traditions long eroded by the migrant labour system, and devalued by the cultural pre-eminence of the English-speaking, urban elite. *Zandile* reveals the rejected child learning the art of storytelling from her Zulu grandmother, then as a teenager executing an untranslated Xhosa praise poem for her school headmaster, and finally, in silence, accepting as she mourns the past selves she takes out of her grandmother's suitcase, as she removes all the little parcels placed there while the woman still lived in hope of her return. Zandile (whose name means 'the number of girls is growing') thereby resists both the dominant discourses of the ruling class, which Fugard finds so hard to escape, and remarkably the alternative, oppositional discourses of black protest theatre as well, creating a version of subjectivity out of deprivation which remains a challenge. Mhlophe has since become an itinerant storyteller performing, and assisting audiences to perform, traditional and new stories at schools and public gatherings with her group Zanendaba ('bring me a story'); and always in a fluid mix of languages, although mainly English, Zulu, and Xhosa. The public response, people coming forward to tell their stories, young and old learning or relearning the verbal tags, formulaic expressions, poems and songs of their fragmented communities, has crossed race, class, and gender boundaries, without erasing difference.

Despite inevitable, increasing commercial and media pressure upon her, Mhlophe's aim to invite identification with everyday experience – primarily but not exclusively of black women and children – through a kind of 'spinstorying' of the present, signifies a version of community- rather than nation-building. This offers a more important signal in the long term than the recent arrival of numerous women within the interim power structures (including the new Deputy Minister of Arts and Culture, Brigitte Mabandla, praised for being one of the most effective voices promoting gender equality within the ANC), since these struc- tures remain tied to a unitary, if not monolithic idea of nationhood, as the lack of progress on gender issues in practice implies. A broader per- spective upon the idea of nation has been offered for many years by the plays of Zakes Mda who, although born in South Africa, has spent much of his life in Lesotho and in exile abroad. A season of Mda's works was presented in various Johannesburg venues to mark his return in January 1995 as Visiting Professor in the influential Witwatersrand University drama department, but he remains remarkably little known in South Africa, for so prolific and adventurous a playwright. His plays have been banned and unbanned, and have appeared in urban South African venues since the late seventies. They often focus upon intimate or family rela- tions as the basis for their critique, unlike the protest work of Soweto playwrights like Maponya and Manaka. Even more important in the pre- sent context, they question national boundaries – as in *The Hill* (revived as part of the 1995 season), which is about the social and economic pre- dicament of the migrant labourers and female underclass of Southern rather than South Africa, thereby including the nominally decolonized and independent territories on its borders.

Mda's recognition that decolonization is only part of a lengthy pro- cess of liberation applies also to the sense of the situation of women displayed in his work. 'It is now time for us to change things', exclaims the

Woman of *And the Girls in Their Sunday Dresses* (1988). 'To liberate not only ourselves, but the men themselves, for we are all in bondage! Yes the men in this free and independent country are in bondage, mostly to their attitudes ... sitting back and swimming in the glories of the past' (27). As so often, this means gender liberation has to wait upon the general change in society. For a much stronger sense of the potential claim for space to speak, you have to turn again to the small band of women struggling to articulate their story.

One of those women is Fatima Dike, whose experience as a stage manager at the Space Theatre, Cape Town, during the early seventies, when Fugard, Kani, Ntshona, and Bryceland were engaged on the 'Statements' plays, helped her develop the expertise for creating two multilingual plays, one set in the distant past (*The Sacrifice of Kreli*, 1976) and one in the present (*The First South African*, 1977), using ritual and spectacle for effect, but without specifying the women's perspective, or departing from familiar theatrical structures. Yet more recently, with her production *So What's New?* (1991, revised 1994; unpublished), eight continuous scenes about three middle-aged township women obsessed with a television soap opera while their businesses collapse and the streets explode, Dike defines a more compelling, formally distinct, satirical vision of the complex formation of women's role in South Africa today. The play resembles *Zandile* in its interweaving of pop culture, gossip, and storytelling to register serious issues of gender and identity, but offers more explicit political comment. Yet in Dike's latest, unpublished work, *Seven Vignettes from the New South Africa*, seen so far only in a fugitive Paris production (June 1995), with the playwright herself performing the seven 'vignettes' or monologues by men and women of varying race and class, her practice is converging with the multivoiced, interweaving, 'curvilinear' narratives which the Fugard of *My Life* has touched, and Mhlophe's group has been engaged.

Deceptively short, even minimalist, Dike's vignettes offer a multiplicity of subjective viewpoints upon the present – from the maidservant who pretends she has voted Nationalist Party so that her 'madam' will raise her salary, to the angry young soldier who served his country's white rulers in the border war. They all affirm or verify the everyday as performable, including the everyday of what is conventionally marginalized as woman's domain – the domain of the small-scale, personal, and domestic, which for this writer-actress need not lose its connection with the more public realm, with the history and politics of a rapidly changing society. Dike herself insists that, in a time of radical uncertainty, with most theatre workers unsure of their ground, 'we're still trying to find a voice for this new era ... but we must not lose our past, a country that forgets its history is lost' (personal interview, 26 March 1995). After all, *So What's New?* originated in 1990 with the release of Mandela as the start point of its story; its continuing development (currently for television) is part of Dike's ongoing attempt to express 'the generations of women, through the apartheid years, to their children growing up now, to *their* children' (interview, 1995).

As the opportunities for active involvement of all the peoples of South Africa in cultural activities increase in the new dispensation, will the theatre, however defined, play a role beyond confirming the changing status quo? The Market Theatre, where almost all the plays I have mentioned have been performed, in 1995 received its first state subsidy, and John Kani, its Director, claimed it would still put on plays 'relevant to our lives', proposing furthermore to bring in a wider audience by bussing from the townships, if necessary. But what do township audiences want? As the subject of Dike's *So What's New?* reminds us, imported commercial fare still dominates popular perceptions of theatre in the country, encouraged by the development of local television as an American clone. And if some leavening of the commercial stodge is provided by local satire (for example, Pieter-Dirk Uys's work in theatre and on television), there seems at present to be an overriding concern to revisit the past through revisions of earlier works such as the Junction Avenue Theatre Company's *Sophiatown*, or *District Six: The Musical*. Critics enthuse over consciously local versions of Shakespeare's *Titus Andronicus* and Büchner's *Woyzeck*: but to what end, in the new dispensation? We should seek ways of speaking no longer determined by the status quo, which still effectively marginalizes the majority.

Often such speech can only be heard in secret or by chance, in a world dominated by the globalizing forces of international power struggles, media hegemony, and the movement of investment. It is up to us, as variously positioned cultural mediators, critics, academics, and 'authorities', to listen for the quiet, maybe hidden way. To enable us to do so with proper self-awareness, to avoid the inevitable imposition of newly excluding values such as those proposed by the Rainbow Nation project behind the Rugby World Cup and analogous recent cultural phenomena, we need simultaneously to assert new values as we rethink the history in which we participate. We need to develop our own permeable, even perhaps curvilinear narratives of the past and the present, looping into the future.

Works cited

Bowker, Veronica, and Mary West. Interview with the cast of *My Life*. *Current Writing*. 7. 1 (April 1995): 54–9.

Cock, Jacklyn. *Colonels and Cadres: War and Gender in South Africa*. Cape Town: Oxford University Press, 1991.

da Gama, Vasco. 'Diary of Vasco da Gama'. *South African Explorers*. Selected and introduced by Eric Axelson. London: Oxford University Press, 1954.

Dike, Fatima. Personal interview. 26 March 1995.

Fanon, Frantz. *The Wretched of the Earth*. Trans. Constance Farrington. Harmondsworth: Penguin, 1967.

Fugard, Athol. *Notebooks: 1960–1977*. Ed. Mary Benson. London: Faber & Faber, 1983.

  Valley Song. London: Faber & Faber, 1996.

  'Some Problems of a Playwright from South Africa'. *Twentieth Century Literature* (Athol Fugard Issue). 39. 4 (Winter 1993): 381–3.

Gray, Stephen. *Southern African Literature: An Introduction*. Cape Town: David Philip, 1979.

Hauptfleisch, Temple. 'Post-Colonial Criticism, Performance Theory and the Evolving Forms of South African Theatre'. *South African Theatre Journal* 6. 2 (September 1992): 64–82.

Kruger, Loren. 'Staging South Africa'. *Transition* 59 (1993): 120–9.

Langellier, Kristin M., and Petersen, Eric E. 'Spinstorying: An Analysis of Women Storytelling'. *Performance, Culture, Identity*. Ed. Elizabeth C. Fine and Jean Haskell Spear. Westport: Praeger, 1992. 157–79.

Masekela, Barbara. 'We Are Not Returning Empty-handed'. *Die Suid-Afrikaan* 27 (August/September 1990): 38–40.

Orkin, Martin. *Drama and the South African State*. Manchester: Manchester University Press, 1991.

Peterson, Bhekizizwe. 'Apartheid and the Political Imagination in Black South African Theatre'. *Journal of Southern African Studies* 16. 2 (June 1990): 228–45.

Sichel, Adrienne. 'Confessions of a Passionate Patriot'. *The Star Tonight*, 21 June 1994: 8–9.

Steadman, Ian. 'Collective Creativity: Theatre for a Post-Apartheid Society'. *Rendering Things Visible: Essays on South African Literary Culture*. Ed. Martin Trump. Johannesburg: Ravan, 1990. 307–21.

Walder, Dennis. 'Resituating Fugard: South African Drama as Witness'. *New Theatre Quarterly* 8/32 (November 1992): 343–61.

Women's Charter, The. *Learn and Teach*, August 1994: 7.

16

South African theatre in the United States
the allure of the familiar and of the exotic

JEANNE COLLERAN

It struck me that to the world at large Africa has always been a dark
hinterland of the psyche, perforce unexplored, a sunken continent of the
unknown or the subconscious on which to project delicious fantasies of
magic and death . . . Every North needs a South – it may even fabricate an
internal one, as we see happening in Europe now – if only to provide for the
movement of disequilibrium.   BREYTEN BREYTENBACH

In an address made to the United States Congress in June of 1990, shortly
after his release from prison, Nelson Mandela read into the
Congressional record the names of those black American leaders whose
struggle anticipated his own. 'We could not', Mandela stated, 'have heard
of and admired John Brown, Sojourner Truth, Frederick Douglass, W.
E. B. DuBois, Marcus Garvey, Martin Luther King, Jr and others – we
could not have heard of these and not be moved to act as they were moved
to act' (Nixon, *Homelands*, 187). On 2 May 1994, after F. W. de Klerk's
concession speech, Mandela spoke at an ANC victory celebration and
again invoked the words of an American civil-rights leader; looking over
at Coretta Scott King, who was with him on the podium, he repeated the
words of her late husband, words with both personal and historical resonance: 'Free at last! Free at last!' (Mandela, *Long Walk*, 540).

Mrs King's company that jubilant night, like Mandela's decision during his American tour to show support for the on-going struggle of black
Americans, underscores the frequent tendency to cast these battles for
racial equality as mirror histories. Yet, just as frequently, Breytenbach's
sense of Africa's psychological usefulness as the 'dark hinterland of the
psyche' is also descriptive of the different value and utility assigned to
South African politics by North American politics and purposes. When
comparisons became odious or when a different kind of political capital
was needed than that bought by eliding the half-shared histories of South
African and American race relations, the response to apartheid could be
usefully reconfigured to signify difference and distance. In either case,

South African politics habitually are read through the refracted lens of American race relations.[1]

The popularity of South African theatre in the United States is one example of how political struggle and the cultural products born thereof become domesticated during the process of international exchange. However much sponsorship of South African theatre performances in the United States has been accompanied by an unambiguously announced concern for human rights, ultimately their presentation exerts a much more equivocal stance. In the main, the appeal these theatre works exert appears bound to two kinds of representational seduction, each an inversion of the other: one is the allure of the familiar and the other is the allure of the exotic. For audiences in the United States, Athol Fugard's enormously popular theatre exerts the allure of the familiar;[2] their depictions of racial antagonisms are cast most often in terms of familial rather than systemic struggle, and thus they fit easily within the usual parameters of both American theatre and American politics. The black South African theatre which has toured the United States, particularly the theatre of Mbongeni Ngema, offers American audiences an alternative, yet equally inviting vision of race relations: this is the allure of the exotic, one spectacularly brokered in terms of a 'real', 'authentic', and 'perilous' witness.[3] In both cases, whether it is Fugard's 'familiar'

1. For further discussion of the vexed relationship between American and South African racial histories, see Rob Nixon's *Homelands, Harlem, and Hollywood*. The premise of Nixon's book is worth repeating here: in his view, 'no other post-World War II struggle for decolonization has been so fully globalized; no other has magnetized so many people across such various divides, or imbued them with such a resilient common cause' (1).

2. Indeed, in 1991, for example, it was possible to see a play by Athol Fugard somewhere in the United States every month of the year: *The Road to Mecca* was performed in the farmlands of the Pennsylvania Amish country; *My Children! My Africa!* in the rust belt of Detroit, and *'Master Harold'... and the Boys* by the Louisiana bayou. This information was provided to me by representatives from both the William Morris and Samuel French agencies; for further discussion of Fugard's popularity see Colleran, 'Athol Fugard'.

3. My discussion centres, obviously, on some of the plays written by black South Africans that have toured internationally and received particular attention in the US. These dramas participate in some of the many forms black South African drama has taken, including protest plays, history plays, rural/mythic plays, and township musicals. Outside of the parameters of this discussion, but still noteworthy because of their conspicuous absence from well-known

theatre or the 'exotic' theatre of black South Africans, the South African
theatre which may have begun as a specific, constructive engagement
with particular issues of jurisprudence has been neutered of its original
political effect, and even, to some considerable degree, of its testimonial
capacity.[4]

In examining how South African theatre 'plays' itself out to
American audiences, I find it important, as an American critic and
theatregoer, not only to think about why imported works of political theatre seem to need to be so adapted to American domestic issues that they
lose much of their particularity and some of their political effect, but also
to think about what happens when local, resistance theatre meets international capital and interacts with established first-world cultural institutions. Ultimately, however, I hope to suggest that the politically disabling
allure of the familiar and of the exotic can be resisted by an investigation,
on the part of theatre producers, critics, and audiences, of the differences
between the original and the current site of performance. Politically
effective theatre, and the important cultural understandings they enable,
depend crucially on our willingness to historicize as well as to empathize,
and to distinguish differences as well as reconcile them.

FUGARD: THE ALLURE OF THE FAMILIAR

For American theatre audiences, Athol Fugard's theatre has assumed the
reputation of the nearly unassailable, a status that was consolidated during an immensely profitable period of creative activity between 1980 and
1990. Three of Fugard's plays were premiered in the United States

and well-connected American stages, are works like Maishe Maponya's *The
Hungry Earth* or Zakes Mda's *Dead End*. For further discussion of black South
African Theatre of Resistance, see Gorak, 'Nothing to Root For', and
Steadman, 'Black South African Theatre'.

4. I use the term 'political theatre' in a particularly narrow sense in this chapter,
defining it as a theatre practice which regards itself as a form of social and
political intervention, and which takes as its subject a particular issue of
jurisprudence, of civil rights, or other aspect of governance, and whose
intent, in performance, is to convey an identifiable political vantage point and
encourage its acceptance among audience members. In drawing the
conclusion I just have, my intention is not to castigate particular South African
playwrights but rather to call attention to what political meanings are lost and
gained in the process of producing and receiving a culturally translated
theatre piece. My discussion throughout is therefore indebted to the work
of Patrice Pavis, especially *Theatre at the Crossroads of Culture*.

during this time, and although Fugard has since decided against having his dramas performed first before non-South African audiences, nonetheless, it was during this interval that his critical success was established and his popularity ensconced.

The American acclaim for Fugard's work, measured by awards and reviews, bordered on nothing less than veneration. Enshrined as the 'liberal conscience of South Africa' (Cody and Schechter, 'An Interview with Athol Fugard', 71), Fugard's major plays of the eighties – *A Lesson from Aloes*, *'Master Harold'... and the Boys*, *The Road to Mecca*, and a revival of *The Blood Knot* – drew major awards and accolades like the following: 'If there is a more urgent and indispensable playwright in the world theatre than South Africa's Athol Fugard, I don't know who it would be' (Kroll, *Newsweek*, 29 March 1982, 52).[5] Frank Rich, theatre critic for the *New York Times*, agreed: 'There may be two or three living playwrights in the world who can write as well as Athol Fugard, but I'm not sure that any of them has written a recent play that can match *Master Harold*' (17 March 1982, C17). For critic Samuel Freedman, Fugard was a 'South African visionary,' (*Vanity Fair* (September 1987): 124) and for William Henry III, he was the 'greatest active playwright in the English-speaking world' (*Time*, 18 April 1988, 81). Fugard has acknowledged the unusual rapport his works enjoy among American audiences, conceding that:

> American audiences and American actors go for the same sort of theatre that I try to write. I don't think it's an accident that I earn eighty or ninety percent of my living as a playwright in America. In England, it's only about ten or fifteen percent. The English don't tune into my plays as strongly as American audiences or critics. (RICHARDS, 'The Art of Theatre VIII', 150)

These same American audiences and critics supported Fugard's decision to work extensively in the United States during this period, and there was little recognition that the 'South African visionary' working in their midst was being dislodged at home by the emergence of a 'new kind of theatre': the theatre of the *Woza Albert!* playwrights, Ngema and Mtwa,

---

5. Vandenbroucke's *Truths the Hand Can Touch*, though now dated, remains the best source for tracing the particulars of Fugard's early career. The awards Fugard won in the eighties include: the New York Drama Critics Circle Award for best play for *Aloes*; the Drama Desk Award and Outer Critic's Circle Award for *Master Harold*; the New York Drama Critics Circle Award for *Road to Mecca*. During this period Fugard was associated primarily with the Yale Repertory Theatre.

and the theatre of Maishe Maponya, Matsemela Manaka, and others. These writers, strongly influenced by the Black Consciousness Movement of the seventies, resisted the representation of black township and location existence by white authors. However much Fugard was lionized in the United States, in South Africa he found himself stripped of a subject.[6]

In retrospect, Fugard's plays during this time appear to be defensive gestures of entitlement: as if to legitimize his right to a theatrical voice, he changed the focus of his dramas to what might more arguably be called his own: his childhood experiences, his Afrikaner heritage, his memories of Port Elizabeth and the nearby Karoo. His decision to stage his works abroad is connected to this assertion of private vision, private right. To Mel Gussow, Fugard defended their American premieres by explaining that the 'origin of the work was so private and so South African that he was hesitant about exposing it to an audience of his countrymen, . . . before he could validate its universality' ('Profiles', 47). To Russell Vandenbroucke, Fugard submitted that while South Africa was 'half owner of the rights' of his earlier plays, *Master Harold* 'belongs to me; this one's mine' (*Truths the Hand Can Touch*, 192).

The terms which Fugard used to defend his choice of subject matter and performance site are revealing. By regarding his subject matter as *both* private *and* South African, Fugard implicitly exerted ownership over his 'private' experience, thereby fending off criticism from some South Africans, even as he publicized these experiences to international audiences as reliably, representatively 'South African'. Further, the validation Fugard explicitly sought for his dramas was not that of representational accuracy nor of achieving some political agency for the population whose lives he has chosen to place upon the stage, though to be fair, all of Fugard's plays, and particularly the earlier, collaborative works, have sought an increase in black franchise. The goals of representational accuracy or political action are secondary, however, to his explicit concern about ensuring the 'universality' of these dramas even though every body on stage has not one but many actual corporeal counterparts, and every gesture and speech has been historically predicated and is politically implicated.

6. The exclusion of white liberals from the emergent Black Consciousness Movement in South Africa is discussed by Rich (*White Power*) and Sole ('Oral Performance and Social Struggle in Contemporary Black South African Literature').

This issue of historical reference and public political discourse has always been a vexed one for Fugard. He repeatedly describes the origins of his theatre pieces as existential rather than historical, and he fervently wants them to deal with the essential 'substance of drama', human desperation (*Playland*, 75). He has stated bluntly that he is a 'storyteller, not a political pamphleteer' (*Playland*, 73). But within a breath of decrying political motivation or historical circumstances as constituent features of his work, Fugard will make statements that recognize the importance of these features: South African theatre, he has conceded, works within an 'almost unique dynamic in terms of the relationship between the event of the stage and the political and social reality out in the streets' (*Playland*, 71). At times, Fugard seems to have convinced himself that this 'unique dynamic' is a form of non-partisan regionalism, a local colouring which produces everything, from plot to setting to dialogue, for one 'storyteller' and from which there may be, ineluctably, a 'political byproduct' (Fugard, 'Some Problems', 385).

By the nineties Fugard resumed premiering his plays in South Africa and writing dramas which directly engaged the State of Emergency politics operative during the waning moments of white governance.[7] Yet, when *My Children! My Africa!*, a drama which argued for the reinstallment of the defeated liberal position within South African politics, was performed in the United States, Fugard again spoke of the play in non-political terms as a 'celebration' of the 'preparedness to forgive' ('Some Thoughts', 389). This celebration was continued in his next work, *Playland*. Talking of the American production of *Playland* at the Alliance Theatre in Atlanta, Georgia, Fugard again glossed over the South African setting and circumstances of the play to remark that 'perhaps the essential American drama is being played out here' (Hulbert, 'The Artist and the City', 22).

What is the effect of the elision of public and private spheres that occurs in both productions of Fugard's dramas and in Fugard's comments about his work? And how are the dramas' politics altered when performed in non-South African venues where this elision goes unnoticed? While it is important to acknowledge Fugard's lifelong commitment to tracing the deformation of all relationships under the perverted rule of *baasskap*, it is also necessary to recognize that his preference for

7. For a discussion of *My Children! My Africa!* as a State of Emergency play, see Visser, 'Drama and Politics in a State of Emergency'.

representing South African history in existential terms nonetheless has political ramifications. Not surprisingly, the dynamic frequently at work in one of Fugard's recent dramas is one which offers therapeutic solutions over political programmes. That Fugard's 'American' plays have taken the form of confessional dramas should therefore surprise few: a culture which values explanation as exoneration as much as American culture does would tolerate nothing less – and desire nothing more.

Arguably, then, the protagonists in the plays of the eighties, from Piet (*A Lesson from Aloes*) to Pavel (*A Place with the Pigs*), through Hallie (*Master Harold*) and Miss Helen (*Road to Mecca*), are versions of the same figure: the beleaguered but blemished good (wo)man who, misunderstood, seeks consolation, forgiveness, support, and community. The plight of these Afrikaner heroes is inevitably intertwined with that of black South Africans; however, the situations of the latter are significantly less foregrounded. Stage presence has always been a prime indicator of a drama's most vested interests, and the relegation of black suffering to backdrop or to invisibility in these plays speaks volumes about the dramas' chief concerns. In *Aloes*, for example, the agony experienced by the Afrikaner, Piet, is the focus of greater interest and to a slight degree, greater sympathy, than the pain experienced by the black South African, Steve. In the allegorical equivalences of *A Place with the Pigs*, black South Africans are not represented at all; in *The Road to Mecca*, a single off-stage presence, that of Patience, is all that calls to mind the black majority (see Blumberg, 'Women Journeying'). In each play, Fugard makes some attempt to figure black suffering into the larger plot line, but inevitably his attention is drawn back to a kind of metafigure that has evolved from these plays: the embattled moral man caught against his will in a fraught historical situation.[8] In the plays of the eighties, the moral man is white.

Obviously, this metafigure can exert an enormous appeal in the US, where a discussion of racism cannot be broached without resurrecting, in white liberal circles, similar spectres of shame, and in conservative ones, explosions of white outrage over affirmative action privilege. But while the subject of racism cannot be broached directly, it is everywhere articulated, inflected in the ostensibly colour-blind yet racially divisive tracts that range from legal to literary expression. Marked most by

8. I argue the validity of reading Mr M., in *My Children! My Africa!*, as the black version of this white prototype in 'Athol Fugard'.

unacknowledged but perceptible dread and fear, the agonized conversation about race in America is particularly receptive to the solace offered by Fugard's iconic figures of guilty goodwill. Dissembling our own history of violent racism, Fugard's white South African heroes are welcomed by Americans like long-lost cousins who have reappeared just in time to remind us that despite our tepid political response to both apartheid and to domestic racism, our capacity for moral outrage is still intact.

THE ALLURE OF THE EXOTIC

Productions of Fugard's dramas in the United States are not the only occasions where South African and American cultural histories are elided; when performances of *The Song of Jacob Zulu*, written by Tug Yourgrau, overlapped the Los Angeles riots, its star, K. Todd Freeman was quick to point out that the event 'pulled the play out of South Africa – it was also America' (Bren, 'Playing Jacob Zulu's Song', 26). Freeman's statement speaks – again – to why South African theatre, and in this case black South African theatre, appeals so strongly to American audiences: its depiction of racial alignments is elastic enough that the plays may be 'pulled out' of the South African context and, if need be, 'put back in' again.

One might think it nearly impossible to hystericize (or, alternatively, to trivialize) South African suffering. Yet, in the instance of Mbongeni Ngema's *Sarafina!*, the combination of its own commercial origins and ambitions, its involvement with non-South African cultural sponsors and entrepreneurs, and its reliance on a formulaic style of stock characters and on sensational plots that could readily embrace new formulas, particularly those ensuring overseas success, worked together to quickly turn it into a political spectacle. By the time *Sarafina!* was performed in the US in 1987, little was recognizable of this work's affiliation with the goals and procedures of committed, critical resistance theatre or of its status as a kind of 'liberation musical' theatre. As the uncritical but laudatory reviews received by *Sarafina!* attest, the musical relied so heavily on its much-promoted status as 'victim art' that it disabled critical commentary. Apparently, no one wanted to defame the 'wonderful kids' from Soweto, as the review in the *New Yorker* called them (Oliver, 130); nor, apparently, did any one want to suggest they deserved better.

To the extent that American audiences think about the various forms of South African theatre at all, the tendency is to consolidate them into a homogeneous enterprise. Having very little personal experience with theatre as a tool of cultural intervention, American audiences remain largely ignorant of the wide range of theatrical activity, which includes community theatre for social issues, such as literacy or housing, trade union theatre, and populist theatre.[9] All of the aforementioned are compressed into the single category of township or black theatre, and thus the impression most American theatregoers have is of a solid, concerted oppositional theatre. The fact that there are several exceptions to this model within black South African theatre, particularly musical theatre, which has a long history of purely commercial motivation, remains unknown.

In the United States, black South African theatre also is assumed to communicate the single, unified vantage point of black South Africans as *authoritative* and *authentic*. Hence, the testimonial weight these dramas bear is more considerable in the United States than it is in South Africa, where critical, committed, and confrontational theatre can be more easily separated from its manipulative imitators.[10] In South Africa, for example, the black South African musical has long been recognized as primarily a for-profit entertainment. According to Anthony Akerman's description of the history of the black South African musical, commercial adventurers quickly realized the availability of the immense profit margins to be had in promoting black musical theatre to both black and white audiences. As Akerman points out, the total weekly salary of the entire black cast would require only 75 per cent of a single night's sales, and thus black musical theatre reproduced the same inequitable economic relations that the rest of industry under apartheid did ('Why Must

9. For descriptions of the varieties of theatre activity in South Africa, see Steadman, 'Collective Creativity' and Orkin, *Drama and the South African State*.

10. Andrew Horn makes extraordinarily valuable distinctions between theatres of manipulation and theatres of criticism. That this kind of critique is more valuable to South African critics is also evident in Gevisser's essay, 'Truth and Consequences', where he also repudiates the kind of theatre represented by *Sarafina!*. Gevisser, a South African journalist and critic, writes: '*Sarafina!* thankfully is dead, but its legacy lives on. Its pastiche of political anger and Broadway-style musical fused into a form of struggle-minstrelsy that has proven to be immensely lucrative and has become the almost inescapable model for how black South African theatre should be made' ('Truth and Consequences in Post-Apartheid Theatre', 11).

These Shoes Go On?', 69). More insidiously, the tradition of black musical theatre that evolved from the notoriously exploitative *Ipi Tombi*, devised by Bertha Egnos in 1974 (Trump, 'Part of the Struggle', 171) and revived in the 1980s by Gibson Kente, operates via the sensational plot lines and stock characters described above to confirm 'white attitudes and prejudices' (Akerman, 'Why Must These Shoes Go On?', 68). Nevertheless, the availability of some work, some salary, some 'recognition' within South Africa, and some possibility of travel abroad, would lead few black South Africans to reject participation on ethical or ideological grounds; indeed the stories of black children vying for a place in a Ngema musical are the stuff of both popular culture and a potent promotional ploy (Akerman, 69).

Within the US, most theatre by black South Africans has been produced in co-operation with a large American cultural institution, such as the Lincoln Center or the Brooklyn Academy of Music. Loren Kruger's insightful analyses of South African theatre describe how it has been promoted in metropolitan centres as a particular kind of testimonial theatre, indeed the direst imaginable. As evidence of this dynamic, Kruger cites Amiri Baraka's description of South African theatre, as one aligned to a 'blood-filled society staggering toward revolution' (preface to Ndlovu, *Woza Africa*, xiii). Baraka's inflammatory rhetoric turns on the unfortunately chosen metaphor of movement, a metaphor which becomes ludicrously inappropriate after seeing one of Mbongeni Ngema's recent musicals, with its signature style of showcasing the extraordinarily energetic, athletic, and rousing style of Zulu dancing. No one staggers in a Ngema production; and whatever political appeal is exerted by these dancers waving spears and wearing animal skins seems far more connected to a bravura display of invincible vitality than by any glancing analysis of the anti-apartheid struggle. Ironically, however much musicals like *Sarafina!* have departed from the tradition of collective, political theatre in South Africa, they nevertheless rely on their loose association with this tradition as yet another index of their authenticity. However much black South African theatre 'performs for New York', to borrow Kruger's phrase, its credibility relies on communicating that, at least at one time, it 'performed for the people'. This tacit assumption has the advantage of silently maximizing the comfort level of the overseas audience. Instead of being directly addressed and thereby directly mandated to react politically, American audiences may maintain the more untroubled, voyeuristic position of watching a *re-performance* of what was originally and intentionally enacted for those *supposed* to respond.

In large and significant ways, however, Ngema's theatre works, especially *Sarafina!* and later musicals, barely fit even the loosest profile of committed or collective theatre. Analyses of committed theatre in South Africa emphasize that radical theatre occurs when a member of the 'majority oppressed group presents to a cross-section of that group a theatrical demystification of events in relation to a broad vision of structural change'; and, further, this sustained critique is *not* 'generated by outside cultural agents' (Steadman, 'Collective Creativity', 317). Performances are thus meant to reinforce political consciousness among members of the oppressed group who constitute the play's audience. In fact, virtually none of the most successful black South African musical exports began in a political collective. In the strictest sense of Steadman's definition, none of Mbongeni Ngema's early theatre, such as his collaborative piece with Percy Mtwa and Barney Simon, *Woza Albert!*, and his next work, *Asinamali!*, were works developed without the considerable assistance of 'outside cultural agents'. However, both pieces played initially and forcefully to township audiences and depicted historically specific instances of apartheid oppression, such as the 1983 violence directed against rent strikes that is the subject of *Asinamali!*[11]

Successful public marketing of subsequent musicals required that there be little attempt to make overseas audiences aware of the mixed genealogy of these South African imports. In fact, three of the most recent South African musicals have hardly been imported at all. Gregory Mosher and Bernard Gerstein, of the Lincoln Center Theatre, offered to produce Ngema's *Sarafina!* not only before they had seen it, but before Ngema had written it (Jones, *Nothing Except Ourselves*, vii). *The Song of Jacob Zulu* was written by a man born in South Africa, but raised from childhood in the States; he visited South Africa for the first time in over thirty years in 1987, and his original 'liberation musical' depended heavily on the talents of the singing group Ladysmith Black Mambazo – to whom he was introduced by American Paul Simon's *Graceland* album. *The Sacrifice of Mmbatho*, by an expatriate white South African, Hilary Blecher, was designed under the sponsorship of the Brooklyn Academy of Music. Best described as an 'ethnic idyll' (Horn, 'South African

---

11. For an account of the origins of *Asinamali!*, see Steadman, 'Collective Creativity'.

Theater', 216) where African values meet Christian ones and where traditional laws are superior to South African jurisprudence, the play underemphasizes the political causes for the 'natural' disasters of drought and poverty that the play depicts. Significantly, its original title, *The Daughter of Nebo*, was exoticized for its American audience.

Sarafina! began with an initial ten-week engagement at Lincoln Center, which according to Laura Jones, Ngema's American collaborator and personal biographer, was extended 'numerous times before the show moved to the Cort Theatre on Broadway, where it played to full houses for a year and a half; then it toured the United States, and a second company was formed to tour Europe and Japan' (*Nothing Except Ourselves*, vii). Encouraged by Harry Belafonte to produce a musical which would rely heavily on the *mbaquanga* music made popular by South African jazz musicians such as Hugh Masekela, Ngema's theatre piece, despite its township trappings, was born in exile and bred for export. In its formative beginnings *Sarafina!* drew on no specific, historical incident, in the fashion of *Asinimali*, nor was it intended, like *Woza Albert!*, for a township audience.

Plotless, until Winnie Mandela suggested it celebrate the resilience and commitment of South African children, the story underlying the musical is extraordinarily slight. In fact, *Sarafina!* is a story so well known in South Africa that it could only be news outside the country, for it is, after all, a fictional reworking of the politicization of children via the Soweto Uprising, and it honours the most well known of South African dissidents, Nelson Mandela. Its 'South African' trappings – the Zulu dancing, the *mbaquanga* music, the animal skin costumes, the cast of (mostly female) children – are more ornamental than anything else, and are included, again as pre-eminently *authenticating* gestures, in order to satisfy the vague expectations of the metropolitan audience assembled to watch the 'real thing'. The narrative of the young schoolgirl's political awakening via the efforts of her energetic, committed schoolmistress is sufficiently reductive that it easily became a Hollywood movie. Not surprisingly, the portrayal offered by the movie's star (and producer) Whoopi Goldberg, and the movie's mixture of rousing music and little plot is virtually identical to Goldberg's other 'inspiring' films about saving young black children: *Sister Act I* and *Sister Act II*. (Fortunately, Goldberg has not yet produced *Sarafina!: The Sequel*.)

In short, *Sarafina!* taxes no historical imagination and enacts no specific political critique. As a pseudo-township musical, or more accurately as a representative of a genre that has been wrenched from its local site of production but nonetheless retains identifying characteristics of its site of origin, *Sarafina!* grafts some features of a theatrical form born in resistance and struggle on to one born of profit and apoliticality, and becomes in the process the worst-case scenario of cultural syncretism. Born of international appetite and not of local struggle, the demand for apartheid drama occasioned the drama itself; the capital availed itself and the audience identified itself long before even the subject of the play was finalized.

The kind of theatre represented by *Sarafina!* makes critical appraisal an agonizing enterprise. When Arlene Croce, writing in the *New Yorker*, refused to see and then review Bill T. Jones's *Still/Here*, a dance meditation on AIDS and other fatal diseases, because she could not find sufficient critical space from which to adjudicate the victims/sufferers/performers involved in the project, her decision was assailed by many of the most prominent American directors and writers. Yet, as compelling as the rebuttals to Croce are, the problem which Croce identified – of the near impossibility of separating what is performed from what is lived and suffered – is the same problem posed by works like *Sarafina!* Even as brutal economic reality and scant opportunity for access to major metropolitan sites of culture and capital make Ngema's impulse to seize the opportunities that come his way understandable, nonetheless there are significant differences between works like *Asinamali!* or *Woza Albert!* and works like *Sarafina!* However much *Sarafina!* was advertised as the child's-eye view of what really happened in South Africa, the fact is that the musical 'arrived' in the US self-shielded from dissenting opinion. In its advertising, it insistently drew attention to the fact that the performance was enacted by the very children who had been brutalized by apartheid, thus placing critics in the hideous position of debating the merits of a work literally blood-smeared. The advertising campaign also insisted on the perilousness of the present undertaking, letting it be known that the children might return from the overseas tours to further repression and reprisal.

It is a delicate task to acknowledge and to assess what kinds of limits to critical judgement are posed by one's cultural, economic, and social positioning. *Sarafina!*, by its promotion of the distant but historical 'real', by the urgency of the South African situation, by the prevailing sense that international outrage could play some role in dismantling apartheid, and most of all, by its pathetic appeal via the use of suffering children, effectually disabled critical judgement in the US. This failure of critical reception was linked to the sense that 'foreign', that is, non-South African audiences, lacked both the capacity to adjudicate the authenticity of what was being performed and the ethical credit to call into question what was so worthy and dire a cause. Yet, increasingly as theatre works are the products of cross-cultural marketing campaigns, and are of born of international collaboration, reservations about criticizing *Sarafina!* and other such productions are not only misplaced, they are an abdication of a crucial responsibility.

In his study of the creative vitality of black South African theatre, David Coplan argues that the *efficacy* of black South African performances derives from the fact that these performances 'are so linked to their social meaning that they are *entirely continuous* with experience itself . . . the illocutionary force, the act *in* rather than the mere act *of* dramatic performance is such that what *happens* in theatre happens' ('Ideology and Traditions in South African Black Popular Theater', 157–8). At the very least, the re-production of theatre works related to this tradition, that is, the restaging of black South African theatre in the United States, if it wishes to be anything other than spectacular display, needs to acknowledge that a certain vital connection has been severed.

Indeed a similar acknowledgement is necessary for any work of imported political theatre. If it is to have any political agency or ethical effect, committed political theatre performed internationally relies on the fragile optimism that something more than just spectacle – than just a show of goods and payments – can be produced and exchanged across national borders. It relies, too, on the delicate faith that the historical and political circumstances it represents will not inevitably incite only the most narcissistic reception or interpretation. Against these two pulls – one toward the self-serving familiar, the other toward the insignificant exotic – committed theatre struggles.

Works cited

Akerman, Anthony. 'Why Must These Shoes Go On? A Critique of Black Musicals Made for White Audiences'. *New Theatre Quarterly* 7 (1977–78): 67–9.

Blumberg, Marcia. 'Women Journeying at the South African Margins: Athol Fugard's *The Road to Mecca*'. *South African Writing: Voyages and*

Explorations (Matatu; vol.II). Ed. Geoff V. Davis. Amsterdam: Rodopi, 1994. 39–50.

Bren, Leslie. 'Playing Jacob Zulu's Song'. *New York,* 12 April 1993, 26.

Breytenbach, Breyten. 'Why are Writers Always the Last to Know?' *New York Times Review of Books,* 28 March 1993, 1; 15–17.

Cody, Gabrielle, and Joel Schechter. 'An Interview with Athol Fugard'. *Theater* 19.1 (1987): 70–2.

Colleran, Jeanne. 'Athol Fugard and the Problematics of the Liberal Critique'. *Modern Drama* 38 (1995): 389–407.

Coplan, David. 'Ideology and Traditions in South African Black Popular Theater'. *Journal of American Folklore* 99.392 (April–June 1986): 151–76.

Croce, Arlene. 'Discussing the Undiscussable'. *New Yorker,* 26 December 1994, 54–6.

Forster, Hal. *Recodings: Art, Spectacle and Cultural Politics.* Port Townsend, Wa.: Bay Press, 1985.

Freedman, Samuel. 'Master Harold,' *Vanity Fair* (September 1987): 124.

Fugard, Athol. 'Some Problems of a Playwright from South Africa'. *Twentieth Century Literature* 39 (1993): 381–93.

Gevisser, Mark. 'Truth and Consequences in Post-Apartheid Theatre'. *Theater* 25. 3 (1995): 9–18.

Gorak, Jan. 'Nothing to Root For: Zakes Mda and South African Resistance Theatre'. *Theatre Journal* 41 (1989): 478–91.

Gussow, Mel. 'Profiles: Witness (Athol Fugard)'. *New Yorker,* 20 December 1982, 47–94.

Henry III, William. 'Enemy of the People'. *Time,* 18 April 1988, 81–2.

Horn, Andrew. 'South African Theater: Ideology and Rebellion'. *Research in African Literatures* 17. 2 (1986): 211–33.

Hulbert, Dan. 'The Artist and the City'. *American Theater* 9. 9 (January 1993): 18–23.

Jones, Laura. *Nothing Except Ourselves.* New York: Viking, 1994.

Kroll, Jack. 'Master-Servants'. *Newsweek,* 29 March 1982, 52.

Kruger, Loren. 'Apartheid on Display: South Africa Performs for New York'. *Diaspora* 1. 2 (1991): 191–208.

'So What's New? Women and Theater in the "New South Africa"'. *Theater* 25. 3 (1995): 46–54.

'The Uses of Nostalgia: Drama, History, and Liminal Moments in South Africa'. *Modern Drama* 38.1 (1995): 60–71.

Lochte, Dick. 'Rebel Rebel'. *Los Angeles Magazine* (September 1991): 154–5.

Nixon, Rob. *Homelands, Harlem, and Hollywood.* New York: Routledge, 1994.

Oliver, Edith. 'The Theatre: He Was Her Man." *New Yorker,* 9 November 1987, 129–38.

Orkin, Martin. *Drama and the South African State.* Johannesburg: Witwatersrand University Press, 1991.

Pavis, Patrice. *Theatre at the Crossroads of Culture*. Trans. Loren Kruger. New York: Routledge, 1992.

Rich, Paul B. *White Power and the Liberal Consciousness: Racial Segregation and South African Liberalism, 1921–60*. Manchester: Manchester University Press, 1984.

Rich, Frank. 'World Premiere of Fugard's New Play: A Merciless Mirror'. *New York Times*, 17 March 1982, C17.

Richards, Lloyd. 'The Art of Theatre VIII: Athol Fugard'. *Paris Review* 31 (1989): 129–51.

Sole, Kelwyn. 'Oral Performance and Social Struggle in Contemporary Black South African Literature'. *From South Africa: New Writing, Photographs, and Art*. Ed. David Bunn and Jane Taylor. Chicago: University of Chicago Press, 1987. 254–71.

Steadman, Ian. 'Black South African Theatre after Nationalism'. *English Academy Review* 2 (1984): 9–18.

'Collective Creativity: Theatre for a Post-Apartheid Society'. Trump, ed., *Rendering Things Visible*. 307–21.

Trump, Martin. 'Part of the Struggle: Black Writing and the Liberation Movement'. Trump, ed., *Rendering Things Visible*, 161–85.

Trump, Martin, ed. *Rendering Things Visible: Essays on South African Literary Culture*. Athens: Ohio University Press, 1990.

Vandenbroucke, Russell. *Truths the Hand Can Touch*. New York: Theatre Communications Workshop, 1985.

Visser, Nicholas. 'Drama and Politics in a State of Emergency: Athol Fugard's *My Children! My Africa!*' *Twentieth Century Literature* 39 (1993): 486–502.

Walder, Dennis. 'Resituating Fugard: South African Drama as Witness'. *New Theatre Quarterly* 8/32 (November 1992): 343–61.

Position Papers

17

Preparing ourselves for freedom

ALBIE SACHS

Paper prepared for an ANC in-house seminar on culture [in 1989]

We all know where South Africa is, but we do not yet know what it is. Ours is the privileged generation that will make that discovery, if the apertures in our eyes are wide enough. The problem is whether we have sufficient cultural imagination to grasp the rich texture of the free and united South Africa that we have done so much to bring about.

For decades now we have possessed a political programme for the future – the Freedom Charter. More recently the National Executive of the ANC has issued a set of Constitutional Guidelines which has laid down a basic constitutional approach to a united South Africa with a free and equal citizenry. What we have to ask ourselves now is whether we have an artistic and cultural vision that corresponds to this current phase in which a new South African nation is emerging. Can we say that we have begun to grasp the full dimensions of the new country and new people that is struggling to give birth to itself, or are we still trapped in the multiple ghettoes of the apartheid imagination?

For the sake of livening the debate on these questions, this paper will make a number of controversial observations.

The first proposition I make, and I do so fully aware of the fact that we are totally against censorship and for free speech, is that our members should be banned from saying that culture is a weapon of struggle. I suggest a period of, say, five years.

Allow me, as someone who has for many years been arguing precisely that art should be seen as an instrument of struggle, to explain why suddenly this affirmation seems not only banal and devoid of real content, but actually wrong and potentially harmful.

In the first place, it results in an impoverishment of our art. Instead of getting real criticism, we get solidarity criticism. Our artists are not pushed to improve the quality of their work, it is enough that it be politically correct. The more fists and spears and guns, the better. The range of themes is narrowed down so much that all that is funny or curious or genuinely tragic in the world is extruded. Ambiguity and contradiction are completely shut out, and the only conflict permitted is that between the old and the new, as if there were only bad in the past and only good in the future. If we had the imagination of Sholokhov, and one of us wrote *And Quiet Flows the Tugela*, the central figure would not be a member of UDF or Cosatu, but would be aligned to Inkatha, resisting change, yet feeling oppression, thrown this way and that by conflicting emotions, and through his or her struggles and torments and moments of joy, the reader would be thrust into the whole drama of the struggle for a new South Africa. Instead, whether in poetry or painting or on the stage, we line up our good people on the one side and the bad ones on the other, occasionally permitting someone to pass from one column to the other, but never acknowledging that there is bad in the good, and, even more difficult, that there can be elements of good in the bad; you can tell who the good ones are, because in addition to being handsome of appearance, they can all recite sections of the Freedom Charter or passages of Strategy and Tactics at the drop of a beret.

In the case of a real instrument of struggle, there is no room for ambiguity: a gun is a gun is a gun, and if it were full of contradictions, it would fire in all sorts of directions and be useless for its purpose. But the power of art lies precisely in its capacity to expose contradictions and reveal hidden tensions – hence the danger of viewing it as if it were just another kind of missile-firing apparatus.

And what about love? We have published so many anthologies and journals and occasional poems and stories, and the number that deal with love do not make the fingers of a hand. Can it be that once we join the ANC we do not make love any more, that when the comrades go to bed they discuss the role of the white working class? Surely even those comrades whose tasks deny them the opportunity and direct possibilities of love, remember past love and dream of love to come. What are we fighting for, if not the right to express our humanity in all its forms, including our sense of fun and capacity for love and tenderness and our appreciation of the beauty of the world? There is nothing that the apartheid rulers would like more than to convince us that because apartheid is ugly, the world is ugly. ANC members are full of fun and romanticism and dreams, we enjoy and wonder at the beauties of nature and the marvels of human creation, yet if you look at most of our art and literature you would think we were living in the greyest and most sombre of all worlds, completely shut in by apartheid. It is as though our rulers stalk every page and haunt every picture; everything is obsessed by the oppressors and the trauma they have imposed, nothing is about us and the new consciousness we are developing. Listen in contrast to the music of Hugh Masekela, of Abdullah Ibrahim, of Jonas Gwanga, of Miriam Makeba, and you are in a universe of wit and grace and vitality and intimacy, there is invention and modulation of mood, ecstasy and sadness; this is a cop-free world in which the emergent personality of our people manifests itself. Pick up a book of poems, or look at a woodcut or painting, and the solemnity is overwhelming. No one told Hugh or Abdullah to write their music in this or that way, to be progressive or committed, to introduce humour or gaiety or a strong beat so as to be optimistic. Their music conveys genuine confidence because it springs from inside the personality and experience of each of them, from popular tradition and the sounds of contemporary life; we respond to it because it tells us something lovely and vivacious about ourselves, not because the lyrics are about how to win a strike or blow up a petrol dump. It bypasses, overwhelms, ignores apartheid, establishes its own space. So it could be with our writers and painters, if only they could shake off the gravity of their anguish and break free from the solemn formulas of commitment that people (like myself) have tried for so many years to impose upon them. Dumile, perhaps the greatest of our visual artists, was once asked why he did not draw scenes like one that was taking place in front of him: a crocodile of men being marched under arrest for not having their passes in order. At that moment a hearse drove slowly past and the men stood still and raised their hats. 'That's what I want to draw,' he said.

Yet damaging as a purely instrumental and non-dialectical view of culture is to artistic creation, far more serious is the way such a narrow view impoverishes the struggle itself. Culture is not something separate from the general struggle, an artifact that is brought in from time to time to mobilize the people or else to prove to the world that after all we are civilized. Culture is us, it is who we are, how we see ourselves, and the vision we have of the world. In the course of participating in the culture of liberation, we constantly remake ourselves. It is not just a question of the discipline and interaction between members that any organization has; our movement has developed a style of its own, a way of doing things and of expressing itself, a specific ANC personality. And what a rich mix it is . . . African tradition, church tradition, Ghandian tradition, revolutionary socialist tradition, liberal tradition, all the languages and ways and styles of all the many communities in our country; we have black consciousness, and elements of red consciousness (some would say pink consciousness these days), even green consciousness (long before the Greens existed, we had green in our flag, representing the land). Now, with the dispersal of our members throughout the world, we also bring in aspects of the cultures of all humanity, our comrades speak Swahili and Arabic and Spanish and Portuguese and Russian and Swedish and French and German and Chinese, not because of Bantu Education, but through ANC Education, we are even learning Japanese. Our culture, the ANC culture, is not a picturesque collection of separate ethnic and political cultures lined up side by side, or mixed in certain proportions, it has a real character and dynamic of its own. When we sing our anthem, a religious invocation, with our clenched fists upraised, it is not a question of fifty-fifty, but an expression of an evolving and integrative interaction, an affirmation that we sing when we struggle and we struggle when we sing. This must be one of the greatest cultural achievements of the ANC, that it has made South Africans of the most diverse origins feel comfortable in its ranks. To say this is not to deny that cultural tensions and dilemmas automatically cease once one joins the organization: on the contrary, we bring in with us all our complexes and ways of seeing the world, our jealousies and preconceptions. What matters, however, is that we have created a context of struggle, of goals and comradeship within which these tensions can be dealt with. One can recall debates over such diverse questions as whether non-Africans should be allowed on to the NEC [National Executive Committee (of the ANC)], whether corporal punishment should be applied at SOMAFCO [Solomon Mahlangu Freedom College (the ANC college in Tanzania)], and whether married women should do high kicks on the stage. Indeed, the whole issue of women's liberation, for so long treated in an abstract way, is finally forcing itself on to the agenda of action and thought, a profound question of cultural transformation. The fact is that the cultural question is central to our identity as a movement: if culture were merely an instrument to be hauled on to the stage on ceremonial or fundraising occasions, or to liven up a meeting, we would ourselves be empty of personality in the interval. Happily, this is not the case – culture is us, and we are people, not things waiting to be put into motion from time to time.

This brings me to my second challenging proposition, namely, that the Constitutional Guidelines should not be applied to the sphere of culture. 'What?!' you may declare, 'A member of the Department of Legal and Constitutional Affairs saying that the Guidelines should not be applied to culture?' Precisely. It should be the other way round. Culture must make its input to the Guidelines. The whole point of the massive consultations that are taking place around the Guidelines is that the membership, the people at large, should engage in constructive and concrete debate about the foundations of government in a post-apartheid South Africa. The Guidelines are more than a work-in-progress document, they set out well-deliberated views of the NEC as enriched by an in-house seminar, but they are not presented as a final, cut-and-dried product, certainly not as a blueprint to be learnt off by heart and defended to the last misprint. Thus, the reasoning should not be: the Guidelines lay down the following for culture, therefore we must line up behind the guidelines and become a transmission belt for their implementation. On the contrary, what we need to do is to analyze the Guidelines, see what implications they have for culture, and then say whether we agree and make whatever suggestions we have for their improvement. In part, we can say that the method is the message; the open debate the NEC wants on the Guidelines corresponds to the open society the guidelines speak about. Apartheid has closed our society, stifled its voice, prevented the people from speaking, and it is the historic mission of our organization to be the harbingers of freedom of conscience, debate, and opinion.

In my view there are three aspects of the Guidelines that bear directly on the sphere of culture.

The first is the emphasis put on building national unity and encouraging the development of a common patriotism, while fully recognizing the linguistic and cultural diversity of the country. Once the question of basic political rights is resolved in a democratic way, the cultural and linguistic rights of our diverse communities can be attended to on their merits. In other words, language, religion, and so-called ways of life cease to be confused with race and sever their bondage to apartheid, becoming part of the positive cultural values of the society.

It is important to distinguish between unity and uniformity. We are strongly for national unity, for seeing our country as a whole, not just in its geographic extension but in its human extension. We want full equal rights for every South African, without reference to race, language, ethnic origin, or creed. We believe in a single South Africa with a single set of governmental institutions, and we work towards a common loyalty and patriotism. Yet this is not to call for a homogenized South Africa made up of identikit citizens. South Africa is now said to be a bilingual country: we envisage it as a multilingual country. It will be multifaith and multicultural as well. The objective is not to create a model culture into which everyone has to assimilate, but to acknowledge and take pride in the cultural variety of our people. In the past, attempts were made to force everyone into the mould of the English gentleman, projected as the epitome of civilization, so that it was even an honour to be oppressed by the English. Apartheid philosophy, on the other hand, denied any common humanity, and insisted that people be compartmentalized into groups forcibly kept apart. In rejecting apartheid, we do not envisage a return to a modified form of the British Imperialist notion, we do not plan to build a non-racial yuppiedom which people may enter only by shedding and suppressing the cultural heritage of their specific community. We will have Zulu South Africans and Afrikaner South Africans and Indian South Africans and Jewish South Africans and Venda South Africans and Cape Moslem South Africans (I do not refer to the question of terminology – basically people will determine this for themselves). Each cultural tributary contributes towards and increases the majesty of the river of South Africanness. While each one of us has a particularly intimate relationship with one or other cultural matrix, this does not mean that we are locked into a series of cultural 'own affairs' ghettoes. On the contrary, the grandchildren of white immigrants can join in the *toyi toyi* – even if slightly out of step – or recite the poems of Wally Serote, just as the grandchildren of Dinizulu can read with pride the writings of Olive Schreiner. The dance, the cuisine, the poetry, the dress, the songs and riddles and folk-tales, belong to each group, but also belong to all of us. I remember the pride I felt as a South African when some years ago I saw the production known as the Zulu Macbeth bring the house down in the World Theatre season in London, the intensely theatrical wedding and funeral dances of our people, performed by cooks and messengers and chauffeurs conquering the critics and audiences in what was then possibly the most elite theatre in the world. This was Zulu culture, but it was also our culture, my culture.

Each culture has its strengths, but there is no culture that is worth more than any other. We cannot say that because there are more Xhosa speakers than Tsonga, their culture is better, or because those who hold power today are Afrikaans-speakers, Afrikaans is better or worse than any other language.

Every culture has its positive and negative aspects. Sometimes the same cultural past is used in diametrically opposite ways, as we can see with the manner in which the traditions of Shaka and Ceteswayo are used on the one hand to inspire people to fight selflessly for an all-embracing liberation of our country, and on the other to cultivate a sanguinary tribal chauvinism. Sometimes cultural practices that were appropriate to certain forms of social organization become a barrier to change when the society itself has become transformed – we can think of forms of family organization, for example, that corresponded to the social and economic modes of pre-conquest societies that are out of keeping with the demands of contemporary life. African society, like all societies, develops and has the right to transform itself. What has been lacking since colonial domination began is the right of the people themselves to determine how they wish to live.

If we look at Afrikaans culture, the paradoxes are even stronger. At one level it was the popular creole language of the Western Cape, referred to in a derogatory way as kitchen Dutch, spoken by slaves and indigenous peoples who taught it to their masters and mistresses. Later it was the language of resistance to British imperialism; the best MK story to appear in South Africa to date was written (in English) by a Boer – *On Commando*, by Denys Reitz, a beautiful account of his three years as a guerrilla involved in actions of armed propaganda against the British occupying army. Afrikaans literature evolved around suffering and patriotism. Many of the early books, written to find a space in nature to make up for lack of social space, have since become classics of world ecological literature. At another level, the language has been hijacked by proponents of racial domination to support systems of white supremacy, and as such been projected as the language of the baas. In principle, there is no reason at all why Afrikaans should not once more become the language of liberty, but this time liberty for all, not just liberty for a few coupled with the right to oppress the majority.

At this point I would like to make a statement that I am sure will jolt the reader or listener: white is beautiful. In case anyone feels that the bomb has affected my head, I will repeat the affirmation, surely the first time it has been made at an ANC conference: white is beautiful. Allow me to explain. I first heard this formulation from a Mozambican poet and former guerrilla, whose grandmother was African and grandfather Portuguese. Asked to explain Frelimo's view on the slogan 'Black is beautiful', he replied, 'Black is beautiful, Brown is beautiful, White is beautiful.' I think that affirmation is beautiful. One may add that when white started saying black was ugly it made itself ugly. Shorn of its arrogance, the cultural input from the white communities can be rich and valuable. This is not to say that we need a WCM [White Consciousness Movement] in South Africa – in the context of colonial domination, white consciousness means oppression, whereas black consciousness means resistance to oppression. But it does establish the basis on which whites participate in the struggle to eradicate apartheid. Whites are not in the struggle to help the blacks win their rights, they (we) are fighting for their own rights, the rights to be free citizens of a free country, and to enjoy and take pride in the culture of the whole country. They are neither liberators of others, nor can their goal be to end up as a despised and despising protected minority. They seek to be ordinary citizens of an ordinary country, proud to be part of South Africa, proud to be part of Africa, proud to be part of the world. Only in certain monastic orders is self-flagellation the means to achieve liberation. For the rest of humankind, there is no successful struggle without a sense of pride and self-affirmation.

The second aspect of the Guidelines with major implications for culture is the proposal for a Bill of Rights that guarantees freedom of expression and what is sometimes referred to as political pluralism. South Africa today is characterized by States of Emergency, banning orders, censorship, and massive State-organized disinformation. Subject only to restrictions on racist propaganda and on ethnic exclusiveness such as are to be found in the laws of most countries in the world, the people in the South Africa envisaged by the Guidelines will be free to set up such organizations as they please, to vote for whom they please, and to say what they want.

This highlights a distinction that sometimes gets forgotten, namely the difference between leadership and control. We are for ANC leadership; our organization's central position in South Africa has been hard won and the dream of the founders of the organization is slowly being realized. Without doubt, the ANC will continue to be the principal architect of national unity after the foundations of apartheid have been destroyed and the foundations of democracy laid. Yet this does not mean that the ANC is the only voice in the anti-apartheid struggle, or that it will be the only voice in post-apartheid South Africa.

We want to give leadership to the people, not exercise control over them. This has significant implications for our cultural work not just in the future, but now. We think we are the best (and we are), that is why we are in the ANC. We work hard to persuade the people of our country that we are the best (and we are succeeding). But this does not require us to force our views down the throats of others. On the contrary, we exercise true leadership by being non-hegemonic, by selflessly trying to create the widest unity of the oppressed and to encourage all forces for change, by showing the people that we are fighting not to impose a view upon them but to give them the right to choose the kind of society they want and the kind of government they want. We are not afraid of the ballot box, of open debate, of opposition. One fine day we will even have our Ian Smith equivalents protesting and grumbling about every change being made and looking back with nostalgia to the good old days of apartheid, but we will take them on at the hustings. In conditions of freedom, we have no doubt who will win, and if we should forfeit the trust of the people, then we deserve to lose.

All this has obvious implications for the way in which we conduct ourselves in the sphere of culture, We should lead by example, by the manifest correctness of our policies, and not rely on our prestige or numbers to push our positions through. We need to accept broad parameters rather than narrow ones: the criterion being pro- or anti-apartheid. In my opinion, we should be big enough to encompass the view that the anti-apartheid forces and individuals come in every shape and size, especially if they belong to the artistic community. This is not to give a special status to artists, but to recognize that they have certain special characteristics and traditions. Certainly, it ill behoves us to set ourselves up as the new censors of art and literature, or to impose our own internal states of emergency in areas where we are well organized. Rather, let us write better poems and make better films and compose better music, and let us get the voluntary adherence of the people to our banner ('it is not enough that our cause be pure and just; justice and purity must exist inside ourselves' – war poem from Mozambique).

Finally, the Guidelines couple the guarantees of individual rights with the necessity to embark upon programmes of affirmative action. This too has clear implications for the sphere of culture. The South Africa in which individuals and groups can operate freely, will be a South Africa in the process of transformation. A constitutional duty will be imposed upon the state, local authorities, and public and private institutions to take active steps to remove the massive inequalities created by centuries of colonial and racist domination. This gives concrete meaning to the statement that the doors of learning and culture shall be opened. We can envisage massive programmes of adult education and literacy, and extensive use of the media to facilitate access by all to the cultural riches of our country and of the world. The challenge to our cultural workers is obvious.

NOTE   This paper was first published in *Spring is Rebellious*, edited by Karen Press and Ingrid de Kok (Cape Town: Buchu Books, 1990).

18

New challenges facing theatre practitioners in the new South Africa

MAISHE MAPONYA

For the purposes of this paper, it is important for the reader to bear in mind
that it was written five years after Mandela's release from prison, and the
start of the negotiations with the liberation movements, in 1990.

INTRODUCTION: PREMISE

It is globally known that the arts, especially theatre, have been one of the
major features in the South African political struggle. From the 1970s,
political theatre took a decidedly sharp critical view against apartheid. It
was in the 1980s that the phenomenon of protest and resistance theatre
performance was intensified within the country and exported to the international market.

This paper will focus on the way in which rhetoric in the arts was used
to achieve power. I recognize that there have been some changes in other
areas and that those changes are highly appreciated. Juxtaposed against
the oppressed's expectation, those changes are too minuscule to warrant
a celebration. I will show that while the liberation struggle recognized the
role of the arts and culture, the developments since 1990 – especially
since the 1994 elections – paint a different scenario in the politics of control. I will tease out questions in an attempt to elaborate on my convictions as one of the contributors to a theatre that has been and is always
geared for change – a theatre that deals with consciousness – a theatre of
resistance.

THE CULTURAL BOYCOTT AS A MEANS OF STRUGGLE

In supporting the call to institute action against minority-rule South
Africa, the United Nations promulgated UN Resolution 237/XXIII of
1968 to urge 'artists to work towards the isolation of South Africa'. The
South African government had not envisaged that, as a result of the
Sharpeville massacre of the protesters against the Pass Laws and the banning of political organizations in 1960, there would be an armed struggle
or that South Africa would be isolated by punitive sanctions.

Between 1979 and 1986 South Africa was gripped by unrest which cut across labour to civics and education. A State of Emergency was declared in 1985. The army and police were deployed in the townships and there was an outcry for their removal by the residents. This excerpt from the poem 'Man-Eater', written in 1985, symbolizes the terror that the deployment evoked and the rejection of arbitrary decisions by the minority government:

> Other people too,
> In Katlehong
> In Huhudi
> In Leandra
> Say they live in fear of
> Ugly brown canvass uniforms
> Behind ugly brown trucks[1]

The deployment of the army in the townships did not improve matters as black councillors delegated by the government were said to be representing the 'system' and were therefore rejected and forced to resign by activists in the communities. The result was a further collapse of order. There were rent boycotts and the councillors were harassed or victimized by communities. Anyone suspected of collaborating with the system would be killed, their properties and houses destroyed by fire. Community councillors in the townships were seen as 'enemies of the people'. The rhetoric was 'in the name of struggle'. The 'necklace' became the most fashionable form of punishment meted out, mainly by students to 'collaborators'.[2]

Stage productions by both black and white writers addressed themselves differently to the issues related to apartheid. The plays were either categorized as protest or resistance theatre. Yet there were also other plays that had nothing to do with political life.

Until the beginning of the 1990s it was clear that there was a consolidated position among opponents of the system, aiming to exert pressure

---

1. Maishe Maponya, Producer, Record Album: *Bušang Meropa (Bring Back the Drums)*.
2. The 'necklace' refers to a tyre that is stuffed with papers and plastics, then doused with petrol. It is put around the victim (as if it were a necklace) and then set alight. Those involved in the act often danced around as the victim burnt to ashes.

on the apartheid regime, despite ideological differences between these opponents.

Naturally, the new political dynamics have had an impact on the role of artists in the new South Africa. Questions that need to be answered are 'How?' 'Why?' 'And to what effect?' In short, what are the issues most important to the theatre practitioner?

Soon after the release of Mandela in 1990, the Cultural Boycott crumbled as a result of positioning or 'political correctness'. Supporters and sympathizers of the ANC were lining up international stars for performances in South Africa. This was being done without consultation with other structures contributing towards the maintenance and effectiveness of the boycott.

Surprising news of the erosion of the boycott hit the headlines of several newspapers in February 1991. The news was surprising because nothing had been said publicly about the developments until this particular two-week period, in which everything was revealed:

(1) *New Nation* (a weekly newspaper, with large black readership), 7–13 February 1991, printed the headline 'Boycott Bombshell', referring to a document signed by the head of the ANC Department of Arts and Culture (DAC), 'giving its support for the concert which could feature top performers like Sting and Bruce Springsteen'.

(2) Another weekly, the *Weekly Mail*, dated 8–14 February 1991, reported that the South African Music Alliance (SAMA), a 'progressive' organization aligned with the ANC, side-stepped the 'cultural boycott *with the approval of the ANC*' (emphasis added) and hosted the Lambada's Kaoma, a Latin American music and dance group.

(3) *South* (a weekly Johannesburg suburb local), 7–13 February 1991, carried the headline 'New Era in S. A. Culture When Boycott Ends'. This was a scoop! At that point, South African artists and supporters of the boycott had already been engaged in discussions with various groups and projects about a new position to be adopted by the UN at a conference to be held in Los Angeles in February.

(4) *City Press* (a weekly, mostly black readership), 10 February 1991, revealed a different *coup* for the entertainment world: the ANC Youth League was engaged in organizing a concert featuring 'MC Hammer . . . Whitney Houston, Phil Collins, Tracy Chapman . . .' The services of Hazel Feldman (the Sun City boycott buster) had already been acquired. She confirmed that she had taken a 'three months leave' and was working on a project 'not connected to Sun City'.

What put a damper to all the hullabaloo of entertainment and quick-buck ventures by impresarios and a one-sided political manoeuvring was another headline in the same newspaper which revealed that two other political organizations, the Pan Africanist Congress (PAC) and Azanian Peoples' Organization (AZAPO) refused to approve the 'ban-busting superstars'. A consensus of the two organizations on the issue could not be ignored by the ANC.

These goings-on were not a surprise, though shocking to those who believed in the undivided liberation. None of these revelations were refuted. But quite interestingly, even after securing ANC approval to perform in South Africa, the groups still went on to negotiate with the Azanian Peoples' Organization for the green light. AZAPO's position was to spite the organizers by refusing to sanction the request. So, most managements abandoned their intentions despite the ANC approval.

(5) *Business Day*, 20 February 1991, revealed that the 'South African Broadcasting Corporation (SABC) [then a government mouthpiece] says it has bought exclusive rights to an ANC concert featuring a number of rock stars in Johannesburg next month.'

(6) *Sunday Times*, 24 February 1991, in an article entitled 'How Much is Enough?', reported that 'top international entertainers are reluctant to come to South Africa to play in an ANC fundraising concert'. It further reported that the managements of the groups claimed that the 'ANC will not guarantee returns and expects too much in the way of donations to social projects'.

These developments had a bearing on the UN Los Angeles Conference to review the academic and cultural boycott, which was scheduled to take place at the beginning of February. The conference was postponed at the request of the ANC.

The controversies called for a response from Mandela. He was then featured in a highly publicized Nguni–Sotho language phone-in programme specifically to clear the air about sanctions, mass demonstrations, and boycott politics, issues that were creating a debate that was gripping the country. These issues had created a climate of unrest, and if the ANC was perceived to have control over its supporters, Mandela had to show it. According to *The Star* of 22 February 1992, Mandela

- defended the right of the ANC to engage in mass action
- reiterated the ANC's belief in a mixed economy
- said that the cultural boycott against South Africa would stay

This attention has highlighted the shift from political struggle to the more mundane issues of the fortune and survival tactics of local arts practitioners within a diverse national culture which is yet to be defined.

In the past, those opposed to apartheid could easily identify the 'enemy' and deal with relations between the struggle and art decidedly. Today the 'enemy' is no longer easily identifiable. What remains is how and from what perspectives can practitioners deal with reconstruction.

Imposed solutions that neglect the dynamics of the legacy we inherit will stifle the arts. There is a dire need for artists from the underprivileged who will have a new sense of the self-consciousness, self-identity, self-definition, self-determination, and self-criticism needed to achieve a position of equity with white arts practitioners. That is a challenge that the new order would have to deal with.

In my opinion the challenges can be divided into the following five categories (these are in no way exclusive):

1. creative aspects
2. bureaucracy and administration
3. responses to political manipulation
4. undoing the white monopoly in the theatre
5. ensuring that the arts are included in the schools' curriculum

1. Creative aspects
If practitioners are to create new and exciting material, they have to come up with new themes to reflect, for example:

- a sense of freedom
- a sense of place (there are new experiences and dreams since the politics have changed)
- the importance of the land
- the impact of time
- the aesthetics of the cultural milieu

2. Bureaucracy and administration
In order to realize the change and its effect, it is my belief that bureaucrats who served the previous regime and defended it need to be replaced by administrators who will have to

- have a sense of democracy
- be diverse in their approach
- shift programmes from their Eurocentric focus to accommodate diversity (and by so doing encourage audiences to be tolerant, accommodative, and diverse in perspectives)

- alter the dominance of male preference in senior administrative positions
  (alter the dominance of white bureaucrats, not just by replacing them
  with blacks, but with qualified effective, critical, and innovative
  administration)
- do away with nepotism
- agree to take big cuts from central government so that the reconstruction
  and development programmes can continue in underprivileged communities
  – but also be prepared to challenge the government to channel resources
  from the cuts to the arts and not to other unrelated departments
- agree to have numbers of redundant and 'time-pushing' administrators in
  PACs (Performing Arts Councils) and CCs (Civic Centres) cut
- make their venues and resources accessible, since public funds were used to
  establish and maintain them

3. Political manipulation

Since the broader public will be engaged in the reconstruction processes, attitudes in running the institutions will have to change.
Therefore

- practitioners will have to be vigilant against partisan politics and political
  posturings
- practitioners should not be seen to be state mouthpieces
- practitioners should not only be seen to be politically sensitive but also
  socially and economically responsible

4. Undoing the white monopoly in the theatre

The general description of the role of whites in the current theatre scene
in South Africa has been a monopoly of privilege. White practitioners
will have to accept the fact that they *cannot* continue

- to be the lifeblood of theatre alone
- to define theatre for themselves and define it for others
- to be unchallenged; and once challenged, they should accede to valid
  contestations
- to hold the arts community at ransom

5. Education

Practitioners should continue to fight to have the arts introduced in
schools (especially underprivileged ones) from primary through tertiary
institutions. The curriculum should be informed by academics, practitioners, and other parties interested in arts education.

NEW APPROACHES

In the underprivileged communities, objectives should be revived to reflect the community performance arts programmes and to encourage communities to develop themselves with 'positive discrimination programmes'. This means that since the majority of the population lives in rural and underprivileged areas, funding and resources should be tilted towards these community areas in need of development. This will ease the burden currently placed on metropolitan areas by the inordinate influx of highly expectant rural dwellers and fortune hunters into the already depleted urban areas. Note, for example, that in rural areas where traditional practices including storytelling, dance, drama, and song are still being practised, albeit on a very small scale, they could be revived and made dynamic with new techniques and be a way for the communities to recreate and regenerate themselves.

New approaches and concepts in education-in-drama and performance, drama-in-education, community drama, and theatre-in-education would enable communities to view their lives in a different light than is the case at present. Practitioners in these circumstances will need to have developed a high sense of critical consciousness in order to contribute effectively towards reconstruction and development.

New themes and styles in addressing ever-rising crime, insensitivity, or disrespect to human life and declining moral values need to be devised.

Since the well-established theatre structures are in the cities and areas where white people were privileged to live, these structures can continue unhindered because some of them are private enterprises. The scenario has changed little since 1994. At best, these theatres host black productions here and there if they appeal to their audience's tastes. The glaring truth is that there is still no single properly built theatre structure in any black township, and community centres in rural areas are almost non-existent. How, then, do people recreate themselves? There is a lack of trained personnel who can run programmes in these areas because of lack of funds. It is unimaginable for black practitioners even to consider getting rights for some of these plays, to produce them, unless one is attached to the major institutions or venues. It feels as if there is another form of 'cultural boycott' being imposed – this time, to ignore the ideals of the dispossessed by telling them about the free market system, reconciliation, multiculturalism, non-racialism, and all the jargon of political correctness.

Thus far, the negotiations have been to secure the confidence of whites at the expense of the black majority, whose expectations are peripherally addressed. Since democracy, the control of the arts is still in the hands of the same white bureaucrats. A new strategy by artists of conscience and community leaders will have to be embarked upon in order to redefine the role of the arts in the new order.

NOTE   This paper was written while I was Visiting Fellow at Northwestern University, Program of African Studies, Evanston, Illinois, USA.

19

Current trends in Theatre for Development in South Africa

ZAKES MDA

With the emergence of the Black Consciousness Movement in the early 1970s, the politics inside South Africa changed from protest to challenge. Theatre not only reflected the change from protest to challenge, but in many respects was catalytic in it. In line with what was happening in the liberation struggle, Theatre for Resistance replaced Protest Theatre as the dominant mode of expression in the country. This happened when the political movement of the time decided to use culture and its products – including theatre – as weapons of the struggle. There was no longer any room, therefore, for Protest Theatre which by its very nature addressed itself to the oppressor with the view of appealing to his conscience. Cultural activists of the time felt that Protest Theatre, practised by both black and white intermediate classes, merely made a statement of disapproval or disagreement, but did not go beyond that. It was a theatre of complaint, of weeping, of self-pity, of moralizing, of mourning, and of hopelessness. It did not offer any solution beyond the depiction of the sad situation in which the oppressed found themselves. The best known practitioner of Protest Theatre was Athol Fugard. In the later phase of his career, Gibson Kente also turned to writing plays with overtly political content, creating Protest Theatre.

The advent of the Black Consciousness Movement in the early 1970s was also the advent of a new militant theatre that went beyond protest. This Theatre for Resistance gained a mass following and became the dominant mode practised by activists from all ideological positions in the spectrum of liberation politics. It was a minimalist theatre that was highly mobile, using few or no sets and props, and a small number of performers – sometimes only one or two actors. The distinctive characteristic of Theatre for Resistance was that it addressed itself directly to the oppressed people – rather than appealing to the conscience of the oppressor – with the overt aim of mobilizing the oppressed to fight against oppression. Its pioneers, Mthuli Shezi, Maishe Mapanya, Matsemela Manaka, and many others whose names never became known individually, since they operated within community groups, had a strong case against Protest Theatre, since by its nature it attempted to reveal the blacks to the whites, and placed the onus on the blacks to prove their humanity. Theatre for Resistance, on the other hand, was 'agitprop', for it propagated a message and agitated for the oppressed to act in order to change their situation.

The agitprop of Theatre for Resistance caught on even with solidarity audiences abroad. A number of South African plays had extensive tours of Europe and North America. Some even had reasonably long runs in off-Broadway and Broadway venues in the United States of America. The style of this highly energetic agitprop came to be known as the style of South African theatre by these solidarity audiences. Many a theatre practitioner in South Africa aspired to take his or her plays abroad, and fashioned his or her plays with that solidarity audience in mind, creating the impression that Broadway represented all that was good in theatre.

During this period almost no Theatre for Development was produced in the country. Indeed this mode of theatre was virtually unknown in South Africa. This was to be expected since in Africa and the developing world in general the preoccupation with 'development' came only after independence. Developmentalism becomes the concern of postcolonial societies when popular politics has come to an end, and the new nation states begin to mobilize the populace for what the leadership refers to as nation-building (in South Africa, 'reconstruction').

However, there were a few early attempts to create some form of Theatre for Development even before liberation. Institutions like the Africa Cultural Centre and Soyikwa Institute for African Theatre had Theatre for Development in their curricula. A forward-thinking practitioner, Matsemela Manaka, produced an early example of Theatre for Development: his musical drama piece on literacy, *Koma*. Although Manaka may not have called it Theatre for Development, nor used any of the terminology that is common in the practice of Theatre for Development in Africa today, *Koma* had a number of characteristics that are currently found in Theatre for Development in Africa. For instance, Manaka took *Koma* to the rural areas where it was performed under the trees at village meeting posts, at the markets, and at village schools. The intention of the play was not to use theatre as a methodology for teaching the target audiences the skills of reading and writing (as one would find in a Theatre in Education programme), but to motivate them to participate in literacy programmes. However, unlike Theatre for Development, the play did not give the target audiences the means of production of the theatre, since the audiences did not contribute to its creation, and therefore could not contribute to the creation and distribution of their own messages.

Although *Koma* was a brilliant play in its mastery of the techniques of theatre, as Theatre for Development it was not effective, in that it required an audience schooled in the modes of Western theatre to decode its messages. The target audiences, however, were the rural communities schooled in the ways of production and enjoyment of their own popular performance modes. *Koma*, therefore, did not open community dialogue on the issues the play raised, since it was a prepackaged production that both posed the problems and offered the solutions. However, it was a worthy pioneer of the form of Theatre for Development that is currently practised in South Africa.

Indeed there is a lot of interest in Theatre for Development in South Africa today. A number of groups have emerged throughout the nine provinces, and many of them hold membership in the Theatre for Community Development Trust, which is an umbrella body. Most of the projects are funded by government agencies, non-governmental organizations, and the corporate world. However, South African Theatre for Development still lags far behind the practice of Theatre for Development in other parts of Africa. It has not yet emerged from the agitprop that was common when Theatre for Development work began in Africa in the early 1970s. This is mainly because it is informed by the aesthetics of Theatre for Resistance. It is therefore very strong on the mobilizational aspects and rather weak on the creation of a critical awareness among the target audiences. It is not created by developmental workers, but by theatre practitioners whose primary concern is the creation of an 'artistic' product, rather than an effective vehicle for community dialogue utilizing the people's own performance modes, which are highly artistic in themselves and on their own terms. With a few exceptions, South African patterns of production and consumption of theatre are informed by Western models, rather than by the common festival of indigenous performance modes that are extant and very popular not only in the rural areas, but also in the urban slums where the majority of the black people live.

Progressive Theatre for Development in Africa is anti-agitprop since its emphasis is on utilizing theatre as a vehicle for critical analysis, which in turn will result in critical awareness, or conscientization. The process of conscientization involves the active participation of the people in transforming themselves by engaging in a dialogue through which they identify their problems, reflect on why the problems exist, and take action to solve the problems. Theatre practitioners, who are variously called catalysts, animators, or facilitators, do not create theatre for the people, as is the case with agitprop in South Africa, but with the people. Catalysts go through the process of information gathering in the target communities, information analysis, story improvization, rehearsals, community performances, community discussions, and follow-up action. Community members are involved throughout this process. Depending on the methodology used, they become active participants in the dramatization itself, by advancing the conflicts among the characters and working solutions into the plays that the catalysts have left unfinished (since the catalyst helps only to pose the problems). In this way the world of the play interacts very closely with the world of the community. People are therefore able to identify their problems within the context of a particular social order, and the theatre provides the means to codify that social reality.

Theatre for Development in South Africa, however, viewed by many practitioners as the extension of the Theatre for Resistance work done during the days of apartheid, and using the same agitprop methods, does not empower the audiences with the means to create and distribute their own messages. Theatre comes to the target area as a prepackaged product that presents both the problem and the solution. These problems and solutions are formulated from the perspective of the theatre practitioners themselves, sometimes with the assistance of 'experts', but without any consultation with the community members. This kind of theatre therefore perpetuates the top-down communication process that only gives the target audiences access to the consumption of messages transmitted by the outside experts, rather than reinforcing the audiences' active participation in the programming itself, and thereby enhancing the community's ability to create and distribute their own messages. In a truly participatory Theatre for Development, however, the message can emanate from any of the participants, be they expert theatre practitioners or the most 'insignificant' community member; and the message can be added to, questioned, or responded to by anyone.

In South Africa there are five different types of practitioners who are involved in Theatre for Development. There are the community-based groups, such as Smal Ndaba's Sibikwa Community Theatre Project in Benoni and Bongani Linda's Victory-Sonqoba in Alexandra Township. These groups are mostly funded by private corporations and by non-governmental organizations at home and abroad.

Secondly, there are the professional theatre companies, based at well-known purpose-built venues, which also undertake from time to time Theatre for Development oriented work as part of their community outreach programmes. These include Walter Chakela's Windybrow Theatre and the Market Theatre. The latter, through the Market Theatre Laboratory, has fieldworkers who work with community theatre groups, not only in the Johannesburg area where the Market Theatre is located, but in cities as far afield as Kimberley and Cape Town. The Windybrow, on the other hand, has a mobile theatre truck which takes theatre to the community.

Thirdly, there are the drama departments of universities who may sometimes do Theatre for Development as part of their training programmes. For instance, the School of the Dramatic Arts at the University of the Witwatersrand has attempted to introduce Theatre for Development to a community group in Dobsonville. Similarly the University of Natal has supported a very successful Theatre for Development AIDS campaign in the rural areas of kwaZulu/Natal.

Fourthly, there are the Industrial Theatre companies such as Blue Moon and Sandra Prinsloo's Productions. These are purely commercial companies that are engaged by the business world, including the multinational corporations, to produce theatre for the promotion of the products and/or services of these corporations. They may produce drama to introduce a new product, such as the launch of a new make of a motor vehicle. Lately they have been increasingly engaged by corporations to do work that is Theatre for Development orientated; for instance, to produce plays for the workforce on such subjects as AIDS. Because these lucrative Industrial Theatre companies use highly paid professional scriptwriters, directors, and actors, they are able to produce an agitprop of very high quality, based on the methods and styles developed by Theatre for Resistance.

Fifthly, there are commercial theatre groups that are professional in orientation, but may once in a while undertake a Theatre for Development project as an extension of their commercial work. An example here is Mbongeni Ngema's Committed Artists. The work of this group illustrates the profit motive that is dominant in the practice of

Theatre for Development in South Africa. Mbongeni Ngema became well known for his Theatre for Resistance plays *Wo*ʒ*a Albert!* (jointly created with Percy Mtwa and Barney Simon) and *Asinamali*, which were well received in the country and abroad. Later he formed his Committed Artists group and produced the highly successful *Sarafina!* This play combined the Theatre for Resistance agitprop with the extravaganza-type song and dance of the Township Musical Theatre that used to be produced by Gibson Kente in the 1960s and 1970s.

In the light of these successes Mbongeni Ngema was commissioned towards the end of 1995 by the Minister of Health, Dr Nkosazana Zuma, to create a play on AIDS which would tour the whole of South Africa. *Sarafina II*, as the play was called, was scheduled to run for one year. Ngema asked for and was granted a budget of R14,270,000 (about US $4 million at the exchange rate of the time). This included his salary of R370,000 (US $100,000) as director, choreographer, and composer; an amount of R100,000 (US $27,030) for costumes, R1,200,000 (US $333,330) for lighting and sound equipment, and R2,245,000 (US $623,610) for a luxury bus, minibus, truck, and trailer.

When this cosy arrangement was discovered early in 1996 there was outrage throughout the country. Firstly, proper tendering procedures had not been followed when Ngema was granted this contract. At first the Minister said that the production was financed by the European Union and therefore need not have followed strict tendering procedures laid down by South African law. The European Union, however, denied that it was fully aware of the details of the play and did not know anything about paying for it, which meant that the Minister had both lied and bla-tantly flouted tendering procedures. The general feeling was that this was a waste of taxpayers' money.

There are many successful projects in South Africa that have cost much less. Hundreds of community-based and non-governmental organizations with proven records in anti-AIDS campaigns operate on shoestring budgets. A women's theatre project, Tivoneleni Vavasati's AIDS Awareness Project operating from Elim in the Northern Province, has been producing AIDS awareness plays for schools and communities in the rural areas and farms since 1991 without any assistance from the government. The R14.27 million budget for *Sarafina II* was higher than the annual budget of theatre establishments such as the Windybrow. The Market Theatre Laboratory AIDS play, *Broken Dreams*, cost the sponsor R76,000 (US $21,000). It has now been running for a year, with an occasional break, playing to ten schools a week before an audience of three hundred students per performance. The projects cited here reached many more people than *Sarafina II* will ever do, at a fraction of the cost.

Ngema's point of view on the matter is that, as a Broadway playwright, he deserves even more than he was paid. He is not prepared to do a second-class production. The critics are merely jealous because he is a black man. The government spends millions of rands supporting Eurocentric culture in the four performing arts councils. Blacks also deserve Broadway standards. One of the well-known critics in South Africa, Geralt MacLiam, supported him in this view (*The Star Tonight*, 13 March 1996). He said that Ngema ranked as a Broadway composer/director with a number of Tony award nominations under his belt, and therefore deserved his fee.

What seemed to escape both Ngema and MacLiam was that the budget for *Sarafina II* was not funding for the arts but funding for health education. Other critics throughout the country understood this very clearly (see, for instance, Kaizer Nyantsumba, *The Star*, 13 March 1996; Mark Gevisser, *Mail and Guardian*, 19–14 March 1996; Annesh Ramklown, *Sunday Times*, 3 March 1996). They said that the production was more a music concert than a play aimed at teaching people about the dangers of AIDS. Others claimed that the play was derogatory to women and portrayed them as schoolgirls in gymslips who loved having sex with many men because it was great fun. The message seemed to be that, if you get AIDS, only God can help you.

Sarafina II cannot function effectively as Theatre for Development. Although there are some lessons on AIDS, they are not integrated in a coherent storyline. The actors merely step forward and recite them. Or they come as slogans in some of the songs. The sheer size of this production works against it. It is not a mobile kind of theatre, and because of the heavy equipment involved and the fact that a theatre has to be constructed at every new venue, the play will have to be stationed at one place for a long period. Hence, in one Johannesburg township it had to stay for three weeks. This means that very few parts of South Africa will see the play. Ideally it can only be performed in cities that have purpose built theatre houses; it will not be able to go to the rural areas. This means that *Sarafina II* is not cost-effective. The R14.27 million is only for the entertainment of a privileged few.

The setting of the play also works against it in other areas of South Africa. Effective Theatre for Development is set in the locale of its target audience, and uses the culture of that area as its point of reference. This brings the problems depicted in the play closer to home, and the target audiences are able to relate to the issues. *Sarafina II* is set in kwaZulu/Natal, which is the home province of both Ngema and Zuma. It is steeped in the Zulu culture, which is remote to people of other ethnic groups throughout South Africa.

Effective Theatre for Development also uses the language of the target audience: *Sarafina II* is mostly in English. There is some Zulu as well, but most of its vocabulary is that of kwaZulu/Natal. There are words that are not even used by Zulu speakers in Johannesburg. The play is done in a language that most of the target audience does not understand. Indeed, some of the English lines are a mouthful even for the actors themselves.

It is impossible to create one single Theatre for Development play that will function effectively throughout South Africa. That is why the Matla Trust Project had seven different groups in different parts of the country doing theatre that was area-specific and language-specific. If the Minister of Health had been well-advised, she too would have distributed the R14.27 million among a number of theatre groups throughout the country, who would perform much more effective plays in their areas, rather than enrich a single individual whose model of good theatre and of Theatre for Development are the formulaic musicals of Broadway.

Theatre for Development has the potential to be the most relevant theatre in a democratic South Africa, since it can be rooted with the people in the marginalized rural areas and urban slums. It utilizes modes of communication and of entertainment that already exist in these areas. It is the theatre of the illiterate since, in its most progressive form, it has no dramatic text that acts as a referent for the performance text. Workers and peasants together form the vast majority of the population of South Africa. Of necessity a truly South African theatre will not be that which is the sole privilege of the dominant classes, but that in which peasants and workers are active participants in its production and enjoyment.

A select bibliography of South African literary writing in English, 1970–1995

The following bibliography has been culled from a much fuller bibliography derived from a database held by the National English Literary Museum in Grahamstown, South Africa. It is designed to reflect some of the most significant literary publication of the period, including anthologies and autobiographical writing – although it cannot, of course, escape a degree of subjectivity in the process of selection. In some instances, collections of an author's works have been cited in preference to individual titles.

Abrahams, Lionel. *Lionel Abrahams: A Reader.* Introduced and edited by Patrick Cullinan. Craighall: Ad Donker, 1988.

Adey, David, ed. *Under the Southern Cross: Short Stories from South Africa.* Johannesburg: Ad Donker, 1982.

Afrika, Tatamkhulu. *The Lemon Tree: Poems.* Plumstead: Snailpress, 1995. *Maqabane.* Bellville: Mayibuye Books, 1994.

Turning Points, with *A Life of Stripped of Illusions* by Arja Salafranca. Cape Town: Table Valley Trading, 1995.

Akerman, Anthony. *A Man out of the Country.* Amsterdam: Frascati, 1989. *Somewhere on the Border.* Amsterdam: Thekwini Theatre, 1983.

Alfred, Mike. *Life in the Suburbs.* Plumstead: Snailpress, 1994.

Altman, Phyllis. *The Law of the Vultures.* Craighall: Ad Donker, 1987.

Asvat, Farouk. *A Celebration of Flames.* Craighall: Ad Donker, 1987.

Banoobhai, Shabbir. *Echoes of My Other Self.* Johannesburg: Ravan, 1980. *Shadows of a Sun-darkened Land.* Johannesburg: Ravan, 1984.

Barris, Ken. *An Advertisement for Air: Poems.* Plumstead: Snailpress, 1993. *Small Change: Short Stories.* Craighall: Ad Donker, 1988.

Becker, Jillian. *The Virgins.* London: Victor Gollancz, 1976; Cape Town: David Philip, 1986.

Behr, Mark. *The Smell of Apples.* London: Abacus, 1995.

Berold, Robert. *The Door to the River.* Cape Town: Bateleur, 1984. *The Fires of the Dead.* Cape Town: Carrefour Press, 1989.

Boehmer, Elleke. *An Immaculate Figure.* London: Bloomsbury, 1993. *Screens Against the Sky.* London: Bloomsbury, 1990.

Braude, Sandra. *Windswept Plains.* Cape Town: Buchu Books, 1991.

Breytenbach, Breyten. *Judas Eye.* London: Faber & Faber, and New York: Farrar, Straus & Giroux, 1988.

Memory of Snow and of Dust. Bramley: Taurus, and London: Faber & Faber, 1989.

Mouroir: Mirrornotes of a Novel. London: Faber & Faber, 1984.

Return to Paradise. London: Faber & Faber, 1993.

A Season in Paradise. London: Jonathan Cape, 1980.

The True Confessions of an Albino Terrorist. Emmarentia: Taurus, and London: Faber & Faber, 1984; New York: Farrar, Straus & Giroux, 1985.

Brink, André. *An Act of Terror*. London: Secker & Warburg, and New York: Summit, 1991.

A Chain of Voices. London: Faber & Faber, and New York: Morrow, 1982.

A Dry White Season. London: W. H. Allen, 1979; New York: Morrow, 1982.

The First Life of Adamastor. London: Secker & Warburg, 1993.

An Instant in the Wind. London: W. H. Allen, 1976; New York: Morrow, 1977.

Looking on Darkness. London: W. H. Allen, 1974; New York, Morrow, 1975.

On the Contrary: Being the Life of a Famous Rebel, Soldier, Traveller, Explorer, Reader, Builder, Scribe, Latinist, Lover and Liar. London: Secker & Warburg, and Boston: Little, Brown, 1993.

Rumours of Rain. London: Howard & Wyndham, and New York: Morrow, 1978.

States of Emergency. London: Faber & Faber, 1988; New York: Summit, 1989.

The Wall of the Plague. London: Faber & Faber, and New York: Summit, 1984.

Brutus, Dennis. *Poems from Algiers*. Austin: University of Texas, 1970.

A Simple Lust: Selected Poems. London: Heinemann, 1973.

Still the Sirens. Santa Fe: Pennywhistle Press, 1993.

Stubborn Hope. London: Heinemann, 1978.

Bryer, Lynne. *A Time in the Country*, with *Parting Shots* by Fiona Zerbst. Cape Town: Carrefour Press, 1991.

Bryer, Sally. *Sometimes, Suddenly*. Ed. Jack Cope. Cape Town: David Philip, and Vancouver: J. J. Douglas, 1973.

Bunn, David, and Jane Taylor, eds. *From South Africa: New Writing, Photographs and Art*. Chicago: University of Chicago Press, 1987.

Burgess, Yvonne. *Say a Little Mantra for Me*. Johannesburg: Ravan, 1979.

The Strike. Johannesburg: Ad Donker, 1975.

Butler, Guy. *Selected Poems*. Johannesburg: Ad Donker, 1975.

Tales from the Old Karoo. Johannesburg: Ad Donker, 1989.

Butler, Guy, and Chris Mann, eds. *A New Book of South African Verse in English*. Cape Town: Oxford University Press, 1979.

Cartwright, Justin. *Freedom for the Wolves*. London: Hamish Hamilton, 1983.

Look at it This Way. London: Macmillan, 1990.

Masai Dreaming. London: Picador/Macmillan, 1994.

Chapman, Michael, ed. *A Century of South African Poetry*. Johannesburg: Ad Donker, 1981.

Soweto Poetry. Johannesburg: McGraw-Hill, 1982.

Chapman, Michael, and Achmat Dangor, eds. *Voices from Within: Black Poetry from Southern Africa*. Johannesburg: Ad Donker, 1982.

Clayton, Cherry. *Leaving Home*. Plumstead: Snailpress, and Guelph, Canada: Red Kite Press, 1994.

Cline, Brendan. *The Six Dead Ballerinas and Other Stories*. Johannesburg: Justified Press, 1994.

Clouts, Sydney. *Collected Poems*. Edited by M. Clouts and C. Clouts. Cape Town: David Philip, 1984.

Coetzee, Ampie, and Hein Willemse, eds. *I Qabane Labantu: Poetry in the Emergency/Poesie in die Noodtoestand*. Bramley: Taurus, 1989.

Coetzee, Dene. *Winds of Change*. London: Hodder & Stoughton, 1995.

Coetzee, J. M. *Age of Iron*. London: Secker & Warburg, and New York: Random House, 1990.

Dusklands. Johannesburg: Ravan, 1974; London: Secker & Warburg, 1982; New York: Viking, 1985.

Foe. Johannesburg: Ravan, and London: Secker & Warburg, 1986; New York: Viking, 1987.

In the Heart of the Country. London: Secker & Warburg, 1977; New York: Harper, 1977 [as *From the Heart of the Country*]; Johannesburg: Ravan 1978; Harmondsworth: Penguin, 1982.

Life & Times of Michael K. Johannesburg: Ravan, and London: Secker & Warburg, 1983; New York: Viking, 1984.

The Master of Petersburg. London: Secker & Warburg, and New York: Viking, 1994.

Waiting for the Barbarians. London: Secker & Warburg, 1980; Johannesburg: Ravan, 1981; New York: Penguin, 1982.

Conyngham, John. *The Arrowing of the Cane*. 1986. London: Bloomsbury, 1989.

The Desecration of the Graves. Johannesburg: Ad Donker, 1990.

Cope, Jack. *Selected Stories*. Cape Town: David Philip, 1986.

Cope, Michael. *Spiral of Fire*. Cape Town: David Philip, 1987.

Cotton, Roy Joseph. *Ag, Man: Selected Poems*. Edited by Gus Ferguson and Alan James. Cape Town: UpStream, 1986.

Everything is Saycred Boere Orkestra Salvayshin is Comining: Poems. Cape Town: A Satyurayterd Seteesz Publickation, 1984.

Courtenay, Bryce. *April Fool's Day: A Modern Tragedy*. London: Mandarin, 1994.

The Power of One. London: Heinemann, 1989.

Couzens, Tim, and Essop Patel, eds. *The Return of the Amasi Bird: Black South African Poetry, 1891–1981*. Johannesburg: Ravan, 1982.

Cronin, Jeremy. *Inside*. Johannesburg: Ravan, 1983; London: Jonathan Cape, 1987 (enlarged).

Cullinan, Patrick. *Selected Poems, 1961–1994*. Edited and introduced by Stephen Watson. Cape Town: Snailpress, 1994.

Dangor, Achmat. *Bulldozer*. Johannesburg: Ravan, 1983.

From Riverlea to Parkview. Johannesburg: Ravan, 1995.

Waiting for Leila. Johannesburg: Ravan, 1981.

The Z Town Trilogy. Johannesburg: Ravan, 1990.

de Kok, Ingrid. *Familiar Ground*. Johannesburg: Ravan, 1988.

Delius, Anthony. *Border*. Cape Town: David Philip, 1976.

Dike, Fatima. *The First South African: A Play*. Johannesburg: Ravan, 1979.

The Sacrifice of Kreli. Reprinted in *Theatre One: New South African Drama*. Ed. Stephen Gray. Johannesburg: Ad Donker, 1978. 33–80.

Dikeni, Sandile. *Guava Juice*. Introduction by Jakes Gerwel. Bellville: Mayibuye Books, 1992.

Dikobe, Modikwe. *Dispossessed*. Johannesburg: Ravan, 1983.

The Marabi Dance. London: Heinemann, 1973.

Driver, Charles Jonathan. *Elegy for a Revolutionary*. New York : Morrow, 1970; Cape Town: David Philip, 1984.

du Plessis, Menán. *Longlive!* Cape Town: David Philip, 1989.

A State of Fear. Cape Town: David Philip, and London: Pandora, 1983.

Ebersohn, Wessel. *A Lonely Place to Die*. London: Gollancz, 1979.

Store up the Anger. Johannesburg: Ravan, 1980; Harmondsworth: Penguin, 1984.

Essop, Ahmed. *The Emperor*. Johannesburg: Ravan, 1984.

The Hajji and Other Stories. Johannesburg: Ravan, 1978.

Noorjehan and Other Stories. Johannesburg: Ravan, 1990.

Faller, Francis. *Weather Words*. Johannesburg: Ad Donker, 1986.

Farisani, Tshenuwani Simon. *Diary from a South African Prison*. Ed. John A. Evenson. Philadelphia: Fortress Press, 1987.

Feinberg, Barry, ed. *Poets to the People: South African Freedom Poems*. Foreword by Hugh MacDiarmid. London: Allen & Unwin, 1974.

Ferguson, Gus. *Carpe Diem*. Cape Town: Carrefour Press, 1992.

Doggerel Day. Johannesburg: Ad Donker, 1982.

Fleischer, Anthony. *Children of Adamastor*. Cape Town: David Philip, 1994.

Forbes, Andrina Dashwood. *Birds on a Ledge*. Cape Town: Buchu Books, 1992.

Fraser, Ian. *My Own Private Orchestra*. London: Penguin, 1993.

Friedland, David. *The Event*. Rivonia: Justified Press, 1991.

I Remember My Running. Hornchurch (Essex): Tully Potter for Poetry One, 1974.

Fugard, Athol. *Boesman and Lena and Other Plays*. Cape Town: Oxford University Press, 1980. [*The Blood Knot, People Are Living There, Hello and Goodbye, Boesman and Lena*.]

Cousins: A Memoir. Johannesburg: Witwatersrand University Press, 1994.

Dimetos and Two Early Plays. Oxford : Oxford University Press, 1977.

A Lesson from Aloes: A Play. Oxford: Oxford University Press, and New York: Random House, 1981.

My Children! My Africa! and Selected Shorter Plays. Edited by Stephen Gray. Johannesburg: Witwatersrand University Press, and London: Faber & Faber, 1990.

A Place with the Pigs: A Personal Parable. London: Faber & Faber, 1988

Playland . . . and Other Words. Johannesburg: Witwatersrand University Press, 1992.

The Road to Mecca. London: Faber & Faber, 1985.

Selected Plays. Edited by Dennis Walder. Oxford: Oxford University Press,

1987. [*'Master Harold'* . . . *and the Boys, The Blood Knot, Hello and Goodbye, Boesman and Lena.*]

Fugard, Athol, John Kani, and Winston Ntshona. *Siʒwe Bansi Is Dead* and *The Island.* London: Hansom Books, 1973; New York: Viking, 1976.

Fugard, Sheila. *The Castaways.* Johannesburg: Macmillan, 1972.

A Revolutionary Woman. London: Virago, 1984; New York: George Brazziller, 1985.

Fuller, Mapulana. *The Porcupine and the Duiker: A Novel of Lebowa.* New York: Vantage, 1983.

Galgut, Damon. *The Quarry.* London and Johannesburg: Viking, 1995.

The Beautiful Screaming of Pigs. London: Scribners, 1991; London: Abacus, 1992.

Gool, Reshard. *Cape Town Coolie.* Oxford: Heinemann, 1990.

Gordimer, Nadine. *Burger's Daughter.* London: Jonathan Cape, Harmondsworth: Penguin, and New York: Viking, 1979.

The Conservationist. London: Jonathan Cape, 1974; New York: Viking, 1975.

A Guest of Honour. New York: Viking, 1970; London: Jonathan Cape, 1971.

July's People. London: Jonathan Cape, New York: Viking, and Johannesburg: Ravan, 1981; Harmondsworth: Penguin, 1982.

Jump and Other Stories. London: Bloomsbury, New York: Farrar, Straus & Giroux, and Cape Town: David Philip, 1991.

My Son's Story. London: Bloomsbury, Cape Town: David Philip, and New York, Farrar, Straus & Giroux, 1990.

None to Accompany Me. Cape Town: David Philip, London: Bloomsbury, and New York: Farrar, Straus & Giroux, 1994.

Something Out There. London: Jonathan Cape, New York: Viking, and Johannesburg: Ravan, 1984.

A Sport of Nature. London: Jonathan Cape, New York: Knopf, and Cape Town: David Philip, 1987.

Gottschalk, Keith. *Emergency Poems.* Introduction by Peter Horn. Bellville: Mayibuye Books, 1992.

Gray, Rosemary, and Stephen Finn, eds. *Sounding Wings: Stories from South Africa.* Cape Town: Maskew Miller Longman, 1994.

Gray, Stephen. *Apollo Cafe and Other Poems: 1982–89.* Johannesburg: David Philip, 1989.

Born of Man. Johannesburg: Justified Press, 1989.

Caltrop's Desire. London: Rex Collings, and Cape Town: David Philip, 1980.

Selected Poems, 1960–92. Cape Town: David Philip, 1994.

Time of Our Darkness. London: Arrow Books, 1989.

War Child. Johannesburg: Justified Press, 1991; London: Serif, 1993.

Gray, Stephen, ed. *Market Plays.* Preface by Mannie Manim. Johannesburg: Ad Donker, 1986.

Modern South African Poetry. Johannesburg: Ad Donker, 1984.

Modern South African Stories. Cape Town: Ad Donker, 1980.

The Penguin Book of Contemporary South African Short Stories. Johannesburg:
  Penguin, 1993.

The Penguin Book of Southern African Stories. Harmondsworth: Penguin, 1985.

The Penguin Book of Southern African Verse. Harmondsworth: Penguin, 1989.

Gwala, Mafika Pascal. *Jol'iinkomo.* Johannesburg: Ad Donker, 1977.

No More Lullabies. Johannesburg: Ravan, 1982.

Haresnape, Geoffrey. *Drive of the Tide: Poems.* Edited by Adam Small. Cape
  Town: Maskew Miller, 1976.

Testimony. Johannesburg: Justified Press, 1992.

Head, Bessie. *The Collector of Treasures and Other Botswana Village Tales.*
  London: Heinemann, and Cape Town: David Philip, 1977.

Maru. Oxford: Heinemann, 1971.

A Question of Power. New York: Pantheon Books, 1973; London: Heinemann, 1974.

Tales of Tenderness and Power. Introduction by Gillian Stead Eilerson.
  Johannesburg: Ad Donker, 1989; Oxford: Heinemann, 1990.

A Woman Alone: Autobiographical Writings. Selected and edited by Craig
  MacKenzie. Oxford: Heinemann, 1990.

Hirson, Denis. *The House Next Door to Africa.* Cape Town: David Philip, 1986.

Hirson, Denis, and Martin Trump, eds. *The Heinemann Book of South African
  Short Stories.* Oxford: Heinemann/UNESCO, 1994.

Hobbs, Jenny. *Thoughts in a Makeshift Mortuary.* London: Michael Joseph, 1989;
  London: Grafton Books, 1990.

Hodge, Norman, ed. *To Kill a Man's Pride and Other Stories from Southern Africa.*
  Johannesburg: Ravan, 1984.

Hope, Christopher. *My Chocolate Redeemer.* 1983. London: Heinemann, 1989.

A Separate Development. Johannesburg: Ravan, 1980; London, Granada, 1983.

Horn, Anette, ed. *Like a House on Fire: Contemporary Women's Writing, Art and
  Photography.* Johannesburg: COSAW, 1994.

Horn, Peter. *An Axe in the Ice.* Johannesburg: COSAW, 1992.

Poems, 1964–1989. Introduced by Njabulo Ndebele. Johannesburg: Ravan, 1991.

Walking through Our Sleep. Johannesburg: Ravan, 1974.

House, Amelia Blossom, and Cosmo Pieterse, eds. *Nelson Mandelamandla.*
  Washington: Three Continents, 1989.

Our Sun Will Rise: Poems for South Africa. Washington: Three Continents, 1989.

Isaacson, Maureen. *Holding Back Midnight and Other Stories.* Johannesburg:
  COSAW, 1992.

Jacobs, Steve. *Light in a Stark Age.* Johannesburg: Ravan, 1984.

Jacobson, Dan. *The Rape of Tamar.* London: Weidenfeld & Nicolson, and New
  York: Macmillan, 1970.

James, Alan. *Morning Near Genadendal: Poems.* Plumstead: Snailpress, 1992.

Jensma, Wopko. *I Must Show You My Clippings.* Johannesburg: Ravan, 1977.

Sing for Our Execution: Poems and Woodcuts. Pretoria: Ophir, 1971.

Kalechofsky, Robert, and Roberta Kalechofsky, eds. *South African Jewish Voices.*
  Marblehead, MA: Micah Publications, 1982.

Kani, John, ed. *More Market Plays*. Johannesburg: Ad Donker, 1994.

Karodia, Farida. *Daughters of the Twilight*. London: Women's Press, 1986.

A Shattering of Silence. Oxford: Heinemann, 1993.

Kavanagh, Robert Msheng, ed. *South African People's Plays: Ons Phola Hi*. London: Heinemann, 1981.

Kgositsile, Keorapetse. *For Melba: Poems*. Chicago: Third World, 1970.

My Name is Afrika. Introduction by Gwendolyn Brooks. New York: Doubleday, 1971.

When the Clouds Clear. Introduction by Ari Sitas. Edited by Junaid Ahmed. Fordsburg: COSAW, 1990.

Krouse, Matthew, and Kim Berman, eds. *The Invisible Ghetto: Lesbian and Gay Writing from South Africa*. Johannesburg: COSAW, 1993.

Kunene, Mazisi. *The Ancestors and the Sacred Mountain*. London: Heinemann, 1982.

Emperor Shaka the Great: A Zulu Epic. Translated from Zulu by the author. London: Heinemann, 1979.

Kuzwayo, Ellen. *Sit Down and Listen*. Claremont: David Philip, 1990.

La Guma, Alex. *In the Fog of the Seasons' End*. London: Heinemann, 1972.

Time of the Butcherbird. London: Heinemann, 1979.

Langa, Mandla. *A Rainbow on the Paper Sky*. London: Kliptown, 1989.

Lanham, Peter. *Blanket Boy's Moon*. Cape Town: David Philip, 1984.

Lefanu, Sarah, and Stephen Hayward. *Colours of a New Day: Writing for South Africa*. Johannesburg: Ravan Press, 1990.

Lemon, David. *Man-eater*. London and Johannesburg: Viking, 1990.

Lewin, Hugh. *Bandiet: Seven Years in a South African Prison*. London: Heinemann, 1974.

Lindfors, Bernth, ed. *South African Voices*. Austin: University of Texas, 1970.

Livingstone, Douglas James. *A Littoral Zone*. Cape Town: Carrefour Press, 1991.

Selected Poems. Johannesburg: Ad Donker, 1984.

Lockett, Cecily, ed. *Breaking the Silence: A Century of South African Women's Poetry*. Parklands: Ad Donker, 1990.

Lovell, Moira. *Out of the Mist*. Plumstead: Snailpress, 1994.

Lowry, Alison. *Natural Rhythm*. London: Heinemann, 1993.

Wishing on Trains. London: Mandarin, 1995.

Lurie, Edward. *Jacob with a 'C'*. Cape Town: Carrefour Press, 1993.

Mabuza, Lindiwe. *Letter to Letta*. Johannesburg: Skotaville, 1991.

One Never Knows: An Anthology of Black South African Women Writers in Exile. Braamfontein: Skotaville, 1989.

Maclennan, Don. *The Poetry Lesson: New Poems*. Plumstead: Snailpress, 1995.

Reckonings. Cape Town: David Philip, 1983.

Macphail, E. M. *Mrs Chud's Place*. Cape Town: Carrefour Press, 1992.

Phoebe & Nio. Johannesburg: Hippogriff, 1987.

Macphail, E. M., ed. *Hippogriff New Writing, 1990*. Johannesburg: Hippogriff, 1990.

Macphail, E. M., and Peter Esterhuizen, eds. *Some Roses, a Hamburger, the AK47 and a Puddle: New South African Writing*. Parklands: Hippogriff, 1993.

Madingoane, Ingoapele. *Africa My Beginning*. Johannesburg: Ravan, 1979.

Magona, Sindiwe. *Living, Loving, and Lying Awake at Night*. Cape Town: David Philip, 1991.

To My Children's Children. Cape Town: David Philip, 1990.

Maimane, A. *Victims*. London: Allison & Busby, 1976.

Makhoere, Caesarina Kona. *No Child's Play*. London: Women's Press, 1988.

Malan, Robin, ed. *Being Here: Modern Short Stories from Southern Africa*. Cape Town: David Philip, 1994

New Beginnings: Short Stories from Southern Africa. Cape Town: Oxford University Press, 1995.

Manaka, Matsemela. *Egoli: City of Gold*. Johannesburg: Soyikwa–Ravan, 1980.

Pula. Introduction by Ian Steadman. Braamfontein: Skotaville, 1990.

Mandela, Nelson. *Long Walk to Freedom*. New York and London: Little, Brown, 1994.

Mann, Chris. *Mann Alive!* With an introduction and interview by Robin Malan. Cape Town: David Philip, 1992.

New Shades. Cape Town: David Philip, 1982.

Maponya, Maishe. *Doing Plays for a Change: Five Works*. Introduced by Ian Steadman. Johannesburg: Witwatersrand University Press, 1995.

Marquard, Jean, ed. *A Century of South African Short Stories*. Johannesburg: Ad Donker, 1978.

Masemola, Thabo Nkosinathi. *Mixed Signals*. Johannesburg: Skotaville, 1993.

Mashinini, Emma. *Strikes Have Followed Me All My Life*. London: Women's Press, 1989.

Matlou, Joël. *Life at Home and Other Stories*. Johannesburg: COSAW, 1991.

Matshoba, Mtutuzeli. *Call Me Not a Man*. Johannesburg: Ravan, 1979; London: Longman, 1981.

Seeds of War. Johannesburg: Ravan, 1981.

Mattera, Don. *Azanian Love Song*. Johannesburg: Skotaville, 1983.

Memory is the Weapon. Johannesburg: Ravan, 1987.

Matthews, James. *The Park and Other Stories*. Athlone: BLAC, 1974; Johannesburg: Ravan, 1983.

Matthews, James, ed. *Black Voices Shout: An Anthology of Poetry*. Athlone: BLAC, 1974.

Matthews, James, and Gladys Thomas. *Cry Rage!* Johannesburg: Spro-cas Publications, 1972.

Mchunu, Vusi D. *Stronger Souls: Poems and Essays*. Introduction by Dennis Brutus. Cape Town: Buchu Books, 1990.

Mda, Zakes. *And the Girls in Their Sunday Dresses: Four Works*. Johannesburg: Witwatersrand University Press, 1993.

The Plays of Zakes Mda. Introduction by Andrew Horn. Johannesburg: Ravan, 1990.

She Plays with Darkness. Florida, South Africa: Vivlia, 1995.

Ways of Dying. Cape Town: Oxford University Press, 1995.

Medalie, David. *The Shooting of the Christmas Cows*. Cape Town: David Philip, 1990.

Metelerkamp, Joan. *Stone No More*. Durban: Gecko, 1995.

Mhlophe, Gcina, Maralin Vanrenen, and Thembi Mtshali. *Have You Seen Zandile?* Johannesburg: Skotaville, 1988; London: Heinemann/Methuen, 1990.

Moerat, Nohra, ed. *Siren Songs: An Anthology of Poetry Written by Women*. Athlone: BLAC, 1989.

Mogale, Dikobe wa. *Baptism of Fire*. Johannesburg: Ad Donker, 1984.

Prison Poems. Johannesburg: Ad Donker, 1992.

Mosieleng, Percy, and Temba Mhambi, eds. *Contending Voices in South African Fiction*. Johannesburg: Lexicon, 1993.

Moss, Rose. *The School Master*. Johannesburg: Ravan, 1981.

Motsapi, Seitlhamo. *Earthstepper* and *The Ocean is Very Shallow*. Grahamstown: Deep South/ISEA, 1995.

Mphahlele, Es'kia. *Afrika My Music: An Autobiography, 1957–1983*. Johannesburg: Ravan, 1984.

Chirundu. Johannesburg: Ravan, 1979.

The Unbroken Song: Selected Writings. Johannesburg: Ravan, 1981.

The Wanderers. New York : Macmillan, 1971.

Mtshali, Mbuyiseni Oswald. *Sounds of a Cowhide Drum*. Foreword by Nadine Gordimer. Johannesburg: Ad Donker, 1971; London: Oxford University Press, 1972.

Fireflames. Pietermaritzburg: Shuter & Shooter, 1980.

Mtwa, Percy, Mbongeni Ngema, and Barney Simon. *Woza Albert!* London: Methuen, 1983.

Muller, David. *Whitey*. Johannesburg: Ravan, 1977.

Mutloatse, Mothobi. *Mama Ndiyalila*. Johannesburg: Ravan, 1982.

Mutloatse, Mothobi, ed. *Forced Landing*. Johannesburg: Ravan, 1980. Also published as *Africa South: Contemporary Writings*. London: Heinemann, 1980.

Mzamane, Mbulelo Vizikhungo. *The Children of Soweto: A Trilogy*. Johannesburg: Ravan, 1982.

Mzala: The Stories of Mbulelo Mzamane. Johannesburg: Ravan, 1980. Reissued as *My Cousin Comes to Jo'burg and Other Stories*. London: Longman, 1981.

Mzamane, Mbulelo Vizikhungo. ed. *Hungry Flames and Other Black South African Short Stories*. London: Longman, 1986.

Naidoo, Indres. *Island in Chains: Ten Years on Robben Island by Prisoner 885/63*. Harmondsworth: Penguin, 1982. Reprinted as *Robben Island: Ten Years as a Political Prisoner in South Africa's Most Notorious Penitentiary*. New York: Random House, 1983.

Ndebele, Njabulo S. *Fools and Other Stories*. Johannesburg: Ravan, 1983; London: Longman, 1985.

Ndlovu, Duma, ed. *Woẓa Afrika: An Anthology of South African Plays*. Preface by
    Amiri Baraka. Foreword by Wole Soyinka. New York: George Braziller, 1986.
Ngcobo, Lauretta. *And They Didn't Die*. London: Virago, 1990.
    Cross of Gold. London: Longman, 1981.
Ngema, Mbongeni. *The Best of Mbongeni Ngema*. Johannesburg:
    Skotaville/Via Afrika, 1995.
Nicol, Mike. *Horseman*. London: Bloomsbury, 1994.
    The Powers That Be. London: Bloomsbury, 1989; London: Picador, 1990.
    This Day and Age. Cape Town: David Philip, 1992.
Nkondo, Sankie Dolly. *Flames of Fury and Other Poems*. Introduction by Patrick
    Wilmot. Fordsburg: COSAW, 1990.
Nkosi, Lewis. *Mating Birds*. Johannesburg: Ravan, and London: Constable, 1986.
Nortje, Arthur. *Dead Roots*. London: Heinemann, 1973.
Nyatsumba, Kaizer. *In Love with a Stranger and Other Stories*. Johannesburg:
    Justified Press, 1995.
Oliphant, Andries Walter, ed. *Ear to the Ground: Contemporary Worker Poets*.
    Johannesburg: COSAW in association with COSATU, 1991.
    Essential Things: An Anthology of New South African Poetry. Johannesburg:
    COSAW, 1992.
Oosthuizen, Ann. *Sometimes When it Rains: Writings by South African Women*.
    London: Pandora Press, 1987.
Opland, Jeff, ed. *Words that Circle Words: A Choice of South African Oral Poetry*.
    Johannesburg: Ad Donker, 1992.
Orkin, Martin, ed. *At the Junction: Four Plays of the Junction Theatre Company*.
    Johannesburg: Witwatersrand University Press, 1995.
Padayachee, Deena. *What's Love Got to Do with It? and Other Stories*.
    Johannesburg: COSAW, 1992.
Parenzee, Donald. *Driven to Work*. Johannesburg: Ravan, 1985.
Patel, Essop. *The Bullet and the Bronze Lady*. Johannesburg: Skotaville, 1987.
    They Came at Dawn. Cape Town: BLAC, 1980.
Paton, Alan. *Ah, But Your Land is Beautiful*. Cape Town: David Philip, 1981.
    London: Penguin, 1983.
Pereira, Ernest, ed. *Contemporary South African Plays*. Johannesburg: Ravan, 1977.
Peteni, Randall Langa. *Hill of Fools: A Novel of the Ciskei*. London: Heinemann,
    and Cape Town: David Philip, 1976.
Pheto, Molefe. *And Night Fell*. London and New York: Allison & Busby, 1983.
Pieterse, Cosmo. *Echoes and Choruses: 'Ballad of the Cells' and Selected Shorter
    Poems*. Ohio: Centre for International Studies, Ohio University, 1974.
Poland, Marguerite. *Shades*. London: Viking, 1993.
    Train to Doringbult. London: Bodley Head, 1987.
Poona, Sobhna. *In Search of Rainbows*. Johannesburg: Skotaville, 1990.
Press, Karen. *The Coffee Shop Poems*. Plumstead: Snailpress, 1993.
Rampolokeng, Lesego. *Horns for Hondo*. Fordsburg: COSAW, 1990.
    Talking Rain. Fordsburg: COSAW, 1993.

Reddy, Jayapraga. *On the Fringe of Dreamtime and Other Stories*. Johannesburg: Skotaville, 1987.

Rive, Richard. *'Buckingham Palace', District Six*. Cape Town: David Philip, 1986.

Emergency. London: Collier-Macmillan,1970.

Emergency Continued. Claremont: David Philip, 1990.

Roberts, Sheila. *Coming In and Other Stories*. Johannesburg: Justified Press, 1993.

He's My Brother. Johannesburg: Ad Donker, 1977. Also published as *Johannesburg Requiem*. New York: Taplinger, 1980.

Rode, Linda, and Jakes Gerwel, eds. *Crossing Over: New Writing for a New South Africa*. Cape Town: Kwela Books, 1995.

Rosenthal, Jane. *Uncertain Consolations*. Plumstead: Snailpress, 1993.

Royston, Robert. *Black Poets in South Africa*. London: Heinemann, 1974. First published as *To Whom it May Concern*, 1973.

Sachs, Albie. *The Soft Vengeance of a Freedom Fighter*. London: Grafton, 1990.

Sam, Agnes. *Jesus is Indian and Other Stories*. London: Women's Press, 1989; Oxford: Heinemann, 1994.

Schreiner, Barbara, ed. *A Snake with Ice Water: Prison Writings by South African Women*. Johannesburg: COSAW, 1992.

Sepamla, Sipho. *The Blues is You in Me*. Johannesburg: Ad Donker, 1976.

A Ride on the Whirlwind. Johannesburg: Ad Donker 1981; London: Heinemann, and New York: Readers International, 1984.

Selected Poems. Edited and introduced by Mbulelo Vizikhungo Mzamane. Johannesburg: Ad Donker, 1984.

Serote, Mongane Wally. *Behold Mama, Flowers*. Johannesburg: Ad Donker, 1978.

Come and Hope with Me. Cape Town: David Philip, 1994.

On the Horizon. Foreword by Raymond Suttner. Fordsburg: COSAW, 1990.

Selected Poems. Edited and introduced by Mbulelo Vizikhungo Mzamane. Johannesburg: Ad Donker, 1984.

Third World Express. Cape Town: David Philip, 1992.

To Every Birth its Blood. Johannesburg: Ravan, 1981; London: Heinemann, 1983.

Sharpe, Tom. *Riotous Assembly*. London: Secker & Warburg, 1971.

Siers, Rushy. *The No-act Play*. Preface by Peter Horn. Cape Town: Township Publishing Co-operative, 1990.

Simon, Barney. *Joburg, Sis!* Johannesburg: Bateleur, 1974.

Sitas, Ari, *Tropical Scars*. Fordsburg: COSAW, 1989.

Sitas, Ari, ed. *Black Mamba Rising: South African Worker Poets in Struggle*. Durban: COSATU Workers' Cultural Local, 1986.

Skinner, Douglas Reid. *The House in Pella District*. Cape Town: David Philip, 1985.

The Middle Years. Cape Town: Carrefour Press, 1993.

Slabolepszy, Paul. *Mooi Street and Other Moves*. Introduction by Robert Greig. Johannesburg: Witwatersrand University Press, 1994.

Saturday Night at the Palace. Johannesburg: Ad Donker, 1985.

Slovo, Gillian. *Close Call*. London: Michael Joseph, 1995.

Death Comes Staccato. London: Women's Press, 1987.

Ties of Blood. London: Michael Joseph, 1989; New York: Morrow, 1990.

Small, Adam. *Black Bronze Beautiful: Quatrains.* Johannesburg: Ad Donker, 1975.

Sole, Kelwyn. *The Blood of Our Silence.* Johannesburg: Ravan, 1987.

Projections in the Past Tense. Johannesburg: Ravan, 1992.

Themba, Can. *The Will to Die.* Selected by Donald Stuart and Roy Holland. London: Heinemann, 1972; Cape Town: David Philip, 1982.

Thomas, Gladys. *Avalon Court: Vignettes of Life of the 'Coloured' People on the Cape Flats of Cape Town.* Braamfontein: Skotaville, 1992.

Tlali, Miriam. *Amandla.* Johannesburg: Ravan, 1980.

Footprints in the Quag: Stories and Dialogues from Soweto. Introduction by Lauretta Ngcobo. Cape Town: David Philip, 1989. Also published as *Soweto Stories.*

Mihloti. Johannesburg: Skotaville, 1984.

Muriel at Metropolitan. Johannesburg: Ravan, 1975. Now published under the title *Between Two Worlds.*

Uys, Pieter-Dirk. *No One's Died Laughing.* Harmondsworth: Penguin, 1986.

Paradise is Closing Down & Other Plays. Harmondsworth: Penguin, 1989.

van Niekerk, Annemarie, ed. *Raising the Blinds: A Century of South African Women's Stories.* Parklands: Ad Donker, 1990.

van Wyk, Chris. *It is Time to Go Home.* Johannesburg: Ad Donker, 1979.

Vladislavic, Ivan. *The Folly.* Cape Town: David Philip, 1993.

Missing Persons. Cape Town: David Philip, 1989.

Watson, Stephen. *In This City.* Cape Town: David Philip, 1986.

Poems, 1977–1982. Johannesburg: Bateleur Press, 1982.

Presence of the Earth: New Poems. Cape Town: David Philip, 1995.

Return of the Moon: Versions from the |Xam. Cape Town: Carrefour Press, 1991.

Wicomb, Zoë. *You Can't Get Lost in Cape Town.* London: Virago, 1987.

Wilhelm, Peter. *The Dark Wood.* Johannesburg: Ravan, 1977.

The Mask of Freedom. Johannesburg: Ad Donker, 1994.

Woodward, Wendy. *Seance for the Body.* Plumstead: Snailpress, 1994.

Ya-Otto, John. *Battlefront Namibia: An Autobiography.* London, Heinemann, and New York: Lawrence Hill, 1982.

Yourgrau, Tug. *The Song of Jacob Zulu.* New York: Arcade, 1993.

Zwelonke, D. M. *Robben Island.* London: Heinemann, 1973.

Zerbst, Fiona. *The Small Zone: New Poems.* Plumstead: Snailpress, 1995.

Zwi, Rose. *Exiles.* Johannesburg: Ad Donker, 1984.

Index

NOTE Titles of works are listed under name of author.